MARBLEHEAD

Samuel Chamberlain

"may your numerous posterity, in the preservation of that Liberty so gloriously purchased, ever venerate the memory of their ancestors."

MARQUIS DE LAFAYETTE
speaking to the people of Marblehead in 1784

MARBLEHEAD

The Spirit of '76 Lives Here

Updated Edition

Priscilla Sawyer Lord
Virginia Clegg Gamage

Illustrated with line drawings by Marian Martin Brown

CHILTON BOOK COMPANY
Radnor, Pennsylvania

Also by Priscilla Sawyer Lord

EASTER THE WORLD OVER
THE FOLK ARTS AND CRAFTS OF NEW ENGLAND
EASTER GARLAND

Key to line drawings
Page 8, pinnace; page 87, heel-tapper; page 88,
James Mugford; page 145, John Glover Cowell;
page 156, Fort Sewall; page 157, Marchant
Schoolhouse; page 169, Fishermen's Monument;
page 227, "Old Brig"; page 295,
Glover's tomb; page 296, John Humphrey's
house; page 319, Devereux Station;
page 332, Map by Sidney Perley.

Copyright © 1972 by
Priscilla Sawyer Lord and Virginia Clegg Gamage
First Edition, Updated   *All Rights Reserved*

Published in Radnor, Pa. by Chilton Book Company
and simultaneously in Don Mills, Ontario, Canada,
by Thomas Nelson & Sons, Ltd.

ISBN: 0-8019-5596-3 *Cloth Edition*
ISBN: 0-8019-5622-6 *Paper Edition*

Library of Congress Catalog Card Number 73-169586
Designed by Cypher Associates, Inc.
Manufactured in the United States of America

*To the families of Marblehead
who have sustained this town and
its vigorous spirit of independence
for three and a half centuries*

Foreword

SEVERAL YEARS AGO in the cabin of a fogbound schooner we renewed our discussion of a favorite subject, Marblehead. In our concern for the preservation of its heritage and for its recognition in colonial history and in the minds of its contemporary citizens, we felt that newly discovered documents and the need for updating demanded a fresh effort to record the character and vitality of the town. Since Samuel Roads, Jr.'s comprehensive *History and Traditions of Marblehead* (1880) and Joseph Robinson's *The Story of Marblehead* (1936), only phases of Marblehead's history have been recorded in articles, lectures, poetry and pictorial presentations.

We began the gargantuan task of assembling a story of three and a half centuries by going whenever possible to primary sources. The superabundance of documents, personal papers, diaries, and so forth has required years of research and selectivity, always with a conscious effort to recognize the difference between fact and legend, yet acknowledging that both convey the spirit of the town. It has been laborious and demanding, incredible and humorous; always exciting and rewarding.

As our research developed, we became more perplexed as to why Marblehead had been so neglected in many histories. Why? The geographical isolation, the lack of aristocratic connections, its nonconformity or the difficulty of unearthing local, documentary evidence? We feel that from the beginning Marblehead held in its rough palm the spirit of American liberty and the concept of individual freedom. The study of this town, we hope, enhances the knowledge of the region and the nation; indeed, as Alexis de Tocqueville pointed out in 1831, the political life of America originated in the town where government was within each man's reach and experience and created a wellspring of the people's power. We admit that "an historian of his own country must always in some sort be considered its advocate," but, we earnestly hope, not at the expense of whatever truth could be ascertained.

Historical research is endless and admittedly we have felt isolated from some particular materials; however, public institutions have been extremely cooperative, in particular the Essex Institute of Salem, Massachusetts, whose director, David B. Little, read the manuscript for historical validity. No inquiry was too trivial for the interested and encouraging assistance of Mrs. Dorothy M. Potter, head librarian, or her assistant, Mrs. Irene B. Norton. At the Marblehead Historical Society Mrs. Frances Lloyd, former executive secretary, helped us to search the enormous store of records.

For a wealth of Marblehead stories, as well as her drawings, we thank Marian M. Brown, and for a critical reading of the manuscript we are indebted to Charlotte F. and Wilson H. Roads. For their aid in publication and editing our deepest thanks to John F. Marion and Elizabeth Powers. To Margaret Foley our deepest appreciation for countless hours of typing and constant enthusiastic encouragement, and to Catherine Collyer and Barbara Hooper Burgoyne for watching over health and home.

Documents reveal facts; people give them life and feeling for which we are grateful to the many families who allowed us into their historic houses, shared their personal "treasures" and answered our questions. Our special indebtedness to:

Abbot Public Library, Marblehead
American Antiquarian Society
Amherst College
Boston Athenaeum
Boston Public Library
Essex County Registry of Deeds
Ipswich Public Library
Lynn Historical Society
Marblehead Arts Association
Marblehead Neck Improvement Association
Marblehead: The Board of Selectmen, Mr. James Skinner, Chairman; Mrs. Betty Brown, Town Clerk; Mr. Benjamin A. Woodfin, Cemetery Commissioner; Mr. Loring Clark, Tree Warden; the Assessors' Department, the Police Department and the Fire Department.
Massachusetts Historical Society
Massachusetts Society of Mayflower Descendants
Massachusetts State Archives
Massachusetts State Library

Museum of Fine Arts, Boston
Metropolitan Museum of Art, New York
New England Historic Genealogical Society
New York Public Library
New York State Historical Society
Peabody Museum, Salem
Philadelphia Public Library
Salem Public Library
Trenton Public Library
Widener Library, Harvard College
Windham Historical Society, Maine
B. Devereux Barker, Jr.
William Henry Barry
Prof. George Billias
Mrs. Janet A. Blood
Jack Breed
Richard P. Breed
Mrs. Camilla B. Campbell
Edward Caswell
Benjamin R. Chadwick
Mrs. Narcissa G. Chamberlain
Samuel Chamberlain
Eugene T. Connolly
Miss Mary Thornton Davis
Miss Lilian A. Dermody
Mrs. Helen Paine Doane
Mrs. Eleanor Gwin Ellis
Daniel J. Foley
Leonard M. Fowle, Jr.
Mrs. Marion Gosling
Miss Mildred Graves
Mrs. Mary Lou Grinnell
Robert C. Harding
William Hawkes, Jr.
Edward N. Holden
R. Stedman Hood
Mrs. Elizabeth Smith Hunt
Mrs. Helen W. Jaques
Norman Kenny
Mrs. Elsie T. LeFavour
Mrs. Patricia Smith Magee
Mrs. Mary E. Nash
Robert Orne

Bowden G. Osborne
Philip E. Parker
Miss Zulette Potter
Bob Sinclair
Mrs. Barbara N. Skinner
Mrs. Marilyn M. Slade
Mrs. Virginia K. Smith
W. Gordon Smith
Mrs. Mary L. Tutt
Richard Tutt, Jr.
Mrs. Marion Paine Walkley
Nancy J. Weiss

Our intent has been to produce an enjoyable, readable account of a fascinating town, fully realizing that it would be presumptuous of us to pose as experienced political scientists or historians. For easier reading we have eliminated the documentary slashed date (1636/37) by placing any event after January 1 in the new style date of the Gregorian calendar. We have taken the liberty of using nicknames, colloquialisms and local color. If, as Samuel Eliot Morison writes, "History is to the community what memory is to the people," our hope is that we have been able to deepen the vibrant memories of Marblehead. History is a moving, live experience in which everyone is playing a part and so no one account can be complete or perfect. There is much more to be said about the town; it is hoped that other family documents will come forth and new voices will be heard to enrich the history of Marblehead.

Contents

MARBLEHEAD

PART I

Marblehead: *Its History*

1. The Original Owners

WHEN THE RED MAN first came to it and when the white man first saw it probably never will be known. But Vikings fished its shores; European explorers sought new lands for old monarchies; pirates, sea rovers, adventurers sailed the seacoast for booty and excitement. Champlain of France outlined its contours, and the Englishman, John Smith, mapped the coastline and first called it New England.

Both maps sketched in a long, almost landlocked harbor at approximately 42° 30′ 27″ north latitude and at what was later called 70° 50′ 18″ west longitude. The deep, straight harbor indentation was barricaded by small islands scattered like pebbles across its entrance; most of them were top-heavy with dark green trees and bright flowers; others were scraped bare by the ancient ice sheet.

That ponderous, thick glacial sheet blanketed the Northeast which had already been shaken, upended, faulted and twisted by earthquakes and encrusted and diked by volcanic eruptions. The incalculable weight of the immense ice cover ground into softer surfaces, cracked off chunks of the hardest rock, dropping them heedlessly at any unlikely spot, and abandoned small icebergs buried deep in insulating sand. Its halting retreat left undeniable local evi-

dence as obvious as its archaic "signature" scratched on the bare
outcroppings of rock. The deep harbor was gouged out in the
northeasterly direction of the glacial retreat while the peninsula and
parallel island of unyielding rock resisted, forming its protective
shores. Time shaped the southeast limits of the harbor where the al-
luvial fill created a shallowness on which the tides would build up a
"barrier beach" or the rough bar that tied the island to the mainland.

The same incessant wave action against the recently defrosted
land eroded the conglomerate and sand leaving great heads of stone
with endless configurations. Swollen with water from the melting
ice, the sea raced into the newly carved coastline to form coves and
bays and to meet the fast-running rivers. The topography of this
place offered many advantages that didn't escape the eyes of the
alert fishermen or traders. Here was an abundance of fish, a deep anchorage with nearby stone ballast, fresh spring water, food and furs;
a place that could be guarded from the high headlands and protected by an islanded entrance sure to discourage invaders. These
same advantages that appealed to the white man had long been recognized by the Naumkeag Indians who encamped here and called it
Massabequash.

The Naumkeags of the Massachusetts tribe and the proud Algon-
quin nation belonged to the woodland tribes who led an easy-going

life of fishing, hunting and farming. Unlike the hawkish Tarrantines, Pequots or Mohawks, the Naumkeags were content to live peacefully, as long as they were not deprived of their hunting and farming lands. Where the Naumkeags came from, or when they began to camp in Massabequash, or first met the white man remains their secret. Their Indian language was euphonious, abundant in soft vowels and difficult for the white man to learn, and there is no evidence of written tribal records. The certainty of their early contact with the white trader was a tragic "trade" of a European disease to which the Naumkeags had no immunity. By 1617 the epidemics (possibly measles and smallpox) had killed off thousands of the tribe and so reduced their numerical strength that the preying Tarrantines, recognizing their vulnerability, attacked in a bloody battle near the Mystic River. They slew the Naumkeag chief, Nanepashemet, and left his tribe in utter defeat from which it would never arise.

Nanepashemet's widow assumed the traditional leadership as squaw sachem, together with her three young sons, called Sagamores. The remnants of the formerly great tribe still returned to their Massabequash settlement for an extended summer, moving inland to avoid the winter on the stormy seacoast. The whole peninsula and Neck were dotted with their encampments, palisaded forts, farms, work areas, burial grounds and shell heaps. The Indian living quarters were prudently located near the sources of food and fresh water, and not far from a defensible headland. At the southwest limits of the peninsula one encampment was built around two ponds just south of a deep, wide river that emptied into the sea. There was the water for grinding stone tools, the meadow for planting and pasturage, and a forest for wood and animal pelts. When the warning drum of a surprise attack sounded, everyone fled into the nearest fort which was palisaded by vertical timbers placed snugly together and supported by an earthwork to absorb enemy arrows. During the fight only a dugout exit was open for the scouts and braves to use for diversionary guerilla tactics.

Further along the river and northwest shore, the Naumkeags piled high the clam and oyster shells discarded from their food, farming, wampum making and handicrafts. That work area was protected against invasion from the sea by another fort built on high ground looking north and west, and in a hollow area not far away was an entire fortified village enclosing many acres of land, a fresh-water pond, and crowded living quarters. Just outside the forts or camps the Naumkeags, with elaborate ceremonials and loud grief, buried their dead whose graves were lined with wampum, weapons, tools and food for their trip to the Happy Hunting Ground—if not condemned to "wander restlessly abroad." The great God, Ketan, would hopefully conduct the noble dead without interference from the evil ones, for the Indians greatly feared the revengeful spirits of Death and Darkness whom the medicine man had not successfully exorcised. As these burial grounds were not sufficiently large to entomb numerous victims of battle, the Naumkeags must never have fought with their backs to the sea and for them Massabequash was just a peaceful refuge.

An indolent summer existence was interrupted by one tribal task, that of replenishing their store of weapons, tools and utensils; so the main "village" of hide-covered wigwams and loosely-connected huts was set up along the southeast shore, a short distance from their quarries. It was an ideal campsite with an abundance of clams, a wide variety of fish from the sea and harbor, lobsters for bait, and sparkling streams and ponds. While lookouts were posted on the rocky headlands at each end of the beach to watch over the women and children, the men paddled or walked to the Neck where the quarries and cliffs gave up a hard hornblendic rock that could be ground or hammered into axes, spearheads, hoes, chisels, knives, arrowheads or utensils for the tribe's winter supply.

The beach encampment may have been once occupied by as many as two thousand Indians whose daily living was unpressured by timepieces or rigid organization. The handsome, lean women did most of the menial work of planting, collecting bait, weaving baskets, raising children, and keeping the home fires burning in the wigwams. There were few prearranged marriages, so the consenting Indian woman was married with the permission of the sachem who, joining her hand to that of a brave, performed a marriage that only adultery could put asunder. If a woman had been born or married into the chieftain's family, no one questioned her right to rule the tribe upon the death of the chief, just as the Nanepashemet's squaw sachem led the Naumkeags. She and the council, and sometimes the powwow, determined the real needs of the tribe, as there was no formal set of laws. A code of fair and honest exchange was understood in the trading, and dire results awaited the one who cheated his Indian brother. Taxes were unknown for rarely were there definite property boundaries, as the benefits of the shore, the forest or the sea were shared by all. Yet, it was understood that half of any tribesman's possessions was available to the chief in disaster or war.

Even with possible ambush around the next bend in the trail, the Naumkeags held no military drills but each brave kept himself and his weapons in excellent condition. He was tall, erect, broad of shoulder with narrow waist, and his piercing black eyes were set off by long, black, straight hair tied back with an ornamental band that held plumed feathers for special occasions. Red skinned he was not, though his dark complexion was frostbitten and weatherbeaten and his face often was rubbed with oil or paint. A kind of tattoo adorned much of his body which was scantily clad in loincloth, snakeskin or wampum belt, beads and ankle-high hide boots—at least until winter cold forced the Indian to add leather breeches, high boots and fur shoulder wraps. The Naumkeag was reserved but friendly, tough yet calm, unless he had been injured or cheated. Then his intense rage erupted in a revenge that was swift and cruel —probably death by the hatchet or club. However, if he were the victim of an attack, an innate pride, dignity and control precluded the slightest expression of pain or fear.

Most of the time the tribesman at Massabequash was carefree, abstemious, healthy and ever ready to abandon work to compete in an athletic contest of canoeing, swimming, running or archery. A kind of rough, body-bruising football easily gathered a crowd that would stay on while the game lasted into the night, producing more broken bones than any one medicine man could handle. The contestants would feast together on fish, meat, fowl, berries, home-grown beans, corn, squash and an unleavened corn meal "bread." The food was roasted, boiled or smoked, the latter being the principal method to preserve food aside from burying it in snow or sand, or hanging it in a cold-running stream. Food was no problem—it was available and simple; work was no problem—take it or leave it. The Naumkeags enjoyed their loosely knit commune of Massabequash and welcomed the white men to it, unaware that the transient traders had been replaced by settlers whose grants stated that they were the new owners of Massabequash.

2. Floundering Among Founders

THE TRADERS—good and bad—had come and gone, with little effect on the Indian encampments, but eventually the white visitors stayed around Massabequash, fished the offshore waters and called it their town. No one, single-minded colony landed here led by a founder fit for a statue. Instead, enterprising, independent men from each of the contemporary New England colonial ventures contributed to the growth and vitality of the new fishing station. To pinpoint the time of the permanent settlement presumes a decision to remain, to build and to establish leadership for future development. That is difficult to ascertain for Marblehead.

In 1629 Francis Higginson wrote "that here is plentie of marble stone . . . our plantation is from hence called Marble Harbor." So the tiny settlement already had a name and activity far exceeding that of a temporary summer fishing camp. It is significant that, as the original town pattern was shaped, Marble Harbor had connections with, but no special obligations to, any one of the existing New England colonies or their churches or colonial officials. It was the independent trader, the dissenter, the unwanted, and the rugged fisherman who put down the roots of this plantation. The only obligation for most was the repayment of their passage and sustenance by working it out for the most ardent backer of the fishermen, the merchant adventurer, Mathew Cradock.

The new world of New England had a fascination for Mathew Cradock, an influential, enterprising London merchant in his late twenties. He seized the first opportunity to become a stockholder during the shake-up of the old Dorchester Company. Later, the Council of Plymouth sold to six men of substance, including John Humphrey and John Endicott, that part of New England that spanned from three miles south of the Charles River to three miles north of the Merrimac River from the Atlantic to "the South Sea" . . . "commonlie called Massachusetts, alias Mattachusetts, alias Massatusetts Bay." With an enthusiasm that pervaded all his future colonial dealings Cradock bought the largest block of shares. When influence was brought to bear in the right places in the royal court, their charter was sealed in March, 1628, and ten months later at the annual meeting, it was voted that: Cradock would be governor; each fifty-pound shareholder would be assigned two hundred acres; John Endicott would be their colonial agent and he would depart as soon as possible for the new northern plantation. Governor Cradock wrote his close friend and cousin, John Endicott, that "we are very confident of your best endeavors for the general good," and then, after suggesting that Endicott bring not only the gospel but also a just and courteous demeanor to the Indians, added, "Be of good courage, go on, and do worthily and the Lord prosper your endeavor."

The endeavor was far more difficult than the Londoners thousands of miles away could imagine. Colonial reports were slow to arrive, but they confirmed needs Cradock had already anticipated: more supplies, more ships, more colonists skilled in fishing, shipbuilding and gardening, regardless of their commitment to the Puritan cause. In 1629 the five ships that departed with people and supplies for the Colony represented another sizeable personal investment for Governor Cradock, because the Massachusetts Bay Company charged only five pounds per passenger (children at reduced rates) and four pounds for one ton of household goods. To repay Cradock it was agreed that, in the division of lands, he would be assigned the first plantation and that the new colonists would work two-thirds of their time for the company and one-third for Governor Cradock. Some of these fishermen and shipbuilders were assigned to Marble Harbor or soon isolated themselves from the incompatability of Salem. Halfway between Boston and Cape Ann and well north of Cape Cod a productive fishing station was established. John Endicott's responsibility as agent was to fill the holds of the returning ships with fish, beaver skins, timber and sassafras. But even before the accumulation of profitable cargoes came the daily struggle to survive by expedient decisions that could not wait months for London's approval. Endicott complained to the home office about these problems.

Governor Cradock's response was a far-reaching decision that would be the yeast in the leavening of the New World for the next two centuries. He proposed that the charter, its authority and its presiding governor be moved from London to the Massachusetts Bay Colony. The motion carried and flung open that "wide doore of libertie."

Mathew Cradock then withdrew in favor of a new resident governor, John Winthrop, whose deputy governor was to be John Humphrey. On Easter Monday of 1630, Mathew Cradock, who had committed his heart along with his fortune, said his farewell to Winthrop on the deck of *Arbella* and disembarked, honored by the captain with a three-gun salute. Why Cradock never crossed the ocean to see his plantation and fishing station no one knows, but it was lucky for the Colony to have a fairy godfather in London. Though no longer governor, he persevered in outfitting ships, arranging cargoes and wages, selecting men, and enthusiastically promoting the Colony and it liberal charter to people of wealth and quality.

Political upheaval and church restrictions greatly augmented the emigration. In 1633, Cradock, as principal adventurer, was summoned before the king's royal council to deliver the patent and passenger lists because persons "ill-affected and discontented with civil and church government are leaving." Cradock appeared but, with his usual business agility, relinquished neither the sailing list nor the patent. The productivity of the colonists was even more impressive after William Wood described it in *New England Prospects:* "Mathew Cradock . . . is at charges of building ships. The last year (1632) one was upon the Stockes of 100 ton; that being finished, they are to build one of twice her burden." And he reported, "Marvill Head is a place which lyeth 4 miles full South from Salem, and is a very convenient place for a plantation, especially for such as will set upon the trade of fishing. There was made here a ships loading of fish last yeare, where still stands the stages, and drying scaffolds; here be good harbour for boates, and safe riding for shippes."

The name had by this time changed to "Marblehead," embracing the entire peninsula, not just the harbor. The center of activity, however, was not at the great harbor, but at Little Harbor, a snug, island-protected cove where the shallops rode safely at anchor and the fish was dried on the nearby ledges and rocky inclines. The man Cradock from "East of England" was personally responsible for most of the settlers of that cove and he owned a house and a fishing warehouse on Little Harbor. In 1634 Governor Winthrop reported in his journal: "February 1—Mr. Cradock's house at Marblehead was burnt down about midnight before, there being in it Mr. Allerton and many fishermen whom he employed that season who all were preserved by a special providence of God, with most of his goods therein, by a tailor, who sat up that night at work in the house and hearing a noise, looked out and saw the house on fire above the oven in the thatch." Isaac Allerton fortunately escaped from the fire but not from the specter of his past colonial ventures. Allerton was one of Marblehead's founders but his residency was short lived.

Isaac Allerton came from the Pilgrim Colony at Plymouth where he played a major role in the settlement, however his tendencies toward speculation and personal "free trade" eventually made him *persona non grata*, which stimulated his removal to Marblehead. It had been a long journey to Marblehead, beginning with his escape with persecuted church reformists to Leyden, Holland, where Allerton took his family and earned his living as a successful tailor. He and others of the English colony in Holland were not satisfied, so their leaders sought a refuge in the New World, working through their underground agent in England, William Brewster. Incidentally, Brewster had a helpful old Cambridge University chum, Robert Devereux, who became the earl of Essex and the ill-fated lover of Queen Elizabeth I.

When the Second Virginia Company was formed, the Pilgrims offered to go to the northern division which was less desirable to other emigrants who sought Spanish gold and the warmth of the southern ports. The Leyden group, including Allerton, tried to stay together and twice attempted to sail from England on their own refurbished *Speedwell*. Each time the vessel leaked so badly it was forced to return. Allerton and those who weren't discouraged by delays and disagreement over the destination, and some hired hands with no religious motivation, finally sailed on *Mayflower*. On the high seas the mutterings and disagreements grew, so that even before a landfall it was decided to draw up a binding contract for the future. The Mayflower Compact delineated their goal and their resolve to combine into "a civil body politick . . . into which we promise all due subjection and obedience." That last phrase was to haunt the fifth signer, Isaac Allerton. Misfortune struck him early, for his newborn son died during the passage and his wife, Mary, during the first winter. When the struggling Plymouth Colony elected William Bradford governor, Allerton was selected as his assistant, a position he held for years while acting as agent.

By this time James I had granted the Great Patent and the new company name was Council for New England. The joint stock arrangement between the merchants and the settlers declared that investors would supply funds and provisions and the colonists would furnish return cargoes, preferably fish. The settlers were expected to produce returns for the impatient investors, but life was hard and first cargoes were mainly wood and furs, but little fish. Agent Allerton became the first overseas commuter but, instead of appeasing the investors, he promoted grandiose schemes for financial speculation for which he borrowed additional funds without approval. Loans at 30 to 50 percent interest soon had the Colony hopelessly in debt.

Allerton's friend, Captain William Pierce, had transported fishing gear and a saltmaker to fishing stations, and when he sailed home to England the ship's hold was full of fish from the more northern waters. Allerton was greatly impressed by the fishing prospects. The Pilgrims tried to set up fishing stages on the north bay shores, but as one leader said, fishing was "fatale" for the Pilgrims, so their trading predicament was worsened. Isaac Allerton's own trading instincts were getting the best of him. He had good friends among his merchant contacts in London. A shrewd operator, he had brought his own goods across under the Colony's insurance, but upon arrival sold them for a personal profit to the colonists. It was hardly the spirit of the Mayflower Compact. The Pilgrims' faith in Allerton was challenged too often for their lasting confidence, so other officials accompanied him to the next London meeting. Still the debt grew, the investment floundered, and their intense suspicions of Allerton were suppressed only because he had married into the family of the highly respected Elder Brewster. Allerton's wife's name was Fear Brewster, an appellation from the fertile imagination of her writer-father who had named his sons Wrastling (with the Devil) and Love (of God).

Plymouth, now mortgaged to the hilt, formed a monopoly called the Undertakers—including Allerton—hoping to rescue Plymouth by claiming all trade, use of boats and fishing posts to the north. Although Allerton had returned to England to enlarge the grant to the Kennebec, the Colony was furious that Allerton "plaid his own game" by indulging in a private venture of buying the vessel, *The White Angel*, manned, according to Pilgrim standards, by "a wicked and drunken crew." They sailed north to a fishing station, Marblehead.

Allerton didn't stay around, but sailed back to England where he was discharged as the Pilgrims' agent. Upon his return to Plymouth Isaac Allerton was exiled from that colony where, it was said, "he scrued up his poore father-in-law's account to above 200 pounds." Undiscouraged, Allerton, the entrepreneur and speculator, fell back on influential friends including Captain Pierce, Samuel Maverick, and Mathew Cradock.

His banishment coincided with a report that Allerton had eight vessels out of Marblehead and was pursuing a brisk trade in fish, a feat the Pilgrims never had accomplished. How much time Allerton spent in Marblehead is unknown because the Allerton family remained in Plymouth until Fear Allerton's death in 1633. The following year Allerton himself was living in Cradock's house in Marblehead, managing the vessels and crews called "Cradock's fishermen." His daughter, Remember, who had lived in Leyden and then Plymouth, undoubtedly met her betrothed through her father's friendship with Samuel Maverick, colonial agent at Noddle's Island (East Boston). Remember Allerton married his brother, Moses Maverick, and in 1633 they set up housekeeping at Little Harbor. Things finally might have gone well for Isaac Allerton and his dreams of a lucrative foreign fishing trade but he was "warned out" of Marblehead by Salem authorities. No record divulges the reasons that can only be conjectured from two current circumstances.

In 1635 the General Court had named Marblehead a separate plantation to punish Salem for its reluctance to banish the dissident Roger Williams and retract their offensive letter. Salem, in hopes of restoring its influence, quickly rid itself of unwelcome nonconformists, among whom might have been Allerton. It was well known that when the Pilgrims turned against a settler, the "weight of their hand and the edge of their tongue pursued the exile like a Fury." As one such exile put it, ". . . this man (whom they have thus depraved) is a spotted unclean leper; he must out lest he pollute the land. . . ." Isaac Allerton's Pilgrim denigration caught up with him and he left Marblehead for New Amsterdam, and then New Haven where he pursued West Indies trade. Fortune never did bless his efforts; probably his greatest opportunity was lost when he was forced to leave Marblehead. The town recorded in May, 1635, that he turned over "to Moses Maverick, his sone-in lawe, all his houses, buildings and stages, that hee hath at Marblehead" which had resulted from only five or six years experience in the fishing business.

Some years later Allerton requested the town's permission to return to live with his daughter, but instead he had to live out his years in New Haven where he died insolvent. A New Haven plaque now commemorates Isaac Allerton as the only *Mayflower* passenger buried in Connecticut. As an early navigator of Marblehead's future course, Isaac Allerton's contribution was a bustling, though infant, fishing business in the capable hands of his son-in-law, Moses Maverick, who was to become a vigorous, shrewd leader of Marblehead for the next fifty years.

Moses Maverick's colonial connections were neither with the Plymouth Colony nor the Puritan Massachusetts Bay Colony, but with a third conflicting English interest that was waiting to pounce on the land grants if the others faltered or failed.

Samuel Maverick, Moses' genial brother who had brought him to America, was the agent for Sir Ferdinand Gorges who headed up the Second Virginia Company. Gorges' official position was a result of his family's financial interests in the Great Council of New England, whose initial colonization efforts had all failed. His long friendship with Sir Walter Raleigh and the earl of Essex had built support for New World plans, but by 1620 a Great Patent already had been awarded to Plymouth. Gorges was not about to retire gracefully from his plan for a great, new, feudal estate across the sea. To secure his plan he financed the Anglican emigrants desiring to come to New England, and to sit on his controversial grant Gorges sent over his colonial agent, Samuel Maverick. Maverick, his brother Moses and other Anglicans, settled on Noddle's Island in Boston Bay, fortified it and "made trouble and they for him," for the habits of the pleasure-loving Samuel Maverick offended all the religious separatists.

One Saturday evening, when Samuel was making merry in the Ship's Tavern in Boston, he was advised to quiet down in keeping with the newly extended Sabbath. Maverick, having caned the constable, moved on to another tavern, only to be ordered out, but in the ensuing argument he heard a seemingly treasonable remark and brought charges. His suit and the Court's counter charges were a capsuled replay of the political and religious tension and government intrigue building up in the mother country.

Samuel Maverick's position could have been in jeopardy as the jurisdiction of his area was turned over to the Massachusetts Bay Company; nevertheless, Sir Ferdinand Gorges, observing the political turmoil in London, had Maverick wait it out on Noddle's Island. It seemed to be no embarrassment to Maverick, but it was a harassment to Puritan Governor Winthrop. Samuel Maverick was known as the most hospitable host on the coast and entertained all comers, Allerton, Winthrop, Pierce, and the lesser known. Once, when Maverick took in an adulterous couple, the staid General Court fined him £100 which it quickly reduced to £60; however, jolly Maverick figured it had been worth more, so he offered an £80 payment.

It wouldn't be strange that the sociable Mr. Maverick and the ubiquitous Mr. Allerton would get along well and for their relatives, Remember and Moses, to meet and marry. The friendly Anglican and nonconforming Pilgrim made a match that introduced another independent strain into the young settlement of Marblehead. It was Moses Maverick who offered one of Allerton's pinnaces to fetch Marblehead's first minister, Mr. Avery, from Newbury in 1635. But, as the vessel was rounding Cape Ann, it was slammed by the high winds and waves of a late August hurricane; the eight members of the Avery family went down with the ill-fated pinnace and Marblehead was forced to wait a little longer for its own teacher-minister.

Two of the largest Marblehead land parcels were soon granted to two long-time shareholders in the Massachusetts Bay Company. The first was the wealthy John Humphrey who from the time of his treasurer's responsibility in the original Dorchester Company until his investment in the Massachusetts Bay Company had colonial ambitions to set up trading colonies in several productive locations from New England south to Virginia to the Caribbean. Though he backed the efforts to finance colonists and relief ships, Humphrey's opportunity to become first deputy to Governor Winthrop was passed up for love. Then, having won the Lady Susan Fiennes, the couple came to the Colony two years later.

As with others of wealth and quality, life in New England was unexpectedly difficult, uncomfortable and even colder than England. Humphrey's yearning for a southern colony and his doubts of northern subsistence, led him to promote a southern transfer of the whole colony, a subversion unappreciated by Winthrop. Yet, when Marblehead plantation was briefly set apart, John Humphrey, the ex-treasurer, was granted three hundred acres in Marblehead from the Clifte to the Forest River to be improved by him and sold to Marblehead "inhabitants as they stood in need of it for equal recompence for his labour and cost." Humphrey, to his own financial loss, did improve the grant, perhaps more than his abutter, Hugh Peter.

Neither Salem, nor its unwilling satellite, Marblehead, had ever seen the likes of a minister named Hugh Peter. Endicott, Cradock and Winthrop all knew this vital, articulate graduate of Trinity College, Cambridge, whose tolerance, wit and community involvement were widely recognized in his exiled Dutch parish and even by the royal court in England. Hugh Peter seemed to be just what Salem needed to abate the bitterness over minister Roger Williams' treatment and preachings. The thirty-seven-year-old churchman brought with him a zest for improvement and accomplishment which he immediately applied to updating local methods of shipbuilding and fishing. A farm marketplace, a general storehouse and salt works came into being with his encouragement and with the supplies he had obtained from Europe. Why not grow hemp? "Why not try?" was Hugh Peter's watchword. And if the involved minister raised "up men to a publick frame of spirit" in business and government councils, no one questioned his religious commitment, for he was Puritan to the core. His brand of Puritanism had warm, human qualities of tolerance and humor and a common touch. Hugh Peter endeared himself to the subdued "liberals" by trying to reduce the harsh sentences. And he could spellbind the loyal and serious Puritans with his unusual, droll and positive sermons. He often said: "The Word of God has free Passage among us, for no sooner in one ear than out the other." This ebullient preacher was granted two hundred acres in Marblehead where he must have felt at home with the fishermen from Cornwall and the Channel Isles, for Foy (Fowey) in Cornwall was his birthplace and his mother was of the ancient Cornish family, the Trefreys. It is tantalizing to recall that one of the early names tried out on Marblehead was "Foy."

Neither Humphrey nor Peter lived out their lives on their lands in Marblehead: one left to encounter greater disappointment in his hopes for a southern colony; the other, Peter, departed with a colonial petition to England only to be swept up in his country's Civil War and tragically cut off in his prime by the royal executioner. Both Hugh Peter and John Humphrey contributed to the early development of the plains area of Marblehead that had seemed uninviting to the fishermen clustered around Little Harbor and Doliber's Cove.

Doliber, the legendary settler without a first name or dates, was said to have left the stifling Puritanism of the opposite shore and taken up a life of liberty, though deprivation, in a hogshead on the point of land named for him. No records exist except in the continuing role of his descendants in the history of the town.

The recounting of the founding of Marblehead has an ambivalence in the comparative effect of each influence. But one conclusion cannot be escaped: it was a mixed bag—from the Plymouth

Separatists, Allerton; from the Puritans of the Massachusetts Bay Colony, Cradock, Humphrey, and Peter; from the Gorges' Anglicans, Moses Maverick; from Salem the escapists, Doliber and other nonconformists; from Cornwall, Guernsey and Jersey, intrepid, free-wheeling fishermen. Marblehead was destined to be a settlement without a common dedication to a single church or colony but with a brash, independent attitude that was going to sorely try Salem, its strict overseer. And not long after it would exasperate the Province and eventually help overturn the throne.

3. Fish Makes the Future

MARBLEHEAD, for its first twenty years, belonged to Salem in a legal and territorial sense, and there it ended. This was no subtle difference, for they were as diverse a pair of settlements as could ever share a common boundary.

On one side were the solemn, scrupulous Puritans who had come to the New World to practice their religion free from repressions by church and state and to carry the Gospel to the Indians. Their knowledge of religion, law, farming and some handicrafts far outweighed their experience in the fishing and trading which would be necessary to produce the profits awaited by the hard-headed London investors. On the other side of the boundary line was a fishing station populated by hardy, plebeian colonists capable of producing the large supply of fish for the Colonies and foreign trade. With little or no religious motivation, these adventurous seamen clustered around their harbor and began their relentless quest for more personal liberty and freedom of the seas.

That this rough, disparate settlement owning its own fish flakes, warehouses and vessels could exist cheek to cheek with the God-fearing Puritans was guaranteed by two advantageous stipulations in the charter: first, English fishermen were allowed to land on the

New England coast and set up fishing stages for drying and curing fish; second, the company could carry supplies to New England free from duties and taxes for seven years and would be exempt from any customs fees over 5 percent for twenty-one years. These generous, sweeping provisions undoubtedly developed from the glowing reports of the fishing prospects beginning in 1614 with Captain John Smith who advised "let not the meanness of the word fish distaste you, for it will afford as good gold as the mines of Guiana . . . and more certainty and facility." And King James, hearing of this, piously added: "In truth 'tis an honest trade, 'twas the apostles own calling."

As John Winthrop approached his new land, he was astonished at the catch of sixty-seven cod in two and one-half hours, each fish measuring one and one-half yards long and a yard around, and he later exulted, "1600 bass in one draught." His sworn enemy, Thomas Morton, wrote in 1636 that at the turning of the tide was seen such multitudes of sea bass "as it seemed one might goe over their backs dri-shod." Small wonder that the fishermen of Cornwall and the Channel Islands signed up to be the first to harvest such enticing fishing grounds. The emigration increased so rapidly that between 1630 and 1641 vessels arrived almost weekly, transporting more colonists in those eleven years than in the entire period from 1641 to the American Revolution. Marblehead got its share of settlers, not of the "apostle" variety, but the sturdy stock who would continually risk their lives on uncharted waters often in old, refurbished British vessels equipped with secondhand fishing gear. Undaunted by these handicaps and the personal privations, by 1632 the tiny settlement was able to produce an entire shipload of cured fish for the European market.

The extreme hardships of these early Marbleheaders can never be underestimated. Clothed only in whatever they had brought from their English homes, plus jackets and boots supplied by Mr. Cradock, they lived in dugouts, caves and wigwams warmed by smoky fires of green wood from the engulfing forest. The dark, depressing forest could hide the enemy and wolves, so the fishermen cut it back as fast as possible and used the wood for fuel, boats, fish fences and the houses they longed to have, just like those in England. With no saw mills or mortar or nails they laboriously built around the rocky ledges, using the boulders for cellar foundations, and tucked against the protective hill single-story dwellings covered by thatched roof, each with one wooden chimney lined with clay, which necessitated a separate cooking area. The windows were shuttered openings, possibly protected by oiled paper or other crude coverings. A few carpenters, coopers and blacksmiths produced the simple implements and tables and benches. A small lamp burned fish oil, animal fat or often a pine knot to illuminate the black night with its menacing sounds and miserable swarm of insects (especially "muskitoes") which were almost intolerable near the woods and marshes. So the incongruous houses clung together near familiar coves, vessels and friends, though the dire necessity for food pushed back the clearing to where they could plant crops with the help of the Indians.

The first, scanty, summer crops of corn and beans planted in rocky, unwilling soil seldom lasted through the long winter; nor did the goats and heifers brought from England survive the weather, the bears or the wolves. Scurvy, death and fear forced some settlers to return home permanently, while others fished in the summer season and spent the winter in England. Those who persevered and put down roots survived only because of the fish. Almost every species from whales to turbot, mackerel to sturgeon, clams to lobsters was found in abundance. In 1634 *New England Prospects* said of lobsters; "their plenty makes them little esteemed and seldom eaten," for both Indian and colonist used lobster for bait. The lowly clam, on the other hand, saved many a hungry family and was "the treasure hid in the sands." Even the pigs appreciated their worth and would rush to the beach at low tide to devour the mollusks. The shallops and pinnaces were small open boats and the hands were few to hold the single lines dropped over the rail. Then began the curing process to clean, split, salt and dry the catch on primitive fish flakes built of round beach stones or a network of raised wooden frames or branches that would allow the air to circulate and the sun to dry the fish splits. Due to a scarcity of imported salt the fishermen laboriously evaporated sea water to preserve the fish for export. Most of the fish was sold and the rest would hopefully last through the times when great drifts of ice and a howling northeast wind confined the boats to the harbor. In the cold months there were few Indians with whom to trade for venison or turkey; however, even fewer returned after another ravaging epidemic of a disease to which colonists seemed immune.

It killed off two of the ruling Naumkeag Sagamores—their names now Anglicized to John and James—and left only the local Sagamore, George, whom the fishermen called "Rumney Marsh" or "No Nose"; only the beginning of hundreds of cryptic, irreverent Marblehead nicknames.

Some of those names splashed out of the keg with its healing, spirit-raising beverage that saw many a fisherman through an icy, desolate and bankrupt winter. Marblehead's reputation was soon established, for some of the first court records reveal complaints of drunkenness and loud, hair-pulling participants brought before Salem's Puritan magistrates.

Though Governor Winthrop had not brought along a system of colonial laws, he had the local authority plus the knowledge of English governance, so in August, 1630, shortly after his arrival, he records "We kept a court." That General Court with historical adjustments has continued until the present day; however, in its earliest days, the court's laws evolved directly from the religious tenets of the Puritans. They themselves had packed more beer than water in *Arbella's* hold, but moderation was expected; yet, even during the crossing Winthrop wrote, "We observed it a common fault in our young people, that they gave themselves to drink hot waters very immoderately." The "hot waters" were usually beer which became the ever-present refreshment, far more trustworthy than water or milk. Suffering with the poor food, cold, insects, wolves, danger and disease, who but the most ascetic Puritan could point a finger at a settler's full tankard? And when decent English beer ran out, local beer was made out of spruce or sassafras, roots, or bark—anything that would ferment and could be swallowed.

Who knows in what beer substitute Thomas Gray and the others from Marblehead were imbibing when they were caught drinking excessively? The records prove the severity of the punishments, especially in the case of Thomas Gray, whose behavior and beliefs resulted in the 1631 order that his "house att Marble Harbor shalbe puld downe, & that noe Englisheman shall here after give houseroome to him or entertaine him." True, he lost his home, but the Marble Harbor Englishmen gave Thomas Gray houseroom until his death, and the town records reveal payments to him, including a "shute of clothes for owled Gray", that would indicate that he was the town's first welfare recipient. Marbleheaders were never known for wasting saccharine sympathy on anyone, but empathy for a fellow townsman who was in trouble or wronged was as much a part of them as the swearing and brawling and cussed resistance to outside authority.

The town seldom reported its offenders to Salem, or, when left to its devices, rarely carried out local sentences. A constable was obviously needed, so Salem soon appointed one of their own men to that unenviable position and began to decree special laws aimed solely at Marblehead's nonconformity. The town had no representation to forestall any repressive measures, for, not being Puritans, they did not qualify for the church membership required to become voting "freemen." The Oath of the Freeman in Massachusetts, approved in 1634, was a precise and noble declaration of a colonial citizen's duties and rights (without even a tip of the hat to the king); but the tolerance that the Puritans themselves craved was not then extended to others. Quakers, Catholics, Dissenters, or irreligious fishermen could not take the freeman's oath and become voters. Marblehead's answer was to passively resist or blatantly ignore intolerant Puritan measures.

The peninsular community almost tasted real freedom when, following the setting off of town boundaries by a committee, the General Court declared Marblehead a separate plantation in 1635, only to dash the town's hopes by reversing the order in less than a year, stating, "It was proved . . . that Marblenecke belongs to Salem."

In 1636 the Puritans decided to establish an educational system. They began at the top with the establishment of a college that they dreamed might one day have the prestige of the English universities which claimed several alumni in the Massachusetts Bay Company. Hugh Peter (B.A., M.A.) and John Humphrey (B.A.), both of Trinity College, Cambridge, were among those assigned to choose the proposed Marblehead site. Their recommendation was a three-hundred-acre grant (owned by Thomas Scruggs) situated "in the outmost bounds of Salem . . . is from the Sea, where the fresh water runs out [Forest River], west and north is the farm next to Mr. Humphrey's bounded by the [Marblehead Common] by the northeast . . . and east. . . ." The competition for the Court's £300 college appropriation was keen and Newtown (Cambridge) won. And not long after, John Harvard willed half his fortune and his four hundred-book library to the new college which, in gratitude, was named Harvard College—and, oh, the difference to Marblehead!

The ordinances issuing from Salem Town were bound to crystallize the difficulties between Marblehead and itself. For, having discovered that John Peach and Nicholas Merritt had fenced five acres in Marblehead against orders, Salem let them improve the land, with the understanding that only Salem could dispose of the acreage. It was time for a realistic decision about the acquisition of land by the fishermen. On November 2, 1636, Salem voted that "for the better furthering of the fishing and trading and to avoid inconvenience we have found in granting land (to plant) to fishermen, that none inhabiting Marblehead shall have any other accomodation of land other than a house lott, a garden lott or ground for placing of their flakes according to the size of the family. Not above two acres and the common use of woods adjacent for their goates and their cattle." Marblehead's concentration on fishing was not about to be diluted by farming just when the fisheries were the fastest growing business in the Colonies.

The business influences of Mathew Cradock and Hugh Peter were becoming more productive in fishing and shipbuilding, for in 1636 Marblehead ship's carpenters completed the third large vessel built in the Colonies—the 120-ton *Desire*. It was a sturdy vessel of hand-hewn New England timbers, equipped with three falcons and one falconet (a kind of cannon shooting a pound or half-pound projectile), manned by colonial seamen and commanded by the renowned mariner, Captain William Pierce. This first large vessel was a source of great pride to the seagoing Marbleheaders, but it sailed out to an ironic fate, a tragic blend of shame and success.

Marblehead's *Desire* performed beautifully, carrying great loads of fish and setting a new record for ocean crossings—twenty-three days to Gravesend on the Thames. The accomplishment was another "first" for the skipper who was recognized on both sides of the Atlantic as the finest mariner and navigator of his day. He was frequently chosen for a dangerous mission, such as the retaliation against the Pequot Indians. *Desire* transported John Endicott's volunteer commandoes to Block Island to "revenge the blood of our countrimen" by devastating the Indian village, burning the cornfields and destroying their canoes. The Indians, with wise respect for the English fire power, hid in the swamps until *Desire* sailed on to another Pequot encampment where each side tore into bloody shreds seventeen years of Colonial-Indian peace.

The official Colonial Seal sent in 1629 to John Endicott had been etched in silver with an oval frame surrounding a modestly dressed Indian figure, arms outstretched with his plea written on a banner above his head: "Come over and help us." This seal, twice in history suspended for political reasons but ultimately revised for the Massachusetts State seal, projected the missionary intent of Massachusetts Bay Company. The primitive culture of the "silly Salvages" afforded much mirth and laughter, nevertheless, the mystery of their origin, appearance, and customs convinced the Puritans that the Indians were one of the ten lost tribes of Israel and destined, at last, to receive the Gospel. This conclusion obliged the Puritans and their leaders to treat the Indians as equals, which resulted in mutual hospitality, extensive trade, legal hearings, and even the use of wampum as official exchange. Yet, the proselytism was generally unsuccessful for, as one Indian chief replied when asked for permission to preach to his tribe, "Make the English good first, then try it on the Pequots and Mohegans, and if it works, I will consider it."

The vicious Pequots were hated and feared by most other tribes who preferred to align themselves with the well-armed English who, in turn, were greatly encouraged in their hopes for westward expansion by having the Massachusetts tribe as their closest ally. The Pequot War in 1636 was less a racial struggle than a mutual Indian-Puritan desire to destroy that fierce tribe in a savage and destructive war.

The coastal interests of the fishermen were not endangered, nor were they worried about friendly Naumkeags, so Marblehead involved itself very little in the Pequot War. A few volunteers brought back tales of the slaughter of the six hundred Pequots caught on the Mystic River while feasting within their palisaded fort which soon became a blazing inferno, consuming most of the braves, the women and children. The Indians who, fortunately or perhaps unfortunately, escaped the fire were among the captives divided among the Indian victors and the Puritan towns. The fifteen Pequot boys and two women brought to Marblehead were placed on a ship loaded with fish bound for Bermuda; instead, heavy storms blew the ship to Providence Island (Nassau). There the Indian captives were exchanged for other human cargo. That ship was Marblehead's first-born *Desire*, skippered by Captain William Pierce. Seven months later, in January, 1638, *Desire* returned and its bill of lading included "cotton, tobacco, negroes, and salt from Tertugos." These were undoubtedly the first black slaves brought into New England by an American-built vessel. As Captain Pierce often brought his large cargoes into Boston for distribution, it is most likely that *Desire* docked there and unloaded its black cargo, probably allotted (rather than sold) to certain families. The cost of the passage might have been sufficient. Marblehead's simple seafarers, unused to domestics in Guernsey or Jersey and owning only small thatched huts, were not likely prospects for black servants. Whereas, Governor Winthrop's advisors, his brother-in-law Emmanuel Downing and Hugh Peter, decrying the labor shortage and unreliability of the Indians, had suggested additional indentured whites or the "Moors."

Undoubtedly, Captain Pierce, "a godly man," had his orders and carried out the Indian-Negro exchange unaware of its significance. Hadn't William Pierce already seen hundreds of blacks carried off by Spanish galleons or distributed in England by the sea rovers or sold by the Dutch to the colony of Virginia? As far as can be determined, this Pequot-Negro exchange was the only incident that could denigrate the distinguished record of one of the most skillful mariners in history.

Captain William Pierce, whose innumerable voyages transported thousands of Englishmen, their household goods, and animals to the land of liberty and hope, could well be called "the ferryman of the Atlantic". The ships were small, the accommodations were uncomfortable and damp, the ocean frightening and rough, and death was an ominous stowaway, but the passengers' courage grew in proportion to their confidence in the skipper. Unbiased and able, William Pierce was sought after by the Merchant Adventurers, the governors and councils and almost every coastal settlement from Pemaquid to Virginia. He was a friend of Allerton, Bradford, Winthrop, Peter, Endicott, Humphrey, Cradock, Winslow, Conant, Standish, and Dissenters who didn't agree with any of them. Plymouth Colony's very survival depended on his persistent efforts to save it from famine. His ships often conveyed Isaac Allerton to England to seek further financing and supplies. However, the fishing equipment that Pierce delivered held little interest for the Pilgrims, except for Allerton who, tempted by the prospects of the fishing trade, broke loose and established his own Marblehead station, undoubtedly with the encouragement of Cradock and Captain Pierce. It was in the outer harbor that Pierce and Allerton welcomed Governor Winthrop's vessel in 1630.

Nothing seemed to daunt Captain Pierce. He towed Mr. Cradock's *Ambrose* from Newfoundland to England, he rescued Separatists escaping to Connecticut in the desperately cold winter, he charted Boston Harbor. Soon after the first colonial printing press (shipped over by the Reverend Joseph Glover) was set up in Cambridge, the choice for the second printed piece in America was *The Almanack of Captain William Pierce*, the first almanac, and by a skipper whose achievements were so highly regarded.

This tribute to the intrepid mariner was just being published in 1640 when *Desire* headed for the West Indies with some disenchanted colonists. Off the coast of Providence Island Captain Pierce spied a Spanish galleon maneuvering for an attack and warned the passengers to go below. He manned the cannon to ward off the attackers, but was killed defending his ship. Captain Pierce was buried at sea from the deck of *Desire* which itself was later buried in historical oblivion. The first out-o'-Marblehead vessel seems to have disappeared with its captain.

The New England trade in human beings that had inadvertently been inaugurated by *Desire* began to expand rapidly in other ports; however, it was decades before Marblehead's population included black servants. For "servant" was the name preferred by the Puritans who held that a "slave" was a criminal or war prisoner with no rights. The Negroes were regarded as strange, exotic creatures whom the sun had blackened or, in keeping with the Biblical reference, had been discolored by Ham's curse. In good conscience the Puritans tried to treat the blacks as equals, but, for all practical purposes, they needed farm laborers, and at a cheaper price. It was the problem of conscience versus need; Marblehead's primary concern was its fisheries.

Pirates caused constant anxiety about the risk of being terrorized at sea. Lying in wait around the next island or cove for any profitable cargo of furs, fish, English goods or salt, pirates menaced New England trade from its infancy. In 1632 Winthrop thought he had persuaded the pirates to confine their deadly livelihood to southern waters.

Anxiety over pirates and foreign enemies resulted in Marblehead's first fortification. Fort Darby, erected on the northwest corner of the peninsula (Naugus Head), was not far from the palisaded Indian fort and probably copied from its design, with the addition of some English fire power. Later a breastwork was built at the entrance to Marblehead Harbor to better protect Little Harbor and the approaches to the Great Bay. From Fort Darby the main traffic between Marblehead and Salem could easily be observed, for by 1637 an official ferry operated from the west shore directly across to the Salem wharf. It is thought that a large, open canoe-like boat was rowed across by the ferryman, his helper and any able passengers who paid tuppence for the trip. This was far easier than tracing serpentine Indian trails the entire length of the wooded peninsula.

The fishermen's trips to Salem were more frequent and even more frustrating. Marblehead lived apart, yet had to pay $\frac{1}{15}$ of Salem's tax assessment for the privilege of having Salem lay out Marblehead lands without providing any improvements. The land demands increased and in 1638 as many as fourteen grants were made in one day, using as the early boundary designations John Peach's Necke, the Forest Side, the Great Meadow, the Necke and the Main. The grantees' names were to frequent the town history—Maverick, Walton, Peach, Knights, Coit, Pitman—and for Nick, the fisherman, "5 acres by the hogstyes in the forest." Controversies were built into the property deeds by such transitory boundaries as the apple-tree stump, a large stone, a small oak or an old Indian marker. Fences were the obvious solution but didn't diminish the argument as they too were movable. So the custom of fence viewing, or walking the boundary, became well entrenched; especially for the "Commons," or the lands of the Commoners who, by virtue of their early arrival, claimed large areas for their exclusive use. The Johnny-come-lately of 1645 had first to make his obeisance to the "old" Commoners for acceptance into town, for a lot and use of the common pasturage. The Commoners felt they alone had carried the responsibility for the continuance of the settlement, its taxes, upkeep of the Commons and payment of the minister's salary.

There was a peculiar dichotomy in the post of Marblehead's first "minister," William Walton. Although he was the teacher and the preacher of the town, no effort was ever made to have him ordained into a specific ministry. Walton, friend and classmate of John Harvard at England's Emmanuel College, Cambridge (where he took his degree), arrived in Marblehead before 1638 and pursued his missionary effort, without ordination, for over thirty years. This kind, judicious and serious man was willing to remain all those years, even though many times his pay was in fish, corn, or half a cow. It can be hoped that Mr. Walton was a good trader the year his payment was a half ton of fish! He lived on the property first owned by Mathew Cradock on Little Harbor, which had been willed to his widow, Rebecca, who then became Mrs. Richard Glover. For £15 she conveyed the land and building to Mr. Walton who already owned pasturage for two cows on the nearby island. In spite of the fact that he educated many of the people and preached the word of God, William Walton never was permitted to marry the local couples—that was Moses Maverick's responsibility as a Court-appointed official. Nevertheless, Marblehead's appreciation of Walton was clearly evident as each year his salary, and often an increase, was decided upon before setting the town rates (taxes). At the time of his death William Walton was receiving £70, annually, which he must have generously shared for his estate listed a simple, scantily furnished home, in which the most valuable item was his library.

There is no record of any pressure by Mr. Walton for ordination, perhaps for the same reason held by the townspeople. Once ordination was accomplished the parish would be subject to the regulations and restrictions of the Puritan mother church and a party to the severity of its judgment.

To throw fear into flagging spirits by making public examples of wrong doers, the Puritans of Massachusetts Bay Colony had a long list of crimes demanding capital punishment, such as adultery, blasphemy, conspiracy, murder, witchcraft, and cursing, or smiting one's parents after age sixteen unless there was justified provocation or unchristian neglect in education. Lesser offenses, like burglary, could result in banishment, branding, or slavery.

Life was difficult enough and death might wait on any shoal or tide; Marblehead hesitated to condemn the common weaknesses in

men: fights and rocks, perhaps, but not pillory or stocks, except
when forced by the General Court to comply. When Margaret
Seale committed adultery with two Salem men and the three were
hauled before the magistrates on a charge that carried the death
penalty, Marblehead witnesses blamed her beastly, drunken husband,
so that the court reduced its verdict to a severe whipping and banishment. To be banished into the woods on foot probably meant
death, but somehow the three escaped that fate, even though Margaret's husband had offered a large reward for her capture. Could
someone have provided a boat?

Salem had had enough. Though the merchants relished the fishing
profits and had pressured the General Court for special incentives to
build the industry, Salem was irritated beyond its Puritan patience
by irrepressible, noisy Marblehead which now could really crow
over the new measures: freeing fisheries' properties from duties and
taxes; releasing fishermen from military training and hogreeving
(collecting the swine roaming through the streets); forbidding the
use of precious cod and bass as soil fertilizer. Salem was glad to shed
the responsibility for Marblehead lands in 1641, when Marblehead
was given permission to lay out its own acreage subject to the approval of a Salem appointee—one more cod-size step in the town's
autonomy.

In 1641 other events were happening to quicken the pulse of a
Puritan. The bright comet that soared through the sky that year
seemed to signal the inauguration of two decades of consolidation of
colonial independence, establishment of its own system of law and
government, and a freedom from English interference not to be duplicated for the next 125 years. Thousands of miles of ocean protected New England from Britain's devastating Civil Wars that fortunately distracted the attention of the home governments from the
Colonies. Quick to sense this and buoyed by their confidence in the
rising star of the Puritan hero, Cromwell, the Massachusetts Bay
Colony strengthened and clarified its jurisdiction by formalizing a
set of one hundred laws into a "Body of Liberties" which delineated
the current legal practices and broadened their interpretation, allowed hearings and discretionary judgments.

Probably just such a judgment caused the outburst of John Coit,
Marblehead teacher and ship-builder, that "it is better to go to hell's
gate for mercy than to Mr. Endicott [Deputy Governor] for justice." Second discretionary judgment: fine John Coit. Marblehead,
not yet a self-governing town, was unable to vote for the three-year
trial of the "Liberties" but Marblehead participated in the 1641 day
of Thanksgiving, not so much for Puritans' gratitude at Parliament's

confirmation of its patent rights, but for the record of 300,000 dried fish sent to market. The favorite among the Colonies, Massachusetts Bay, was further blessed by the House of Commons with an uncommon advantage: because the plantations of New England had established themselves without cost to England, all merchandise to and from New England would be free from all customs duties until further notice.

"Further notice" caused incessant colonial anxiety as power shifted around in the mother country, for the final outcome was still questionable and the delay in overseas notification might be fatal to their future. The necessity for mutual help and defensive strength compelled cooperation in the first confederation of New England colonies. The new United Colonies of New England proclaimed friendship in mutual aid in defense and war under the guidance, but not jurisdiction, of the governor of Massachusetts. Concern for the protection of seaports was a paramount issue. William Walton and Moses Maverick, "in behalf of the inhabitants of Marble-head," by-passed Salem and petitioned directly to the honored Court. Couched in respectful, effective language worthy of Mr. Walton's Cambridge degree, the petition pointed up the necessity of securing the Marble-head harbor, not only for the safety of the inhabitants "wanting all means to defend them against the assault of the weakest enemie: but especially in regard to the Great Detriment; that probably may come to the whole countrie, in case the Harbour be left open." Marblehead, it continued, would not presume to tell the Court what to decide, but, "we hope the Lord will appoint salvation for wals and bulwarkes." The motion passed: Marblehead could fortify itself by a breastwork and the General Court would deliver two cannons and suitable ammunition. Not long after, the Court couldn't resist commenting on Marblehead's lack of martial discipline—an oft-repeated complaint about Marblehead's disinterest in drilling, tidy uniforms and perfunctory preparation, yet her men's performance in combat was never questioned.

A subversive campaign against Salem domination was ever pursued with further Court petitions implying lack of support by Salem, as in the 1646 complaint of consumption of Marblehead timber by strangers. The petition was signed by the most active and influential townsmen: William Walton, Moses Maverick, David Curwithin, constable, John Bartoll, John Peach, Arthur Sandin, John Legg and an unidentified, Walsingham Chilson. These citizens were running Marblehead as if it were independent. Salem's Town Meeting finally conceded on December 12, 1648, by granting Marblehead full independence, subject to the approval of the General Court.

From that moment, the separation of the two communities was acknowledged to be more than a boundary line; it was a deep ravine of differences inherent in their religious and educational backgrounds, social and economic positions, their attitudes toward personal freedoms and conformity, and their reasons for emigrating to America.

At last, Marblehead was "on its own hook"; of course, it really always had been. Few in the Puritan Massachusetts Bay Colony pretended to understand the fishing town populated by rugged, uneducated, irreligious fishermen and their equally sturdy wives. No church or state authority seemed to intimidate the townspeople who, inexplicably, showed not the slightest desire to attain the doctrinal position of a godly "freeman." They just acted as if they were free men who guarded not the Puritan *status quo*, but their own liberty and that of their town. The boldness and daring of their daily adventures on the sea penetrated their beings and the prospect of official disapproval turned not a hair; it was just a question of how to maneuver around that governmental reef. Why did strict, stern colonial officials tolerate this nonconformity for which the Quakers and other dissenters were prosecuted? The answer was centuries old: they needed Marblehead—its profitable fish, its food supply and its unremitting battle with the mother country for colonial fishing and trading rights and freedom of the seas. Let the fractious fishermen fight those battles and keep their radicalism at sea.

The divergence was supported by the natural geographical isolation of the peninsula town—"so solitary and detached, that it is not a thorough fair to other places"—and the inborn traits of its people. This physical and cultural isolation preserved Marblehead's customs, life style and dialect, and developed a strength and self-sufficiency as solid as the rocky terrain into which the settlement forced its roots.

The town huddled around Little Harbor and along the western side of the great harbor with its unadorned, unpainted houses perched at cockeyed angles against the rock and tucked back from the wind and sea. The choice of land for the productive fish flakes seemed equally important and almost every headland was crocheted with raised wooden frames, or "flakes," holding up many varieties of fish to the sun and air. The pathways followed the convenience of men's feet around the boulders, or the marsh or stream, between the tightly spaced houses directly to the wharves or fishing stages. Other homes were lined up along the Indian trails that soon widened into cartways. Marblehead could have not cared less for its symmetry or system.

Out on the water was what really mattered. The harbor and coves were dotted with Indian-style canoes, shallops, pinnaces and the larger sloops and ketches. The entire concentration of the town was on fishing and the ships that carried the men and their catch. There were skilled fishermen, experienced skippers, shipbuilders, coopers, blacksmiths, sailmakers and the vital middlemen, the merchants. The involvement of the fisherman's entire family was an accepted fact—his wife and children watched and stored the dried, cured fish, tended the animals and garden, and tried to keep his home warm and safe. Every "grummet" of food and firewood would be spared until replenished by the next voyage. The months-long fishing trips or trading voyages to coastal colonies or distant ports left the fisherman's wife dependent on her own resources and she grew in self-reliance and fortitude which prepared her for the oft-repeated walk to the wharf to account for the returning boats and their crews. Many a man was lost at sea; and those who had weathered the storm and shoals or escaped from the pirates, Indians, or foreign plunderers made a terse report or a futile gesture. Accordingly, the widow might pull herself back up the rocky steps to a tiny house abounding with children, where, bereft of the solace of distant relatives, she might try to face the sparse winter with a swig of Arthur Sandin's beer. Her neighbors would speak little of her loss, but would close in around the family with whatever they could spare until the fisherman o'er the hill, who had lost his wife in childbirth, presented his offer of marriage. Their combined properties would improve the lot of both. And so began the maze of intermarriage of Marblehead families that defies disentanglement. Many of the men and women married three or four times, usually producing a sizeable family each time, reduced in number only by the high infant mortality. And if the deceased infant's name was John, 'twas no reason not to name the next son John without any numerical indications to reduce future genealogical frustrations. After all, *they* knew.

No documents or gravestones can reveal the heartaches of the early town, but those who were not buried at sea were laid in the burying ground on the hill between the pond and Little Harbor. The shallow soil between the outcropping of rock was unlikely ground in which to lay the dead, except that, true to English custom, the burial ground was adjacent to the place of worship. This, according to colonial custom, was a secular meeting house built on a high headland, a strategic lookout toward land and sea. From this reassuring landmark issued the bell's warning of attack, fire, or the news of victory or defeat by man or the sea. The first bell ringers,

Edward Read and Francis Linsford, were paid forty shillings a year to "warne the Towne" and care for the meeting house.

This small, rude meeting house must have been built about 1638 after Mr. Walton's arrival, and by 1648 it had the first call on the town's taxes for upkeep. With the growth of the place extensions were added to the accompaniment of usual hassle over the work and the seating. Carpenter Robert Knight's bill was finally paid (after defects "cleered") for timber, work on the bell and meeting house and three shillings spent for a day of arbitration.

When the 1659 seating was "donn," Town Meeting appointed nine men, including the constable, and five more to collect for the seats. Those seats were hard benches in an unheated building perched on a hill where the northeast wind found no delay. Personal foot warmers came along in the form of large, fuzzy sheepdogs, which may have something to do with a later ordinance limiting the size of the dogs, though no one was ever appointed dog measurer! Those who wished came on the Sabbath to hear Mr. Walton's serious book learning; those who preferred a more orthodox Salem service boarded Tom Dixey's west side ferry to Salem. Many a husband missed the ferry by attending "Tom Bowen's church" at the wharf where Tom, the town's way warden and wayward tavern keeper, stayed open for special Sunday service. The authorities kept arresting Tom Bowen and threatening eternal doom. After all, hadn't Archibald Thomson set out on the Sabbath from Marblehead on a clear day and with a smooth sea, carrying a load of dung in his canoe which, strangely, was overturned and only the Almighty knew the cause of the end of Archibald? Better to stay home and walk to the meeting house for Mr. Walton's kind but solemn words, interwoven with deep affection for Marblehead and moderating advice on self-improvement.

After Salem had cut the mooring line in 1648, Marblehead sailed into official self-government by electing its first selectmen: Moses Maverick, Samuel Doliber, John Peach, Francis Johnson, John Devereux, Nicholas Merritt and John Bartoll. The issues of the earliest town meetings were to echo down the decades: taxes, land, boundaries, citizens' rights and obligations, animals, increments, town buildings and challenges to strangers. Specifically, the town, gathered in the meeting house, voted: a four-rail fence for town boundaries, the stinting of Commons land for pasturage among the forty-four Commoners; the establishment of a tax rate based on Mr. Walton's salary and upkeep of the meeting house; the appointment of herdsmen and also way wardens to enforce the ordinance that all the citizens repair the roadways or pay a *per diem* fine that would be used "for the refreshinge" of those who showed up; and a ruling to tax "strangers" for their use of Marblehead timber or fish flakes, or other "conveinencies."

Thus began a tradition of over three hundred years of Marblehead Town Meetings interrupted only twice by oppressive foreign authority. The meetings were called whenever conditions demanded decisions and for centuries for annual elections. Every male citizen (women's voices have been heard only recently) had a platform for his recommendations, rebuttals, refusals, reforms or rebellion. The majority of ayes had it and the nays take the hindmost—until next "meetin'."

The townsmen, or selectmen, elected to set the town's early course were not chosen because of wealth, church or social position, or party affiliation (there were none), but because of the respect in which they were held as individuals, whether they were fishermen, merchants, traders, shippers, coopers, blacksmiths, millers, or farmers. There were no lawyers or doctors and few trained in law or government; some could not write their names, so they placed their mark firmly on the records. The selectmens' sole responsibility was to bring their good judgment, experience and effort to bear for Marblehead, and there was no office immune from public criticism or even threats of court suits for overspending. An early town meeting vote read, "It is agreed that the 7 men are not Limeted in things that is for the good of the Towne."

The existing records of the first town meetings reveal the simple, democratic steps taken by the Commoners to organize and finance a town government, appoint officials, enforce the ordinances and protect the rights of the citizens. Every page discloses their attitudes, customs and language. The division of land, such as the swamp next to John Legg's, lists the five owners of every acre and reads like a census of Plains Farm landowners. The hassles over grants, boundaries and fences kept appointees so busy one wonders when they fished.

Appointments were annual, including grand jury men, and any pay came in unusual forms—corn, butter, wood, clothing or fish. Even the old custom of turning up the turf to indicate a change in title had to be performed before town witnesses. Watchful eyes discouraged the encroachment of strangers, and transient fishermen who were only fishing the summer season were taxed in 1657. "Furriners" were denuding the peninsula of wood so new ordinances demanded that no stranger or inhabitant fell trees in the Commons or pay five shillings fine and return the timber to the town. Later, no trees could be "feld" for fencing or building without permission and

none until old wood was "burnt upp." The inhabitants were to ring
the swine, clear the horses from the Commons, cooperate with
herdsmen, repair the ways, do their stint and attend town meetings.
A two shilling fine was laid on each absentee from town meetings
(which were rarely held during the summer fishing season); the fines
to be collected by the constable whose own name might be on that
public list. Everyone was expected to come to set the rate.

Marblehead town rates or taxes were collected the first year, 1648,
by John Harte and others who kept casual, personal accounts that
soon didn't add up, so the town ordered the annual accounting
under the eye of all former constables. By 1657 the tax collectors
were Messrs. Maverick, Lattimore and Codner, whose responsibility
was eased by appointing Francis Johnson as commissioner, and to
him each inhabitant was to submit the "vallew of their estats"
within a fortnight or be assessed by six judges.

All these decisions were recorded by a clerk chosen because he
could write, not spell. The delightfully phonetic minutes fortunately leave a true record of the local dialect—the rolling *r*, the
guttural sound, the transposing of vowels and the "in" ending for
"ing" or "une." So it was that, "att a gennerall twowne meting this
7 of feaburary . . . farder it 'tis agreed oppon that Francis Linsford
have the sum of fower pounds alowd him for the yeare." And then
there is the ferry regulation prompted by the exasperation of the
cue waiting on the wharf:

> "The Towne Consideringe the inconveinencie of many Crowdinge
> into the firrie boate wth the danger wch may increw by people press-
> inge into the boate It is theirfore ordred this day that those that come
> firste to the furry place shall firste goe over. . . ."

A very personal town leadership combined with open, compulsory town meetings provided a vital experience in independent self-
government which would prove a dynamic battering ram against
the dried-out, inflexible redoubt of royal authority. The period from
1640 to 1660 was an open invitation to the whole Colony to try on
independence. While the home government's attention was diverted
from affairs of New England the Colony moved swiftly to develop
its self-defense and a system of laws appropriate for a maturing colonial government. The first colonial coin, the "willow" shilling, was
issued, while Marblehead still prospered with its popular exchange,
fish.

Marblehead soon found itself in the midst of the trade duel
sparked by the English Navigation Act in 1651 which protected the
British monopolies by requiring all goods (sugar, cotton, tobacco,

ginger, etc.) for the Colonies to come via England and in English or colonial bottoms, for no foreign ship was to enter colonial seaports. The Massachusetts General Court retaliated with duties on wines, anchorage fees and forbade any Massachusetts vessel to trade in Bermuda, Barbados, Antigua and Virginia. Both sides had difficulty in enforcing duties and restrictions without customs collectors, relying on just a few naval officials, some of whom feared the local seamen or found that gold coins covered their eyes to smuggling. The trade keystone, the fishing business, was still protected by a special importation contract for salt. Fish could be exported, though the profit was diminished by the exorbitant price of English goods and supplies.

Marblehead fish had made a name of itself in Europe and the Colonies—the quality, the flavor, the dependable delivery; the town sought to keep the edge of competition by appointing cullers and packers to regulate the quality of fish, its packing and to require the master's stamp on his barrels of mackerel. The fish was separated into three markets—the dun fish or Jamaica fish for the islands, local specialties for colonial consumption and the best cod for Europe and the "Romish" countries that paid the highest prices. Coastal fishing in cool weather brought in the only fresh fish for local sale. The hard work, the dangers, the smell, even the derision were worth it—just to have new Royal Commissioner Samuel Maverick report back to the king, Charles II, that Marblehead was "the greatest Towne for fishing in New England."

4. Israel Imperiled

THE FAVORITE had fallen from favor. God must be "shaking the heavens over his head, and the Earth under his feet . . . it is in a manner dissolved bothe in Religions and Relations." The restoration of the Stuart king, Charles II, with its strong Anglican influence, sent a shock wave through Puritan New England that was keenly felt in Salem and Marblehead, especially when the news came that their friend and advisor, Hugh Peter, had been beheaded, disemboweled and his head left to rot on London Bridge. The anxiety that swept the Colony in no way diminished the Puritan determination to clutch their charter.

Even nature was taunting the confidence of the Colony, for the scare of the recent earthquake that cracked chimneys and shook the very ledges to which the houses clung was just becoming a memory when "great dreadful comets" appeared in the sky as if to warn of plagues and frightful vicissitudes. When the largest comet ever seen made a second appearance, the governor declared a fast day to prevent the "foreboding of some calamity." A twenty-one-year-old—Samuel Cheever, Harvard, 1659—was among the graduate tutors who, motivated by their studies of Ptolemy and astronomy (with a generous helping of astrology) published *Almanacks*. The second "almanack" by S. Cheever, Philomate, in 1661, dated "the second year after Leap Year and 5610 years since Creation" calculated the positions of the moon, sun and stars and predicted the weather, unusual phenomena and appropriate sentiments that they might engender. On that September 27, 1661, an eclipse would blanket the area and the "Greatest Obfuscation" would occur at 10:21 for a total duration of two hours and thirty-three minutes. One might ponder:

What's here presages dire fate (not think it strange)
If not be men, to men, be made some change.

Marblehead's fishing fleet would still be at sea that day, and one of Cheever's nonreaders, Richard Thistle, seventeen, would be standing at the rail of the ketch *Mary* with his hand line tempting the big cod they'd seen at dawn. As the seas grayed and the sun's warmth retreated from a strange, unknown occurrence overhead, he would look down into the sloshing sea, capturing figures in the fog and his Hannah's voice in the night wind, and dark tales of silent, derelict ships slipping through those waters. Then he would recall the story of a fisherman who was carrying his pail of fish to his sweetheart when he met her on the way. Taking his gift, she vanished up the dark, narrow path. Hellbent for her home on the cove, he collided with the news that she was gone those many days and her shrouded body lay on Burial Hill. It was enough to give a man the mollygrubs. The shudder that would move down the strong spine beneath a leather jacket and oil-cloth apron would cause him to thrust his line into the next man's hand and flee below to the keg of courage.

Back at Nick's Cove, Hannah, with feet as cold as the foothold of rock—for the morning sun left only its circular rim—would stare at Point o' Neck as if *Mary* were rounding it under full sail, or would never round it again. The town would seem strangely quiet until the fishwife voice, heavy with pipe smoke, would holler to tilt the flakes to the sun before it was gone forever.

But that dire doom held off. Marblehead went on supplying the main food staple for the Colonies and taking advantage of the freedom to export fish. Persons from other depressed towns were asking for land and the town's steady growth forced decisions on Town Meeting: first, for a highway to be laid out to Salem that would go west over the Indian trail through the meadowland around the ponds (Tedesco Street) and join the north road; second, that a town wharf in the cove between John Codner's and John Northey's stage "shall be for a Common landinge place for the use of the publick good . . . forever."

The town was spreading out from Little Harbor. The waterfront on the Great Bay now became a deep anchorage for larger vessels, and to the south and west houses, gardens, orchards, pastures were changing hands and they weren't all Commoners' hands. A few stout souls decided they'd build on the "Necke." The selectmen usually acted as a land court unless hotheads appealed to the Salem Quarterly Court; moreover variations or abatements were often granted for shops, seasonal warehouses, the old and the poor.

In 1666 the mounting tension caused by the prowling French, Dutch and pirate ships is evidenced by a new item in the town budget, the fort, which would reappear regularly for the next two centuries. The second largest expenditure in a total budget of £167 was £39 for the carting and landing of twenty-five hundred foot of boards and one thousand foot of planking "for the fortt." It was simply a last defense for the harbor if any enemy vessel should maneuver the hazardous offshore islands and, though seldom used, the fort stood as a sentinel of reassurance to the town.

Lookouts were kept on the Neck to watch to the east and south, though that was a lonely post, for only a few families lived there. By 1669, the Commoners thought better of the island and not only claimed all the land not specified in earlier Salem grants, but also laid out a convenient way for the drift of cattle.

The homogeneous fishing interests of Marblehead could not be better illustrated than by the 1669 petition to the General Court opposing the imposition of new duties of 1 percent on all imports and exports and two cents per bushel on all imported grains. Fish was finally hit and Marblehead hit back. No grievance was slighted in the petition: the fishermen had been invited to move south; free trade had attracted merchants, but the loss would now be borne by fishermen and seamen; other colonies, like New Amsterdam, were encouraging free trade. It was pointed out that fish and corn were necessities, unlike tobacco and wine; the cost of customs and weighing officials would increase—a stern reminder of privateers' need of hard money for defense; finally, a warning that any colonial customs system might "bee monopolized afterwards by such as may not bee acceptable to us." The petition signed by 140 men of Marblehead was influential in the reconsideration of some provisions of the almost unenforceable order. British naval officials swooping in and out of seaports could hardly be efficient collectors and no local person would ever be an applicant for the hated job. The whole Colony realized that survival was implicit in the continuance of fishing and trade, so propriety and obedience be damned! Smuggling became a respectable, accepted colonial outgrowth of the destructive trade restrictions. The black market took on excesses of greed and brutality and the Colony finally found itself decreeing death to pirates. The penalty discouraged only those who were caught, and the next seventy-five years reek with hair-curling tales of piracy. Marblehead, a seaport of dark coves near islands with wood, fresh water and stone ballast was worth the pirate's risk, especially among tough fishermen who would strike a bargain and mind their own business. Other townspeople did just that when they saw new hard money appear in town, though most gave a wide berth to a pirate's shack or vessel. Some of the young fishermen who had it figured that "better a short choke than a long life at a merchant's desk" couldn't resist the temptation to become buccaneers. And the gory yarns quickened the cold winter's night spent before the great fire in the ordinary or "publick" house where the action was. It took Marblehead two hundred years to even worry about becoming more abstentious.

The best known and respected men of the town owned the publick houses, beginning with Moses Maverick who got permission in 1638 to sell a "tun of wine." Arthur Sandin sold "strong water" and his own beer right across from the wharf, but Town Meeting later requested additional places for the accommodation and entertainment of strangers with a—

Coil up your ropes and anchor here,
Till better weather does appear.

The strangers (on whom the town kept tabs) brought to town news, money, excitement and sometimes a good fight. They worked up a terrible thirst from taproom samples of salt fish, supped on local sea fare, and retired to a room upstairs shared with several men. Latecomers slept on the sandy floor or a hard, long bench; the grog was effective sedation. More licenses, costing £2 annually, were issued to Marblehead by the General Court then, having collected the revenue, it ordered that no Indian be served, the beer be wholesome and a list of immoderate drinkers be posted outside the tavern. No such Marblehead list was ever found, nor, in spite of arrests for drunkenness, did anyone walk around wearing a *D* on his chest. The Salem Court stated that there were too many "tippling houses" in Marblehead, but few were closed even upon the death of the owner, if his widow or son could carry on. The warm sociability at the tavern buoyed up Marbleheaders through tides of joy and sorrow, for hardly an occasion passed without ample refreshment.

Weddings and funerals, launchings and landings, seating the meeting house, raising the house walls or raising the roof, welcomes and departures, elections and town meetings all provided excuses for conviviality.

Marriages were an opportunity for the whole town to celebrate, sometimes for as long as a week. The local magistrate performed the ceremony and the celebration might begin with a mild sack-posset bowl but end with any "strong water" available. Then the newly marrieds were taken to the nuptial bedroom by the men and women of the bridal party who marched around the bed throwing corn, shoes, or any local substitute. Funerals, with little or no religious accompaniment, were attended by all and concluded with a "banquet" meal and plenty of liquid spirits. The "liquor" budgeted for Town Meeting often specified a gallon of brandy which may account for the appointment of William Beal as clerk to "Comand Silanes" by law and the imposition of a fine of "12d." on the offensive or disorderly members attending. Brandy was probably cider brandy or applejack, the popular choice following the scarcity of beer from refusal to import high-priced English malt. It must have reminded the oldsters of their songs:

Oh, we can make liquor to sweeten our lips
Of pumpkins, of parsnips, of walnut tree chips.

But now the orchards, not the fields, supplied the basic ingredients —pears for perry, peaches for peachy and apples for cider, which, with the encouragement of frost and time, turned in jovial applejack. Apple orchards, scattered all over the Marblehead peninsula from harborside to John Devereux's and the plains, produced good crops for home-brew squeezed from apples in a carved-out hogshead or pressed in the great hollow log at the "cyder mill." It was popular, plentiful and cheap, but without the status of the new "Kill Divil" copied from the West Indies. That "hot hellish and terrible liquor" called rhumbullion, distilled in the Colonies from imported sugar and molasses, was selling for just over a shilling per gallon. It had it all over that Salem jug of "whistle-belly vengeance," nevertheless, it was a long time before the rum-booze replaced the hard cider that enlivened the town meetings facing hot, controversial issues of expansion and the challenge to the Commoners' "elite" authority.

The growth of the town forced the meeting house to be expanded twice within three years; the second time, in 1672, by a "lentoo," adding considerably more seating which would be assigned by a formidable committee of the selectmen and Mr. Cheever. It proved a thankless effort, for hardly anyone was satisfied with the arrangement which acknowledged status, success, longevity and marital status. Richard Norman must have been a brave man to accept the duty to quell the disorderly parties or fine them on the spot. Contentions had been simmering over the privileges that the founding families, or Commoners, had secured for themselves, while the "purchasers" of the plains farm obtained pasturage only by paying fees which went not to the town but to the Commoners. These latecomers, or "non-Commoners" had little land and less influence, but their numbers and demands were growing. It was agreed to sell some of the Commons for houses not "prejudicial to the Towne;" yet, the non-Commoners were not meant to respond to the loud beating of the drum calling the Commoners to the town square to divide other Common lands. The only recourse to settle the divisive land troubles was the Courts, which in 1674 issued a judgment confirming the claims of the earliest settlers up to 1648, allowing cow pasturage to the second group from 1648 to 1660, and recognizing the non-Commoners' right to use of the Commons. It was also declared that the Commoners' recent land acquisitions were void. This decision was ratified at Town Meeting and a formal list of 114 house owners and their cow commonages was issued. That land dispute settled, the town could implement improvements for the general good.

The first rulings about public health specified that all dead animals—horse, dog, cat or swine—be buried in the ground or at sea within twenty-four hours; also that Dr. Richard Knott, who seemed to treat man and beast, be granted a parcel of land for his use as long as he followed his employment as doctor in town.

Traffic on the narrow, winding streets was endangering the children and anyone galloping a horse through Marblehead streets would be penalized. In 1679 John Ashton became the first recorded town crier to be paid 40 shillings in silver for crying the hours and ringing the curfew bell at 9 p.m.—the initiation of Marblehead's highly ignored "chicken whistle." Other town positions were created: the official salt measurer, the leather sealer, the corder of wood, the horse herder, the hog-reeve, the clerk of the market, and the first official teacher.

As far back as 1647 the Massachusetts Bay Colony pursued the Puritans' hopes for general education by ordering establishment of schools based on population but, though it was supposedly compulsory, schooling was not free until years later. Whether Marblehead managed not to fulfill population specifications, or realized that most of its school-age children were otherwise occupied, the town limited itself to informal tutoring by John Coit, William Walton and Samuel Cheever until 1675 when Edward Humphrey was voted £5 a year for keeping the school. The school was probably held in his house for short sessions at convenient intervals during the year, for Mr. Humphrey's income had to be augmented by being bell ringer and maintenance man for the meeting house. Someone must have questioned his credentials, for a couple of years later Humphrey's pay was contingent on fulfilling qualifications "as the law required." It seems he didn't qualify, so the school appropriation disappeared until the selectmen were empowered to hire "a Lattin skollmaster for the teaching of our children in the Lattin tong and to gieve such in Coridgement as thay can agre with on for not exeding fieve pounds." Doctor Chadwick won that appointment for the next year.

The tax rate bounced up and down, dependent on the times and needs of the town: the meeting house, Mr. Cheever's salary, the fort and a myriad of budgetary items that succinctly reveal the year-to-year story of the plight of the fishermen's widows, clothes and wood for the elderly, financial losses, official salaries paid in mackerel, shoes, stockings (replacing those eaten by the rats), and some money "left in small dribletts." Funds had to be borrowed from leading citizens because tax collection was difficult from fishermen whose expenses, losses, and risks mounted as the mother country stifled colonial competition and punished their resistance to mercantile suicide. Enough problems stung the Colony that summer of 1675 without the explosion of King Philip's war with its heavy toll in lives, devastation, and the financial burden on a colonial government unable to afford large military expenditures and internal disruption.

While the Puritans in western Massachusetts fought bloody battles with King Philip and his allied tribes, Marblehead—smug in its own peaceful Indian relationships and deep in its own maritime struggle—showed little interest in war enlistment. By fall, Marblehead was notified that it owed £10 in war taxes and was to impress at least fifteen men into war service with a certification of their equipment, from clothing to muskets and cutlasses. A Marblehead contingent reluctantly departed for the savage encounter with an eventual loss of one killed and one wounded. The second draft met with resistance as some of the leading citizens refused to go and others had friends testify as to their poor health. Warrants were issued for the Marblehead Impressment Committee's failure to fill the quota and each member fined £10, which at the war's end was cut in half. To the General Court's request that Marblehead consider building its section of a colonial "Maginot line" stockade from Charles River to the Merrimac, Moses Maverick replied that it would be too great a burden and a superfluous charge to the town. Yet, the town was not wanting in its own defense preparations, for it built a watch house, purchased a barrel of powder and bullets, twelve bags of powder, made Ensign Norman a selectman, and supplied a gallon of brandy to those hauling the great guns. Militia ranks began to appear in the town records, as the well-known leaders became captains, lieutenants and sergeants.

With the death of King Philip and the abject surrender of most New England Indians, the wretched captives, including Philip's wife and children, were marched to the seacoast for shipment to the West Indies. The only evidence of the following incident was a letter in which the incurably inquisitive Increase Mather reported hearing that in Marblehead, on a Sabbath night outside of meeting house, the women fell upon two Indian prisoners and barbarously murdered them. "If the Indians hear of it, [our] captives among them may be served accordingly," he gloomily predicted. Not that the women of Marblehead weren't capable of fiery, primitive reactions, but with no other source the rumor smacks of a Bostonian's idea of Marblehead's subculture. The recipient of the letter, John Cotton, puritanically explained away the Indian war as God's displeasure with the unconscionable ways of New England youth. The displeasure must have deepened, for as trade conflicts and colonial frustrations multiplied, a new oppression arrived in 1676 in the form of Edward Randolph.

Randolph, as royal agent, compelled the General Court to enforce the English acts of trade and customs collection which he undertook to personally expedite. In 1679 Henry Bartholomew was appointed collector for Marblehead to collect one shilling per ton on ships from other ports, but the magistrates switched the choice to Hilliard Veren, who then couldn't, or apparently didn't, perform the odious duty. Soon after, the magistrates threatened to annex Marblehead for making entry of ships as a port of delivery, and then, in desperation, appointed three Marbleheaders to survey the ships' goods before unloading. There is no record of success or failure but the officials were long-time residents: two selectmen, Ambrose Gale and Captain Samuel Ward, and Richard Reed. Customs collection was a performance in futility for a hundred years in Marblehead where harassment and circumvention of this official intruder was an accepted sport. It was strange how often the collector fell into the sea, or his boat was lost in the harbor, or a vessel was unloaded while he was delayed at the tavern. While the pinch on foreign trade was severely damaging other ports, Marblehead stuck to its fishing and by 1688 a great season produced 8,400,000 pounds of fish worth £37,500 in sterling.

Nevertheless, the town couldn't escape the anxiety spreading throughout the Colony from Randolph's determination to deny the charter and dispute earlier land grants. Many towns, including Marblehead, decided to clear their land titles back to Indian ownership by purchasing the area from whichever local Indian leader could be located. Sagamore George, or Winepoykin, the only survivor of Chief Nanepashemet's family, with a minister's help, had just been bought back from the West Indies where he had been sent into slavery after his internment at Deer Island during King Philip's Indian War. After eight years as a slave, Sagamore George, now a broken, old man, bargained with the Marblehead selectmen, but died before signing the deed. In 1684 his widow, Ahawayet, and other relatives signed for the tribe's sale of all of Marblehead for approximately £16 or about one fifth of the annual salary being paid to Mr. Cheever.

But Marblehead had always been generous beyond its means, in poor or profitable season, with its unordained preacher-teacher. An intelligent, tolerant William Walton participating in, but not dominating, town affairs had patterned the preacher's role which Mr. Cheever then followed with the same warm devotion and affection. Together the two men represented eighty-six years of Marblehead's first century. Young Cheever, a Harvard graduate, was well received in Marblehead and was soon voted a larger remuneration than his famous father, Ezekiel Cheever, received as head of Boston Latin School. His young son Samuel became a freeman, married, fathered ten children, and lived out his life as a neighbor of a town founder and benefactor, Moses Maverick. After sixteen years among the townspeople, Mr. Cheever was requested by the churchgoers to seek ordination and gather a formal, independent church. In May, 1684, "The brethren at Marblehead finding a great inconvenience in going to Salem applyed themselves to Samuel Cheever . . . that he take office of Pastour and themselves might so congregated into a particular society for the enjoyment of all the ordinances of this place, as in other Townes and places in the Country." Fifty-four members, having confessed their faith, entered into a covenant for private and public worship, conversion, and obedience to the rules of baptism and communion. New members were admitted after a "satisfactory account of their works of grace."

There in the church records of the "gatherers" are found many of the same settlers' names that pervade the minutes of Town Meetings: Maverick, Stacey, Dixey, Pitman, Gatchell, Pedrick, Reed, Gale, Conant, Legg, Russell, Merritt, Blackler, Doliber, Darby, Beal, Ward, Bartoll and Roads. The given names of their baptized children divulge traditional and even Puritan influences: Deliverance, Tabitha, Remembrance, Hannah, Sarah, Arrabella, Abigail, Mehitabel and Obedience, whose brothers were given simple names of John, Samuel, William, Richard, Benjamin, Joseph, Christopher and Ebenezer. Turning down other opportunities, Samuel Cheever remained in Marblehead in great harmony and mutual affection and "to win souls to Christ, he took no pains to please the fancy, but delivered the mind of the Spirit with great plainness and cogency"— never missing a single Sabbath service for forty-eight years.

In spite of severe winters, disease, shipwrecks, wars and sea marauders, the leaders of Marblehead were blessed with longevity which gave the town a continuity and strength. At first the town offices were passed around among a few early settlers.

It is difficult to choose a sampling of town fathers who gave enthusiasm and vitality to the town for almost half a century. Ambrose Gale arrived not long after Marble Harbour had been settled and was successful as a fisherman, planter, merchant and a large landowner. He used the headland jutting out to the east of Little Harbor for his fish flakes and landing, then released a parcel for a breastwork and fort which for almost two hundred years was called Gale's Head. Gale was elected selectman in 1656, his eleven terms ending in 1682, plus a series of appointments with the titles of Commissioner for the 1677 Census and of Small Causes for the General Court, Tax Collector and Surveyor of Goods. He acted as a bondsman for town finances and supplied the town with all manner of goods from nails, glass, gunpowder, to brandy for Town Meeting. He gathered with the First Church and became involved as a diffident witness in the witchcraft trials, and one of his last responsibilities was to raise the funds and plan the seating for the new meeting house in 1695. But of quite a different sort was John Codner.

Codner emigrated before 1640 and built his house quite a distance from Little Harbor activities. In a cove (which soon bore his name) he obtained a large plot of land along the shoreline of the Great Bay which was used for his fishing stage, an English-style house, orchards, and a farm. He is said to have been the person who first made the footpaths that became Front Street and State Street—a route he walked through his farm in order to get to the Indian huts on Harris Court. He was selectman, constable, petitioner and promoter for the public landing on the main harbor. A fisherman, Codner owned *Black Bess* and other shallops which brought in fish enough to cover his flakes up and down the shore. His daughter married Ambrose's son, Benjamin Gale, whom he named in his generous will as "my loving son-in-law."

Another favorite son-in-law was young Lot Conant married to William Walton's daughter, Elizabeth, who had been raised in Eng-

land and then came to her father's Little Harbor home. The young
Conants settled in Marblehead where the older Roger Conant could
review his memories of the earliest days before Walton's fire. Meanwhile, at a neighbor's house, the younger Roger was courting Elizabeth Weston who had come from abroad to live with the Moses
Mavericks. This was the Roger Conant who had been honored with
twenty acres from Salem as the first white child born there and
Marblehead welcomed him with an equal grant. Both Lot and
Roger Conant soon became involved in Marblehead government.

Then there was John Peach, a first official and often reelected selectman. Undoubtedly, because of his land, farm and flakes in the
uninhabited northwest peninsula, Peach was asked to help lay out
the highway to Salem and a cartway toward the west shore. The
controversies he faced as a fence viewer couldn't match the "ruffle"
at his seating of the meeting house.

This authority he shared with another early grantee, John Devereux, who was said to have been of noble stock, the fifth son of Walter Devereux, Viscount Hereford. In 1636 he was granted twenty
acres and soon after leased Hugh Peter's large farm which he later
purchased. First chosen for the board of selectmen, then constable
and juryman for trials, petty and grand juries, boundary runner and
fence viewer, especially for the Commons that bordered on his extensive land. His own boundaries were beginning to present impedi-
ments to the use of the Neck and middle meadowland. An abutter,
John Legg, would soon have similar boundary problems, though he
too participated in many phases of town government as selectman,
constable, tax collector, leather sealer and the prosecutor of timber
ordinances, planner of the lentoo and, finally, a commissioned officer
in the local militia.

Widely different backgrounds could have deeply divided these
and other town fathers, but their determination to put down deep
roots of personal liberty and self-government bound them together
in spite of disagreements, court cases, boundary battles, cow chaos
and tax tiffs. They were deeply concerned with town betterment,
and the hazards of the sea, Salem, the General Court and kings were
bravely navigated and a few ever quit the place. They and the town
sailed a daring course with Maverick's steady hand at the tiller.

The town father for all times was Moses Maverick. He couldn't
have been more than twenty-three when he became part of Isaac
Allerton's family and his fishing business. The lure of Marble Harbour, its beauty, its prolific fishing and its people held him there for
all of his life. Moses Maverick devoted over fifty years to building
Marblehead into the most famous fishing port on the Atlantic coast.

Not that Moses didn't share in the benefits; the records prove that he became a successful trader and large landowner. Having started with the banished Allerton's holdings, Maverick's own warehouses, fishing stages and Little Harbor real estate burgeoned to include a good part of the Plains Farm. His generosity was such that the earliest records disclose his assumption of town expenses when ends didn't meet. He often advanced the town considerable sums for its projects and the reimbursement was slow. His tax bill was usually the highest, from 1644 when he owned the greatest number of cows (three) to his death in 1685. No position was too unimportant and no responsibility too burdensome: from the elective offices of selectman with terms from 1648 to 1677, town clerk, juryman, census commissioner to his appointments by the General Court as Marblehead's first justice of peace and magistrate who performed all the marriage ceremonies prior to 1684. At the top of local petitions was written the name of Moses Maverick, who often delivered them to the General Court regardless of the unpopularity which their challenging content prompted. Small wonder that by 1672 Marblehead's town clerk inadvertently recorded in the minutes "father Maverick."

The death of Maverick and many of the original colonial "fathers" was an unfortunate coincidence with a climax of the alarm and resentment of England toward its distant and defiant New England Colonies. The colonial sacrifices and struggles for personal independence and prosperity were going to be momentarily crushed under the heavy wheels of royal oppression, and in that anguished crisis of confidence and security it took only a brilliant, inflammatory demagogue to lead New England to the occult headquarters of the scapegoats responsible for the imperilment of this "Israel."

5. Satan Attacks New England

As MARBLEHEAD and other towns of the Bay Colony neared the end of their first half century, the desperate struggle for mere survival was ending. Dogged perseverance and a craving for liberty had reaped, "with the blessing of God," an encouraging degree of prosperity.

The tangible indications of success in fishing trade, shipbuilding and self-government seemed proof of the truth of the sermon text that the New England colonists were "the chosen people" of the New World and that God was pleased with them.

The mother country was not so pleased. Even the political turbulence at home didn't distract England from her mounting disapproval of the Colonies' lack of respect, cooperation and obedience. After all, weren't these distant subjects ignoring the king's representatives, avoiding navigation laws and duties, defiantly smuggling goods, and steadily growing more independent in trade, government and religion? The mailed fist stretched across the ocean to crush such initiative.

Edward Randolph's appointment as royal special agent developed into a cold war between Randolph and the colonial customs and government officials. Cast in the role of the detested royal spy, he was insulted or ignored. Randolph's revenge was to report the treasonable attitude of Massachusetts and relentlessly pursue the prosecution of the Colony, ending with the revocation of the Massachusetts Bay Company Charter in 1684. It was said that the Puritans held their sacrosanct charter as second only to the Bible; the Marbleheaders probably put it first.

Every condition in the new regime hurt "the greatest fishing town in New England." Customs inspections were more strictly enforced, town meetings were forbidden (except for elections), land grants by the General Court were put in jeopardy and all the disassociated colonies were consolidated under the title "The Dominion of New England," which would be ruled by officials of royal appointment, including the governor.

The king's governor was Sir Edmund Andros, experienced and imperious, and determined to bring about the submission of the emigrants. With his arrival the Colony was transformed into an armed camp with royal authority omnipresent—on the streets, in the churches, in the courts, and on the docks.

To those who had just fought the sea, the elements, the Indians, the land claimants, and poverty to secure their liberty, submission came hard. However, their indignation and aversion to arbitrary royal prerogatives were contained long enough to send Increase Mather, influential churchman and president of Harvard, and Sir William Phips, the recently dismissed high sheriff of the Colony, to England to enumerate their grievances and petition for a new charter. Meanwhile, the former governor, Simon Bradstreet, formed a "Council of Safety" to warn Marblehead and other towns of an emergency and to issue a declaration demanding Andros' surrender.

Surrender he did, but only after the anger of the colonists exploded into violence on learning of the fall of the Stuart government in London. The Boston street crowds captured Randolph and narrowly missed the well-concealed Governor Andros. His rule and the Dominion of New England collapsed as a result of what was called justified resistance, not rebellion.

The seamen never missed any chance to declaim their rights and carried the news home on the vessels that daily plied the waters between Boston and Marblehead. As the principal fishing port, Marblehead had an unending aversion to any outside interference or unauthorized duties. The next town meeting signified through their representative, Nathaniel Norden, that their civil government requested the right to resume the exercise of their government according to their former charter rights. And to stress the point, Marblehead soon withheld half of its provincial taxes. The same town that several years before had instructed Moses Maverick to report to the General Court that new fortifications were "needless" by now had installed three large guns. A petition was granted for local troopers led by Marblehead officers: Nathaniel Norden, Robert Bartlett, Andrew Tucker and Robert Goodwin. Against whom the military force would be directed was a tantalizing conjecture.

During the interim government of the acting governor, Bradstreet, the aggressive William Phips won the approval of Bradstreet and the Massachusetts General Court for an expedition against the French at Port Royal, an action that might soften the attitude of the British royal councils during the consideration of the new charter.

The first Canadian expedition was an easy victory for Phips and Massachusetts. A weakened French garrison surrendered without a fight, but provided the excuse for a hero's welcome and a joyful celebration.

Dissatisfied, Phips now promoted an assault on Quebec and orders were issued for more majors, captains, soldiers and sailors—hopefully, a good many from Marblehead. It was rumored that the French were cruising along the New England coast and possibly had landed on Cape Cod, so coastal vessels were ordered out to seek the enemy or pirates. Then Captain John Alden (son of the Mayflower Aldens) appeared at Marblehead to take the town's guns for the Canadian expedition. His report of his reception caused the General Court to order Captains Legg and Norden to be summoned to account for "suffering the drums being beat, and not suppressing the insurrection" by which his Majesty's officers had been obstructed from removing Marblehead's guns.

The town's guns would have been put to little use, for well-fortified Quebec was ready. Phips was forced to withdraw, only to see his retreating fleet demolished by a severe storm. Defeat, debts and depression hit the Colony; England wouldn't assist, so the first New England paper money was issued. Marblehead's principal exchange remained fish. The next blow was the delivery of the new 1691 charter, deeply discouraging in its restrictions on trade, loss of provincial authority, royal choice of a lifetime governor with broad veto powers, and the stipulation of voting rights based on property and estates. Voting specifications by church or town were nullified. It appeared the Anglicans, or even the Quakers or Catholics, would now be more troublesome.

New England's atmosphere became increasingly tense and divisive, unhappy and suspicious. In every direction lay trouble and change: the frustrating new charter, rumors of French and Indian attacks, high taxes and worrisome debts, piracy, and disturbing challenges to the authority of the well-established Puritan Church.

That renowned Puritan minister, Cotton Mather, brilliant, articulate, energetic egocentric, had earlier issued another of his sermons (later published) entitled, "The Glorious Revolution of 1688." When his father, Increase Mather, released the latest charter conditions, the glory of the rebellion dimmed in Cotton Mather's anxiety about the Anglican ascendency in a Puritan land. There surely was evil abroad in New England now, and Mather scrutinized the source; it was, of course, his ever-present, potent adversary, the Devil. Mather had a public running battle with Satan; and surely there was tangible evidence in events, nature, and the meeting houses that Satan's hellish assault was succeeding. Witness the dejection of the people, the smallpox ravaging Boston, the drought and famine after a severe winter. God, Mather concluded, had turned his face away from his blessed New England.

Revelations of Satan's inroads were publicized in Mather's widely read account of Boston's witch, Goody Glover, and her "possession" of the Goodwin children whom he had studied in his home. Described in unrestrained hyperbole, the vivid, frightening exposé coupled with fiery evangelistic sermons reawakened the centuries-old and scantily concealed conviction that witches did exist at the Devil's behest—to sign his book, spread his wickedness and initiate weaker spirits to his bale. The colonists could recall that witches by the hundreds had to be routed out of Europe and a royal English edict in 1604 had said, "Death to witches!" Stories of witchcraft in Connecticut and Massachusetts had been whispered about and believed by most, for all true Puritans understood the inherent depravity of Man and the daily offensive by the Devil on his soul. And Cotton Mather made sure that New England remembered this.

He painted the highly colored, imaginative backdrop with soul-searing sermons, crystallized fear and threatened doom. The Reverend Mr. Samuel Parris supplied the script and cast; the Province brought in the principals; the church gave its stamp of approval; the people made up the captivated audience. So the witchcraft tragedy played out in Salem Village erupted into a frenzy of fear and hatred that ricocheted throughout the Province.

Salem Village (later Danvers) was only nine miles from Marblehead, but it could have been a continent apart so disparate were the religious attitudes. Although Marblehead was isolated by its geography and its nonconformity, its two roads to Salem and the west shore ferry were the supply routes for news and gossip. It didn't

take long to hear of the tumult at Salem Village which probably locally provoked a curse or a shrug. Unpuritanical Marblehead could
understand anyone acting up after dismal, three-hour sermons brim-
ming with fearful foreboding of "the Devil and Death," especially
by that hell raiser, Mr. Parris. Marblehead's only minister, Mr.
Cheever, was a gentle man of peace who "joined no party except
against vice and immorality." Town children kept busy working at
the fish flakes or wharves where the hairy tales of distant voyages
and the superstitions of the local seamen could satisfy the imagination of any adolescent. While fishermen fathers were away six to
eight months a year, every other hand was occupied at home.

The "witch" Marblehead had muttered about was irascible Mrs.
Erasmus James who, when she was called a witch, among other
things, sued her neighbor and was awarded damages. Then down
near Little Harbor there lived a testy old crone with whom the wom-
enfolk were always having trouble. She was the wife of fisherman
Samuel Redd and, though her first name was Wilmot, the fishermen
inexplicably christened her "Mammy." There were rumors that
Mammy could curdle milk or sour butter, or even sicken a baby
when she let her temper fly. Few paid serious attention to one more
odd character. Live and let live; Mammy was probably more bitch
than witch.

Suddenly on May 28, 1692, the local constable, James Smith,
showed up in town with a warrant signed by Magistrates Jonathan
Corwin and John Hathorne to apprehend Wilmot Redd for examination on the charge of having "committed sundry acts of witchcraft on bodys of Mary Wolcott & Mercy Lewis and others in
Salem Village to their great hurt." If Mrs. Redd had ever traveled to
Salem Village, it must have been on Tituba's broom.

Tituba, a West Indian woman who had become Mr. Parris' servant while he was an ambitious though unsuccessful merchant, had
a ready supply of West Indian voodoo and sorcery. Her tales and
gyrations made her aromatic kitchen the only lively diversion in the
Parris home, and the village girls gathered into a "club" that reveled
in her exotic fancies. Their stifled imaginations ran wild, and when
nine-year-old Elizabeth Parris' nightmares and odd behavior persisted,
the doctor's diagnosis was "bewitched." That word inflamed the
ostentatious Mr. Parris and he demanded that the girls name the
witches who infested the village. Tituba, the sorcerer's apprentice,
was the first witch's name "cried out." She smartly confessed and
became a prosecution witness. Her confession was undeniable proof
of Satan's success, but who were the other conspirators? Names,
names—of the aged, of the ill tempered, of the beggar woman and

her five-year-old child—tumbled out. Then the "afflicted" accusers turned on employers, the wealthy, or the dissenters like Martha Corey who laughed, in a most un-Puritan manner, saying "she scorned to watch what she couldn't believe." Obviously, the coven of witches had spread to other towns where informers readily supplied the names of allies of the Devil. One of these names, from a never-to-be-known source, was Wilmot Redd of Marblehead.

On May 31, 1692, Mrs. Redd was delivered by the Marblehead constable to Nathan Ingersoll's house in Salem Village for a preliminary examination and her first face-to-face meeting with the "afflicted children" who reacted with noisy, uncontrollable hysteria. Eleven-year-old Abigail Williams, Elizabeth Booth (eighteen), Susan Sheldon (eighteen) and John Indian, Tituba's husband, fell into fits which were cured as soon as Mrs. Redd was directed to touch them. Mercy Lewis (seventeen) complained of pinches. Elizabeth Hubbard (seventeen) and Mary Wolcott (seventeen) said "Witch" Redd had threatened to hit them with Satan's book (of signed agents); Ann Putnam testified to Wolcott's and Lewis's distress. When Wilmot Redd was asked what she thought ailed these persons or if they were bewitched, she simply said, "I cannot tell." The magistrates urged her to give an opinion to which she replied with restraint: "My opinion is they are in a sad condition." With no defense counsel and no evidence to the contrary, Mammy Redd of Marblehead was indicted as a witch.

The formal indictment stated the wife of Samuel Redd was accused of "detestable arts called Witchcraft and Sorceries wickedly, mallitiously and felloniously used, practiced & exercised at the Towne of Salem" . . . against Elizabeth Booth and Elizabeth Hubbard . . . whom she "tortured, afflicted, consumed, pined, wasted and tormented." Wilmot Redd was then committed to the overcrowded Salem jail on Prison Lane. William Dunton, the jail keeper, had never been so busy or important, but he still found time to sell rum and grog at Sam Beadle's tavern down the lane (Beadle's was sometimes used for pre-Court examinations), and tavern business boomed as the excitement mounted. For soon a village's agitation developed into a county's frenzy and a province's mass hysteria.

The apprehension of some ministers resulted in a meeting with the influential Increase Mather on August 1; they came away with the announcement that there was little danger of innocent people suffering. Meanwhile, the counterattack on the Devil was being intensified in the pulpits of the producer, Mr. Parris, Mr. Noyes of Salem and the passionate orator, Cotton Mather. The panic in "the hour and power of darkness" found little relief in Cotton Mather's calamitous analysis that "there never was a poor plantation more pursued by the wrath of the Devil than our poor New England."

A special court of oyer and terminer was appointed by the peripatetic Governor William Phips, who, having been assured by Cotton Mather of victory over the Devil, went north to subdue the Indians. His judiciary appointments included some of the most important and illustrious men in the Colony. Only three—Jonathan Corwin, John Hathorne and Major Bartholomew Gedney—lived in Salem; the others, including Wait Winthrop, Peter Sargent, Major John Richards and the eminent Samuel Sewall, came from Boston. The presiding judge was stern, unrelenting Deputy Governor William Stoughton. All were well-educated, successful Puritans who undoubtedly accepted the traditional belief in witchcraft, but also were fully knowledgeable about English law. Yet, few valid legal procedures were followed at the witchcraft trials. Preliminary questionings took place in houses, taverns or the parsonage; few records were kept of the early examinations, but were merely recalled; the din and disorder in the courtroom never quieted; the judges themselves before the trials discussed the cases with prosecutor, his witnesses and the "betwitched girls"; the accused was allowed no defense counsel; the testimony of a five-year-old child was once accepted for a conviction.

Judge Samuel Sewall and his nephew, Court Clerk Stephen Sewall, were in correspondence with an old friend, Cotton Mather, concerning the admission of "spectral" evidence, or apparitions. The author of *The Wonders of the Invisible World* was not about to refute "spectral" validity and so encouraged the judges. Perhaps any means were fair when in battle with Satan himself.

Samuel Sewall, the punctilious diarist, the righteous man, the orthodox conservative, would not listen to the disapproving voice of another friend and minister, Simon Willard. He and the other impressive, red-robed judges sat in Court, now in Salem Towne, and unquestioningly accepted apparitions, gossip and slander as evidence against the likes of a fisherman's wife, Wilmot Redd.

Four months later, the indictment witnesses were summoned from Marblehead to testify at the trial of Mammy Redd. Men and women from eleven families were officially notified. A few were lucky enough to be at sea, one was ill, others didn't appear, but the court records show that, at least, three witnesses gave testimony.

The daughter of Ambrose Gale, one of Marblehead's most outstanding citizens, Charity (Mrs. John) Pitman, age twenty-nine, recounted that five years before, a Mrs. Symmes of Marblehead thought her servant, Martha Lawrence, had stolen some linen and, accompanied by Charity Pitman, had followed her home to Samuel Redd's house. There an argument ensued and Mrs. Symmes threatened to take the servant before Magistrate Hathorne. Wilmot Redd threw her out, but not before she wished Mrs. Symmes might never again *"mingere,* nor *cacare"* (polite court Latin for "urinate nor defecate"). Charity Pitman related that Mrs. Symmes soon after was taken with "a distemper of the dry Bellyake and so continued many months during her stay in town. . . ."

Sarah Dodd, Charity's sister-in-law, testified that she had heard of this and added that Mrs. Symmes threatened to take Wilmot Redd to court for her own misdemeanors. Then followed Ambrose Gale, a respected churchman and well-to-do citizen who had loyally served Marblehead for almost thirty years as selectman. He disciplined his testimony to affirming that Mrs. Symmes had lived in Marblehead at the time and had become so afflicted in her health.

Depositions from the earlier examinations of the "bewitched" girls were submitted with one more penetrating question added: How did they know her name and town? Their reply was simple: When this woman appeared to them, she told them she was Wilmot Redd from Marblehead.

But Mammy Redd would not confess to being a witch, despite prison gossip that those who confessed escaped execution. Instead, she sat awed before the eminent judges and a ruthless prosecutor, mystified by the frenzy of the young girls and the obvious fear of the audience. She could only answer, "I know nothing of it." There being no defense, the prosecution closed its case and awaited the judges' decision.

The Court summoned Wilmot Redd from prison on September 17 and condemned her to "hang by the neck until she is dead." Her execution and that of seven others was set for September 22. A witness reported that the cart carrying the condemned became stuck during the climb up Gallows Hill (or perhaps a nearby highland) and 'twas said "the Devil hindered it," but not for long. Terrified as Mrs. Redd must have been, she never confessed to being a witch. So she was hanged before the huge throng who had traveled a day's journey and filled the local taverns while awaiting the executions. No one discouraged the crowds that included children from attending, for it was a recognized deterrent to sin; Cotton Mather, witnessing an early execution, had castigated the crowd's surge of sympathy for George Burroughs, formerly the Salem Village pastor. But, on that September 22, he and several of the judges were at the Sewall home planning a witchcraft publication, as another kind of deterrent.

Some of the milling crowd knew that the horror didn't end with limp bodies hanging from their ropes. In a macabre ritual a court-appointed committee (of men or women, depending on the sex of the corpse) examined the body for the physical brand-marks of the Devil. A witch's teat masquerading as a mole, a callous, a scar or muscular sensitivity belatedly clinched the prosecution's case. The bodies were usually thrown over a cliff to deepen popular shock; consequently, only a search in the darkness or a fee slipped to a guard enabled the relatives to bury the body in a family plot, rather than the common grave. It's doubtful that Mammy Redd's body was claimed, for no one appeared to pay her jail fees for board and jailer's maintenance—the "room" was free. The brash, rude, old "witch" of Marblehead seemingly had no friends. In later years no one came forward to claim the recompense granted by a guilt-ridden General Court, nor was her name ever included in petitions to wipe from the Massachusetts records the convictions of the victims of the witchcraft hysteria.

No Marblehead vital statistics, no town records admit to Mammy Redd's existence. The local official obliteration is complete, but not in the minds and tales of the later generations and the children's doggerel:

Old Mammy Redd
Of Marblehead
Sweet milk could turn
To mould in churn

That only one of Marblehead's citizens was executed for witchcraft can partly be attributed to the town's lack of interest in the antics of the "bewitched" girls. Yet, there were other local people involved in the months of terror and, by some strange fate, most names are recorded in the yellowed, handwritten records of the gathering of the first organized church in 1684.

The gatherers established the principles of their church and promised that they would walk "in brotherly love, to watch over one another's soul" . . . "and to submit ourselves to the discipline and government . . . to the ministerial teaching. . . ." Eight years later these two principles would seem paradoxical when interpreted with the eloquent magnetism of a Cotton Mather. Among the names on the original church lists are several who are in the witchcraft trial records: from Wilmot Redd's case—Anna Symmes, Charity Pitman, Ambrose Gale and Sarah Dodd; from Philip English's indictment—William Beale, George Bonfield and Sarah Buckley.

Sarah had arrived from England in 1643 and later married William Buckley, a shoemaker. After living in Ipswich and Salem, they moved to Marblehead where the fishing business was thriving and the population growing rapidly. William Buckley must have done his work well, for at the Town Meeting in March of 1678 he was appointed "leather sealer" for Marblehead. His wife, Sarah, a "good woman," met with the original church gatherers in 1684; as there were only fifty-four of them, no doubt she was well acquainted with Mr. Cheever, her minister. When the Buckleys moved to Salem Village, he recommended her as a communicant to her new church and regretfully marked his records "removed."

There, as members of Mr. Samuel Parris' church, they couldn't avoid the controversy that swept the village as the agitation over Mr. Parris, his salary, and so on, spun out from the bitterness within the meeting house.

After Mr. Cheever's gentleness, the Buckleys undoubtedly were shocked by Mr. Parris' personal tirades and accusations—even against Ezekiel Cheever, their former minister's brother. Later, for reasons never to be proven, the "afflicted" girls struck out at the Buckley family.

Ten days before Wilmot Redd was "cried out," Abigail Williams accused Sarah Buckley, a sixty-year-old woman with "scragged teeth" of biting her many times. Mary Wolcott and Ann Putnam were unable to speak; Mercy Lewis saw Mrs. Buckley lighting upon her feet at night and Susan Sheldon related that she had been torn and brought Satan's book. In the tiny house in the village the people heard the girls' fits cease as they were touched by Sarah Buckley, whose horror was compounded by one of the girls (Elizabeth Hubbard) accusing the Buckley's daughter Mary of sorceries. The magistrates, ignoring the not-guilty plea, arraigned Sarah Buckley and Mary Buckley Whittredge on the same day, May 18, and had them carted off to the hot, dirty and crowded jail where mother and daughter were to remain for eight months, until the following January, 1693.

Although Sarah's husband, William, had lost his land, cows and goods in the customary confiscation of a "witch's" home, he had not lost courage. Turning to the Church, he sought a certification of Sarah's character from the minister at Ipswich where she had grown up. The sympathetic Mr. William Hubbard wrote on June 20, 1692, that he had known Sarah since she had been brought from England as a child, and that he never had known her to be unchristian in word, deed or conversation. In strong words he closed, saying, "[I] am strangely surprised that any person should speak or think of her as one worthy to be suspected of any such crime. . . ." The effectiveness of his letter was nullified in July by a Benjamin Hutchinson of Salem Village whose wife had pains in her head, teeth, and all parts. Hutchinson called in Mary Wolcott who solved the problem by seeing specters of Sarah Buckley and Mary Whittredge upon his wife. Then, when Wolcott had a fit, Mrs. Hutchinson said the pain left her and the torment was transferred to Mary Wolcott.

Hutchinson petitioned the sheriff to restrain their evil spirits in jail, so irons and shackles were clamped on both women. Their family was then charged seven shillings for each of the heavy irons along with their maintenance (such as it was), with the suspected embezzling of funds for the jailer's addendum.

The special court and jury sat in September and heard the depositions of Benjamin Hutchinson and Mr. Parris' report of the "substance" of the May 18 examination, and then the frenzied accusations of the "afflicted." If the "kitchen club" had been caught up in imaginative voodoo rites, the girls now were completely hysterical, or comatose, spun tight in their own web; perhaps wild with fear of real bewitchment or the ministerial threats that "sinful children are more hateful than vipers . . . and are never too young to go to Hell." Better to point out possible witches!

The court urged Sarah Buckley to confess to being a witch, but she only murmured that she did not hurt them and was innocent. If the Court was hesitant, Susan Sheldon guaranteed the indictment by screeching, "There is a black man whispering in her ear." Now indicted, Sarah and her daughter returned to their fetters, while her husband searched for help.

Just before the trial date, he secured two more letters from ministers: the first, from John Higginson of Salem who wrote, "being desired by Goodman Buckley to give my testimony . . . I cannot refuse to bear witness to the truth . . . [I] have always looked upon her as a serious, Godly woman." The other letter came from Marblehead on January 2, 1693, from Marblehead's minister, Samuel Cheever, who spoke of Sarah's "pious conversation during her abode in this place and communion with us." The quiet Mr. Cheever must have had to gird himself to oppose Cotton Mather, the most brilliant and famous pupil of his father Ezekiel Cheever, known as the most outstanding teacher in New England. Nonetheless, Cheever's letter went to the Salem Court from Marblehead's meeting house.

No doubt, the churchmen's words delayed the Buckleys' case long enough for the whirlpool of panic to widen and snatch up the important, the rich, the officials, churchmen or their wives. This superior court, though composed of almost the same judges, met in the changed atmosphere. For Governor Phips, back again from his military adventures, had found his wife accused because of her request for kinder treatment of prisoners. The special oyer and terminer court had been dissolved, some prisoners released, the superior court was instructed not to admit "invisible" spectral evidence. Constable Smith of Marblehead had been instructed on December 23, 1692, "to assemble freeholders and other inhabitants and choose four "good and lawful men that had real estate of 40 shillings per annum, or personal estate of £50 to serve as jurors." The next week the constable reported the Marblehead selection for the grand jury was Richard Reed and William Wood; for "Tryalls", Richard Grose and William Beale.

William Beale is thought to have migrated from Plymouth Colony to the fishing station. He ran Marblehead's main grist mill and owned considerable land on the west-shore side. Beale, now age sixty, had held several town offices from constable to selectman, but this jury appointment is puzzling, for just a few months before he had sworn out a deposition against Philip English, a wealthy Salem merchant and shipmaster, who, with his wife, was a victim of the Salem Village girls' accusations. The Philip Englishes were allegedly witches who tormented them in the usual occult ways.

Beale signed a long, complicated report of an argument a year earlier with Philip English over his land boundaries in Marblehead. Although the rich English offered Beale a "piece of eight" to testify against Richard Reed's land claim, Beale refused. Reed returned from the Canadian expedition only to be arrested because of the land encroachment. William Beale, whose son was ill with smallpox, moved in with his neighbor, George Bonfield, where in the shadows of the chimney corner early one morning the specter of Philip English appeared to threaten him. That same day his son died; not long after there was a second son's death. The latter son also had been struck with choking which had been witnessed by two Marbleheaders, William Jackson and William Daggett.

William Beale recovered, but on riding the disputed boundaries with Reed's son he was struck with a gushing nosebleed unlike any since childhood. This deposition of Philip English's bewitching influence was confirmed under oath in January, 1693, as were those of the village girls, but the trial could not be completed, for the Philip Englishes had vanished. Influential friends had them transferred to the Boston jail where, with the help of two churchmen and letters of introduction from the governor, they escaped to New York. There they waited until the witchcraft "delusion" ended and, upon returning, English sued for the restoration of his confiscated estate.

Not so fortunate was Sarah Buckley. She endured the final trial and was declared "not guilty" with the jury bill mentioning Mr. Cheever's letter. Impoverished and broken in health, Sarah died shortly after. The family finances never were regained, though her son was later awarded damages of £15, part of the cost of freeing his mother and sister by payment of the jailer's fees. When the courageous William Buckley died, his minister's diary records ". . . very poor. He had not his portion in life. Lord, forgive."

"Lord, forgive" was now seeping into the New England conscience and a public fast day had been declared for repentance. The queen herself (Mary II) praised Governor Phips for releasing the prisoners, which then made some people question his delay, as though the hanging crowd had not flocked to the executions.

Inhabitants of many towns petitioned to remove the infamy from the accused, a sentiment echoed in a ministers' petition, first signed by Marblehead's Samuel Cheever, for "there is great reason to fear that innocent persons then suffered and that God will have a controversy with this land on that account." Cotton Mather's reaction was, "Why after all my unwearied pains to rescue the miserable from the lion . . . of hell . . . must I be driven to the necessity of an apology?" He was soon passed over for Harvard's presidency. Mather's dear friend, Judge Samuel Sewall, "to take the Blame and shame of it" stood in church while his confession was read and the jurors signed a document asking forgiveness of all. The "afflicted" Ann Putnam confessed her guilt but the inventive Tituba and the others seemed to vanish, as did the name of Salem Village eventually. A comeuppance from his parish and the church council was all that was left for Mr. Parris, who later departed from the exhausted village. The catharsis of fear and hate and superstition brought most of the principals to public confession and the Province to depression and shame. The shame that caused most records to be hidden or obliterated did not soon vanish from the colony. Only the dead and injured and broken found no solace in the various bills for recompense and official absolution introduced from 1703 until 1957.

In these bills the name of Marblehead's executed Wilmot Redd never appears. Yet, every day children and adults of Marblehead visit the deep, rock-ledged pond that bears her name, probably because her small house and lot abutted on the southeast side of the pond. Next to the old Burying Ground and topping a hill overlooking Barnegat, Redd's Pond is the only witchcraft association that lives on, though, considering the accused persons, witnesses, jurors, and constable, Marblehead's involvement was deeper than ever publicized. Yet it must be recognized that the town, as a whole and officially, never became badly entangled in the widespread hysteria.

The rugged, realistic fishing port, often chided for its irreligious attitude, was not stampeded into witch hunting its neighbors or enemies. Unlike Andover or Gloucester, Marblehead refused to invite the "afflicted" witch spotters to town. The right to be different was inherent in Marblehead's make-up. Would that the rest of Essex County had been so independent of mass conformity! As Marbleheader Justice Joseph Story said almost 150 years later, "this sad catastrophe . . . an affecting, enduring proof of human infirmity."

6. "Don't Step on Me"

When Mather's Mephistopheles departed from New England to the noises of belated, holy ejaculations, he must have laughed. His spiritual pollution of the New England atmosphere had spread into provincial depression, personal and economic, that was evident in self-doubt, loss of confidence, and stifled resentment toward royal authority.

Town meetings were limited; the Massachusetts General Court was reduced to a legislative body intimidated by a royal governor's veto and the necessity of relaying their acts to England for approval, which, even on a swift vessel before fair winds, meant a possible three months delay with no assurance that Parliament would bother to debate the issue. England's interests lay in trade, a tighter control of her colonial possessions and a dynastic coalition in Europe; three purposes that precipitated a series of wars from 1689 to 1763. Unfortunately, each European war had its counterpart in America with only begrudging support from the Colonies.

The Canadian expeditions had taken their toll early in William Phip's seesaw victory and defeat. The colonial fleets, including Marblehead's, had suffered serious losses, and ransom was demanded for the stranded crewmen and ships. The maritime towns were struggling to maintain their fortifications while expending additional money for advance scouting boats. The colonists, chafing under legislative limitations, found some solace in the Non-Residency Act specifying that the representative to the General Court must be a local resident, for "if government, taxation and legislation depend on the consent of the governed, then the people's chosen leaders must truly represent them, live with them and respond to local interests." Marblehead always made good use of its representatives who presented petition after petition defending its maritime rights or fisheries. Late in the seventeenth century a plea was submitted to omit small, open boats from taxes because of fishery losses and the number of men drafted for his Majesty's service. Swallowing their pride, the Marbleheaders now admitted to "Extreme Povertie . . . and disabilitie to paye" and foresaw the "Utter Distruction of fisheing." Later the town successfully claimed a rebate on their £80 expended for the fort during this "unhappy war"—after all, it was for general public security. Business was bad, money scarce and immigration down to its lowest point in history. Even nature seemed part of the conspiracy, for the 1694 season produced rotten weather, few fish and further fleet losses. A quintal (hundred weight), called a kentle by Marbleheaders, of scale fish like haddock or pollack was bringing twelve shillings, mackerel twenty-two shillings, and a cod quintal went for twenty-four shillings.

A respite in the war and a new governor who was susceptible to merchants' influence gave Marblehead an opportunity to recoup and to turn to local improvements. At the annual town meeting in April, 1695, it was voted that, not the town funds but the peoples' donations be used to build a new meeting house, for the old one held only half the assembly pressing against one another, which was especially grievous in the summer heat and created "great disorders." When 126 subscribers (Legg, Gale, Waldron, Hooper, Merritt, Getchell, Girdler, Bartoll, Pedrick, Homan, Humphrey, Trevitt, and others) contributed over £500, the meeting house was guaranteed and the committee was given the power to seat the congregation according to their liberal payment: men on one side, women on the other and all in assigned seats, such as: the committee in "the pew next to the Pulpitt staires," Ingalls in the pew "to the Eastward of the South East Door," and Edward Dimond in the lower floor gallery. As the new building was oversubscribed, it was voted to tear down the old meeting house and use the materials for a schoolhouse in a more convenient place—this with a stern admonition to render an exact account for both. At a public meeting on December 26, 1698, that account, including six shillings for paper to read on occasions and "nailes" for publication (posted notices) and an anonymous gift of window glass, were happily accepted and the town had two new facilities.

The schoolhouse was not empty for long because Mr. Cheever and the merchants were successful in getting a young Harvard graduate (1698), Josiah Cotton. He boarded with the Reverend Mr. Cheever, for his income was £15 annually plus a weekly fee from each pupil. Josiah stayed most of six years. Although he found the people generally inclined to give their children education, the scholars were thin among them; yet, he had the satisfaction of tutoring Mr. Cheever's son right into college. The young Cotton at nineteen had almost fallen into the intemperance and "extravagance in that place." His temptation must have been reduced somewhat by the new 1700 tax—this time a retail sales tax on all wines, liquors and strong drink and a demand for the tavern's inventory, retroactive for six months. Marblehead innholders joined Essex County in protesting the impossibility of such an accounting and sneered at the "multiplicities of Oaths." No one was going to swear to past stores; the tax remained and made smuggling even more attractive. Some years later, now minister, Josiah Cotton, concluded that Marblehead was one of the best country places to keep school in, providing a man be "Firmly fix't in principles of Virtue and religion." That Josiah Cotton learned more from his stay in Marblehead and in imitation of the quiet, prudent Samuel Cheever than from his forensic uncle, Cotton Mather, was apparent in his advice to young ministers "to avoid all meddling too far and to carry it with equal hands towards all." The incorrigible meddler, Uncle Cotton, was still bustling around, ignoring the actuality that secular authority, new religious denominations, and an illicit underground of rogues and respectables had long since wilted his Puritan mandate.

The rogue's credo, "We live hard and die hard and go to Hell afterwards," was a way of life for the pirates, English sea dogs or French buccaneers, who had long concentrated on the rich Spanish gold cargoes of the Caribbean rather than the slim pickings of New England. The English Council for Foreign Plantations changed all that by systemizing the trading acts, appointing special officials, levying heavy duties and enumerating legitimate cargoes. Smuggling seemed justified for survival to the remote and self-taught individualists of New England. Forced into midocean trade, swapping of cargoes in a foggy Newfoundland bay or a lonely Tortuga cove became an accepted practice; the return cargo was good for quick, risk-priced sale to respectable seaport merchants. The black market was too tempting to be ignored by pure plunderers: what in a hot

war with France was called "privateering," in New England deteriorated in the cold war trade into "piracy." In spite of laws for capital punishment New England produced its own batch of daring, un-
scrupulous pirates and the scent of smugglers' money tempted
southern sea rovers.

As early as 1689, Pirate Thomas Pound, out o' Boston, took the
Marblehead ketch *Mary* just off Half-way Rock. Deciding to trans-
fer to *Mary* and sell her fish cargo, Pound forced the fishermen into
his ship. They sailed home with the news of the sea robbery. The
Marblehead and Salem militia sallied forth in a futile pursuit of the
pirate and Marbleheader, John Darby, who had volunteered to join
Pound although he was abandoning his wife and four children. In
Tarpaulin Cove at the Vineyard Pound was cornered and most of
the crew were killed, including the neophyte pirate of Marblehead,
John Darby.

'Twas a tale told nightly in the taverns, embellished with gore, always competing with hushed rumors and whispered names. A pirate's shack squatted further down the way, doubloons and pieces of
eight were thrown on the bar while small boats rowed quietly into
the dark coves for water and food. Only a fool or accomplice would
go far abroad those eerie nights. No one had budged from house or
tavern to save the woman passenger shrieking, "Lord Jesus save me!
Mercy!" as the savage pirates murdered her in Oakum Bay. They
buried her body in a nearby swamp and having replenished the
ship's stores set out to sea again in their Spanish prize. Only the
Marbleheaders were left to hear her screeching again and again on
each haunting anniversary of her death. Footsteps echoing between
the tightly huddled houses, the misty face of a "cut-tail" lost at sea,
gruff shouts in the night, nightmares of drowning in icy, unknown
waters were as real to the superstitious seamen as the voice of Ole
Dimond echoing down from Burial Hill.

The wind carried Dimond's bull-horn voice down every alley in
Barnegat, clear out over Little Harbor and by some unquestioned,
mysterious force to his vessels at sea. It was said that his shouted orders carried across the water saved many a vessel from disaster. Ed
Dimond had been in town for quite a spell and had a land grant on
Charles Island, fish flakes near Doliber's, his own fishing boats, and
had joined the church. Wizard that he was, he was known to fore-
tell the future and point out an evil trespasser—a power seemingly inherited by his grandniece, the famous seer, Moll Pitcher—but
Ole Dimond's prophecies never foretold the future of Marblehead's
most perplexing pirate, Quelch.

London-born John Quelch was the mate on the eighty-ton brigantine, *Charles*, being outfitted in Marblehead for a privateering mission approved by Governor Dudley and financed by Boston merchants. Its captain, Daniel Plowman, was suspicious or ill, or both, and twice sent word to Boston that "it will not do with these people". Nevertheless, before the owners could check on *Charles* a second time, the vessel sailed out of Marblehead and headed for southern waters. Captain Plowman was buried at sea, with no questions asked; then John Quelch took over command with amazing skill and success, for in four months off Brazil *Charles* captured nine prize ships laden with £100 of gold and £1000 in specie, plus fabrics, rum, and ammunition. In May of 1704, loaded to the gunwhales, the vessel returned to Marblehead, where the news traveled fast about the gold "treasure from a wreck," the absence of Captain Plowman, and the crew's glib revelations. The next packet to Boston carried the reports to the skeptical owners who sent the attorney general to investigate. Quelch and several of the crew were taken in Marblehead, charged by Judge Sewall in Lewis' Tavern in Lynn, and jailed in Boston.

The value of the treasure occasioned a special printed proclamation from Lt. Gov. Thomas Povey on May 24, 1704, warning any of her Majesty's "loving subjects" of the severity of the punishment awaiting anyone who would "entertain, harbour or conceal" any of the crew or treasure. With gold surfacing in Marblehead and Boston, a court of inquiry was held at Captain Brown's home in Marblehead in a determined effort to turn up the treasure or the men. The investigation uncovered the hiding place of some crewmen on Cape Ann and a posse rode out on horseback, while Col. John Legg's company—delaying only long enough to grant Judge Sewall's wish that they be blessed by Mr. Cheever—set sail for Gloucester. Their prayers were answered in the capture of the pirates at the Isles of Shoals with only forty-two ounces of gold dust aboard.

The thirty-eight-year-old Quelch requested a legal delay and defense counsel and was assigned James Meingies, a wily Scotsman, who presented a strong case based on the conditions of privateering. Although three Negro cooks who testified that they were held forcibly were freed by the Court, Quelch and the crew were found guilty. With all the clamor and excitement of a carnival the crowds gathered on Copp's Hill, and on the river below over one hundred boats maneuvered for a better view of the gallows. Cotton Mather delivered and printed the appropriate "just desserts" sermon, though John Quelch found it tedious and was unmoved to confess. Instead, he proclaimed his innocence by saying, "I am condemned only upon circumstances" and, turning to the crowd, he admonished them to take care how they brought money into New England only "to be hanged for it." As Quelch's body was left to swing in the breeze as a warning to prospective pirates, the treasure was claimed by the Province for payment of pirate bounties to the governor and other officials; then, according to goldsmith Jeremiah Dummer, 788 ounces of gold dust were turned over to the Crown. A later legal assessment called the Quelch case "judicial murder." The tightrope between piracy and privateering had become Johnny Quelch's hangman's noose.

The Colonies were by now involved in the parallel version of Europe's War of Spanish Succession, which, in America, was attributed to Queen Anne. As in the other indecisive wars, this was confined to the northern frontier and eastern seaboard, so the northeast seaports were seldom free from war alerts or defense expenditures. Thereupon began a long jousting match between Marblehead and the Province to decide who was going to foot the bill. The Province appropriated £40 to repair the Marblehead fortifications, provided the town would put in £60. The town shot back a petition decrying the "miserable decayed state" of the fort and its armament and insisting that further financial pressure would "damnify the Principall Manufactory." That petition failed. A few months later Marblehead went back complaining that the collectors of the "powder tax" from ship entries were remitting the money to Salem or for her Majesty's castle and forts at Boston. The demand that powder tax collected at Marblehead should remain there to support its fort was voted on affirmatively, but, said the Assembly, Marblehead must insist there be "great exactness" in tax collection with no one escaping.

The hackles of the General Court were again raised when Marblehead would not submit its muster rolls (probably for further impressment), and the legislature voted that "their acting contrary thereunto is a grievance" to be reprimanded by adding "£46, 9s., 7d." to the town tax and forbidding any further provincial support of the fort. The town's financial condition precluded expensive maintenance, so when a Captain Forbes arrived to annex the stores for another Nova Scotia expedition he reported obtaining only one demi-culverin (small cannon) "without everything."

At the start of the eighteenth century the Marblehead vessels that dropped their sails as they slid by that fort were not a profitable, proud fishing fleet. Rather, they were only a number of deteriorating small boats that furnished profitable fish cargoes for the large Salem and Boston merchantmen moored in the harbor and eventually headed for West Indian ports. Privateers and English men-of-war also put into Marblehead for supplies and frequently dropped off French prisoners for Justice of Peace John Legg to deliver to Boston for confinement. With Nova Scotia finally in English hands Queen Anne's War ended in 1713 with the guns on Gale's Head loudly proclaiming peace. It was the ensuing peaceful hiatus of thirty-one years that proved providential for Marblehead.

The traffic in the harbor was already a source of constant conflict between the natives and the outside traders. Not unusual was the case of *Province Galley* which, even with the help of a pilot, moored too close for the blow that came up that March night. John Stacey's unmanned *Dragon* dragged beneath *Province's* bowsprit. Its crew, working in a snow squall and aided only by candled lanterns, bent a hawser to the small sloop and rode her to the stern where the line snapped and *Dragon* broke up on the rocks and sank. John Stacey sued, but had little satisfaction even after years of litigation.

Far less welcome were British merchant vessels competing with colonial shipping already severely set back by the last war. Even so, the Marbleheaders' need for hard money didn't force cooperation with royalist traders. English captains reported inexplicable difficulties in purchasing Marblehead fish: *Thomas and John* could bargain for only half a boatload; *Grundy* waited two months and ended up with no more fish than the other empty London vessels, *Mary and Johannah* and *Tyson*. Innkeeper William Nick, with an assist from local hard cider, persuaded the crew of *Port Royal* to desert. And loud guffaws must have carried across the harbor the night that the fishermen sold a full load to *Goodfellow* just before they succeeded in inducing her master, Jeffery Farmer, to stay in Marblehead for good! Marblehead was impatient to get on the move again, needing only a spark of leadership to strike out into active trading instead of sloshing in the doldrums of two decades of profitless fishing.

It was a churchman who prevailed upon the town and its merchants to relieve the "poor, ill-clothed" conditions by entering into direct competition for the West Indian trade. It was going to take some doing to find risk capital and to shake the populace out of their habitual role; however, John Barnard was the man to do it. It was no youthful, inexperienced cleric who had come to assist the aging Mr. Cheever, but a well-educated (Harvard, 1700), well-traveled man of thirty-three. As chaplain, Barnard had been with the troops in Nova Scotia where he had narrowly escaped from both a French ambush and the Indians. Soon after that he survived a severe hurricane and French sea attack at Barbados. From there John Barnard sailed for London where he was in the company of successful merchants and traders who, unable to entice him into their business, offered him a church. But New England was his birthplace and he returned to it full of fresh ideas and a tolerance which no longer conformed with the orthodoxy of his friends, the Mathers, who subsequently blackballed him for the ministry of Boston's North Church. "I was born a dissenter," Barnard said later; so he felt at home in Marblehead, even when his confirmation as minister in February, 1715, caused the first church schism. The Minister Selection Committee had finally accorded Barnard sixteen votes, the minister's son, Amos Cheever, nine and Edward Holyoke, two. Almost immediately, Mr. Holyoke's ardent supporters disqualified themselves to form a new church, the Second Church, and build their own meeting house, without the concurrence of the town. Richard Skinner, Richard Trevett, Samuel Stacey, and John Legg joined in asking that Edward Holyoke be ordained their minister in the spring of 1716.

That wasn't the only religious upheaval in town, for already a Church of England, St. Michael's, had come into being, fostered by the wealthy visitor, Francis Nicholson, and Marblehead families like the Bowdens, Calleys, Girdlers, and Chapmans. Of the thirty-three signees, twenty-nine were captains of vessels, some perhaps English masters frequenting the port. The diversity of church affiliations was bound to become interrelated with town politics as the town tax support of the First Church persisted. Parson Barnard, a tolerant man, cut from the cloth of a Hugh Peter, remained friendly with the various churchmen putting the general good of Marblehead first. When invited to accept an affluent pulpit in Boston, he replied, "I look upon myself so strongly engaged to Marblehead from their kind treatment of me, that no prospect of worldly interest shall prevail with me to leave them."

Barnard opened up a worldly interest for his people by inveigling an enterprising merchant, Joseph Swett, to break the Boston bondage and sail Marblehead fish directly to Barbados. Swett, who was described as "a young man of strict justice, great industry, . . . and enterprizing genius," reported his success, the profits and prospects. With this evidence Barnard restimulated widespread interest in Marblehead's deep harbor, prolific catch and rugged mariners with the result the new families like the Ornes, the Lees and the Minots moved to town and invested in new vessels for the West Indies trade. Artisans, tradesmen, merchants, craftsmen came on the tide of commercial optimism and participated in a period of unparalleled growth. The small, lateen-rigged sloops gave way to an original design called the schooner—a larger, stronger vessel carrying plenty of sail and capable of transporting cargoes long distances. The forty- to fifty-ton schooner that had a wide, heavy hull, low waist and raised afterdeck became known as a Marblehead heeltapper; however, many other rigs, ketches, brigs, barques and brigantines came 'round Point o' Neck from their three-months voyage to Antigua, Barbados, or any island offering a good trade—even from Portugal and the Baltic.

Local shipping with its valuable vessels and cargoes now attracted the "brethren of the Coast," and the black Jolly Roger flag began to fly offshore more often; no borderline privateers, but bands of cruel, roving ruffians whose greed and inhumanity were vented in bloody, sadistic attacks on the vessels of any nation. Pirate Sam Bellamy on *Whidaw* was said to have taken three shallops and schooners from Marblehead; while his cohort, John Phillips, captured Captain Ben Chadwell's Marblehead schooner, *Good-will*—both with better luck than the English sea dog, William Fly, who favored Captain Girdler's fishing vessel over his own *Fame's Revenge*. He underrated Captain Girdler's seamen for, having greedily ordered his crew to attack another vessel on the horizon, Pirate Fly remained behind alone with the Marblehead prisoners. In an unguarded moment, they overcame him and sailed him into Boston in chains—the same ones he wore when he later swung from the gallows at Nix's Mate.

Who should request that William Fly be first brought to his church for a pious upbraiding but the unctuous Cotton Mather! Captain Fly refused to budge, but Preacher Mather got to him before the execution with a copy of his published sermon—probably the one prepared for Sam Bellamy, "Instructions to the Living from the Condition of the Dead." Mather seldom missed an execution and often walked with the condemned through the streets of Boston where his publications were being hawked.

Marbleheaders never let piracy keep them from the sea, although no one wanted to meet up with the mad villian and pirate, Ned Low. His barbarous, drunken crew reveled in mutilation of prisoners, and Low himself sadistically thought nothing of cutting out a man's heart, roasting it and, at the point of the cutlass, forcing the mate to eat it. Ned Low's reputation attested that he gave no quarter except in a psychotic reversal regarding fathers of children. 'Twas said Low had a daughter in Boston whom he could never see again—a fate he wouldn't decree for the children of Marblehead fishermen, so he sent their fathers home in a discarded vessel. With tricks and speed, Low had already taken twelve vessels off Nova Scotia when he came on the eighty-ton schooner *Mary*, owned by Joseph Dolliber of Marblehead and skippered by Captain Flucker.

There she lay, quiet on the Sabbath morning, as was the custom of Marblehead vessels and, without a hint of trouble, Captain Low came alongside. At a signal his pirates rushed topside and overcame the Marbleheaders and Low took over the new schooner, renaming her *Fancy*. The prisoners he separated—the married men were to head home in his empty boat; the six single men would join his pirate crew. One (Fabens) escaped, two others disappeared, and the fate of the other three ran the gamut of piracy. Young Joseph Libby joined up and records say he was a full-fledged buccaneer on several vessels until he was captured. When he refused to lead the authorities to Low, he was condemned and executed.

Nicholas Merritt, while he was serving a hated old pirate, asked to man a captured sloop with nine other crewmen. When their escape plan was carried out, the sloop put into a Portugese port where they were then imprisoned for months. Finally, weakened by an attack of smallpox and utterly broke, Nicholas Merritt was released by the local consul and sailed home from Lisbon. By the time Merritt arrived at Marblehead, the twenty-one-year-old reformed pirate was a God-fearing sailor who never did find his treasure chest.

The sixth Marblehead captive, Philip Ashton (though he claimed he never had signed up with Pirate Low) had months of wild, hair-raising adventures from Cape Sable to Brazil. Later, *Fancy* was turned over to Pirate Spriggs and Ashton went along with it, hiding in the hold to avoid the gory battles and waiting for an opportunity to escape. Finally, at Roatan Island in the Honduras he was permitted to go ashore for water and cocoanuts. Young and speedy, the nineteen-year-old raced into the brush and hid for five days until the disgruntled pirates sailed away. The joy of escape dissolved quickly into lonely misery of nine months of bare subsistence on fruit, eggs and water and no fire, knife, shoes or cover. The insects and snakes were maddening, but far less dangerous than the bands of marauding pirates seeking escapees. A poor swimmer, Ashton had to wait for a canoe to float in to move to a larger island. His adventures there dragged on for months amidst a group of rum-sodden refugees until the day he spotted several vessels anchored in the lee of Bonacco Island. When a small boat came ashore for water, Ashton overheard those New England accents and threw himself on the mercy of the crewmen of the brigantine whose home port, luckily, was Salem.

Two years and eleven months after his capture by Pirate Ned Low, Philip Ashton returned home to Marblehead as a man from the dead. Parson Barnard held a special service of thanksgiving, and Ashton recounted his incredible tale. His story, *The Strange Adven-*

tures and Deliverances of Philip Ashton of Marblehead, was published in Boston. Daniel Defoe created *Robinson Crusoe* about the
same time; however, the fiction of Crusoe's trials on the deserted island never lived up to the real-life adventures of Marblehead's Philip
Ashton. True to the tradition of his town, he went right back to sea
and fished for most of his life.

If Philip Ashton's adventures had kept him away any longer, he'd
have hardly recognized the place. Marblehead had revived and no
longer postponed its town projects. Town Meeting was called for
10:00 a.m. on a spring morning for elections of selectmen, whose
roster now included new families who would deeply influence the
course of that century: Joshua Orne, Francis Bowden, Ebenezer
Hawkes, Amos Dennis, and others accepted the 1723 responsibilities
of selectmen, hogreever, fish culler, leather sealer, wood corder, and
tithing man, clerk of market, fence viewers and the newer positions
of auditors, surveyors of highways and boards. The expansion of
town and trade presented new problems among which was a vital
decision on property sales. In 1724 Marblehead was divided into
three divisions, "lower," "middle" and "upper," with numbered lots
measured by poles, feet and inches according to the quantity and
the quality of the land. For generations the plots within these divisions changed hands, enlarged, were inherited or lost to mortgages
until the deeds had their own story to tell.

The excitement of prosperity brought change but not upheaval.
A new road was connected to the Boston highway and another to
the ferry; on old Windmill Hill (Washington Square) the selectmen
laid out a training field . . . "for that use forever"; the meeting
house was again enlarged; and a schoolhouse built and the appointment of a teacher and his salary were soon to be on each annual
warrant. The town ordered vessels not to "hove ballast" into the
harbor and all seamen were warned that the town would prosecute
"Pitch Penny" in the streets. Colonial mail came not only by boat
but, by 1729, over the Post Road that followed the coast from Philadelphia to Piscataway. Marblehead mail dropped at Salem was
picked up by a local rider and taken to a central place, perhaps the
Town House.

It was incumbent on a successful, enterprising seaport to have a
seat of government, so in 1727 Town Meeting turned down a new
schoolhouse and voted instead to build a town hall on the site of the
old jail in the center of town. The harborside was bustling with
action—sailors, cargo, captains and merchants—and it would be
a short walk to the Town House, not over the old, corduroy cart-

way but a narrow road with the appropriate name of New Wharf Road, later King Street.

Out of the salty mix of mariners and traders came a man of letters (using the pseudonym, "A Native of New England") who published widely read almanacs from 1721 until 1737. Marbleheaders must have known it was a member of a prominent local family, Nathan Bowen, whose mentor may have been a local minister, Edward Holyoke. Holyoke, as a young Harvard tutor, had published several almanacs in which he sought to undeceive the world after other authors' "shameful inaccuracies," for, he said, "ignorant people have the knack at Figure flinging, Witchery and Conjuration." Although he carefully recorded the royal dates, tides, weather, and featured the stars with their "apoge" and "perige," Edward Holyoke's almanacs never led the field as Nathan Bowen's did for eighteen years. Bowen's small, annual book began by enumerating the time interval following great events: 4,014 years since the Great Deluge, 2,827 since the building of London, 2,044 from the Death of Alexander the Great and 10 from the Great Fire in Boston. His effort was "fitted to the horizon of Boston, the metropolis of New England . . . but may without Sensible Error (tides excepted) serve all the Adjacent Places from Newfoundland to Carolina." Although the weather might be "as inconstant as women," he didn't hesitate to predict it imaginatively by "fickle . . . dirty . . . weeping . . . a topsail gale or . . . what not" and March's deceitful days evoked eerie comments: "The Old Jade strides a broom and rides before the Wind," or, "In empty houses young cats are old witches."

Bowen's popular publications were printed in Boston and sold at the Sign of the Bible in Cornhill and at the Booksellers Shop. Competitors once caused Mr. Bowen to preface his book by saying that the annual writer must either be "truly heroic or audaciously impudent" and that the world would probably honor him with both. As the years rolled by, the renamed *New England Diary* listed wine cask measurements, highways, Newton's Laws of Motion, anatomy, paradoxes, and spot news such as the new Charlestown Penny-Ferry where the landing offered good entertainment "for Man and Horse." Yet, nowhere, even after the author included his true name and address, did Nathan Bowen, the town's shopkeeper and clerk of the market, and a town official, ever mention his native Marblehead.

The General Court probably wished they had never heard of Marblehead with the rash of town petitions being submitted. Ninety-eight townsmen, including the old captains and the new traders like Proctor, Smethurst, Parker, Howard, Twisden, Turner, Kim-

ball, Courtis, Bassett and Breed signed an emphatic petition. With
little timidity and less modesty, the document presented to Lt. Gov.
William Dummer (who originally had landed at Marblehead in
1712) made two demands: that the narrow beach of sand and ballast
stones at the western end of the harbor be repaired, so that the sea
would not break through a permanent passage, as had been feared
during the recent severe storms; that the decayed wooden fort at the
mouth of the harbor be replaced by a small fortification for the security of the trade, protection from pirates and enemies, and preservation of town health by providing a checking station for possible
infections before vessels entered the harbor. The town's petition rea-
soned that it was a "well-known constant practice of the English
Nation agreeable to their Constitution to look upon all the Vallua-
ble harbours, as the care of the Publick, and by a National Act to
Repair and defend them." The language reeks of Marblehead's renewed confidence; no longer "povertie," but Marblehead, "The special Seat of one of the Greatest Branches of Our Trade . . . there is
no harbour in the Country that can claim the Preference, and therefore none more worthy of the Care. . . ." The legislature agreed,
after a committee's visit, to advance several hundred pounds to
Marblehead, not for the fort, but for the southwest sea wall; the
appropriation plus the £250 from the town, was to be handled by
appointed trustees.

An earthquake hit Marblehead that year, but the financial trustees
probably mistook it for the ruckus that erupted from Marblehead's
innate skepticism about the security of large amounts of public
money. When a later appropriation of £550 came through, the
direction to the three trustees were that the money was to be kept
in a chest with two different locks and keys; the chest was to be
kept by one trustee and the unmatched keys by the two others. No
one man, only all three, could open the fort money chest. The con-
tention became so bitter that Joshua Orne and Joseph Swett resigned and Nathan Bowen and Thomas Gerry bravely joined Giles
Russell as guardians of the chest. Money was fast becoming one of
the Province's greatest scarcities, except when the Crown nodded
affirmatively to finance another colonial conflict that would assure
English possession of northern America.

Boston was bearing the brunt of onerous harassment by royal officials over the collection of duties that inflated prices or took goods
completely out of circulation. The violence that erupted verged on
open rebellion and the seat of provincial government was moved to
Salem. The northern Bay seaports were still thriving with Marblehead moving rapidly into first place. Although fishing and trading

vessels jammed its main harbor and Little Harbor, tons of goods escaped the royal collector's ledger by being smuggled into dark coves, islands, or the Neck. Hardly a house went up in Barnegat or near the wharf that didn't have trap doors, fake cellar walls, secret staircases, or even a tunnel to the beach. In defiance of harsh royal edicts there was a large smugglers' network, involving most Marbleheaders to some degree.

The volume of foreign shipping carried misfortune, too, in the form of contagion. Boston was fighting smallpox and in 1730 and 1731 Marblehead was set back by an epidemic that spread swiftly through the town, in spite of having shut down the Salem ferry and closed the town gates on all the highways. Men were hired to guard the town entrances twenty-four hours a day, dogs were not allowed to roam around spreading contagion, and those nursing the sick were forbidden to walk the streets unnecessarily. The more affluent left for the country; the more scientifically minded tried the novel innoculation as the disease continued its rampage. One British gentleman in Boston, Mr. Dalton, paid Dr. Steward £200 to come to Marblehead to stem the epidemic, for few homes escaped and the mortality rate soared. Only one or two selectmen were able to conduct town business with the aid of the justice of the peace who was empowered for the only time in history to call town meetings. Those were brief and to the point, mostly voting on smallpox ordinances. The disease was spent after many months; however, decades later town memories of that smallpox horror were bitterly revived.

Marbleheaders were "hooked" on their town, whether it offered prosperity or poverty, peace or war, land or no land. They would rather build as close as a common wall than move away. The General Court, therefore, must have been incredulous when in 1734 the town's representatives, Abraham Howard and Joseph Blaney, petitioned for a grant of northern land, listing as their reasons: the smallness of the Marblehead acreage, inhabitants so numerous "they were straitened in their accomodation," and recent discouragements in the fishery. As Massachusetts was intent on defending its northern frontier (Maine), the General Court readily granted six square miles to sixty men to be selected by a committee charged with choosing those most likely to settle in New Marblehead under the conditions specified: that each contribute £5 toward a survey; that the ten-acre lots be built upon; that lots be set aside for the support of the minister, the church and a school; that the defense of the grant was to be expected by an organized town government—all within a given time limit. Sixty Marbleheaders, mostly substantial citizens, accepted the grant with those prerequisites. Their motivation is problematical: was it land speculation, timber profits, or a refuge in case of enemy attack? It was hardly a noble defense of another frontier with the danger riding each tide splashing against their own shores. Or could it have been a veiled threat to the Province and the royal governor following the repressive duties of the Molasses Act? The "settlers" list included ministers George Pigot of St. Michael's and Edward Holyoke of the Second Church, merchants Robert Hooper and Joseph Swett, gentlemen Nathan Bowen and James Skinner, innholders Nathaniel Bartlett and John Stacey, joiner Isaac Mansfield, hat maker Frothingham, and a wide assortment of sailmakers, glaziers, shoremen, blacksmiths, and even a sea captain or two. The tract was all forest, yet there wasn't a husbandman or woodsman among them. How many proprietors ever saw New Marblehead or attempted to settle is unrecorded, but, years later, having survived the French and Indian War, the settlement's two leading citizens were Marbleheaders—William Mayberry, the blacksmith, and Thomas Chute, the tailor. The latter became New Marblehead's leader, church gatherer, militia captain, innholder, and merchant. He was persistent and undiscouraged by the terrors of the forest or Indians and was subsequently honored by being chosen the first selectman. By then, Chute and Mayberry owned the largest acreage; lots had been sold or just settled upon by those willing to clear the forest and plant large farms. Years later, realizing the original provisions of the grant were unfulfilled and taxes were unpaid, the Marblehead proprietors accepted their wilderness failure and met at John Reed's tavern to sell their lots for taxes and the highway charge. Most of their rights were released to the twenth-nine settlers living in New Marblehead, later renamed Windham, Maine.

There were plenty of reasons for the proprietors to remain in old Marblehead. Immigration was up again, and foreign trade— undiminished by English duties—brought new affluence and recognition to the town.

Marblehead even built another and shorter road to Salem over Rowland's Hill and around the highlands and north of the Dungeons to where the Forest River emptied into the sea. There was a great demand for venturesome seamen and skippers who could make a good trade and then outsail pirates, privateers, and British naval patrols. The homeward voyage brought salt, cotton, wine, lemons and limes, indigo, fustic, molasses and sugar. The last items were reaping large profits for the French islands and, with that as an excuse, England had imposed a high duty on all foreign sugar and molasses, primarily imported for rum distilleries. The Molasses Act angered the Colonies as one more unreasonable trade barrier, though it soon proved unenforceable. The rum still flowed and was put aboard the slave traders to be exchanged with African chieftains for slaves usually destined for the islands or American southern farms.

Marbleheaders didn't relish or require the slave trade, though black servants became more numerous in town after the turn of the century. The provincial black population (probably a few hundred) was a source of concern to the General Court and private individuals like Judge Samuel Sewall who published *The Selling of Joseph*, maintaining that "all Men . . . have equal Right unto Liberty, and all other outward Comforts of Life" and that "Man Stealing is ranked among the most atrocious of Capital Crimes: What louder Cry can there be made of the Celebrated Warning, Caveat Emptor!" Yet, his old friend, Cotton Mather, was writing in his diary that he had received "a singular blessing in the gift of a likely slave."

The Massachusetts General Court attempted to discourage the importation of black people by promoting white indentured servants in order "to put a period to Negroes being slaves" and had also ordered a high duty on imported Negroes, a ban on exchanging Indians for blacks, and granted equal rights and responsibilities (military service, and so on) for freed slaves. Yet, in the towns suspicion of the blacks, their customs and the fear of disruption of the social order generated rulings that blacks be off the streets after 9:00 p.m., "manumitted" or freed slaves must be given £50 to prevent their becoming town charges, and sexual intercourse with blacks and intermarriage were outlawed.

In Marblehead the wealthy families had slaves (or servants, as most preferred to call them) throughout the eighteenth century. The recorded ownerships appear in letters, diaries, newspaper ads, legal papers and wills: for example, Mereah, who was owned by Samuel Russell, bore a son Scipio, who was, according to probate court testimony, promised to Elizabeth Greenleaf "before it was born." But the same Mr. Russell had so valued the loyalty of Agnes, his black servant, that he arranged for her to be buried in the family plot in the Old Burying Ground with a monument to mark her passing. Most blacks were given ancient or bizarre names like Cato, Pomp, Prince, Pompey, Cesar, Primus or Coffee and put to work at household chores, the fish flakes, gardening or, occasionally, on a fishing boat.

A visitor's diary records his pleased reaction to the room of a well-treated Negro in Marblehead, describing it as spacious and comfortably furnished, "in every way adapted for a gentleman of his degree and complexion." Some Negroes, rootless and lonely, ran away and were sought through Boston advertisements signed by well-known families like the Devereux, Bubiers, Reeds, Homans, Staceys, Gales, Trevetts. Other men, women and children were sold through ads, seldom mentioning price. Most ministers had black servants whom they hoped to bring to baptism, though one notable failure was a resentful woman slave of the Reverend Mr. Bours who tried to kill him as he slept. Next day he sold her and used the money for a portrait of himself, happily still alive.

Negroes who didn't live within their master's home had their small houses at the back of the town not far from the Negro Burying Ground, later the site of the Alms House. The number of persons or their manner of living are not disclosed in official documents, for neither the census nor vital records listed Negroes, and their illiteracy prevented any personal accounts of their plight, which in Marblehead was far preferable to the nightmare of the slave-trading ports or the southern auction block.

In 1737 two of Marblehead's ministers were approached for the presidency of Harvard. John Barnard graciously refused to leave Marblehead and suggested Edward Holyoke of the Second Church, over the chauvinistic objections of some Boston ministers. The Harvard Corporation approved the candidacy of Holyoke; however, when his parishioners withheld their permission for him to leave, the corporation appealed to Parson Barnard to appear before Holyoke's congregation. Barnard urged them not to deter Holyoke's God-ordained destiny "for the sake of universal serviceableness." His effective persuasion reversed the decision, so Edward Holyoke became Harvard's fourteenth president and served for the next thirty-two years. Though Barnard was said to have "restrained every imprudent sally of youth" by his example and his very presence, the more austere Holyoke defined the submission of the people by saying, "We demand of you that you honor and reverence your Pastor." The strict proprieties of Harvard had appeared unenforceable, but the new President Holyoke tried mightily by laying on large fines for profanity, cards, drunkenness and forgetting the sermon, but his difficulties were confounded by having to dismiss two of the governing board for intemperance. His was a notable presidency, highly praised in the Latin interment sermon by a Harvard colleague who had his linguistic problems with Marblehead: "Marmaracria, oppidium maritimum, saxis abundans, etc. . . . or Marmaracria, a maritime town, abounding in rocks; from which circumstances it is called in the true purity of the New England idiom, Marblehead; a

most grating word, and intolerably offensive to classical ears."
(Wonder if he ever heard them speak?)

President Edward Holyoke often boarded Marblehead students in
his home; the first of those was fourteen-year-old John Palmer, Jr.,
son of a prominent Marblehead merchant. His youthfulness (not his
financial condition), must have been the reason, for Palmer died as a
young man and the inventory of his estate indicates the degree of
affluence rapidly attained by Marblehead merchants in the first half
of the eighteenth century. John Palmer's closet held scarlet and
green jackets with gold lace, black velvet jacket and breeches, plush
and leather breeches, three wigs, beaver hat, silver-hilted sword and
buff gloves. His rooms were handsomely furnished with mirrors,
sconces, crimson and leather chairs, valuable clocks, china punch
bowls, pictures, and books. His estate inventoried 137½ ounces of
pure silver, a pink-sterned schooner listed for £226, a black horse
valued at £6 and a Negro couple, Dinah and Tom and their two
children whose total worth was estimated at £132. A portion of that
estate had been inherited from his successful grandfather, Richard
Skinner, whose own father, James, had arrived in Marblehead in
1664 and had been a fishery merchant until he drowned in Boston
Harbor in 1701. Richard Skinner had married innkeeper William
Wood's daughter and became a well-known town official who
owned shares in several fishing vessels. One of the first to enter the
Mediterranean trade, Skinner soon accumulated considerable wealth
which was made public when his estate was probated, listing two
"mansion houses" and four small ones, three schooners, large
acreage, fish fences, warehouses, an impressive household inventory,
177 pounds of pewter, 131 pounds of tobacco and 4 barrels of
"syder." With ten living children and numerous partnerships, it was
eighty-two years before Richard Skinner's estate was settled.

Because Parliament's acts of credit favored the big merchant with
ample security, sizable fortunes were few, though prosperity spread
throughout the town into the small clapboard house or even fisherman's shack. Marblehead's fisheries were seldom the target of the
royal anger, as the need persisted for its vessels and seamen in colonial conflict with French or Spanish interests. In 1742 another approaching clash may have prompted the order that within twelve
months "a good and sufficient breastwork" with a twelve-gun platform and all necessary warlike stores be built and financed by £550
from the Province. If Marbleheaders did not maintain or repair the
fort on Gale's Head, this money was to be repaid by the town. To

oversee the construction and quietly investigate the smuggling, the collector of the port of Boston, Sir Harry Frankland, frequently sailed to Marblehead where he lodged at the nearby Fountain Inn. Frankland's expediting of the fort or customs collection is not as well documented as his romance with the native servant girl, Agnes Surriage, whom he took back to Boston upon completion of the harbor defense.

The declaration of King George's War (Europe's War of the Austrian Succession) activated the fort and European privateers forced the use of convoys and unarmed fishing craft as spy ships. The English resented the imposing French fort at the entrance of the St. Lawrence River and determined to take Louisburg, emphasizing its ominous threat to New England fisheries. Marblehead and Salem merchants had been trading with the French and now looked upon Louisburg as an "economic outpost." Governor Shirley urged an expedition for the Crown, while the General Court Committee took a more pessimistic view: the difficulty in raising funds and volunteers; the irreparable damage from possible failure to defeat the French heavy armament; the undeniable responsibility of Great Britain to pursue her own war. Their vote was negative and Benjamin Franklin wryly agreed that "some seem to think that forts are taken as easily as snuff." Unintimidated, Shirley, while seeking British initiatives, sent William Vaughan, an ambitious Boston merchant, to Marblehead to persuade one hundred leading fishermen to petition the General Court to reverse its decision. Marblehead merchants not only signed the petition, but, carried away with the daring plan, also promised a sufficient number of vessels to transport the troops within fourteen days. Boston and Salem merchants added to the pressure for a surprise attack and the General Court by a narrow margin "embraced the favorable opportunity." Shirley had boasted of New England's abilities and had won the heart of every Marbleheader by saying that five or six well-fed Marblehead men could catch as much fish as ten or twelve Frenchmen in the same length of time. Governor Shirley then tried to appoint John Barnard a chaplain, but his congregation would not permit the sixty-four-year-old minister to endanger himself. The recruiting of men and vessels, for a price, started off well in Marblehead, then dwindled as it became obvious that the fisheries could not spare either. Various recruiting inducements were offered in wages, rum, bounties, and an enlistment bonus of one-half pound of ginger and one and one-half pounds of sugar. The wives were involved by being offered the opportunity to claim half or all of her husband's monthly pay and a promise of four months' pay if widowed. The first flush of excitement and adventure and the prospect of forever ending French competition resulted in sufficient enlistments for a Massachusetts expeditionary force of two thousand men who sailed northward, delayed now only by ill winds and stormy seas. The incredulous, embattled French withdrew into the great fort and a siege began that daily became more nerve racking for both sides. The French were depressed by their inept, elderly commander and absence of relief; the New Englanders chafed at the delay, the diverse strategy of the American commander, William Pepperell, and the Englishman, Peter Warren, and the shortage of food for troops and prisoners. Some fishermen preferred to leave, carrying French prisoners to Boston and Marblehead. No tremendous battle ever occurred, for Louisburg surrendered.

New England now had its northern outpost and the British controlled the St. Lawrence; yet, instead of mutual celebration, there was obvious disillusionment over recognition of the colonial expedition. New England sailors felt superior over the tardy English arrivals. They reveled in the American daring and accomplishment, but Britain seemed unimpressed as it pursued the European war front. The victory celebrations were saddened in Marblehead by the number of widows and children left from the loss of the snow, *The Prince of Orange*, which capsized during the blockade, dooming the entire crew and Captain Samuel Rhodes.

In truth, any celebration was premature. The occupation force at Louisburg succumbed to a disastrous epidemic and Massachusetts was on the verge of bankruptcy. Impressment of American seamen by the British Navy was intensifying to an alarming degree, sufficient to cause sailors' riots in Boston. During a "press," townspeople would attempt to hide the seamen in their cellars or secret staircases; nonetheless, hundreds were overwhelmed in the taverns or streets and dragged aboard British vessels from which one captain brazenly shouted back his sentiments, "Kiss my arse." Some years after, Charles Reddin of Marblehead, who had been impressed on an English sloop, was granted a claim of sixteen shillings per month for the twenty-three months he had spent in a French prison after the British ship's capture. However, the people had not yet seen the real superfluity of their effort until the 1748 Aix-la-Chapelle Treaty returned Louisburg to France in return for England's claim on distant Madras. The angry indignation of Massachusetts would, hopefully, be subdued by British financial aid for New England war debts, a hope impossible to realize in the Colony's deep disenchantment with the mother country's cavalier treaty settlement. A reinforcement of confidence in New England military ability and renewed French

West Indian trade were New England's war gains, along with flick-
erings of a great awakening of American spirit far beyond that
sought by the religious revivalists.

In the confusion emitted from upsurge of religious diversity the
traveling evangelist appeared on the scene speaking anywhere, at
any time, and in straight, plain talk posited the gospel religion—

And when the Gospel Charms he doth display,
On Wings of Faith believing Souls away.

The excitement in this "Great Awakening" that moved away
from Puritan gloom and uncompromising authority was quickly apparent from the large spontaneous attendance, especially at the night
lectures. Jonathan Edwards preached brilliantly, and magnetic
George Whitfield was said to have been so eloquent that he could
bring tears by merely pronouncing "Mes–o–po–tam–ia." Mr.
Whitfield accepted the invitation to preach in Marblehead, and
noticing that the audience was less visibly shaken than was customary, he laconically commented, "Marbleheads—Marble Hearts."
George Whitfield didn't tarry long enough to discover that Marblehead had never been launched into the unswerving orthodoxy and
instead had cruised around on its own sea of liberty for over a
hundred years—with most of its ministers aboard.

There were other travelers who visited the famous fisheries town
briefly and reported at length. One of these, the New York merchant, Captain Francis Goelet, posing as an observant man of the
world, found that the clapboard houses sheltered an abundance of
children, "the most of any place for its bigness in North America
. . . and that they were principally nourished on cod's heads." Goelet saw five topsail vessels and ten schooners in the harbor and reported that seventy other vessels were fishing. Over six hundred
men and boys were employed in the fisheries which supplied
enough splits to cover the several thousand flakes on every headland
and hill . . . their profitable perfume pervading every lane and way.
The scent must have offended Goelet whose final comment, "It's a
dirty, irregular, stinking place," was made when he was safely back
in New York.

What that fish smell conveyed to the local people was that Marblehead was third in New England in ship clearings and exported
more cured fish than the total tonnage of all New England. Marblehead was in its Golden Age of trade at the middle of the century
and every facet of town life reflected the general prosperity and the
emergence of a merchant aristocracy. Fortunes could be made in a
few years by the young, enterprising, and lucky traders who intro-

duced Marblehead to an exciting era of affluence. It was a new day since Joseph Swett's experimental voyage to the Barbados and though he himself never gained great wealth, his daughters married the three richest merchants in the town: Jeremiah Lee who, together with William Lee, accounted some years for half the ship entries; Robert Hooper, who was considered "king" of the New England trade; Benjamin Marston, successful in his own right and in partnership with the other two. The Pedricks, Reeds, Skinners, Staceys, Ornes and others made their fortunes in the coastal or foreign trade. A Marblehead wharf could have been considered "a gang-plank to the world." A typical voyage logged by a Marblehead vessel might have been to Bilbao, Spain, where Marblehead fish would bring a good price from the Roman Catholics and the opportunity to load up on salt for the fisheries. Sailing on to Malaga, the rest of the fish would be traded for wine, raisins, lemons, olives, and oil, part of which would then be sold in England. The resulting hard cash purchased cambric, linen, wool and, particularly, badly needed metal supplies. Homeward bound, the vessel then raced a well-known course, dodging the French, the pirates and, finally, the customs collectors. The exciting welcome at the Marblehead wharf was matched in the counting rooms or at the end of the tunnel. And carefully packed in most incoming vessels was the precious personal cargo of the owner for his new home.

Handsome mansions designed with ballrooms, glassed cupolas, splendid doorways, wine cellars, tiled fireplaces, and beautiful gardens were being built around the Training Field, or just back from the owner's wharf. English brick and early English Georgian style appeared along with traditional clapboard. And the men and women who lived there ate well, drank imported wines and dressed elegantly in colorful European clothing. They were the patrons of the goldsmith, silversmith, cabinetmaker and all skilled craftsmen from the incomparable Samuel McIntyre to the local wigmaker. Records reveal that a theft at Barber Coes included eight brown and three "grizzle" wigs and an assortment of feathered tops and ribbons. Wig styles offered great choices: the peruke, brigadier, foxtail, giddy feather top and Grecian fly made from human, goat or horse hair. Although the price was high and the maintenance tedious, wigs were worn by the wealthy, their children and servants, and even by soldiers and sailors. The limners left the first pictorial images of the Marblehead gentry—for gentry they were, and addressed as such —Sir, Gentleman, Esquire, Deacon, Colonel or even King—and for the first time in Marblehead a more inflexible class structure was being stratified by property and income.

Yet, there was little early evidence of separation, for prosperity and continued success of all the townspeople were so tightly interwoven. The captain, togged in his long jacket and high hat, commanded the respect of every citizen as he walked up King Street. He was skipper to courageous men, master of his vessel on uncharted seas, navigator, ship's preacher and doctor, and, on distant shores, a trader. The lives of the crew, the safety of the vessel and the profits from the voyage were all in the master's skilled hands and no one realized it more than the merchant-owner. Captains' pay was minimal, as they contracted for a percentage of the voyage's profits and the right to trade their own goods from the lazaret. Their own Marblehead houses were remodeled or torn down for new, handsome homes equal to their station. The indispensable seamen and fishermen of Marblehead were largest in number and shortest in cash; their families built up debts during the long absences, and the boring, long days ashore waiting for a berth or the weather to swing around were often spent in drinking and spinning yarns at the tavern, or sometimes betting on coasting races on the outlying snowy hills. Only a grouty old Marbleheader would ever refuse to bet on any opinion, event, or even the next fishing catch. The wives who stuck their heads through the scuttle on the roof, speculated on the identity of the vessel sailing 'round Point Neck. It was the town crier who sent them flying to the roof as he made his rounds, relaying by bell and voice the time, the news, the ship arrivals. One crier is said to have called out his own personal announcement forbidding anyone to harbor his wife, "she having left my bed and board." Next day, his wife did the same rounds crying out, "I, Sarah, declare that I have not deserted John's bed and board, because he never had a bed, and I furnished him board." Such quiddling news usually didn't make the town crier's headlines. However, ship arrivals were vital to the whole community. It was this mutual maritime concern that closely knit together all segments of the town.

The merchants took the lead in bringing about long overdue fire protection for, although the town ordinance specified that chimneys must be cleaned every three months, oil lanterns and candles in cheek-to-cheek wooden houses were a constant fire hazard. A board of fire wards was established to improve on the fire-fighting methods of the current, spontaneous, serpentine bucket brigade. The board provided a fashionable activity for wealthy merchants and responsible landlubbers, and they met weekly to plan protective measures. The 1751 town meeting voted to purchase a fire engine; however, Robert ("King") Hooper, whose generosity was already benefitting the schools and church, donated the hand pump Friend to the town.

Many a man had his name proudly gilded on his leather fire bucket, and if he were a regular volunteer fireman he was not draftable for military service, hogreeving, and the like.

The following year another siege of the smallpox pestilence spread through the town, although its effects were lessened by many citizens seeking unofficial inoculation out of town. At the merchants' urging the first effort to isolate the disease at a hospital resulted later in a building, offensively called "The Pest House."

Merchants, captains, tradesmen and fishermen all worked together in these decades to preserve the town's independence of action, even when that included dangerous smuggling and open defiance of royal edicts. Their immediate adversary was the informer; their remote foe, the exasperating British government.

The "6 penny" per month Greenwich Hospital tax on each seaman often went uncollected, especially from the fishermen, yet the irritant festered with no likelihood that any Marbleheaders would ever gain admittance to the royal hospital. In 1732 the town had voted money to support Benjamin Boden's suit against Collector William Fairfax relating to the "6 penny Act." Boston's impressment riots had brought on the British Riot Act to reduce violence, and royal authority was steadily being strengthened to keep law and order in the Colonies. An unusual young man, Ben Franklin, who had recently invented an iron stove, had been named Royal Deputy Postmaster General and was soon to appoint Woodward Abraham the first postmaster of Marblehead. With the onset of another intercolonial war, Franklin, at a congress in Albany in 1754, had attempted to unite the Colonies, but without success. The same year additional taxes were levied by the British on the colonies' consumption of rum and spirits which was even less bearable in the knowledge that the income financed the British troops being readied for another conflict with France for control of North America.

From the start of the French and Indian War (England's Seven Years War) the British improved on their earlier efforts to eliminate the French by taking the offensive on land and sea. To prevent French control of the Mississippi and Ohio valleys, or their recapture of Acadia, the British carried on several campaigns at once which involved many more colonies, not just those nearest the northern frontier. Pennsylvania and Virginia were fighting in formal British style to capture Fort Duquesne, while New England was again expected to press the battle against Louisburg and Quebec. Britain now set definite quotas of men and money and Massachusetts' empty treasury forced the issuance of more questionable bills of credit.

To protect their supply of muskets and powder Marblehead built its own powder house in 1755, an unusual, circular brick building set well back from the shoreline. One hundred and twenty-four Marblehead men were mustered for the Nova Scotia (or Acadian) expedition, while those at home were fighting their own battle against the embargo on fishing on the Banks. Merchant, master and fisherman signed a petition requesting that the embargo be lifted because the legislature should realize that the spring-fare sailings were ready, provisions would spoil and men's spirits would sink. And why, why would anyone let the French have all that fish for the European market? The legislature knew well that Marblehead would take its chances against the French and lifted the embargo one week later. Fishing that year was mighty risky and those who were still at sea late that fall season experienced a shock never felt before. Suddenly their vessels shuddered and shook as if they had hit a shoal, though soundings proved forty fathoms of water beneath them. An earthquake of severe intensity had thunderously struck the entire coast with series of jerks of the earth's crust that toppled chimneys, broke stone walls and cracked beams. The ledges and boulders in town cracked and shook, causing little damage except an outburst of seacoast superstition and strange weather. In December severe snowstorms kept vessels outside the harbor where they cut the mizzen and main to save the ship, but were unable to keep crewmen from freezing. The snowfall was three to four feet deep and, as drums declared a town emergency, the populace with shovels flying cleared a way to Salem for provisions and help.

More French warships were reported by the spying fishermen. England, fearing a sympathetic French uprising in Acadia, burned supplies there and scattered the French "neutrals" among the coastal towns, dropping thirty-seven people at Marblehead. The group was placed in rented houses and barns a mile from town near the Salem Ferry landing and careful account was kept for the Province of their upkeep in food, wood, shoes and medicine. Meanwhile, the townspeople worried about these people's lack of employment, their restlessness, and the possibility of rescue by a French warship which Marblehead fortifications could not repulse. A petition for the removal of "neutrals" was granted after several months and Samuel Chipman sent a bill for £24.13.11 for conveying the French people to Medford, Natick and other inland towns. Joseph Lemmon's claim for eleven months rent and Sam Roger's for dinner at his inn were honored, together with a charge for two bowls of punch for Messrs. Bowen and Foster who accompanied the French refugees. The fear of the French in town had been enhanced by the number of Marblehead men who had left in the second draft for the war with Col. Jeremiah Lee's company. Fishing boats were the prey of French privateers that sometimes were then overtaken by a British man-of-war. A Marblehead vessel might change hands three times on one voyage—or be detained for ransom. The same kind of dangerous and exciting chase was occurring in the West Indies, so the trader's shipment was a dice throw for all or nothing, until combined British and colonial naval superiority and troop strength overcame Louisburg and, a year later, Quebec. Marbleheader Ashley Bowen, who had sailed the sea since the age of eleven, described the Quebec strategy of setting seven boats afire to float into the colonial fleet that had forty vessels alongside. Marbleheaders and other mariners took to small boats and towed some of the fireboats ashore while some of the fleet hoisted anchor. Some Marblehead men were injured, but the fleet was saved for the counterattack and the Marbleheaders witnessed the fall of the city.

Then, in 1763, suddenly the imperial axe fell on the game of cat and mouse that the maritime towns had been playing with Britain for decades. A large number of the British naval ships remained off New England to enforce the Sugar and Molasses Acts and curtail smuggling, especially at Salem and Marblehead where the man-of-war *Jamaica* had been stationed to clamp down on the collection of duties and to search for smuggled goods. With the elimination of France from the Continent, Great Britain's behavior toward her recent colonial allies became more possessive, authoritative and frustrating. Britain felt that continental expansion would solve her population surplus and provide a market for the new industrial goods plus offering a source of food and raw materials. Her colonial subjects had their own ideas.

The colonists and, particularly the Marblehead fishermen, were relieved that France had finally withdrawn from the northern borders and fishing grounds and that America was no longer dependent on England for military protection. Because of expeditionary forces and foreign trade the colonists from widely distant towns had intermingled. There was a growing American confidence, an increased mobility and exchange that was permeated by a feeling of unity and a sense of common purpose.

7. "Times That Try Men's Souls"

ON THE MORNING of August 1, 1763, the *Boston Post-Boy* printed a euphoric story announcing that Governor Bernard had proclaimed a day of Thanksgiving at the behest of King George III to celebrate the peace that now reigned in his kingdom. In the post-war depression following the French and Indian War the people of Marblehead, viewing their damaged fleet, the poor, the war widows and the scarcity of hard money, might have been more thankful if rumors of British cruisers off the coast and permanent garrisons of troops were not so persistent. It was soon obvious that Great Britain was entrenching its colonial power by stronger and broader administrative powers with thinly veiled military reminders of the might of His Majesty. The support of royal officialdom and troops would require greater colonial revenue, hopefully to be produced from the enforcement of the longstanding Navigation and Trade Acts and more assiduous customs collection. The British expenses were estimated at £300,000, and the first step toward reimbursement was enactment of the Sugar Act which increased the duty on sugar and other victuals and reduced the molasses duty; however, no longer would haphazard collection of duties be tolerated.

Shortly before, the merchants of Marblehead, Salem and Boston in a united front had petitioned the General Court to persuade Parliament to lessen the tariffs because a trade decline would further disrupt the fisheries which supplied the cargoes to be exchanged for West Indies sugar and molasses, the principal ingredients needed by the rum distilleries. Having been ignored, the Merchants Committee, while awaiting enforcement of the new sugar duties, encouraged public protests within their communities. It was more than coincidental that Marblehead's Town Meetings that year were moderated by Jeremiah Lee and King Hooper; though the minutes show that local shipping had not yet been seriously affected, for the town's problem was to clear the wharves for speedier unloading of the vessels crowding the harbor.

The Sugar Act revenue was disappointing, providing less than one-fourth of the troop cost so the British Parliament, without so much as a word of debate, passed the Stamp Act and furnished the fuse for the colonial cannon already loaded with angry indignation. The people bitterly resented the abolishment of their traditional right of trial by jury and the establishment of juryless admiralty courts. Upon the announcement of the stamp tax the vocal young, the articulate educator, the affluent merchant, the lawyer, the debt-ridden newspaperman, the restless mariner and the southern planter now had a common grievance. All legal and business forms were taxed, as were church certificates and newspapers by page size and advertisement. Months before the stamp enforcement date the roar of colonial protest crescendoed with a cacophony of words like *liberty, safety, rights* and slogans of "Liberty, Property and No Stamps" or "Keep Alive a Spirit of Liberty."

A Marblehead committee, with Jeremiah Lee as chairman returned to the September 24 Town Meeting with a resolution instructing the town's representative to the General Court to promote and join dutiful remonstrance to the king and Parliament and take decent measures to repeal the Stamp Act; however, barring riots and outrages, he was not to indicate any "willingness of your Constituents to submit to any internal taxes." Trade duties were admittedly odious, yet, in the opinion of the Colonies did not imply the unconstitutionality of internal (and infernal) stamp tax which provided America with the enduring issue of taxation without representation. A Stamp Act Congress attended by nine colonies enunciated fourteen resolutions built around the premise that "the increase, prosperity and happiness of these colonies, depend on the full and free enjoyment of their rights and liberties."

The British Parliament was intensely divided in its belated debate, with William Pitt vainly speaking for the colonial position which was duly appreciated by the colonists, who not only christened vessels after him, such as Marblehead's *Pitt Packet*, but also wrote:

"I thank thee, Pitt, for all thy glorious strife
Against the foes of LIBERTY and life."

Marblehead mourned the fateful November 1, 1765, when the Stamp Act became law with flags at half-mast and bells tolling and people demonstrating in the streets. As John Adams put it, the "presses groaned, pulpits thundered, our towns voted and Crown officials have everywhere trembled." Stamp officials resigned or even recanted in public, but the official repeal of the Stamp Act arrived too late to subvert the embracing unity of its opposition. From Marblehead to South Carolina the pattern of future protest had been drawn: Town Meetings, resolutions and petitions, street action organized by activists like the "Sons of Liberty," opposition in the press, a general convention or Congress, threats of boycott and encouragement of independent home industry. In the tumult of protest for individual and colonial rights Marblehead was always right at home.

Young John Adams discovered that when he visited Marblehead that year, though his diary concentrates on its appearance. He found the road from Salem "pleasant indeed . . . grass plots and fields are delightful. . . . The streets are narrow, and rugged and dirty, but there are some very grand buildings." Those who occupied those buildings were still reaping the profits of foreign trade, even under duress. Though the town streets were not of cobblestone or brick, they were being formally laid out by the selectmen and even slightly widened, if possible, considering the houses and ledges strewn along the way. The annual town warrant recorded the local decisions concerning: the establishment of longer hours and improved methods of weighing and storage at the market (where pork could be kept only two days in the colder weather); the advisability of a sixteen-foot-square steeple on the new meeting house; the difficulty in keeping the town clock regulated; the twenty-shilling fine, per tide, for any vessel delaying unnecessarily at the wharf; and the important appointment of five trustees to direct school affairs.

As the first formal school committee, the trustees were advised that the town would now pay for all poor children if it could be determined who they were and how to educate them, and thence to organize three more schools for "teaching reading, writing and arithmetick." One fifth of the 1767 Marblehead annual budget of £1500 was appropriated for public education which was now accepted as the town's responsibility, instead of its traditional, limited grant of schoolmaster's salary and a schoolroom with all other expenses covered by the students' weekly fees. Poor children's fees often had been paid by generous benefactors. Within a few months the three new schools taught by Messrs. Ashton, Phippen and Jayne had admitted eighty males who proved they could read the Testament, and almost as many females who could read off different Psalter verses. Nearly one hundred and sixty pupils having been enrolled, the public schools were overcrowded; they were too hot in summer, too uncomfortable in winter. Five new trustees went about seeking "a proper place" and additional teachers, Joseph Smethurst, Joshua Prentiss and Samuel Hancock, "late of Harvard College." Marblehead's education of its children was no longer lagging behind as it had done for decades.

Marblehead was shocked anew by Parliament's effort to restore its prestige and authority by the Mutiny Act and the Townshend legislation that contained several abhorrent provisions, particularly that the income from the new duties on glass, lead, paper, and so on, would be used to pay the salaries of governors and judges in America. Marbleheaders were too wise in the ways of provincial government not to realize that their last hold on these officials was pried loose when official salaries could no longer be withheld by disgruntled citizens. They were further depressed at the prospect of a large Board of Customs Commissioners stationed in Boston and equipped with writs of assistance to enter and search vessels or private homes without warning.

The colonial gloom was lighted up by the fiery reaction of James Otis, whose impassioned letter was widely circulated in Marblehead, and Town Meeting of July, 1768, formally thanked Otis and the House of Representatives for their steady resolution in maintaining provincial rights. Marblehead agreed that the latest British measures were inflammatory and that "it is most certainly the duty and interest of every people who would not tamely part with their rights and Liberties to interfere in the matter and let the world know their sentiments in such a case."

The world should have heard Marblehead's peculiar profanity when the salty mariners came up against the strict customs conditions in the ports of Salem and Marblehead. John Nutting, collector for both ports, received his instruction from the head man in Boston, Henry Hulton, in the form of a forty-page manual beginning with "the Collector is to take no gratuities" and he was to be diligent in searching, seizing goods or vessels, entering houses or warehouses and penalizing resisters. The burden of proof, the manual stated, would always be on the owner of the imported goods, twenty-four of which were enumerated—running the gamut from furs to pitch, hats to hemp, molasses to copper ore. The collector's instructions applied to imported (and, added belatedly in ink, "exported") goods which were to be examined as the vessel left or entered harbor. On his sworn oath the vessel's master must not misrepresent the cargo under penalty of £100 fine. To attempt such an inspection in two busy harbors required a large staff with such titles as tide surveyors, hand waiters, searchers, watermen or riding officers. Marblehead customs employees, Philip Thresher, John Butler, and Andrew Phillips were to report to Woodward Abraham, former postmaster, any illicit cargo or unusual shoreline activity. These Marbleheaders were either immune to insults or cooperative, as Phillips' dismissal for incomplete reporting would indicate.

Customs surveillance was an ineffective deterrent in Marblehead, as an official in despair reported to Boston that "every Owner and every Master of every Vessel . . . are concerned with smuggling." The islands and circuitous coastline were still a godsend; smuggling continued to be an ingenious underground operation and a coating of warm, sticky tar that sprouted feathers was near at hand to use on any informer.

The royal officials would try other checks. An order was issued for a complete list of Marblehead's inhabitants and their rateable (taxable) estate. In spite of an innate reluctance to part with private information, the town voted to "conform" by directing each person to call at Nathan Bowen's office with the necessary information. No evidence of any other compulsion was recorded. By the following year the tax assessments would have changed considerably, for, just when the fisheries were producing at such a rate that the number of town-appointed fish cullers had jumped from thirty-three to forty-four, disaster struck at sea. Storms of tremendous force with devastating waves and high gales twice ripped apart the northern fleet with a sickening loss of one hundred and twenty-two men and boys who went down with twenty-three vessels. The town forgot the Crown and all else while it grieved with the seventy widows and one hundred and fifty fatherless children. The people's voice, Town Meeting, spoke for all when it called for tax abatements and contributions for the bereft families.

Small wonder, then, at the agitation inspired by the news that the arbitrary old Greenwich Hospital tax would be strictly enforced and extended to include all fishermen. A formidable committee of merchants, Robert Hooper, Jeremiah Lee and Benjamin Marston, were asked to take action which they did by protests to the governor and by drawing up a nonimportation agreement against British goods, exempting fisheries' supplies and coal, but retaliating against the Townshend dutied goods, particularly tea. All except four Marblehead merchants signed the agreement and the publication of their names resulted in three reversals. To dramatize the boycott of tea, a cart carrying a large tea chest painted with derisive slogans was driven through Marblehead "Lanes" and "Ways" and then symbolically directed to Boston. The mounting wave of excitement rolling over Marblehead was providing a natural outlet for the pugnacious struggle for liberty that the town had been waging for one hundred and forty years, for much smaller stakes.

Bold, impetuous seamen were not easily satisfied with the merchants' printed protests and resolutions, when hardly a voyage escaped obnoxious harassment by the British, even to rummaging through a man's private sea chest. If another shove toward radicalism was needed, the incident early in 1769 provided it. Captain Thomas Powers' brigantine, *Pitt Packet*, was homeward bound from Europe when the British man-of-war, *Rose*, cruising around the Bay, sent officers aboard *Pitt Packet* with the intent of impressing Marblehead seamen to serve in the British Navy. The unarmed seamen defiantly shut themselves in the forepeak and after being shot at by a "Limey" lieutenant they used the only weapon at hand, a harpoon, to finish him off. Overwhelmed by *Rose's* crew, the Marbleheaders were carried away to prison in Boston. Essex County mariners were aroused to a furor which was kept at a nearly riotous pitch by the brilliant maneuvering of John Adams and James Otis who had volunteered for defense counsel. Refusing the alternative of a jury trial in England, they chose a trial without jury in Boston, while demanding that the background for the judge's decision be made public. The Marbleheaders were acquitted on the excuse that the slain lieutenant had no specific orders to impress seamen. Even as they left the courthouse there were British field guns across the street facing the court of justice doors.

Overt attacks, wharf riots, and loss of control by the more conservative merchants undoubtedly influenced the now powerful combination of Lord North and King George III to rescind the unproductive Townshend duties—except on tea—which would aid its East India Company and also retain the principle of royal taxation. Most events were overshadowed by the Boston street battle on the night of March 5, 1770. A taunting mob of four hundred frustrated colonists armed with rocks, clubs, and bricks were faced by eight British guards who were ordered to load their muskets, and the crowd was told to disperse. No one could account for the command, *"Fire!"* yet in that significant moment five Americans were killed, four white men and one black man destined to be acclaimed early martyrs of the American struggle. The Sons of Liberty and their skillful agitator, Samuel Adams, arranged the Boston Massacre funeral attended by thousands of aroused citizens from surrounding towns, including Marblehead. Every tongue on both sides adjudged the fiery temperament of the people and the British agreed to remove the troops from the city. A calm seemed to settle over the Province.

With a sigh of relief most of Marblehead returned to the business of living and earning a living. The annual March meeting, moderated by Ben Marston, voted a £1300 budget, made many appointments, including a new position of Deer Reever. Captain John Glover was again made leather sealer and his brother, Jonathan Glover and Azor Orne served as assessors. That same year a special committee handled the complaints against "the Publick Schools" and among those serving were Captains Joseph Pedrick and James Mugford, Joseph Hooper, John Prince and Stephen Phillips. They reported that, although the complaints of severe punishment and imprudent conduct by the teachers had some validity, their official town duties had perhaps demanded too much time, but the situation now looked optimistic.

Many citizens, whether they drank tea or something stronger, still rankled under the tea tax and its implications. At two Town Meetings held three days apart in May, a committee of seven, Elbridge and Thomas Gerry, Azor and Joshua Orne, John Gallison, Jonathan Glover and James Mugford, recommended a nonimportation of tea agreement that was unanimously accepted. In strong language it expressed: the unconstitutionality of the tea tax, approval of legislature's and merchants' remonstrances against injustice, a threat to force reshipment on importers and to publish their names, and, finally—referring to the Boston Massacre—the town declared its readiness to support civil opposition to such injustices "with our lives." Seven hundred and twelve signed for their families; only ten reneged. Those four women and six men were listed in the *Essex Gazette* report and were refused liquor licenses—a serious fate in Marblehead.

The opposition to the tea tax seemed to cool down, as increased shipping activity and fishing tonnage improved business conditions. Town Meeting voted educational improvements and extension of highways. Gaiety reigned in the splendid mansions and the newfangled stage-coach brought friends into town to help everyone celebrate Training Day, Election Week, Thanksgiving Day; however, not Christmas, which was still considered "Romish" or European and was simply listed in the almanacs: "December 25: Christ Born."

Those years were saddened by the loss of an old and true friend of Marblehead, the man that others called "the bishop of that place," Parson John Barnard. The Reverend Mr. Barnard's death at the age of eighty-nine closed fifty-four years as the minister of the First Church in Marblehead, which he could never be induced to leave either by Harvard, the provincial governor or Boston churches. In his autobiography Barnard admitted that, upon arrival, his opinion of Marblehead was best kept to himself, but, as with so many others, the independent spirit, the courage, and unassuming kindnesses of its people captured his heart and he could not depart except in death. The town had been "in irons," but Barnard's zest and enthusiasm were the winds of change that had set the town on a swift winning course. Parson Barnard lived to see Marblehead as the second largest town in the Province, sixth largest in the country, and recognized from one side of the Atlantic to the other for its fisheries, its shipping, intrepid men and daring seamanship.

John Barnard had set an example of tolerance, especially toward the new churches where, he said, he found only a few "bigots." Accordingly, the ministers of all the churches attended his funeral which was planned by an Interment Committee of Robert Hooper, Esq., Jeremiah Lee, Esq. and Mr. Eben Foster. The funeral was scheduled for January 29, weather permitting, and John Barnard was laid to rest among his people on Burial Hill. His death closed a remarkable chapter in town annals, for Marblehead's first three ministers, Walton, Cheever and Barnard, had begun and ended their ministries in Marblehead—covering a span of 132 years—which speaks volumes for "that place."

The parson's handsome house was located on the street named for the genial genius, Benjamin Franklin, who that same year had presented to the British some scientific information that had long been the personal observation and a navigational aid to American shippers. The Board of Customs in Boston had complained that their mail packets were taking two weeks longer on their westward voyage than American ships, so Postmaster General Franklin collated his observations, logs, soundings and currents and drew up a chart of the Gulf Stream which the British vessels had been bucking. The printed charts were furnished to the mail packets, not so much to speed royal instructions to customs collectors, as to inject a conciliatory note in the strident relations between the mother country and the Colonies. Franklin and other men like George Washington hoped for a reconciliation or a compromise instead of a bloody confrontation. Their voices were lost in the political turmoil and power struggle in England, while the speeches and shouts of the Sons of

Liberty were reported regularly. The Massachusetts hotbed of individualism and dissent became the focal point for royal repression and every mandate acted as a bellows for the fire of independence. When the new and unpopular Governor Hutchinson accepted his salary from the king, in a direct violation of the Colony's charter, provincial disgust was vehemently expressed by Samuel Adams at the Boston Town Meeting moderated by John Hancock. Adams proposed that a Committee of Correspondence be organized to communicate with the towns and publish to the world the violation of their sacred rights. Just such acrimonious repudiation permeated the circular letter received by Marblehead urging the people to realize that "we are struggling for our lost birthrights and inheritance."

A Marblehead citizens' petition requesting Town Meeting elaborated on Adams' points by accusing Parliament of despicable neglect and a repugnant use of power over the money and property of their subjects and "crammed down their throats." The entire petition was inserted in the warrant. Town Meeting adjourned to have a committee draw up the resolutions which angrily denounced "sending troops and ships to parade about the coast and street" and the dismissal of the Massachusetts Legislature, and further asserted that "this town is highly incensed at the unconstitutional, unrighteous, presumptious and notorious proceedings." At the next session the newly created Committee of Grievances declared that Boston's *State of Rights* pamphlet should be read annually at Town Meeting "to inform posterity (should their rights and liberties be preserved) of how much they are indebted to many eminent patriots." Youthful spirit and enthusiasm carried the vote and Town Meeting ended with a stirring appeal to support their God-given rights, and with the warning that "we desire to use these blessings of Liberty with Thankfulness and prudence, and to defend them with intrepidity and steadiness."

The high excitement of the meeting must have continued in Henry Saunders' Green Dragon where, according to the *Essex Gazette*, "all gentlemen, strangers and others may depend on meeting with good attendance and entertainment." The entertainment that December night would be the animated exchange of the latest news and hopes, and Marblehead sailors' accounts of their punches in the Boston's wharf riots would vie with the skippers' uproarious tale of outwitting customs and the fishermen's disgust with damage suits backlogged in the courts. Marblehead liked a good scrap and the shouted slogans could be heard at King Hooper's, a good place for a quiet meeting of the worried merchant aristocracy. The opposition they had fostered against royal trade duties had now, with that radical Sam Adams raising the lid, proved a Pandora's box. They felt that Town Meeting resolutions had too much "intrepidity" and too little "prudence"; and before long the recent quiet stability that had somewhat revived trade would disappear in riots, repression and recession. Disruption would further endanger their credit and trade and the whole town's prosperity.

With ship seizures increasing many merchants could no longer ally themselves with the more intemperate element, who called themselves patriots. A letter denouncing Marblehead's rash action and refuting the claim of a majority vote was signed by twenty-nine town merchants and published in the *Essex Gazette*. The next day the "patriots" vigorously denied these charges. Sides were being drawn up and claims of bad faith, accompanied by open antagonism, were fragmenting the solidarity of the town. The language of Town Meeting minutes exposes the gradual political swing from "His Majesty's subjects" to "American British Colonists" and thence to "Americans" and "Patriots"; the conservative description evolved from the Merchants' Committee who spoke for "English Liberty" to "Respectable Gentlemen," and then to suspected "Enemies of the Country" and, finally, to "Tories."

Tension mounted with sparks flying at every turn and in 1773 an uncontrollable explosion of emotion and fear almost ended the political services of several men destined to become conspicuous patriots. That hated disease, smallpox, again was discovered in town and threw panic into the hearts of the taut townspeople. The selectmen voted to "impress" houses, as needed, for the care of smallpox victims, and—a saddening decree for the town's children—ordered all dogs be killed immediately on the suspicion of spreading contagion. Azor Orne, John Glover, and Elbridge Gerry petitioned for an inoculation hospital on Cat Island, either publicly or privately owned. The latter course was voted with many stipulations to reduce possible contagion: burn clothing, limit ferry service, order a thirty-day period of quarantine. The populace lacked an understanding of inoculation. When the public tar and feathering of those who had stolen infectious clothing magnified their terror, opposition built into panic that caused one of the Cat Island proprietors, Colonel Jonathan Glover, to place a cannon in his front room.

One night arsonists succeeded in burning down "Castle Pox" at a loss of £2000 to the four owners; and the suspects were jailed in Salem. As five hundred "Headers" advanced toward Salem to rescue the prisoners, the Salem militia was drummed to arms and only a speedy withdrawal of charges by the hospital proprietors brought peace to the borders. It was a far cry from the Salem–Marblehead

congeniality of the previous October when the Marbleheaders tore
over to Salem with their two fire engines and scores of volunteers to
help quench the fire on Essex Street. In the smoke of the charred
buildings the Salemites invited one hundred and thirty-two Marblehead volunteers to breakfast which was bolstered by three gallons of
rum and three jugs of gin. The smallpox skirmish didn't upset Salem
nearly as much as it did Marblehead and the prominent proprietors
whose disillusionment cut deeply into their confidence in the town.
They resigned from the Committee of Correspondence and Elbridge
Gerry withdrew his name from the General Court election. Only
the unwavering enthusiasm and eloquence of the Boston patriots
reactivated their personal involvement in the cause of freedom for
America.

If, as it has been said, molasses was an "essential ingredient" of independence, surely it must have been dissolved in tea. The reduction in the cost of the colonial tea did not diminish the determination to prevent the East India Tea Company from monopolizing the
tea trade. The merchants and the smugglers would be hard hit by
direct competition, yet the issue was primarily the taxation principle
which Marblehead's Town Meeting defied by claiming "that Americans have a right to be as free as any inhabitants of the earth."
When resolutions and protests left the Massachusetts governor unmoved for almost a month, eight thousand people gathered in Boston, including a Marblehead contingent of high-calibered thoughtful
men. As the crowd watched from the shore, the disguised band of
white American "Indians" (Dr. Elisha Story among them) boarded
Dartmouth and two other vessels and threw chest after chest of tea
into the waters of Boston Harbor. No one was harmed, nothing else
was stolen, but ninety thousand pounds of tea steeped in the Bay
waters for the Boston Tea Party. The British were enraged. Parliament ordered repayment and an end to Massachusetts' "rebellion"
by installing a military governor, Thomas Gage, legalizing British
troops in Boston, abolishing Town Meeting (except for elections),
and firmly closing the port of Boston. The provincial government
was moved to Salem and the customs collectors to Marblehead
where departing Governor Hutchinson was entertained by Robert
Hooper, Esq. and the local Loyalists.

Most merchants were not yet ready to abdicate their influence or
abandon their business interests, and merchant Thomas Robie was
even elected town treasurer. Robie, who specialized in imported
china, glass, wallpaper, cheeses and gunpowder, had a large inventory of imported goods which had already annoyed the nonimportation proponents. His correspondence with his conservative cousin,

Jonathan Sewall, told of his abhorrence of serving in the militia and he was urged to seek public office as an exemption. To Thomas Robie's concern over the turn of events in Marblehead, Sewall had replied that he hoped to come into possession of material to "enable you to be a Terror to evildoers . . . and to look down with a smile of contempt on Town Meetings, colonels, captains and militia, clerks, and especially, on modern patriots, falsely so called. . . ." Robie's carefully worded letter in 1773 regretted that he did not find life (in Marblehead) "so desirable as I once did."

Most merchants had hoped to persuade the Colony to reimburse the East India Company and had expressed fear for the safety of private property in the growing unrest. Their continuing support of England was flaunted by a letter in the May 25, 1774, *Essex Gazette*, praising the departing Governor Hutchinson for his "general good." The "subscribers, merchants, traders and others, inhabitants of Marblehead" who signed were strange bedfellows—five Hoopers, Nathan Bowen, Benjamin Marston, Thomas Robie, Isaac Mansfield, Sr., joined by Jonathan Glover, John Pedrick, John Gallison, John Prince and several later supporters of the rebellion. Governor Hutchinson's reply to the Marbleheaders, "Gentlemen of respectable Characters," was published in the same issue.

The town broke wide open over this act and in strongly worded resolutions stated: "Be it known to the whole world, its present generation and every future one . . . that the justification of the Governor and his stand on the Greenwich Hospital Tax was designed to destroy the harmony of the Town by . . . seeds of dissension, animosity and discord." Although sprinkled with the words "insulting" . . . "malicious" . . . "effrontive" . . . and "obnoxious," the statement still left the door open for public retraction saying that these were "otherwise affectionate and thoughtful men."

All but ten of the signees were moved to recant publicly, two saying they wished the devil had taken that paper before they ever saw it. Some others, bravely or foolishly, flaunted their royal loyalty by welcoming the new military governor to Salem and dining with the British officers. King Hooper had built a fine country house in Danvers where he entertained Governor Gage, so angering the irate citizens that a warning shot later pierced the door of his country home. Communication between the Tories and Patriots was breaking down as each side became more inflexible in its position.

The propaganda battle for the support of the vacillating moderates was fought in the press which became an effective weapon in all the Colonies. Articles from brilliant and educated men were published under pseudonyms, causing the royal officials to use innumerable means to close down the newspapers. Pamphlets on public questions appeared on the streets augmenting the broadsides and signs into a huge barrage of words to inspire and unite. There was a period of comparative restraint when the words of "separation" or "independence" were being rehearsed only in men's minds, but the stage was set in the press for their entrance cue.

May's provincial elections made John Gallison Marblehead's representative, with a mandate from his constituents to discard the idea that might makes right, to fight against the Port Bill and charter revision, and to recommend a congress of all the assemblies on the Continent. Gallison was asked to report back the sense of the House "upon the absolute authority . . . claimed by Great Britain over the Colonies." Although town resolutions were still qualified with appropriate phrases to avoid charges of treason, the tone was challenging and the words foreshadowed Marblehead's involvement: "The worthy patriot does not fully show himself when the State is secure and tranquil, but shines illustriously in the midst of attacks and dangers. . . ."

There were many immediate ways to "show" themselves: by making storage space available in the Powder House and Town House for Boston merchants, by taking nightly cartloads of fish to Boston's poor, by enlarging the Committee of Correspondence, and by requesting Jeremiah Lee, Azor Orne or Elbridge Gerry to decide which one would attend the Continental Congress and, finally, by ingeniously circumventing the royal governor's order forbidding more than one Town Meeting a year. The Marblehead moderator never called for final adjournment, but simply adjourned temporarily until a specified date and hour. Four or five meetings a month or even twice a day for forty-six continuous meetings went right on under the noses of a regiment of British Regulars stationed on the Neck to force an end to Town Meeting. The clashes in town and the people's threat to march on the Neck to "exterminate the entire body" eventually convinced the British commander of the wisdom of withdrawal. The tradition of 127 years of Marblehead Town Meeting didn't melt away before the political heat exuded from British redcoats, but just in case of emergency the Marblehead militia was being readied for action, from the "smoke-dried" company who could only "whip the snake" to what the elderly John Barnard described as a regiment of seven full companies ". . . well-clad, bright, vigorous, active . . ." and so well-trained that one general had remarked that "throughout the country . . . he had not seen . . . so goodly an appearance of spirited men." Militia training was now extended and each man had to report for two hours, four times a week. There was some discussion about hiding the town's powder where it would be safe; the only trouble was no one could find the powder, so the town asked every citizen to look around and, please, to return it. Every male inhabitant was ordered to procure this equipment: a firearm, bayonet, pouch of thirty rounds of shot and a knapsack. A Committee of Inspection was chosen for military reorganization and to give the alarm, if possible, with four days notice. The work of this committee immediately conflicted with the convictions of some of the Loyalist officers who felt that arming against the greatest power in the world was, at best, ridiculous or futile and, at worst, tragic or fatal. Some resigned; others were forced out by legal interpretations giving the town the authority to grant new commissions.

During the fall, 1774, two significant Congresses—the First Continental Congress in Philadelphia and the Massachusetts Provincial Congress in Salem—affected Marblehead's course of action. In each courage and caution were skillfully combined in navigating the narrow channel between bloodshed and complete submission. In Philadelphia, efforts to apply full colonial pressure resulted in the Association which would press for national nonimportation and local enforcement in hopes of reversing trade conditions to those of 1763. To accomplish this the Congress recommended national austerity, nonconsumption of tea and local manufacturing efforts, such as production of nails which England had withheld for seven years. Each colony was requested to ratify the Association which the Massachusetts Provincial Congress swiftly accomplished; meanwhile taking far bolder steps on its own. As the focal point for British retaliation, Massachusetts was more immediately concerned with its safety and defense. The Provincial Congress, which had no legal standing but which assumed legislative power with the people's approval, organized militias, ended tax payments to royal representatives and established executive committees. Marblehead's Elbridge Gerry served on the committee to consider the general state of the Province and the Committee of Safety. Azor Orne and Jeremiah Lee were the other Marblehead delegates and Lee assumed the chairmanship of the local enforcement committee which found most importers cooperative. Auctions of imported goods in transit when the order was issued were popular in Marblehead; the cargo of *Champion* from London brought £2410 for its books, duck, medicines, and so forth. Other vessels unloaded raisins, lemons, figs, wines that would soon be rarities. If the committee's auctions showed a profit, that money went to the Boston Committee for Relief. There was alert vigilance about tea consumption, as Thomas Lilly learned to his embarrassment when he was caught buying tea. This was promptly burned in public as he signed a confession and promise to obey. Lilly returned to his work with clear resolve to drink something else. The town's adherence to frugality meant no parties, dances or even marriage or funeral banquets, unless the participants wished their names published the next day at the Town House. Militarily, the town's location made defense of its fisheries and merchant fleet vital to the Province; so the Congress appröpriated £800 for enlistment and training of Marblehead Minutemen "in the arts of war." Captain James Mugford was paymaster under the direction of Joshua Orne, Thomas Gerry and Richard Harris who worked out a system of daily payment (limited to three days per week) from two shillings to a private to six shillings for a captain. The fashionable, sociable drills and parades of the past decade shifted to serious military training and discipline for a time that was close at hand.

On a cold February Sunday in 1775 the British transport, *Lively,* dropped anchor off Homan's beach and remained almost as quiet as local church services. Suddenly, the Sabbath calm was broken, as troops of the 64th Regiment rushed topside, bayonets fixed, and formed for the march to Salem to confiscate cannon and ammunition. That was a Sunday when it was fortunate that so many Marbleheaders were not churchgoers, for observing the disembarking troops, they ran to the church doors where drums picked up the general alarm. Major Pedrick raced from church to his stable at Washington and Pickett Streets for his fastest steed and, as he rode swiftly along the Dungeons road to warn Salem, he was recognized by his daughter's British suitor who ordered "file right" to cause the major no delay in his haste to a "sick friend." Pedrick found the Salemites at church where the bells were set to ringing out an alert. The North River Draw Bridge was raised to prevent the British from reaching the hidden cannon; militia, ministers, and hundreds of citizens gathered to greet Colonel Leslie's regiment, knowing that Marblehead's militia was bringing up the rear. Leslie's demands to lower the bridge were countered by refusals to budge the chains; meanwhile, every available barge was being removed.

Young Robert Wormstead of Marblehead could not restrain himself any longer and, drawing his sword, skillfully fenced and disarmed six British Regulars. The normally subdued Salemites taunted from windows; the street exchange became more heated, and Colonel Leslie turned to commence firing. Salem's Captain Felt shouted "Fire! You'd better be damned than fire . . . if you fire, you are all dead men." Surrounded by Minutemen and mobs, Leslie was persuaded by calmer minds to accept an alternative: to save face by marching across the disputed bridge and then return without seeking the cannon. That military gesture accomplished, tight-lipped British soldiers marched the four miles back to their ship through Marblehead's militiamen who were lined along both sides, shivering noticeably—almost enough to jiggle the trigger of a loaded musket. No gunfire occurred and the British fifed their men aboard *Lively* with the prophetic tune, "The World Turned Upside Down."

The British import sales were dropping fast. In fact, in one year the £562,476 importation total collapsed to a mere £71,625, so retaliatory royal decrees, especially aimed at insubordinate New England, cut off trade with other nations and prohibited fishing on the Banks. American vessels and fishermen were warned by the Massachusetts Provincial Congress to stay close to home, so, instead of the Marblehead spring fare, all hands were around to propel the rapid succession of events of 1775.

Jeremiah Lee and Elbridge Gerry had been carting powder and guns to the Concord storehouse in good old Marblehead hogsheads labeled "Fish." They and Azor Orne had arranged to meet with Samuel Adams and John Hancock at Wetherby's Tavern in Menotomy on April 18. The Marbleheaders stayed overnight at the tavern and observed British officers "out on some evil design," so a warning was sent to Hancock to escape. A few hours later British troops stopped outside the tavern and a search was ordered. Clad only in nightclothes, the Marblehead Committee members shivered in the cornfield until all danger of discovery had passed. The next day the "shot heard 'round the world" brought bloodshed and shock to Lexington and Concord, but the resourceful Minutemen regrouped and peppered the retreating British all along the return march to Boston. Disorganized and stunned, the British crossed Charlestown Neck where it is thought some Marbleheaders joined the fight and the siege of Boston although the Provincial Congress had emphasized the necessity of the coastal units staying on guard to defend the seacoast against naval attack. Captain John Glover was alerted to prevent military information from reaching *Lively*, which had reappeared off Marblehead.

If any hope of avoiding open warfare remained, the British Parliament had to be made aware of both sides of the Lexington conflict, so Elbridge Gerry was asked to take depositions from those in the action and then send the report aboard a London-bound vessel that would try to sneak past *Lively*. Under the cover of night the ship

escaped and began its race to England, arriving before General
Gage's official report but without having the desired effect or influence on Parliament.

The local situation worsened as press gangs trapped Marblehead
seamen on the streets of their own town and the British vessels
lobbed some shot into a wharf and tavern, while unemployment and
scarcity of provisions affected most households. What had been
called the Tuesday Night Club now met at the Prentiss-Story house
on Mugford Street to perform their duties as the Committee of
Safety and to relay intelligence reports received from the Provincial
Congress in Watertown. Secrecy was imperative; fear of detection
by the discontented Anglophile merchants grew. Some of King
George's "loyal subjects" had found quarters for British soldiers, so-
cialized with officials of the royal government in Salem and even
fraternized with the officers of *Lively*. It seemed as though many
wealthy Tories put economic stability and fraternization with the
British far ahead of the intense love of liberty so deeply ingrained in
Marbleheaders. A notable exception was Jeremiah Lee who worked
closely with the Gerrys, Ornes and Glovers and the townspeople,
offering his fortune, his influence and himself in the fight against oppressive acts and military occupation. But on May 10, 1775, the
same day that the Second Continental Congress initiated its crucial
meeting Jeremiah Lee succumbed to a severe fever and Marblehead
lost a patron, a civic leader, a financial backer and a true friend who
might have been effective in persuading other merchants attached to
Great Britain, either through their ledgers or their hearts, to join the
fight for freedom.

No Loyalist could have misunderstood Town Meeting's sharp
order to its Safety Committee "to attend to the conduct . . . of Ja-
cobites in this town . . . report names . . . take effective measures
either for silencing or expelling them from this community. . . ."
Marblehead emotions were reinforced when word reached town
that the Philadelphia Congress had avowed the rebellion, appointed
George Washington as commander, specifically warned against giving aid or supplies to the British, and urged the towns to disarm or
arrest those endangering their safety. Now a signed allegiance could
be demanded of all citizens and the British sympathizers, or Tories,
would have to "fish or cut bait."

Most Tories were predicting devastating effects of a war between
an unformed country and a great European monarchy, yet some
were finally moved by Parliament's inflexibility to throw in their lot
with the "cause"; others retreated into silence and the comparative
safety of inland towns, and the outspoken or collaborators later fled

from Marblehead, usually by boat. Ideologically, families were tragically split apart, usually by generations, as the older members clung to royal traditions and the young seized the dangerous alternative of independence. Married couples were often separated as the brunt of unpopularity was usually directed at the husband who escaped to an unknown fate, leaving his wife with friends and in charge of his children and property. Not all Tories were influential, educated or wealthy; some were simple tradesmen and many were members of St. Michael's, the local Church of England. Its minister, Rev. Joshua Wingate Weeks, who had gone to London to be ordained, had an unswerving loyalty to his church and king. As early as the 1769 *Pitt Packet* incident he had written, "political matters embitter the minds of the people." When hostilities occurred at Lexington, he still urged his parishioners to "have nothing to do with this rebellion" and many concurred. After the Church of England was denounced as an enemy and St. Michael's closed, the Reverend Mr. Weeks endured three imprisonments, and when a later order for the arrest of thirty Marblehead Tories was issued, he escaped to British headquarters in Newport, Rhode Island.

Among those thirty scheduled for arrest were: John Wormstead, relative of young Robert who fought so bravely at Bunker Hill; Woodward Abraham, shopkeeper and former postmaster; Edward Bowen, most of whose family had moved to Amesbury; and Richard and Michael Coombes. The latter had baited the townspeople with sarcastic remarks and was known to have supplied timber for British fortifications. Finally, a citizens' group set out to take Coombes, who raced to a sympathetic neighbor's home for protection. As the crowd attempted to invade the Bowden home, Mrs. Bowden stood her ground, ordered them out, saying they endangered the life of her ailing daughter. Challenged, Mrs. Bowden swore the man was not under her roof and the crowd moved on. Michael Coombes wasn't under her roof; he was standing upon it behind the chimney. Coombes persistently avoided the oath of allegiance, secreting himself for three years, after which he departed alone for Penobscot and London. His war claim to the British government for his shipping losses was settled for one seventh of their value, barely enough for him to return to Marblehead where he died in 1806.

Two distinctly different Loyalists were Agnes Surriage Frankland and Ashley Bowen. Following Sir Harry Frankland's death, Marblehead's "Lady Agnes" did not return to her native town but joined the coterie of royal officials. After the Bunker Hill battle Agnes had nursed the British wounded, an act that marked her as a turncoat

Tory and hastened her departure for England. Far different was the roving mariner and artistic journalist of Marblehead, Ashley Bowen, who had sailed the world over and now decided to stick with the Crown. He was a burr under the sea jacket of most 'Headers—especially as he made no effort to leave town—so Bowen could find little or no work as a rigger and shopkeepers often refused to sell him provisions. Twice drafted and trained, he was still suspect and, finding no bondsman, Ashley Bowen was given a sea assignment on a guard ship. Sympathetic friends found him a berth on a vessel that may have been supplying the enemy but, lacking any proof, his town accepted him in later years. Their fury was concentrated on the merchants whose wealth and support were badly needed in the mobilization of men and equipment to fight King George III.

A particular target was Thomas Robie who had recently bought the impressive brick mansion around the corner from the Lees. Robie had stubbornly antagonized the townspeople by refusing to sign the Stamp Act protest or Nonimportation Act, then he charged the town an exorbitant price for gunpowder. The resentment of the town was constantly rekindled, especially, by the Robies' cold reaction to the "bewitching charms of the Great Goddess, Liberty." As the family set sail in 1775 for Halifax, the welcoming refuge of Royalists, a crowd surrounded the wharf hurling epithets until Mrs. Robie is said to have angrily retorted: "I hope that I shall live to return, find this wicked rebellion crushed, and see the streets of Marblehead so deep with rebel blood that a long boat might be rowed through them." The enraged roar that greeted that farewell must have echoed in the Robies' ears in Halifax where even while hating the "disloyal scoundrels" at home, they longed to return from their "captivity."

Of the three most prominent Marblehead merchants, only Jeremiah Lee had embraced the idea of independence. His partners and brothers-in-law arrogantly scorned the revolutionary movement and eventually both King Hooper and Benjamin Marston were no longer tolerated in Marblehead. Departing about the same time from Marblehead was the renowned artist, John Singleton Copley, who had agreeably painted such successful Marblehead magnates as Hooper and Lee, posed in their beautiful homes and dressed in fine, brightly colored imports. Copley never returned, nor did his son, who in time became the lord chancellor of England. Portrait artist Copley had gone to London, but Hooper sailed for the Maritime Provinces accompanied by only a few of his family who were sharply divided in their personal loyalties. Years later King Hooper returned to Marblehead, never to recoup the great Hooper trading fortune or his lofty status. Some of the other Hoopers remained in Massachusetts, more or less silent, except son Joseph, who owned a successful ropewalk in Marblehead and through his cordage business became independently wealthy. Joseph Hooper displayed his affection for the British before the townspeople and was suspected of giving information to the blockaders. The hateful Restraining Act had agitated the town to a frenzy when one of their own native sons authored a published protest against "disloyal Whigs" and the people of Marblehead. The author was Joseph Hooper who signed all the Royalist letters to the *Essex Gazette*. Arson was attempted three times at his new home on Back Street (Elm Street) caricatured as "Tory Hall," until Hooper armed himself and one night killed an alleged assailant. In fear of his life Joseph Hooper hid amidst the fish in the hold of one of his father's ships in order to escape to Bilbao, Spain, from where he made his way to England. He married a wealthy English woman and tried unsuccessfully to establish a paper mill in Suffolk. His divorced American wife was awarded one third of his confiscated Marblehead estate, for the son of King Hooper had no desire to return.

Hooper's uncle, Benjamin Marston, (Harvard, 1749), married Sarah, the daughter of Joseph Swett, and used his inheritance to establish an impressive importing business and build a handsome mansion on Watson Street. His status, he felt, called for a coat of arms, which the rest of the family ignored. This fascination with nobility and England didn't prevent his protesting the Greenwich Hospital tax or acting as town moderator, yet the trouble stirring caused him to liquidate some of his property as early as 1771. He spoke out against the bold resolutions challenging the English prerogatives, and his frequent trips to the royal governor caused enough suspicion to make the committee break in and search his office for espionage evidence. After his wife died that year, Marston hid with friends to avoid signing the oath of allegiance, then sailed in an open boat to Boston where General Howe protected him.

From that day, energetic and charming Ben Marston led the life of a refugee seeking a congenial colony in Nova Scotia or New Brunswick where he could establish a business and enjoy the people. He held public office in the Maritime Provinces, but his dreams were never realized. On several occasions Ben Marston made unexplained trips to the West Indies and, while homeward bound, was taken into custody by a privateer for his part in a spy operation. Much of the war he spent in jails in Plymouth, Bristol and Boston from which he wrote of his total disbelief in Washington's promise

of a French fleet, "there will be one from the Moon as soon." The
"sad, incorrigible Tory" again shipped out of Marblehead in 1777,
this time in an exchange for an important American prisoner. Later
he was twice jailed in Philadelphia; his good fortune at being released was usually balanced by his misfortune in the Maritime Provinces. Jailed for debts on his postwar return to Boston, Marston
traveled to London for a war-claims settlement. The award was so
small that he couldn't afford a passage home. Then three more business ventures fell through, including his interesting invention of "an
artificial horizon for Hadley's quadrant which would permit the determination of the sun's altitude when the real horizon was invisible."

Nothing worked now for Ben Marston; England was miserable
and he longed to return to his native country, but money was still a
problem, so he signed up for a colonization scheme in Africa. For
£60 sterling and five hundred African acres Marston would set up a
"great commercial System with the Native Africans on reciprocal
advantages, to cut up by the roots that most wicked traffic, the
Slave trade." This from the experience-molded, mature Marston
who had earlier listed three Negro "servants" in his war claims!

In his last letter home, before he went to his death from fever in
Africa, Benjamin Marston wrote, "there is not remaining the least
resentment in my mind to the Country, because the party whose
side I took in the Great Revolution did not succeed, for I am now
fully convinced it is better for the world that they have not" . . . "I
don't mean by this to pay any compliment to the first instigators of
our American Revolution." It was hard for the Tories to forget
their fears, though no Marblehead Tory was ever injured or killed.
It was agonizing, too, for the Patriots to tolerate any menace or deterrent to this magnificent and perilous opportunity.

The Massachusetts Spy, or American Oracle of Liberty, printed
the provincial proclamation for a day of fasting and prayer. By a
town vote Marblehead, too, held such a day "on account of the
grievous state of affairs."

Almost every household in the town felt the pressure for enlistment, as Col. John Glover had been ordered to have his regiment
ready to march at a moment's notice and the town had already
voted blankets and provisions. Congress was advised that Glover
had gathered ten companies, mostly from Marblehead, and three
quarters of them had workable firearms. On the day before the
Bunker Hill battle John Glover was officially commissioned head of
the 21st Regiment and ordered to remain at Marblehead. When the
alarm of battle spread on that hot June day, Capt. Samuel Trevett's

artillery company set out from Marblehead for Boston and joined the attempt to hold the Hill against successive British attacks. Finally, bombarded and cut off from their supplies, the Americans fell back, leaving British carnage and many dead Americans on the field, including Marblehead's William Jackson and David Carmichael. Most of the wounded were rescued and among them was Robert Wormstead whose first military encounter had been at Salem's North Bridge. Four days later, Colonel Glover was commanded to move his regiment to Cambridge headquarters, and, to the tune of drums and fifes, four-hundred-and-five strong, they marched away from the Marblehead Training Field, confident and colorful in their blue pants and jackets with leather buttons.

Very little protection was left for the town itself, so the citizens raised two more local companies to be stationed at the fort. That redoubt was in a sad state, but within a week one hundred men built a stronger breastwork with funds from the town and private citizens —all under the watchful eye of the British vessel, *Merlin*, which was searching returning vessels and fishing craft. The British naval vessels confidently came and went as they pleased here and in Boston, without challenge by the powderless patriots.

Ammunition, metal supplies and saltpeter had been long enumerated imports and the short supply was now acute in the Colonies. Marblehead's representative, Elbridge Gerry, experienced in the mercantile business and warehouse supplies, had pressed the Provincial Congress to stockpile saltpeter and plan a powder mill in Revere. General Washington, deeply troubled by the scarcity, welcomed the proposals of Marbleheaders that armed privateers be outfitted to capture British supplies. Washington, then Congress, commissioned Marblehead's John Glover to lease and arm merchant vessels as authorized privateers.

The Glovers' *Hannah* had been in West Indian trade and was available, so Marbleheader Nicholson Broughton was placed in command and the vessel was manned by seamen from the Marblehead Marine Regiment. Having been outfitted at Beverly, Marblehead's *Hannah* bravely set out on September 5, 1775, to take on the British Navy, only to be chased back into Gloucester by the familiar British man-of-war, *Lively*. Undaunted, *Hannah* was more successful two days later when she captured the British *Unity*, full of provisions, arms and powder which were rushed to Cambridge. The confusion over the prize money for a recaptured vessel led to such misunderstanding and protests that the ensuing row brought on arrests and punishments. A few weeks later, with a fresh crew, *Hannah* tried again but that voyage was ill-fated for, while being pursued by the enemy's *Nautilus*, America's first official vessel went aground and was later stripped.

Meanwhile, Colonel Glover was making arrangements for additional Marblehead vessels for what he called "ye navy": Archibald Selman's *Elizabeth*, renamed *Franklin;* Thomas Grant's *Speedwell*, called *Hancock;* John Twisden's *Hawk*, now *Warren*, and *Two Brothers*, owned by Thomas Stevens, christened for the deceased patriot, *Lee*. Three out of four vessels of the American "fleet" were skippered by Marblehead captains—Broughton, Selman, and Manley—with experienced Marblehead mariners for crew. The financial account for Glover's "navy" was listed as the "United Colonies of America." This tiny naval fleet from Marblehead was now solely responsible to America and was being readied to take on the strongest naval power in the world.

In late October of 1775, *Hancock*, commanded by Nicholson Broughton, and *Franklin* under John Selman, set sail with two sets of orders: the first was the official authorization to gather coastal information and to take British prize vessels with the provision that one third of the cargo value would be divided among the officers and crew by shares (to avoid the controversy that had beset *Hannah*), and to preserve ammunition they were not to engage armed vessels. Also, any prisoners taken were to be treated with kindness and humanity. A second set, or sealed orders opened at sea, advised of intelligence reports that two brigantines loaded with armaments from England were probably headed for Quebec, and *Hancock* and *Franklin* were ordered to intercept them. If the British vessels had "passed," *Hancock* and *Franklin* were commanded to remain offshore to take any prizes, except government transports.

Stormy weather, loss of a mainmast hastily replaced by a great tree, and the vague intelligence information caused the Marblehead vessels to miss the assigned brigantines; however, they managed to capture ten valuable prize ships. Learning that several large cannon were mounted at St. John's, where officials were recruiting for the British, the spirited Marblehead skippers headed in, hellbent on a real achievement. They discovered the cannon were too cumbersome to handle. However, other supplies were taken for the war effort, and it was rumored that the crew helped themselves. Then, impulsively, the captains arrested the acting governor and a judge, calling them hostages, and proudly set sail for home. Later, to their amazement, George Washington, whose fiery temper matched his hair, reprimanded Broughton and Selman for having exceeded their authority and the captured officials and the ships were released. American relationships were very touchy with the Northern Maritime Provinces and Washington did not wish to disrupt any plans being considered by the Congress. The unexpected rebuff of their patriotic, though overzealous, accomplishments was a crushing blow to Selman and Broughton. They resigned their commissions in Glover's regiment.

By November Gerry's bill had passed and expedited the outfitting of the 72-ton, topsail schooner *Lee* commanded by Captain John Manley of Marblehead. Flying the new "Pine Tree" flag *Lee* rounded Point o' Neck on its maiden voyage and immediately gave chase and recaptured an American vessel which was sent into Marblehead. The British ordinance brigantine, *Nancy*, was sighted off Gloucester and was swiftly captured by *Lee*, barely one third her size. *Nancy* was a bonanza for the poorly equipped American troops: 100,000 flints, 32 tons of lead, 2000 muskets, bayonets, fuses and several field pieces which Colonel Glover rushed to General Washington to strengthen the ring around Boston. When the prize cargo began to arrive by the wagonful in Cambridge, an uproarious cheer ripped through the camp and it was spontaneously decided to hold a christening. One of the oldest generals hoisted himself onto the largest field mortar, poured rum down the throat of the cannon and christened it "Congress." The howls of laughter came within earshot of the British who shook their heads over the trivialities of these simple revolutionists. General Washington said, "Nothing surely ever came more apropos," and John Adams, writing later of the significant capture, said: "I assert that the first American flag was hoisted by John Manley, and the first British flag was struck to him."

Manley's naval career had just begun, for soon after he captured four more important prizes carrying shipments of badly needed food, rum, coal, dry goods and important British naval papers. General Washington's recognition of Manley's feats resulted in the January 1, 1776, commission as commodore and his transfer to the faster vessel, *Hancock*. Manley's prize record continued, but later in the month, when dangerously reduced in manpower, he was pursued by an armed British frigate ordered to end the career of this daring Marbleheader. Manley, after trying to hold off under the heavy cannonade took a calculated risk and beached *Hancock*. Commodore and crew waded ashore, covered by gunfire of the local militia. When the British attempted to fire *Hancock*, colonial muskets held off the small boats, so the frigate retired with its wounded. Manley's men refloated the damaged vessel and returned it to port for repairs, after which the winter weather prevented new encounters.

That year of 1775 had overflowed with tirade and tumult out of which a general purpose was becoming crystallized as protest developed into armed opposition. Noble and brave words came out of Philadelphia: "Our cause is just. Our union is perfect," and added that "for the defence of the freedom that is our birth-right . . . for the protection of our property, acquired solely by the honest industry of our forefathers, . . . we have taken up arms."

On that Thanksgiving young Isaac Mansfield, Jr., descendant of a seafaring Marblehead family, preached the sermon to the soldiers encamped at Roxbury. As in so many pulpits throughout the land, Mansfield applied a Bible text to the critical American dilemma: "And now I am become two bands." After reviewing the list of colonial grievances he spoke words that many a soldier might grimly recall during the next months: "In a state of war, the final victory by no means depends upon early success." Mansfield decried the current distress of the blockaded seaports cut off from food supplies and their livelihood and constantly endangered by British naval vessels and raiding patrols.

Such was the distress of the seaport of Marblehead that there were collections for the relief of the poor and suggestions to use roots and peat for fuel now that the coastal lumber vessels were held in their ports. Income had plummeted; husbands and sons were with General Washington or at sea on privateers; shops were closed, and unemployment was widespread, except in defense work. General Washington, aware of the worries of his Marblehead men whom he called a "rugged, story-telling" lot, thoughtfully sent $390 "to the relief of the distressed, sad wives and children of the soldiers from Marblehead." Short army enlistments allowed men to return home to earn some income or arrange credit; nevertheless, this detracted from the army's organization and strength. There was no age limit; boys like Abraham Wood, who was described at his enrollment as being fifteen, of light complexion and four feet, eight inches tall, signed up with grizzled fifty-year-old seamen to join Colonel Glover or the naval commanders.

In the face of somber developments as Britain hired German auxiliaries, beefed up their colonial forces and ordered confiscation of American ships, Marblehead increased the size of its Committee of Safety to watch for Tory spies. The patriots faithfully followed the spreading rebellion through newspapers, broadsides and pamphlets. Suddenly everyone was electrified by an anonymous forty-seven page, two-shilling pamphlet, *Common Sense* that said out loud in clear, unvarnished language that America should declare its independence, not only to unite the Colonies and encourage European aid, but also to fulfill America's moral obligations to the world. Two years before, Marblehead's Town Meeting had voted that it must make its voice heard by the world; now, Tom Paine was telling the whole country that it could change the destiny of others by its example. It was an awesome, challenging destiny to warm a revolutionary spirit during that fuelless, cold winter in a port that relied on its fisheries and trade for its life.

Seamen signed up to serve under Captain James Mugford, highly respected skipper and former town official who had recently returned from impressment on a British vessel. There Mugford had overheard talk of the great "Powder Ship" scheduled to leave England and now he sought permission to pursue that vessel. In May he was cruising on the sixty-ton, armed *Franklin*, when he came on the three hundred-ton *Hope* headed into Boston. Getting everything he could out of *Franklin's* canvas, Mugford bore down on the British vessel and boarded her while almost within range of British frigates. The prize *Hope* was guided in through a narrow channel known to local mariners and ebb tide grounded her. Captain Mugford sent word ashore and every kind of barge, sloop and rowboat appeared to help unload the British vessel of gun carriages, carbines and powder, plus desperately needed tools: shovels, handsaws, hatchets and spades.

Putting out to sea later, *Franklin* went aground in the same treacherous gut and the British fleet moved in for revenge. The Marblehead crew fired the broadsides, then fought off the boarding parties by every ingenious means. The seasoned mariners cut the lanyards, soaped the nettings and hooked the masts of the small boarding boats and swayed them until they were swamped or the sailors fell into the sea. Captain James Mugford was mortally wounded by a British cannon, yet insisted on staying on deck to urge his men on, gasping: "I am a dead man—don't give up the vessel—you will be able to beat them off." And they did until an ebbing tide forced the British back; and when high tide floated *Franklin*, the damaged vessel with its dead captain limped back to Marblehead where it was met by throngs of sorrowful townspeople.

Meanwhile, Commodore John Manley had gone back to sea in the repaired *Hancock* and was collecting prize vessels off Cape Ann. Manley was then ordered along with other American vessels to lay outside Boston Bay during General Howe's evacuation and to attack only small craft; however, there was only one he could approach outside the convoy. Shortly after, his urgent request for a speedier armed ship was granted with the new *Hancock*, a thirty-two-gun Continental frigate built in Newburyport. In Manley's new vessel he battled and captured several more valuable British ships until he ventured alone off the Halifax coast. There three British frigates with a total armament of ninety-six guns to his thirty-two chased and caught *Hancock*, although Manley had even pumped the bilge to gain speed. Captain Manley was imprisoned until 1778, after which his ill luck pursued him aboard the privateer *Cumberland*, resulting in another imprisonment in the Barbados. Having bribed his way out, he and the crew stole a sloop in which they sailed back to Boston where Manley now lived. A command on the privateer *Jason* was available and Skipper Manley stood out to sea on the 200-ton vessel with 120 in crew whose superstitions about sailing with a two-time loser seemed confirmed when a smashing squall hit them off the Isle of Shoals. "The sails shivered" and a sudden wind shift "hove us on our beam ends, and carried away our three masts and bowsprit." The squall ended as quickly as it had started, but on board trouble had just begun. The superstitious seamen mutinied; Manley fought back and regained control only after slashing three crewmen with his cutlass. To forestall desertions repairs were made at sea; *Jason* then cruised along the coast taking various prize vessels and several times barely escaped from the British blockaders until finally Manley lost the battle to the British *Surprise*. This time John Manley was put on a guard ship and taken to Mill Prison in England where he was held until 1782.

Released in a prisoner exchange Manley rejoined the Continental Navy in which he remained until his death in 1793. In a letter to Manley, Washington's words were: "Your general good behavior since you first engaged in the service, merits mine and your country's thanks."

The evacuation of Boston by General Howe in March raised hopes until the new British strategy became more obvious: to retain the blockade of seaports, but to remove the action from the focal point of resistance, New England, and then split the Colonies in two by attacking from Canada and taking New York while fostering collaboration in the South.

In Philadelphia, the Second Continental Congress was struggling with almost insurmountable problems of money, supplies for the army and navy and serious disagreements among the delegates. Elbridge Gerry, the representative from Marblehead who had wrestled with supplies for the first Provincial Congress, was appointed to the committee to superintend the treasury—only there wasn't a treasury; just a hope to find the ways and means. Gerry's business experience and maritime connections enabled him from the beginning to obtain, if anyone could, old sails and duck for tents, powder, blankets and ordinance. After Boston's evacuation he said, "America has gone such lengths she cannot recede. . . ." The concept of separation was spreading, as Gerry must have informed his friends and townspeople, for at Town Meeting called to commemorate Bunker Hill Marblehead voted, "If the Continental Congress think it for the interest of these United Colonies to declare them independent of Great Britain . . . the inhabitants of this town will support them . . . with their lives and fortunes." This was the kind of backing Elbridge Gerry could expect. That strong, local government that neither the royal governor nor his troops had been able to destroy was to be the cement that solidified the American foundation. It was also the part of Elbridge Gerry's education which would strengthen his convictions about independence, but magnify his distrust of federal power.

The son of Thomas Gerry, a Marblehead merchant and shipowner all his life, Elbridge Gerry had played and worked around the Gerry wharf and warehouse, attended local schools and earned his B.A. and M.A. at Harvard. His Master's thesis questioned whether the Colonies would endure the oppressive British duties, a subject he probably often chewed over with his friend, the impatient, progressive Sam Adams. In the stockpile of experience for independence there were few ingredients that Gerry missed— association with the outspoken, freewheeling mariners, town offices, moderator of Town Meetings when tempers of conservative and liberal were running hot, committees of correspondence and safety, representative to the General Court, representative to the Massachusetts Provincial Congress and then to the Second Continental Congress. He had been quick to join the earliest agitation for a spirit of resistance to clench constitutional rights, and when every approach to Britain met with rebuff and disdain, Gerry moved into the conviction that separation was inevitable.

To help New England fight back with her own men and ships Gerry pressed the Massachusetts and Philadelphia delegates for maritime appropriations and naval retaliation albeit only the diminutive fleet from Marblehead. In May and June of 1776 the magnetism of liberty was drawing more delegates closer to an open declaration, while others resigned or departed for instructions. On July 1 the committee reported a draft for a debate lasting three days after which Thomas Jefferson's "title deed of liberties was confirmed which was in reality a solemn, forcible, impressive recognition of truth that was familiar." An angry, Tory-tinged delegate swore that they then became rebels enough to expect "pendency" (hanging) not independency. There on the famous Declaration of Independence parchment where the words begin: "When in the course of human events . . . ," in the far right row of signatures, under Samuel Adams and John Adams, was written the signature of Elbridge Gerry, the man from Marblehead.

By stagecoach, post rider and packet the bold and stirring words of the Declaration of Independence were sent out to the people of America. The news from Philadelphia and then a verbatim copy of the Declaration reached Marblehead and the place went wild. Muskets were fired until the wise warning of a powder shortage; the town crier must have been hard put to speed good news yet, somehow, the townspeople gathered in a spontaneous meeting to wholeheartedly acclaim their independence. It was later ordered that every word of the Declaration be written down in the town records and then posted and read in all the churches.

The town that had been in love with liberty for almost 150 years exploded in unbridled enthusiasm. Forgetful of their deprivation, swarms of elated Marbleheaders paraded through the zany streets, hesitating only long enough at the homes of lingering Tories to give a message to the king, "to Hell I pitch it." Everyone wanted to ring the church bells; then someone thought of the closed, silent church, the king's church. Racing to St. Michael's, a boisterous group broke in, tore the royal coat of arms from the wall and tolled that Tory bell until it cracked from top to bottom. Any British cruisers at anchor offshore and hearing the clanging bells must have thought the place was afire. It was—afire with the tingling, delicious excitement of freedom. Oblivious of trepidation, Marblehead was afire with the spirit of '76.

The patriotic people of Marblehead would need to return to that glorious day's wellspring of hope and inspiration many times during the hardships of the next five war years. They were totally involved in a people's war being run without a formally constituted government or international recognition, without national taxes or funds, without a trained army or commissary and without a singularly dynamic leader to forge national solidarity. The old royal government had been tossed out even before a new one could be planned; yet, there remained that backbone of colonial strength, a century and more of experience in self-government by Town Meeting. As one nineteenth-century historian wrote: "Its institution of town-meetings was the most perfect system of local self-government that the world had ever known." Marblehead Town Meetings continued uninterrupted by the war with a noticeable difference: the minutes became brief and concise and contained little of the intense discussion or the proponents—a wise procedure in a seaport whose records might soon be captured by the British. The town clung to the continuity of self-government by handling the familiar local issues and facing crisis after crisis of its new "nation." From 1770 the Gerrys, Glovers, Ornes had led Marblehead and its patriots in their resistance to the British; now with Elbridge Gerry in Philadelphia and John Glover with General Washington, Azor Orne and Jonathan Glover were prominent in town affairs.

There was a remarkable correlation in the careers of these two men. Both were wealthy ship owners and merchants. Azor Orne had openly shown his convictions on the Committee on Grievances and had barely escaped capture at Wetherby's Tavern before the Lexington battle. He and Jonathan Glover had been elected to the Committee of Correspondence; then they became embittered casualties of the Marblehead "Smallpox War." Having survived that raucous upheaval, they were persuaded to rejoin the colonial "rebellion" and later became delegates to the Provincial Congress where Orne served on the Committee of Safety and Supplies. Jonathan Glover was also a member of the Inspection Committee of the Association and later Marblehead's member on the Massachusetts Board of War. Both men, though members of the local militia, were not in the Continental Army or Navy because of public responsibilities. Cognizant of the British threats to burn Marblehead as a defiant and rebellious seaport, Orne and Glover rushed to improve the town's security by training the seacoast companies of the militia, raising temporary fortifications on Bartoll's Head and Twisden's Hill, and stationing guards. They knew the sea and coast; they owned larger trading vessels and, no doubt, Gerry and the Provincial Congress often sought their assistance.

In 1776 Jonathan Glover was appointed coagent for Salem, Beverly and Marblehead to handle prize ships sent into these ports, sharing the commission from the sale of the cargoes. By the following year he was owed over $55,000 by the Marine Committee; not long after, Marblehead was greatly in his debt, for as the town treasurer he advanced his personal income to pay town expenses, appropriated, but not funded because of insufficient tax collection. The wives of soldiers and sailors were left without income; bills of credit were doubtful tender without a treasury. Hundreds of fish fences lay bare and unattended; warehouses echoed in their emptiness; small fishing boats rotted at the docks. On the other hand, waterfront activity was not fully suspended, for privateering was paying off in profits and patriotism. Privateers needed to be refitted or repaired which exacted the greatest ingenuity, considering the lack of nails, lumber and metal parts. The local merchants were trying to locate provisions for the townspeople, and supplies desperately needed for the seacoast militia and men enlisting in the Continental Army.

On July 18, 1776, in a Marblehead call to arms issued by Captain John Selman, all males from sixteen to sixty-five years belonging to the training band or alarm lists and living within the limits of his militia were warned to appear Tuesday next at 2:00 p.m. on the town's training field to choose four sergeants and corporals, a clerk, and a drummer and fifer. And, pursuant to the General Court's resolve, one man out of every twenty-five might be enlisted or drafted into the service of the United Colonies to serve until December 1, 1776. Anyone not appearing would forfeit £10 within twenty-four hours. The Marblehead men who could sign for the short enlistment and hopefully (according to John Adams), a short war, were needed to join Col. John Glover's Marblehead regiment now in New York.

After three months in Halifax the British had sailed south to New York, thirty-two thousands strong and confident. Washington, with half as many men and none of the naval mobility of the British fleet, was hoping to defend New York from the south-western tip of Long Island. Stationed at that defensive position was the largest military force America had ever gathered; however, when General Howe's surprise attack on August 29 crumbled their position, the Americans—many inexperienced farmers and undisciplined militiamen—raced behind the fortifications on Brooklyn Heights. An immediate follow-up attack would have finished that fighting force; nonetheless, General Howe entered into a strategic pattern, perhaps ingrained by his formal, eighteenth-century military training. Tactical delay proved an ineffective means to defeat desperate men whose informal training had been outwitting Indians, pirates, customs officials, and the unexpected on the sea or in the wilderness. But General Howe did not press his advantage; he halted for the night. Storms held off the British vessels, and Washington, having relayed deliberately misleading orders, planned a daring night retreat with John Glover, commander of the Fourteenth Continental Regiment that had just reinforced Fort Putnam.

An officer of an exhausted fighting unit recalled that the fort's reaction to the Marblehead regiment's arrival was "these were the lads that might do something." It was something that they did unexpectedly that night of August 29, 1776, that saved the entire besieged American force. With the skill and calm courage of experienced mariners the Marbleheaders raced against the tide change, the stormy winds and the short summer night. Flat-bottomed boats and whatever else could be maneuvered by oar or sail, manned by men from Marblehead and Essex County, evacuated nine thousand Americans in nine hours. During the last few hours a blessed fog providentially draped off the daylight and discovery. Men and material were saved for the future by the bold amphibious withdrawal planned by General Washington, who knew that his only chance for a successful escape was in the hands of Colonel Glover and his seasoned mariners. This impressive accomplishment convinced Washington of the mobility the Marine Regiment could contribute to his army. He hastily set up boat stations on the Manhattan shoreline and requested Colonel Glover to remove the wounded and sick before the main forces withdrew from a possible Manhattan trap. The latter plan never came off because New York connections did not produce the necessary sloops for the operation coded "Marblehead-Orange."

Glover's regiment, now acting as an army unit, were marched toward Harlem, after depositing their gear and tents at the river's edge for someone else to transport by boat. They never saw those supplies again. As they approached Harlem, Glover could see the disarray of the battlefield as the frightened militia, deaf to commands, had panicked under Howe's vicious bombardment and were fleeing. The stocky, smallish colonel stood his ground and coolly absorbed the shock of panic-stricken novice soldiers; reversing their rout, he proceeded to prevent British landing parties from dividing American forces at Kip's Bay.

During another gratuitous delay by General Howe Washington regrouped troops at Harlem Heights until a sudden flanking operation began. On October 14 John Glover's brigade was ordered to Pelham Bay, one of the enemy's possible landing areas. With a few fieldpieces and 750 men Colonel Glover, without a higher command post for guidance, was faced with British artillery and troops that outnumbered his, five to one. Tactically, the shipowner and leather sealer from Marblehead handled the situation like a military school veteran by drawing the enemy units into a skirmish, then retreating. The inrushing British were caught time and again in cross fire from Americans hidden behind the stone walls of Split Rock Road. All day the engagement kept up with heavy casualties inflicted on the British and this delay was sufficient to permit Washington's army to escape encirclement. Col. John Glover had earned his place as a military leader with an innate sense of strategy and indomitable coolness and courage.

Acting as a rear guard for Washington's retreat at White Plains, Glover's brigade—including Marblehead's Fourteenth—harassed and raided the enemy. Dangerous engagements during the New York withdrawals were almost preferable to slogging through the rain-soaked, clay mud of New Jersey to a cold, ill-equipped encampment on the other side of the Delaware River. The disheartening, perilous year of 1776 was drawing to a close, its memories brightened only by the joyful Declaration of July Fourth and the patient persistence of General Washington, ever retreating yet never succumbing to the largest British army that had ever landed on American soil. The Continental Congress, quickly transferred to Baltimore, seemed unresponsive to the desperate conditions of an army whose strength and supplies appeared to exist only on official paper. Many strong, persuasive men who might have strengthened the Congress were serving in the armed forces or others, like Ben Franklin, were abroad seeking out international friends. Privateers —some disguised as patriots—preyed on British supply lines, but could seldom prevent the men-of-war or transports from adequately reinforcing the British or Hessian mercenaries. In some sectors as much as a third of the colonial population, seeing the outnumbered, ill-prepared patriots' army, were siding with and supplying food to the probable winner. Washington and Glover realized that the current enlistment period ended with the year of 1776. Winter recruiting possibilities were gloomy, for the hotbed of the Revolution, New England, felt far removed from the action, and long-delayed news and letters were no substitute for involvement. A discouraged Washington had written his brother that it seemed "the game was pretty nearly up"; yet, it was not like the man to give up. His agonizing desperation demanded a daring gamble.

Exhibiting serenity and confidence, Washington outlined to his experienced and loyal staff at the Delaware River camp his plan for three-pronged attack on Trenton scheduled for early morning on December 26, 1776, when the Hessian troops would be recovering from their traditional Christmas festivities. Three simultaneous river crossings would assure encirclement and the capture of prisoners and equipment, while General Putnam's Philadelphia troops would begin a march toward New Jersey to divert the enemy. Every detail was calculated for a precise dawn attack: complete silence in the march, no one to break ranks, white paper markings on officers' caps, three days' cooked rations, new flints, ropes and spikes for taking cannon, exact positions for field artillery and the protective guard around disembarking troops. General Washington and Col. Henry Knox would cross at McKonkey's Ferry where Col. Glover's rugged Marblehead regiment was assigned the responsibility for transporting twenty-four hundred men, plus the horses and artillery. The Fourteenth had never flinched before danger; Washington put his full trust and his own safety in the hands of his friend John Glover and his seafaring men. As a young officer reported, "Colonel Glover's fishermen are to manage the boats just as they did in the retreat from Long Island." It would require three coordinated river crossings and swift regrouping on the New Jersey side to assure the success of the surprise offensive.

It would have been surprising, regardless of the holiday merriment, if Hessian Commander Rall had believed reports of such a wild, adventurous scheme—to be carried out by poorly equipped men using borrowed boats to cross a dangerous, icy river in the dark. It couldn't be expected that he would have understood their longing for liberty to which a single victory might lend reality. It's told that Tom Paine's words from *The Crisis*, which had just been published in Philadelphia, were spoken to those men shivering with cold, rags tied into makeshift shoes and fingers numbly grasping snow-covered muskets. Who better would understand "These are the times that try men's souls . . ." and that "tyranny, like Hell, is not easily conquered"? There were tears in the eyes of the determined soldiers silently moving toward the river bank in hopes that Paine was right that "the harder the conflict, the more glorious the triumph."

It now appeared that only the weather might triumph, for by 6:00 p.m. a soldier's diary recorded, "It is fearfully cold and raw and a snowstorm is setting in. The wind is northeast and beats in the faces of the men. It will be a terrific night. . . ." The swift current of the Delaware was carrying jagged ice floes that struck sharply against the Durham boats which were ruggedly built thirty- to forty-foot canoe-type craft used for hauling river cargo and requiring a crew of four or five on the steering oars placed at both ends. The high wind must have reminded the Marbleheaders of other northeast gales at home that had demanded all their skill and strength to stay afloat; yet, here were the added problems of large ice floes and freezing snow on the oars and in their eyes. Then Washington learned that the other two crossings had been postponed or abandoned, and young John Glover, Jr. brought the word that Sullivan's men couldn't shoot their wet muskets. Firmly, Washington answered, "Tell General Sullivan to use the bayonets. I am resolved to take Trenton." Washington gave the orders; Colonel Knox of Boston bellowed boarding directions to the men; the Marine Regiment shoved off—again and again fending off ice and collisions until it was time for General Washington to cross. Captain William Blackler's boat, manned also by another Marbleheader, John Roads

Russell, was boarded by Washington, Knox and the other officers, and, to relieve the tension Washington is said to have shouted at the three hundred-pound colonel, "Shift your backsides, Knox, or we'll all be upset." Which would have suited Colonel Glover far better than the anachronistic, though inspiring, visualization implanted in American minds by "Washington Crossing the Delaware" by the German painter, Emmanuel Leutze. In that painting the flag shown had not yet been designed; the uniforms are inaccurate, as is the boat design; the river width and its shore are foreign; the manning of the boat unbelievable; and if Colonel Glover had seen one of his men with his leg over the side and his commander in chief standing with his foot on the gunwhales, enough hell would have broken loose to have caused a court-martial. So much for pictorial fantasy.

Colonel Glover managed the dangerous operation without losing one of the twenty-four hundred men. And, while General Washington waited silently and with desperate earnestness on the New Jersey bank, all the horses, artillery and supplies were delivered safely. No one knows how many trips the Marbleheaders made across the river; nevertheless, almost exhausted they regrouped and marched to their assigned position at the Assunpink Creek bridge where they hoped (although late) to cut off the Hessian retreat. Joshua Orne and others collapsed in the snow and would have frozen but for companions who pushed them on. The surprise was complete; the enemy ran in great confusion; their commander Rall was mortally wounded. The gamble was won; Trenton was taken. Having captured almost one thousand prisoners, Washington ordered Colonel Glover to transport all the men back across the Delaware for safety. The river was still ice laden; the storm had not let up and the rough trips were no less demanding, except for the high spirits of the tired men and a fresh confidence in that ultimate triumph. One officer praised the discipline, aptitude and confidence of the Fourteenth Regiment; and Colonel Knox's gleaming memories were articulated: "There went the fishermen of Marblehead, alike at home upon land or water, alike ardent, patriotic and unflinching. . . ."

Knox did not speak of his and Washington's disappointment when Colonel Glover and many of the Marblehead regiment left several days later when their military enlistments terminated. Most men had had no clothing issued; they had not been paid; family letters from home bemoaned the deteriorating conditions in Marblehead and dwelled on the lures of privateering. Personally, John Glover after a year and a half of action was physically exhausted and extremely worried about his sick wife, their many children and his financial reverses. The departing Marbleheaders, longing for the smell of the sea and a brisk wind to carry them home, tried to coax the top brass into permitting them to sail back to New England in the Continental frigates stymied in Delaware Bay. Request refused for fear of capture; most men were fated to a long, cold march home or, hopefully, a horse or wagon. Nevertheless, the arduous trip home was eased by the thought of the town's excitement when the tales of "the Fourteenth" at Long Island and the Delaware were told again and again with every chilling detail. The fishermen from Marblehead had sure shown those landlubbers from New York and Pennsylvania how to handle a boat—even in a damn flat-bottomed river boat surrounded by ice cakes!

When John Glover, who had marched away to service as a prosperous shipowner, saw his depressed town, he must have realized that this British blockade was working and those at home were suffering more than anyone could remember. Relief came from public funds and donations from wealthier families; yet, people in and out of the workhouse were reported on the verge of starvation and the poor had again been urged "to Digg Stumps and Turf out of the Swamps for fuel."

Despite all the local problems, townspeople and the more affluent ship owners had contributed to the "Canaday" expedition, to enlistment bounties and to repairs for the fort. Then, a petition was sent off to the General Court, telling it in no uncertain terms that the town wanted cannon and ammunition, so "we may under Heaven be able to make such Defence as will do us Honor, if not frustrate the attempts of those Brutall Dogs of War."

The townsmen could probably not repeat the performance of one earlier December day when the "Dogs of War" had been foiled by clever chicanery. On that occasion, at the sighting of the British vessels, *Lively*, *Hinchinbrook* and *Nautilus* cruising outside the harbor, Marblehead went into action, for British Admiral Graves was probably about to burn Marblehead, just as he had Falmouth. It was the only time in history that Marblehead women and children were evacuated while men worked feverishly at the fort. With typical bravado the fort's cannons were turned toward the enemy vessels and gave every impression of Marblehead's preparedness to lob shot into any British vessel crossing the harbor entrance. Or the shot might just reach the first vessel to go aground off Cat Island. After hours of naval picketing, while the British captains observed the frantic preparation and threatening cannons, the three vessels headed out to sea. The tension broken, cheers and laughter erupted, for the cussed "lobsterbacks" would never know there was no powder to fire the cannon!

Which reminded everyone of the time that the old "Son of Liberty" and Tuesday Evening Club member, Dr. Elisha Story, stole the cannon from the Boston Common. One of the most highly regarded young men in the community, Elisha was an enthusiastic "Son of Liberty" and plotted with several others to capture some British fieldpieces. Having distracted the guards, Dr. Story's band took the cannon right from the Common to a hiding place on Boston Neck. Suspicion and arrest followed quickly, yet Elisha Story talked his way out of treason by swapping information on the cannon for his liberty. Some of the earliest secret patriots' meetings were held at his home where the men who attended the Boston Tea Party planned their disguise. Dr. Story made an odd-looking "brave," but the raid was only the beginning of his devotion to the cause of liberty.

Incredible was the only word for another Marblehead patriot, Samuel Tucker. No sooner had Tucker shoved off in *Franklin* than his youthful experience on a British man-of-war enabled him to recognize and outmaneuver British merchant ships. After *Franklin* had been turned over to Captain Mugford, Captain Tucker was transferred to Manley's old *Hancock* on which he increased his prize record, taking two brigs off Boston Light and assisting in the capture of the British transports, *George* and *Annabel*, carrying units of a Scottish Highland regiment. That battle lasted several hours until the British surrendered with severe loss in men and equipment and *Annabel* ran aground on Allerton Point. Captain Samuel Tucker seized vessel after vessel carrying valuable stores, such as, one brig laden with £25,000 sterling, articles of clothing ranging from thirty thousand shirts to seventeen thousand suits, soap and wine, candles and barley. It was claimed that in all Captain Tucker took thirty to forty prize ships in 1776. When Washington's early navy was being phased out, Samuel Tucker was commissioned commodore in the new Continental Navy and given command of the frigate *Boston*.

Less fortunate was John Lee, captain of the commissioned privateer *Nancy*. Commanding this small vessel carrying only six guns, Lee's skill and ingenuity were responsible for thirteen prizes, most of which were taken off the European coast and sent into Marblehead's favorite foreign port, Bilbao, Spain. His crew told of Captain Lee's cleverness in a night encounter with a much larger British vessel that was deceived into surrender, for Captain Lee had strung out lanterns from the bowsprit to stern and in the darkness the tiny

Nancy became an overpowering enemy. John Lee's boldness carried him dangerously close to the English Channel where he was suddenly pursued by the British admiral's flagship. Lee's guns, ordinance, and equipment went overboard to lighten up; but the English were coming down upon him, so Captain Lee beached *Nancy* in hope of escape. Instead, he and the crew were soon prisoners at Forton Prison in England.

This bad news about his older brother, John, greeted Col. William R. Lee when he arrived home. He had just been promoted in rank after having served as a senior captain in the "Fourteenth," from the Long Island evacuation until the battle of Trenton. Now, as Colonel Lee, he was back to recruit officers and men for a new regiment. General Washington had chosen well, for Lee represented the wealthy Lee family who, beginning with Jeremiah Lee, had stayed with the cause of freedom. William R. Lee had started in his uncle Jeremiah's counting room, advanced into management of much of the Lee shipping, married Mary Lemmon from Marblehead, and now lived in his grandfather's mansion at 185 Washington Street. It was Lee's recruiting efforts and Glover's conscientious concern for his good friend Washington that brought pressure to bear on Marblehead for more army enlistments. At the first meeting (Town Meeting of 1777) the people were asked to accept increased assessments on their estates to raise additional bounty for enlistments. This would help the soldiers' families, as would the price controls that were put into effect on items such as, clothing and wood, and later on services, like horseshoeing.

The sea was where a man should be, as any Marbleheader knew; nonetheless, patriotism overcame their reluctance to slosh through the spring mud of upper New York State where the military campaign was now being waged by the British under Gen. John Burgoyne. The acme of the 1777 "recruiting" was accomplished by the commander in chief, General Washington, who gently and firmly persuaded John Glover to forsake army retirement and accept Congress' commission as brigadier general. "I may tell you without flattery," wrote Washington to Glover, "that I know of no man better qualified than you to conduct a Brigade. You have activity and industry . . . you know how to exact that duty from others." So once more John Glover left his family and joined the brigade at Peekskill.

Typical were the assignments given to General Glover: to hold a perilous lookout position near an enemy fort; to plan a river-boat supply line, to sail his whole brigade up the river and then to harass General Burgoyne. Burgoyne later testified to General Glover's effectiveness by reporting that "not a night passed without firing, and sometimes concerted attacks upon our advanced pickets." However, Glover's men from old Massebequash had little understanding of Indians, so undoubtedly the woodland trickery of Britain's Indian allies added a terrifying, new element to the fighting.

Glover's brigade then fell back to Van Schaick's Island where the food was abominable, the Yankees and Yorkers baited each other into fights, and all the men were poorly clothed and equipped. In his depression John Glover wrote to Jonathan Glover and Azor Orne reviewing the military situation, and, in his discomfort, he chided them bitterly, "I should have been happy to have seen more of my friends . . . particularly Messrs. Glover, Orne and Gerry . . . but (their) being engaged in Public Service has prevented." While the rain leaked through his hemp hut, musing over the Tuesday nights with a warming fire, pipes, tobacco, wine and good punch, Glover concluded—as any weary field soldier might—"They possibly can do more good at home, I'm sure they will not be so much exposed and will live better." But, by contrast, he was optimistic about beating Burgoyne, and he had only a month to wait for the net to close around the unsupplied and unreinforced British.

After many skirmishes and two battles in which there were costly casualties on both sides the British Army surrendered to the Americans at Saratoga. Gates, accepting Burgoyne's word that his men would never again fight in America, ordered General Glover to march General Burgoyne, his German counterpart Baron von Riedesel and the captive army of over five thousand to Cambridge, Massachusetts. Glover's joy in victory was drained by the news that his eldest son, who after several land campaigns had turned to privateering, had been lost at sea. Alone and weary, Glover tried to absorb his tragic loss. His innermost reactions and distraction may account for his strangely undisciplined behavior on the march to Cambridge.

Burgoyne had an appropriate nickname, "Gentleman Johnny," and, as a well-bred English gentleman, connoisseur, and excellent conversationalist, he absolutely charmed the lonely John Glover. In the ambivalence felt in some of New York State about the "rebellion" the opposing American and British generals were all entertained for a week in Albany. Subsequently, the march was too leisurely; both armies were unruly and scoured the countryside for food and wood. Finally, growing dissatisfaction and complaints by Baron von Riedesel tightened up discipline as the march neared Worcester. By this time General Glover was convinced that Burgoyne should visit the seaport towns and together they would go to England to convince the Crown of the war's futility. Neither proposal was approved at headquarters. When General Glover and General Burgoyne rode into Cambridge together, the people hailed the British defeat and the parade of prisoners with cannon fire and church bells. The receiving officer was Col. William R. Lee of Marblehead.

The Saratoga victory meant self-confidence and renewed consideration abroad. Foreign ports were opened for safe anchorage and quick sale of prize cargoes. Marblehead captains looked forward to that boon, for 1777 hadn't brought much to the town except privateering shares and trouble. Smallpox was abroad again. This time immediate measures of inoculation, destruction of stray dogs, moving the infected to the Neck, a "pox house" in the Middle Division seemed to stifle the epidemic. That year soldiers' needy families were granted "necessities of life" up to half of the man's wages (as if his pay really would materialize or would be worth a "Continental" when it did!) Captains Manley and John Lee were in prison while Commodore Tucker combed the seas for British transports. Discouraging reports from Elbridge Gerry caused some concern and skepticism, although Marblehead had every reason to have faith in its national representative.

From the age of twenty-seven, when he became a school trustee, Elbridge Gerry served Marblehead, Massachusetts, and the nation with an ardent zeal and meticulous diligence seldom witnessed. Young Elbridge had not gone to sea as had the other Gerrys; instead he applied his education and training to the success of the Gerry business—the trading, the warehousing and distribution of the goods unloaded at Marblehead. It was this same business efficiency and perspicacity that Gerry futilely tried to apply to the disparate interests and delegations of the Second Continental Congress. No one could have worked harder on the details and correspondence preceding the Articles of Confederation. In the fall of 1777 Gerry was an effective "whip" to assure sufficient votes for passage of this "firm league of friendship" that limited Congress to war and naval operations, coining money, postal organization and other activities that would not reduce the predominant role of the states in trade, taxation and tariffs. In the congressional debate were germs of the problems to be faced by the later Constitutional Convention; nevertheless, the Articles of Confederation contained the mortar for the future in the common citizenship for all Americans and the idealistic concept of perpetual union. Elbridge Gerry's hometown supported the articles by enthusiastically voting ratification at Marblehead's Town Meeting on January 20, 1778.

That third year of the Revolutionary War found Marblehead

conditions worsening; most of its men were still deeply involved in the war. At Cambridge Col. William R. Lee struggled to keep order between the Americans and Burgoyne's defeated army; Gen. John Glover attempted to straighten out the maze of expenses incurred on the Saratoga to Cambridge march which were to be charged to the British. Fraternizing was common among the British and American officers and it was rumored that General Burgoyne was entertained at the William Lee's in Marblehead. In any case, Lee's hospitality had tangible results. His imprisoned brother, Captain John Lee, was secretly contacted in Forton Prison and allowed to escape after being given seventy-five guineas by an unknown friend— somebody who just might have been a friend of "Gentleman Johnny" Burgoyne's.

William Lee had refused the post of adjutant general as being unsuitable for him, or, perhaps, because the Lee shipping business was without a helmsman and headed for bankruptcy. He resigned his commission a few months later; however, his resignation did not take effect until after the Rhode Island campaign to which he and John Glover were both assigned. Glover's local responsibilities, which had kept him from joining Washington's winter encampment at Valley Forge, undoubtedly led up to his decision to resign. Again, it was refused by the commander in chief, who wrote: "I have too high an opinion of your value, as an Officer, . . . My earnest wish is that you continue in it." General Glover did continue, this time at West Point where he and the Polish engineer, Kosciuszko, constructed an important defense post until Glover was ordered to join Marquis de Lafayette in Rhode Island.

Earlier that year, France had signed the Treaty of Alliance with the embattled and emerging nation across the sea and now planned to augment America's land and sea forces. John Adams was sent as a diplomatic emissary to Paris aboard the frigate *Boston* commanded by Commodore Samuel Tucker of Marblehead. The Navy Board, evaluating the importance of the mission and its vital papers, sternly admonished Tucker: ". . . on all occasions have regard to the importance of his security and safe arrival." Those words must have haunted the commodore on that nearly ill-fated voyage; first, when barely outsailing three British pursuit vessels, then riding out a three day northeaster that split a foresail and carried away the main topmast and, finally, encountering Britain's *Martha* armed with fourteen guns. As *Boston* maneuvered to deliver a broadside, Commodore Tucker espied his official passenger, Mr. Adams, armed with a musket and standing on deck ready to do battle. Tucker's first suggestion to go below quickly turned into a loud, clear order with

"I am commanded by the Continental Congress to deliver you safe in France. . . ." John Adams, admirer and friend of many Marblehead patriots, must have understood as pure Marblehead any added expletives. He obeyed. *Martha* surrendered and while a prize crew returned its rich cargo to Boston, Commodore Tucker safely delivered John Adams to Bordeaux.

Marblehead's distinguished skipper pursued his own anti-British campaign off the French coast during the negotiations for French vessels, troops and military advisors. Commodore Tucker bagged several more rich prizes, once while using a temporary French crew. He then teamed up with other American vessels to capture at least fifteen valuable prize ships. Some months later, in a rendezvous at Nantes, Tucker met *Providence* and then at Brest, joined *Ranger*, recent command of John Paul Jones. The American frigates and sloop of war acted as a miniature naval attack fleet, and, all confidence, they sailed for home. During the Atlantic crossing their coordinated efforts cleverly defeated several large British merchant ships which were sent into Portsmouth, New Hampshire.

During that summer of 1778 France, having allied itself with America, declared war on Great Britain, forcing her to concentrate military forces on the Continent. When French assistance materialized into eleven vessels and four thousand marines under Count D'Estaing, it appeared that, at last, America could seize the initiative. Washington and D'Estaing coordinated a French naval attack on Britain's Newport base with a land offensive by General Sullivan. General Glover's assignment to Rhode Island filled an obvious need; the large amphibious operation to land troops on the island base would demand hundreds of skilled seamen and expert supervision. Glover and others were asked to recruit two hundred to three hundred men from Marblehead, Salem and Boston. A promise of three dollars per day for a limited fifteen-day enlistment produced the required number of boatsmen, and on a foggy August 9 they ferried Sullivan's troops to Newport. Then everything went awry. Sullivan made his move prematurely; D'Estaing was forced to halt disembarkation to escape a trap by the approaching British fleet. Shortly after, the two fleets were hit by a gale and heavy seas that wrought such damage that both withdrew for repairs. During that two-day storm General Glover's brigade, responsible for the left wing of the attack, was immobile; then it pressed forward against the British, momentarily expecting the return of the French fleet.

When the news of the French reversal became known, General Glover and other officers signed a bitter protest addressed to Count D'Estaing, fearing "ruinous consequences." The short enlistment period was ending, but most Marblehead and Salem boatsmen were persuaded to remain long enough to carry out the evacuation under the man they trusted, General Glover. The Americans had to fight their way out. Glover's brigade held together under heavy fire and repulsed the enemy advance long enough for the volunteers to successfully ferry out one more retreating American force. Col. William Lee commanded the Salem volunteers in this, his last military action before retirement and it was also the last major campaign of General Glover's career. His next effort to resign after the death of his wife, Hannah, was met with only a brief congressional furlough to arrange for his motherless family. The disappointing conclusion of the first chapter of French-American cooperation plunged the wobbly "union" into deeper discouragement.

America's rebellion against Britain was foundering. Congress, bickering and splintering each proposal by sectionalism, lacked strong leadership, steady direction and financial stability. The requisitioning by states of enlistments and money (to which Elbridge Gerry had been assigned) was proving unworkable and antagonizing. The soldiers were unpaid and mutiny was in the air. Exhaustion and uncertainty seeped into the most patriotic towns. Marblehead had trouble finding men to run for selectmen; the constable took the responsibility for calling Town Meeting; one school would barely survive—providing hard money could be found for the teacher's salary. The April meeting voted to take the Gun House for the use of the town and then the privilege of disposing of it to aid the town treasury. A public fast and church services sought Divine help and guidance.

Somehow, in June of 1779, Marblehead provided its share of men and ships for the ambitious Massachusetts expedition against Penobscot, Maine, where a British force had entrenched itself to close off that American coastal base and to harass nearby seaports. A crushing defeat desolated the Massachusetts expedition; the men were bottled up in the Penobscot River and forced to burn sixteen American vessels to prevent their capture by the British victors. Even under these depressing conditions Massachusetts continued its efforts to reorganize its colonial government into a formal state. Azor and Joshua Orne, Thomas Gerry and Jonathan Glover were asked to be the Marblehead delegates to the Massachusetts Constitutional Convention which, hopefully, would return a strong, acceptable constitution unlike the legislature's earlier proposal that had been rejected by the town.

New Year's Day of 1780 dawned with little joy and even less hope. On that morning General Glover's Second Massachusetts brigade, which had been moved from its defensive position in Providence to the vicinity of the Hudson Highlands, mutinied. Glover had said that he would not be answerable for the consequences of a situation where eight hundred men must endure "the sweets of the winter campaign" without shoes or stockings and often without bread. Soldiers began to leave, but en route they were finally persuaded to return. Their ailing commander, John Glover, was given sick leave late in January.

At home in Marblehead the winter couldn't have been worse. Edward Bowen's journal vividly reported that the harbor was frozen eight inches thick as far out as the fort and that the people were crossing the ice by cart and oxen to forage on the Neck, for two thirds of them were without meat or wood. Bowen wrote of the confusion over the Massachusetts monthly scale of dollar depreciation, and gloomily related that four small sleds of wood had cost him "what men call dollars—260 of them. So much for Liberty." Indian meal sold for seventy dollars per bushel and rum for eighty dollars a gallon. The Continental coins were said to consist of twelve parts tin and one part lead; the state's paper money, such as the eight-dollar bill, promised payment of eight Spanish milled dollars by 1786 plus a 5 percent per annum interest. There was no end in sight; the army was still on the defensive, privateering was not closing the supply line, British sympathizers came out of the walls. Commodore Tucker and Marblehead seamen who could be persuaded to forsake privateering for the Continental Navy were at Charleston, South Carolina, vainly trying to contain the British expedition attempting to cut off the southern states. A seige by the British fleet ended in the capture of Charleston and Commodore Samuel Tucker's surrender and imprisonment.

These dark days of 1780 suddenly became an actual reality on May 19 when a strange, unexplained darkness covered New England and a weird, yellow-gray cloud darkened the light from 10:00 a.m. to 4:00 p.m. "Black Friday," as it was called, inspired a twenty-two stanza broadside that moaned:

What great event, next will be sent
    Upon this weary land
He only knows, who can dispose
    All things at his command.

Three days later Marblehead was holding Town Meeting. Its delegates presented the new state constitution with a bill of rights and Marblehead voted for adoption. Massachusetts and Marblehead hoped to hold together no matter what happened in Philadelphia.

America's tide of independence was at its ebb. Everywhere morale was low and recruits were few; the South seemed lost except for the guerrilla bands keeping liberty alive. The French fleet had departed again, unharmed and ineffective; Benedict Arnold had betrayed his country; Congress couldn't enforce the states' "specific supplies" plan and, when some stores were obtained, distribution collapsed. In disgust, Elbridge Gerry, who had been defeated in a parliamentary maneuver to force the states into the open with a firm allotment and conforming prices, resigned from the Second Continental Congress and returned to Marblehead for the first time in four and one-half years. He may have hoped to elude the anxiety and frustration inherent in the national paralysis, so well illustrated in Congress itself. Gerry had, from the beginning, deeply involved himself in the grass roots rebellion, yet, he was plagued by the unconquerable fear of a new tyranny filling the gap left by the expulsion of the Crown.

Elbridge Gerry was a native Marbleheader, and, yet, he was not a typical Marbleheader. He had not liked the sea although he lived among mariners; he had not joined the military service although his father had been captain of the fort; he had been nourished by the courage and historical continuity of his town, yet he spent only a few years there between 1776 and his death in 1814. He and Marblehead did have in common an overwhelming desire for independence and freedom, without tyranny from outside their country— or from within. Yet, the complexity of this man, the inflexibility of his positions, the belated reversals, the lack of humor or common touch made Elbridge Gerry, though respected, not a well-loved figure.

Socially, Gerry was especially appreciated by the ladies. The agreeable, dignified bachelor endowed with good manners and a Harvard education was a favorite guest at the more luxurious social events in Philadelphia that belied conditions of nearby Valley Forge. The well-to-do Mr. Gerry had a private servant and team of horses and arrived in the manner of a fashionable gentleman whose grooming and dress spoke of expensive materials and good tailoring. He had given up using a wig and wore his hair in the current style —powdered, combed back and tied in a queue. With ruffled shirt and gold cuff buttons, well-tailored coat and silk vest and black silk pants with silver knee buckles Gerry cut a fine, though not robust figure. It is not surprising that Gilbert Stuart would paint Gerry as a lean, rather handsome figure of a man. The ladies found him attentive and gracious and, in New York, Ann Thompson, daughter of an affluent New York merchant, agreed to marry Elbridge Gerry, then forty-two. They stayed briefly in Marblehead and then moved to Cambridge. Gerry's social acceptance was never duplicated in political circles. There even his closest associates and friends found him puzzling, if not infuriating; nevertheless, few ever questioned his ardent patriotism. They questioned just his misdirected zeal.

Gerry felt that Benjamin Franklin was "too French" and that Washington was an admirable commander deserving of Congress' energetic support; however with frequent, suspicious glances at the extent of his "kingly" power or the influence of the military. Jefferson, John and Samuel Adams were Gerry's friends; nonetheless, his recalcitrance irritated them beyond all patience. Washington angrily claimed "vanity and duplicity," Jefferson gloomily reported "Gerry changed sides," and John Adams' wise summation was that Gerry had an "obstinacy that will risk great things to secure little ones." Then as now, Elbridge Gerry was a controversial man, except, perhaps, in his own town.

Shortly after Gerry's return on September 4, 1780, Marblehead held its first official state election and cast its votes for John Hancock for governor. The lethargic, reluctant revolutionary was still remembered by members of the Committee of Correspondence, so Gerry refused Hancock's patronage appointment to the justice of peace office, nor would he run for state senator. Persuaded to serve in the House, where he felt closer to the people, Gerry represented Marblehead in 1780, refused in 1781, accepted in 1782. He was further honored by election to the new American Academy of Arts and Sciences and reappointment to the Massachusetts congressional delegation which he did not rejoin until considerably later. Gerry obstinately awaited justification of his stand on parliamentary procedures, tended to his personal business and worked on local town committees.

Gerry and Samuel Sewall pressured the legislature and wealthier taxpayers to provide food—especially beef—for servicemen. After the public reading of General Glover's letter from his New York state encampment describing his ill-clothed men and desertions, Marblehead's great heart showed through in its vote to sell its Bubier Plains land to John Sparhawk for £223 and to hire a rider to take the money to Glover for enlistment bounty. General Glover was met on the way and he urged use of the money at home, as recruits were impossible to find in rural New York. Yet, at home a state committee, having completed a survey of Marblehead, reported: men numbered 831; other persons not in business, 477; missing, 121; imprisoned, 166. Family statistics were: 1,069 women, 387 widows, 2,242 children of whom 672 were fatherless. The survey resulted in a state tax abatement and reduction in the enlistment quota. In spite of that no one would accept the job of tax collector.

There wasn't an auspice that hinted that 1781 would be a providential year. Marblehead skippers and crews were unrelentlessly attacking British vessels off the European coast, in the West Indies, near Halifax or anywhere along the Atlantic coastline where an American vessel could dodge the British Navy. Pages could be filled with the adventures of Captain Richard Cowell, Captain Robert Wormstead, and Captains Bray, Dennis, Collyer, and Dixey. Their crewmen, many of them descendants from the early settlers' families like Goodwin, Girdler, Doliber, Graves, Bartlett, Bowden, Merritt, Hooper, Harris, Martin and Bessom clung to the thread of continuity woven through nearly two centuries of fighting and dying on the sea for freedom.

All the while General Washington remained steadfast, firm and enduring; seldom the victor, he was never vanquished. His official support improved in a burst of energy and reorganization within Congress, spurred on by new delegates and appointees. Imaginative and resourceful American military leadership took advantage of British delays and blunders, then suddenly found itself in a position to take the initiative. In a coordinated American-French offensive imbued with every element of success—leadership, strategy, timing, experienced troops, enemy miscalculation and a providential share of good luck—General Cornwallis and his British force were besieged at Yorktown. There on October 19, 1781, Cornwallis surrendered. His men laid down their arms as the British band played the same old tune that in 1775 had filled the air when Colonel Leslie's embarrassed regiment marched between the Marblehead militia: "The World Turned Upside Down."

Word of the tremendous Yorktown victory caused great excitement; yet Marblehead's joy must have been tempered with a deep skepticism of British negotiations and a tremendous sense of loss. The proud, prosperous town of ten years before was in financial ruin and physical deterioration was evident on every wharf and way. Scores of Marblehead men were dead, wounded, missing or imprisoned in England, Halifax and the West Indies. Any word of young sons, sons, husbands and brothers would be slow to reach the families during the next two years of negotiations during which sizable land forces continued to hold their positions and privateers took no chances in that limbo. In fact, two of the last maritime engagements involved Marbleheaders. In 1782 a captured American crew managed to free themselves from a British ship's prison and gleefully take over His Majesty's brig *Lively* and sail her to Havana

where Marblehead's John Prince disposed of the ship and cargo for
$20,331. The other incident was a defiant, skillful escape of *Hague*,
(commanded by Commodore Manley) under a bombardment by
four British vessels while aground near Guadaloupe. Manley is said
to have freed *Hague*, hoisted the Continental flag with a thirteen-
gun salute and sailed safely to New England.

New England and its fisheries were a vital issue in the peace negotiations, as Elbridge Gerry had anticipated in a 1779 peace approach. His proposal for the security of the fisheries read, ". . . that
inhabitants . . . should continue to enjoy the free and undisturbed
exercise of their common right to fish . . ." on the banks off Newfoundland. Marblehead on Gerry's advice now circularized the seaports with a letter on the importance of the treaty's fisheries clause
and urged pressure on the legislature and Congress. New Englander
John Adams took care of that issue and wrote Gerry frequently
during the 1782–83 negotiations, finally victoriously announcing,
"Thanks be to God, my dear Gerry, that our Tom Cod are safe."

Elbridge Gerry resumed his congressional seat shortly before the
delivery of the peace treaty; then, along with the few other men
present who had signed the Declaration of Independence, Gerry
presented the treaty to an approving Congress. The day of Peace
Celebration dawned on Marblehead to the bells clanging and a cannonade from the fort; then every waking moment overflowed with
glorious festivities. Prominent citizens indulged in emotional toasts
to freedom, punctuated by a thirteen-gun salute and an oxen dinner
and rum punch from a bowl that never ran dry were free to all at
the Town House. The town's illumination by night was topped by
making a great bonfire of the wooden watchtower. For one brief,
expansive moment the depleted present was forgotten in bright vi-
sion of America's future.

The fragile union was marred with cracks from sectionalism,
shocking financial difficulties, unappreciative compensation to its
military men, taxation, and fear of the enemy outside and within.
Trust of the British would be long in coming; meanwhile, the seacoast didn't drop its guard. The 1783 *Fleet's Packet Almanac* explained the network of signals on the coastline for the enemy alarm.
During the day a series of flags would be hoisted on the headlands
from Cape Ann to Boston; at night, cannon fire, rockets or a beacon
fire would signal towns of the discovery of a fleet of topsail vessels;
expresses were to be sent to Boston. Such a fleet just might appear
to incite a civil war between the underground Tories and the exhausted Revolutionists; the civil strife had never ceased to be a fac-

tor throughout the War for Independence. Marblehead resisted the return of its refugees, whose support and money might have shortened the war or saved their men. Elbridge Gerry helped to draw up resolves to prevent refugees from disembarking without the sanction of the Inspection Committee.

It wasn't long before some British Loyalists trickled back and town emotions ran high. Memories flooded in when the Robies began returning. Mrs. Robie came first and was safely conducted by a relative, the Reverend Isaac Story, to her home where others were now living. Mary Robie, daughter of Marblehead's minister, Simon Bradstreet, writing to her husband still in Halifax that the few callers had been kind and in her isolation and fear, said: "I cannot express how strange everything appears to me, but seeing Marblehead, I assure you has by no means tended to lessen Halifax in my estimation, yet I think I could be contented to live here if the family were settled here as formerly. . . ." That was no longer possible, for William Lee had to smuggle Mr. Robie into town to assure his safety. Finding his house and personal property confiscated and that money put into the empty town treasury, Robie sued the town through his legal counsel and relative, Samuel Sewall. Isaac Mansfield was appointed the town's agent; a small settlement was made and certain individuals were charged with special assessments. Tensions were relieved when the Robies moved to Salem. Other Tories drifted back and some sued; these suits were defended by Sewall and Mansfield acting for Marblehead. Some, like Joseph Hooper, never returned and processed their claims through the British government which awarded Hooper £4200 on his claim of over £10,000 for his Marblehead houses, ropewalk, stables, land and Negroes. The town's settlements with the Tories were only a small part of widespread financial upheaval.

The whole recovery period for Marblehead was "operation bootstrap"—where would the money for school teachers, the new fire engine "Endeavor," soldiers' relief and repayment of town loans come from? There was a long discussion about selling the wharf and stores on the town landing, and an account for bounties of £1649 advanced by Marblehead was submitted to the State Legislature for reimbursement. The town debt of £2700 would be repaid in installments to townspeople who had been generous enough to lend money to Marblehead throughout the war—Azor Orne, Jonathan Glover, Samuel Sewall, Robert Hooper (not "King"), Captain Israel Foster and Archibald Selman. The workers who had rebuilt the fort in 1776 had never been paid so, rather than have the fort's timbers and equipment carried off, Marblehead voted to

take up the public platforms and "sell the stuff for most they can."
It would take years for a town whose prewar shipping tonnage
of 12,313 had sagged to 1,509 tons to recover its tax base; never
would most of the foreign trade return, but since 1629 there had
always been *fish!*

The early signs of normalcy appeared in that enduring gauge of
the town—Town Meeting. Elections had a full slate, and hogreeves, fence viewers, fish cullers, cordwood dealers, fire wards,
and market clerks were back in business. Suffrage was still limited to
the minimum colonial stipulation of income or property but then
the minutes began to read "male inhabitants of 21 and upwards."
Officials were obliged to take an oath of allegiance abjuring former
allegiance to the king and supporting the "free and independent
State." The churches decided the time had come to collect for pew
rents; in the postwar period the important, respected committees
were no longer composed of mostly wealthy merchants and masters,
but now included mariners, tinplaters, shoremen, cordwainers or a
tailor. The war had shaken up the social structure that the mid-
1700's foreign trade affluence had created; in demanding the best of
all men the Revolution had "set them on thinking, speaking and acting in a line far beyond that to which they were accustomed." War
heroes like John Glover and William Blackler became selectmen;
privateers brought back experience and drive to reestablish the fisheries. Financial investors were not knocking at the town gates; famous friends were.

The year after the peace, Marquis de Lafayette visited Marblehead and the town's reception was overwhelming. Crowds met him
at the Forest River, bells rang, cannon were fired from Workhouse
Rocks where Lafayette left his carriage and joined the parade and
the marching band to the Training Field. There free rum punch
evoked a multiplicity of toasts oft repeated at the formal reception
at the Lee Mansion. The selectmen apologized for the condition of
the town as a "misfortune, not a fault." Lafayette responded with his
admiration of Marblehead "which so early fought and so freely
bled" and expressed his tender concern for the town ". . . may your
losses be a hundred-fold repaired by all the blessings of peace. . . ."
Another reception took place at Elbridge Gerry's home, followed
by a lavish Marblehead banquet. The customary thirteen toasts to
the Colonies remembered France, the Commonwealth, Congress,
Marblehead's war dead and "firm Assertors of Liberty, in every part
of the globe." The French nobleman ended his visit with an affectionate toast to Marblehead and "unbounded success to their fisheries."

The economic depression retarding the recovery of the fisheries and shipbuilding had its parallel in the conflict of debtors and creditors and ruinous taxes in rural western Massachusetts; law and order was dismantled by desperate farmers using revolutionary technique to disrupt courthouses and threaten the Springfield arsenal. There was widespread fear for public order and those who had formerly opposed a standing army now requested Congress to enlist troops. Shays' Rebellion was put down by the local militia, but the occurrence awoke the complaisant to the need of a national government to prevent the collapse of the new nation. Marblehead Town Meeting voted approval of the militia's action taken to end the insurrection and offered to furnish its quota of militiamen. Not long after, the voters chose the delegation to be sent to the Constitution Convention in Philadelphia to strengthen the Articles of Confederation. Elbridge Gerry of Marblehead would be one of the four delegates representing Massachusetts.

The gloom in the country mirrored the deep-seated apprehension for the success of the great experiment in independence. One expression was: "We have contended with the most powerful nation and subdued . . . the best appointed armies; but now we have to contend with ourselves. . . ." Elbridge Gerry was shaken by Shays' rebellion in his own state and felt a need for national organization, fearful though he was of domination by any distant authority. In fact, his own state had at times treated Congress like a foreign power. In Philadelphia Gerry, one of the few delegates who had signed both the Declaration of Independence and the Articles of Confederation, was now without his revolutionary friends, John Adams, Samuel Adams and Thomas Jefferson. Old Dr. Franklin sat as subdued as possible, and George Washington presided impartially and attentively and as restrained as a trained jurist. Fifty-five intelligent, experienced men wrangled throughout the hot summer; issues created opposing factions from large and small states and rural and commercial interests. Elbridge Gerry's reaction was: "We are in a peculiar situation. We are neither the same nation nor different nations."

Gerry, at first, seemed favorable to the federal plans and proposed "establishment of a federal legislative, judiciary and executive." On the other hand, as definite proposals were drawn up for federal or national powers, Gerry began to ferret out each controversial detail and his stand against concentrated federal power showed signs of hardening and eventually became his main target.

The season of disagreement dragged on while sectional interests and minutiae seemed to obfuscate their purpose, until even long-winded Gerry warned the Convention that "something must be done or we shall disappoint not only America but the whole world." Resolve after resolve was challenged; yet postponement could not be brooked. Gerry's stand against a standing army and slavery were notable; he feared that a military elite, such as the Cincinnati Society could evolve into military tyranny. As for the counting of nonvoting "slaves" in representation figures, the Marbleheader bitterly questioned whether if blacks were held to be property and yet counted in representation, why shouldn't the cows and horses of the North have the right of representation? Nevertheless, the fatal "⅗" compromise was voted.

Finally, the day arrived when the Constitution was ordered to be engrossed; but not before Elbridge Gerry stood up to elaborate the eleven reasons for withholding his approval. On the crisp, cool Monday morning of September 17, 1787, the Convention convened to sign the document for a future government and with a deep solemnity the delegates inscribed their signatures. Some, like Caleb Strong of Massachusetts, had left; others abstained. The man from Marblehead, signer of the daring Declaration of Independence, after explaining his painful feelings and fear of civil war, was the only Northerner present who refused to sign. Dr. Franklin, as the signing concluded, commented that he'd finally decided that the sun painted on the back of Washington's chair was, in fact, a rising sun.

The furious fight for ratification by the states rocketed each resolution into bright limelight, dividing the people and state delegations into angry camps. The Federalists had eloquent spokesmen; the Anti-Federalists had few constructive proposals, concentrating on the negative aspects of sweeping powers that threatened local governments and individual liberties. Feared, too, was the power of wealth, the military and the demagogue.

Massachusetts held its Constitutional Convention in Boston and Marblehead Town Meeting sent, as delegates, John Glover, Azor Orne, Jonathan Glover and Isaac Mansfield. Elbridge Gerry had written his reasons for refusing to sign the Constitution to the Massachusetts Legislature saying, ". . . the liberties of America were not secured by the system . . ." ". . . nevertheless, in many respects, I think it has great merit, and by proper amendments may be adapted to the exigencies of government and preservation of liberty." Gerry, living in federalist Cambridge, was not elected a delegate; and although he attended *ex officio,* to his deep regret he was not called upon. After a lengthy solemn debate by delegates ingrained with the Massachusetts Bay Colony's spirit of independence and suspicion of outside authority, a series of "Bill of Rights" amendments were adopted and the Constitution so ratified by a vote of 187 to 168, a majority of only nineteen, four the "aye" votes of the Marblehead delegates.

It is interesting to observe that two months later the town's gubernatorial election gave Hancock a fourteen to one advantage over the native, Elbridge Gerry, though, admittedly, the switch could have resulted from the local sensitivity to Gerry's bringing home a "furrin" socialite as his wife and subsequently moving his residence to his Cambridge estate, Elmwood. Gerry's friends feared for his reputation in a popularity race for United States senator; nevertheless, a hard-fought campaign elected him a representative to the United States Congress, where he found few appreciative friends. After two terms Gerry retired to enjoy his family and farm and to reestablish his business. The constitutional antagonists had formalized themselves into two parties and disputation swirled around every issue except one. One man was above party and by the unanimous vote of the electors was elected the first national leader, President George Washington.

The cause of unity must have been served by the first president's extensive tour in the fall of 1789. Washington went out of his way to visit Marblehead where his retired general, John Glover, now selectman, led the great throng welcoming the president of the United States at the town's entrance. After a collation and toasts at the Lee Mansion the president visited the fish yards where citizens and officials apologized for the depressed conditions of the once great seaport. Washington remarked that the town had the feeling of "antiquity," yet he was puzzled at the preponderance of wooden houses where stone was so abundant. The "Patriot Ruler" was given every indication of Marblehead's blessing and sincere affection; a few days later he wrote his thanks to the people of Marblehead. Washington, noting the benefits the efficiency in the new government should bring to the fisheries, gave his "unfeigned wishes" for prosperity. He concluded, "Your attachment to the constitution of the United States is worthy of men, who fought and bled for freedom, and who know its value."

Congress was also giving some attention to the fisheries and Marblehead; first by the Tonnage Act, fostering the use of American built vessels, then the Bounty Act for owners and fishermen with the crew getting five eighths of the payment for each season. Congress established a Marblehead customs district that would include Lynn, but the collector would reside in Marblehead. Native Richard Harris held the job briefly until the appointment of Elbridge Gerry's brother, Samuel, who served for eleven years, using part of the

Gerry's warehouse (101 Front Street) as the Customs House. Though the Gerry patronage appointment was controversial, Marblehead's main problem was to reverse its century-old attitude toward customs collectors whom they had previously cheated, harassed, avoided or dunked in the harbor. Their own American appointee should make the difference, especially as he approved bounty payments and issued certificates of American citizenship to mariners. The collector's status improved so rapidly that as a United States official he was often called upon to accompany governors, senators or important foreign visitors on tours of Marblehead, its fisheries and to extend the town's hospitality. Two years after President Washington's visit, Vice President John Adams journeyed to Marblehead and was appropriately toasted as a "protector of the Fishery."

Recovery for the fisheries was tortuous; the effects of war privateering on the fleet and scattering of its seamen were long lasting. In spite of continuing harassment by the French fleet in the West Indies and British impressment of Americans as "English" sailors, business for the seaport was improving and so was concern for its town conditions. With the approval of the legislature a lottery was held to provide funds to secure the isthmus at the southwest end of the harbor.

In 1794 the fort at Gale's Head was turned over to the United States government. The famous engineer, Rochfontaine, was sent to survey the area and recommend an improved fortification. His plan for a redoubt for harbor defense included parapets two feet thick and eight feet high that would require, at least, twenty thousand bricks. There was a prevailing dread of war—the French Revolution had exploded abroad and both French and English privateers were hampering the recovery of United States trade. The state call for a militia found the Training Field in use once more, and Colonel Orne with Major Swazey held military reviews of three hundred men and officers all in blue uniforms and carrying rusty firearms bare of bayonets. Colonel Lee, whose home was at the parade grounds, often received "foreign" guests who found the hospitality polite and generous, but the local entertainment a bit intemperate and profane in the songs and stories of the sea and distant ports.

The subdued sobriety of the war years was fading and Marblehead was hitting its stride again. Yale president Timothy Dwight in his *Travels in New England* remarked on the physical decay of the town, and commented that the fishermen worked hard much of the year and then "frolic away the remembrance of their hardships during the winter."

A current broadside announced a new frolic—the exhibition of the first elephant ever brought to America. Bengal, India, had been the home of the 3000-pound mammoth who ate 130 pounds a day and drank porter; his daily quota was 30 bottles from which he could pull the corks himself. The billing was: "He surpasses any terrestrial creature and in his intelligence, makes as near an approach to man, as matter can to spirit. . . ." Adults 25¢, children 12½¢; Marbleheaders came in droves.

It wouldn't be long before many mariners would be seeing the exotic sights of the Far East for themselves, for, although the larger, long distance trading ships were embarking from Salem, they carried many a skipper and mariner from Marblehead. One of those was Captain John Marchant who made the voyage to distant Batavia where he fell ill and died. The captain had left a promissory note owed him with Col. William Lee who, in case of Marchant's death, was directed to turn it over to the town poor. Later, unused funds were transferred to the town for the construction of a primary school named after Captain Marchant.

The relocation of the funds would have been understandable to Marchant, who had shipped out when Marblehead schools were in the doldrums. So a group of concerned parents and benefactors, Col. William Lee, Samuel Sewall, Marston Watson, Dr. Elisha Story, and others established a private secondary school to teach classical languages, arithmetic, English, geography, with bookkeeping and music varying the curriculum. It was the third academy opened in Essex County after Governor Dummer and Phillips Andover, and its doors remained open to both boys and girls for seventy-six years. Preceptor William Harris (Harvard, 1786), having been ordained into the Episcopal ministry, also served as rector to the reopened St. Michael's Church. Some years later the Reverend Mr. Harris left for a New York parish where he was later tapped for the presidency of Columbia University.

The Massachusetts Legislature incorporated the Academy in 1792 and its financial aid was in the form of a land grant in Maine which Samuel Sewall later purchased for five thousand dollars. The coeducational experiment at the secondary school worked well and one of the most famous pupils, Justice Joseph Story, said he was "struck with flexibility, activity, and power of the female mind." The long day stretched from 6:00 a.m. until 6:00 p.m., yet the scholars were expected to obey strict rules ranging from not loitering on the way to school to rising and bowing to all visitors. Laughter, whispering, giggling were disrespectful, whereas, profanity was deemed reprehensible.

Another "institution" with a long-lasting effect was the Marine

Society of Marblehead whose membership was confined to Marblehead skippers, fifty-seven of whom had joined by 1798. After the initial fee of five dollars the dues were twenty cents per month, which would be suspended in case of capture or shipwreck. The Committee on Observation provided for a compilation and exchange of marine information from the written reports of its captains regarding variation of the needle, currents, tides, soundings, lights, rocks and such. These men of authority were warned of quarreling at meetings, no drunkenness and a fine of forty cents per "cuss." When Captain John Dennis was first president and Isaac Mansfield, clerk, the skippers' main concern was the seemingly inevitable war with their former ally, France.

President John Adams appointed his old friend Elbridge Gerry to a commission to France along with General Pinckney and John Marshall. Jay's treaty arrangement with England had eased that American tension; now Adams sent his emissaries to the French court with a foreboding plea for "harmony and unanimity." There was anything but that among the commission itself or its diplomatic contacts. Caught in a complicated French intrigue entwining secret agents with covert demands for bribes and pretreaty loans and Talleyrand's high-handedness, the commission was split wide apart. Two members departed and Gerry remained behind believing that he could contrive some rapprochement to avoid war, as he alone of the representatives was acquainted with Talleyrand. The Marbleheader was not only outwitted by the French but also actually detained, as Adams said later, "as much as a prisoner in the Bastille." Gerry supplied the secret agents' names, identified by X, Y and Z, then after more diplomatic fencing he returned home to a United States aroused to an angry pitch by the reports of the other commissioners of French corruption, Talleyrand's demands and the unwarranted secrecy.

Elbridge Gerry, whose diplomatic ineptitude was not viewed in the light of his patriotic zeal—except by Adams—was the butt of the anger and frustration of the young sovereign country. His wife was subjected to hate mail and threats concerning the family's safety; Gerry was hung in effigy and stung by ostracism from many circles. Vindication efforts seemed futile as Congress again called on Washington to command, authorized naval reprisals and arms. Then a second mission to France met at a more auspicious moment; the crisis was resolved, although spoliations claims remained unsettled. Elbridge Gerry had returned to Cambridge.

As French and English privateering diminished, its place was taken by those sea dogs who had picked up the scent of profits—

the pirates. Operating off the European coast, in the Mediterranean
and the China seas, the buccaneers discovered that the Marblehead
seamen were as scrappy and uncompromising as their fathers and
grandfathers had been off Tortuga.

The incredible, extraordinary century was ending and Marblehead had ridden on the pendulum of affluence and poverty, old op-
pressions and young independence, war and peace, victory and depression. Ending, too, were the lives of their war leaders. Azor Orne
was sincerely eulogized as a warm friend and benefactor to his town,
his church and his nation; John Glover, honored general and citizen
leader, passed away at sixty-four, worn by personal sorrows, illness
and the long effort to recover his losses. And, seventeen days before
the year of 1799 ended, the death of "The Father of His Country"
plunged Marblehead into deep sorrow expressed by black armbands,
bells tolling and vessels remaining at their moorings. A great procession moved along the old streets as the artillery fired its last salute to
George Washington—and to what the last twenty-five years of
that century meant to Marblehead.

8. Freedom of
the Seas

THOMAS JEFFERSON came into office on a policy of peace
and economy under the banner of Republicans (later called Demo-
crats), an outgrowth of the Antifederalist movement; Marblehead
voters backed him all the way. Neutrality treaties with England and
France reassured the seaports which rapidly set out to extend their
trade and enjoy that rarity, freedom of the seas. Marblehead had
struggled up from another bout with smallpox that had claimed sixty-
four lives while commercial losses mounted from the quarantine.
Depleted finances and Marblehead's traditional resistance to lengthy
ocean voyages resulted in smaller vessels than those being built
for other ports. The one-hundred- to two-hundred-ton schooners,
brigs, or brigantines used for three- to four-week passage to Europe
were supplemented by vessels of lesser burden for Indies trade or
fishing. Some of the owners were new; nonetheless, the vessels were
skippered and manned by men of old Marblehead seafaring families:
Nathaniel Lindsey, Jr., son of a captain of a Continental company
and town selectman, skippered the schooner *Two Brothers* and later,
Print; Joshua B. Prentiss skippered four different schooners during
the first five years of the century; Captain Edmund Bray's 187-ton
Orient was, in 1801, the first ship entry at the Marblehead Customs

from the East Indies. William Mugford commanded the 340-ton *Ulysses* out of Salem. Three days out on a passage to Marseilles a tremendous storm hit *Ulysses* and tore the canvas, strained the seams and carried away the rudder and stern post. While drifting aimlessly, Captain Mugford rigged an ingenious rudder that guided the ship into port. The unusual steering apparatus brought scores of curious masters and owners to *Ulysses'* dock; some made drawings, others cut models. The American Philosophical Society of Philadelphia, headed by Thomas Jefferson, formally recognized his invention and courageous feat by awarding him the Magellanic Medal with the inscription, "Nothing should be despaired of, tomorrow we shall sail again on the mighty sea."

Danger was aboard every voyage. Salem's navigational expert, Nathaniel Bowditch, surveyed the shoreline to better chart the shores and harbors; the Marine Society of Marblehead petitioned to install landmarks, monuments and trees, especially on the outlying islands for safer entry. A measure of financial security could be found in the newly formed Marblehead Marine Insurance Company whose stock certificates were held by the successful merchants. For a premium of $15.50 John Roads could cover his schooner *Mary* (worth $1,000) for five hundred dollars while fishing and during a twenty-four-hour unloading period; an additional premium covered his general supplies. However, no coverage was allowed on perishables like fish, grain, rice, flaxseed or fruit. Yet, *Mary* was insured against the seas, men-of-war, pirates, fire, rovers, assailing thieves, surprisals, arrests, detainment of all kings and princes, barratry of the master and other conditions in small print.

The future looked brighter when President Jefferson concluded the Louisiana Purchase with the provision that some of the money be used to settle old claims for French ship seizures. Marblehead now had a safe place for that claims money in the first Marblehead Bank, incorporated in 1804 and located in the Lee Mansion. No claims money trickled into Marblehead; yet, the bank's statement was hopeful that prosperity was ahead for trade and the fishery which now employed a thousand seamen.

An invigorated spirit was abroad in Marblehead. There was even plenty of "spirit" in the town bills: the August to October costs for a highway crew itemized a water bucket for 25¢, 3 brooms for 37½¢, powder 28¢ and 32½ gallons of rum at $1.00 per gallon. And when the committee "ran the bounds" the journey to Salem cost $1.66, the bread and fish, $5.00 and the rum, $7.00.

The "strong water" didn't seem to have fatal effects, for the "Bill of Mortality" for Marblehead, published in 1808, showed 57 marriages, 222 births and a death total for the year of 118 persons, 19 of whom had been lost at sea. The highest mortality was among infants; the most destructive disease was tuberculosis ("consumption") and then "fevers." Only one person died by violence, and three from debauchery—and those were women. The reporter commented that "the air is proved to be wholesome, though the wind blows upon the town over salt water from 18 points of the compass."

The school costs for the North, South and Center Schools were modest: a male teacher received $33.33 per month, the women teachers about half that amount, though some of them conducted a primary school in their own homes. School vandalism was on the increase and glazier Robert Harris was kept busy replacing eight by ten window panes for twenty-five cents each. Several local people belonged to a Boston library company in which they had purchased shares and paid dues; and Captain John Prince carried the books to and from Boston by water, but he found collecting the library's fines a nuisance. In collaboration with Dr. William Bentley, Isaac Mansfield had written the history of Essex County and in preparation for that Mansfield wrote the first brief history of Marblehead which was published in the Massachusetts Historical Society Collection of 1802.

Peace on the seas was short lived, for the Napoleonic Wars had erupted again. Both France and England adopted policies under which American shipping was arbitrarily subject to search and seizure; the British, claiming deserters were shipping out on American vessels, boarded Marblehead fishing boats and impressed "Englishmen." American responses inflamed the country's early venture into party politics which, in the campaign of 1805, spilled its bitterness and invective into the streets, the pulpits and local politics. The defeated Federalists seemed determined to disrupt the Jeffersonian hold on Marblehead; so just before 1806 Town Meeting every household woke to find on its doorstep an unsigned pamphlet addressed to all the inhabitants. It blasted the selectmen for bad management, tax increases, and holding meetings that were merely cloaks for political caucuses. The language was abusive, so the meeting excitedly authorized the constables to publicly burn the pamphlets. When the pamphleteer was discovered to be William Reed he was taken to court. Charges of libel were exchanged with charges of a "riot," resulting in "no bill." The political ferment had only just begun.

Although ship seizures and impressment increased, a nation without naval protection or a volunteer army was hardly prepared to take on two international giants. President Jefferson abruptly with-

drew all American shipping from the seas by the 1807 Embargo
Act. Anguished howls from New England merchants and traders
could be heard all the way to Washington—"In this dreadful situation of affairs, what in the name of God will America do? . . .
stand by and see her commerce plundered?" Talk of rebellion
brought the sloop-of-war *Wasp* to Salem Harbor to enforce the embargo though illicit trade was continuing in coastal darkness or over
Canadian borders. Marblehead's support remained with Jefferson,
yet petitions for bounties or for conversion of vessels for naval use
battered representatives' doors. Within fifteen months the seaport of Marblehead was almost in shambles again—empty vessels
tossed at their moorings, sail lofts and ropewalks closed, warehouses
overflowed with fish that couldn't be sold. In spite of inflammatory
opposition from other seacoast towns Marblehead stuck by its Town
Meeting resolution: "That we will support the government of the
United States . . . and we do hereby tender our all whenever our
country calls. . . ." Most Marbleheaders judged the real cause to be
not the embargo, but tyrannical Great Britain and France and, as in
1776, they would rather "die Freemen, than live as Slaves." They
suffered until Jefferson's embargo was repealed; the next Nonimportation Act forbidding trade with only the two offending countries
brought some relief. Yet, almost immediately several Marblehead
ships bound for other countries were captured by British cruisers
and taken as prizes in foreign ports.

When Jefferson commented on the embargo repeal, he irately
stated, "I ascribe all this to one pseudo-Republican, Story. . . ."
The president meant Joseph Story of Marblehead who had composed the first formal protest and characterized Jefferson's attitude
as "visionary obstinacy." Joseph Story was twenty-nine at the time
and serving as a member of the Congressional House of Representatives, to which he had been elected by the Jeffersonian Republicans;
however, the news from New England convinced him of the destructive effects of the embargo, including the possibility of secession.

This spirit of regional independence was readily understood by
Joseph Story. He had been born in Marblehead during the War of
Independence and had lived among people who emptied themselves
for independence and freedom. His father, Dr. Elisha Story, one of
the radical Sons of Liberty "held every office he would consent to."
An amiable and good man, Dr. Story had ridden out every wave of
indignation, sorrow or joy in Marblehead. Married twice, he had fathered many children, including Joseph.

After graduation from Harvard young Story went into Samuel

Sewall's law office in Marblehead to prepare himself for the bar. When Counselor Sewall, who had been elected to Congress, resigned to accept a seat on the Supreme Judicial Court of Massachusetts, Joseph Story continued his legal practice in Salem. He was chosen, at twenty-seven, for the Massachusetts Legislature, followed two years later by election to the United States Congress. His vacillation on the embargo cost him the next congressional nomination; however, his talents were used by reelection to the Massachusetts Legislature where he became Speaker of the House. That year, 1810, Marblehead men occupied important posts: the governorship (Gerry), the Speaker of the House (Story) and a justice's seat on the Massachusetts Supreme Court (Sewall). This was a new kind of legislative and judicial leadership from Marblehead which had long provided the ships' masters, naval commanders and military officers. The next step up for these three men came a few years later when, concurrently, Elbridge Gerry served as vice president and Samuel Sewall was chief justice of Massachusetts, the third member of his family to be appointed to that office. After being educated in Marblehead and at Harvard, Sewall married Abigail Devereux, and practiced law in Marblehead where he frequently served as a town official and later was elected to the United States Congress, from which he resigned to accept the judicial appointment which death ended the first year.

At that same time Justice Joseph Story of Marblehead was sitting on the United States Supreme Court. The thirty-three-year-old, volatile, auburn-haired Story relished his good fortune in serving under the leadership of Chief Justice John Marshall who appreciated the intensity and industry of the young jurist. His opinions became noted for their lucidity and the depth of his support of the Constitution. In 1829 he was appointed Dane Professor of Law and his influence provided impetus to the development of the Harvard Law School. Still later, he and John Quincy Adams were the moving forces to organize a Harvard alumni assocation and were the first to hold its two top offices.

A man of vitality and drive, Justice Story not only taught when the Supreme Court was not in session, but sat for circuit court sessions in the New England states. In that capacity Story wrote landmark decisions in the fields of prize claims, admiralty and patents.

Justice Story's fame grew during his lifetime as he fulfilled his calling as a judge, teacher and writer. His law books were so widely recognized that they were printed in several languages in Europe. Honorary degrees were bestowed by Brown, Dartmouth and Harvard and a fellowship from the American Academy of Arts and Sciences. His historical interests led Joseph Story to be one of the co-founders of the Essex Historical Society in Salem in 1821.

It wasn't all "tea and skittles," however, for Joseph Story lost his beloved first wife and later four of his seven children. He was inwardly torn by political issues, yet obliged to withhold public comment except when his antislavery feelings once burst forth. He often said that pronouncing a capital punishment judgment actually made him physically ill. In the raucous changes of the Jacksonian period Story's anxiety and frustrations moved him into unallayed conservatism which may have been partly accountable for his being passed over by President Jackson for chief justice of the United States. Justice Joseph Story died in 1845; his memorial was the admiration of jurists everywhere—the British commendation as the "Blackstone of America" and the accolade of "one of the ten outstanding men in judicial history."

When Story first entered Congress his hometown was churning with the political implications of the embargo, British attacks and violent party politics. It spilled over into the churches where change was also fermenting. The Marblehead Baptist Church was organized in 1810, some years after the first Methodist preachers had visited the town and somewhat later erected their church. The current upheaval in religious doctrines caused most members of the Second Congregational Church to follow their pastor in Unitarianism. There was a storm of competition in the meeting mania; the fiery "New Light" was burning brightly in "Hot Fast Sermons." Women, especially, were excited about the religious revivals and would often be seen on the Salem Road bound for night lectures. Medical men declared the baptismal "dip" in the freezing waters of the harbor pure fanaticism. Just as in the new nationalism, with its upsurge of population, westward expansion, and emerging industry, orthodox religious patterns were being rudely shaken up—sometimes by political strife.

The Federalist strength had waned; Elbridge Gerry of the Jeffersonian Republicans was elected governor of Massachusetts thirty years after he had resented being overlooked for Governor Hancock. The governorship gave him patronage and power which he used moderately and thoughtfully the first term; in the second term, Gerry's sensitivity to the Federalists campaign attacks caused him to wield the "spoils" system flagrantly for the good of his party. In the moment of the tragic flaw Gerry permitted himself, according to a contemporary biographer, to give a tacit approval to a redistricting bill, benefiting Antifederalist representation in his Essex County. The *Salem Gazette* pounced on the governor with

Appleton's cartoon of the district in the shape of a salamander renamed "Gerrymander." There was nothing new in the custom of political redistricting, but, this man Gerry with political service of some thirty-nine years was to be forever hung on the petard of a clever visualization of a political maneuver that is still called gerrymandering. And Marblehead's votes did move three senators over to the Republican side, yet, Governor Gerry was then defeated by that salamander and his approval of the War of 1812.

Interference with trade, the infuriating impressment of sailors and more ship seizures wracked the east coast; but, the real war hawks were in the newer western states where the British were inciting Indian attacks. Sectionalism and jealousy were rampant; Congress in early 1812 authorized additional army and militia troops. By a quirk of fate the news that the British trade orders had been withdrawn was on the way to America when the United States Congress, at the behest of President Madison, declared war on England. The declaration passed by a scant margin of six votes and a similar declaration against France luckily failed by two votes. The unprepared and disunited country was forced to fight an "unnecessary war." With Britain locked in war with France the first year the American Army had the initiative, though not the victories. Reinforcing their efforts was the small United States Navy of twenty vessels—and revitalized privateering.

Unlike the many antiwar seaports, Marblehead could never find itself siding with anything British and supported Congress' action as a last resort. There were sixteen Marbleheaders already impressed and twenty others missing and suspected to be in British hands. Marblehead outfitted the vessels *Industry, Snowbird, Lion* and *Thorn*. Commodore Samuel Tucker now in Maine, at sixty-five, came out in a sloop and took in the British ship *Bream*. Salem vessels like *America* had many Marblehead seamen and *Growler* had a Marblehead crew and Captain Nathaniel Lindsey. The naval vessels *Essex* and *Constitution* listed plenty of Marbleheaders among their officers and crew. Vessel after vessel that could have brought foreign trade or profitable fishing to Marblehead were fighting Great Britain again, many in engagements off the coastline of the Maritime Provinces. There was *Concordia* (owned by four of the Blackler family and John Pedrick), 386 tons, 3 masts, 2 decks, 110 feet long, fighting off Halifax; *Orient*, carrying thousands of dollars in specie, was captured and her men imprisoned; *Betsey* was taken off Newfoundland. As many as four privateers a day might weigh anchor and stand out from Marblehead, most of them causing the British Navy great embarrassment until Great Britain was able to enforce

an effective blockade. And the popular sailors' chanty went like
this:

> Then under full sail we laugh at the gale,
>   And the landsmen look pale, never heed 'em.
> But toss off the glass to a favorite lass,
>   To America, Commerce and Freedom.

Marblehead Town Meeting, realizing the proximity of British
blockaders, organized a Committee of Safety as they had in the Revolution and requested Major Ranney, commander of the fort, to
throw up four additional breastworks. To protect Little Harbor, the
large bluff of rocks across from Old Burying Ground, so called Bailey's Head (Fountain Park), was fortified by a battery and designated as Fort Washington. A forty-two-pounder was platformed
on Skinner's Head, a small cannon on Goodwin's Head and another
on Fort Glover (Gilbert Heights). Guards were stationed on the
eastern shore of the Neck; at a British sighting they were to fire a
single shot. On All Fool's Day that year the town boys set off a
false bomb and hid to watch the excitement. The fort came alive, a
detachment raced to the Neck and the townspeople loaded their
muskets and headed for the highlands. No British; no boys! On
June 1, 1813, news flashed through the town that vessels offshore
were maneuvering for battle positions—they were identified as the
American *Chesapeake* and the British frigate *Shannon*. Seemingly
evenly matched, the vessels came within fifty yards when *Shannon*
opened fire and was, in turn, hit by close broadside. The furious
cannonade lasted fifteen minutes, leaving both vessels reeling from
extensive damage and casualties. *Shannon* recovered more quickly
—its captain had commanded her many years with a tough, experienced crew especially drilled in gunnery. On the other hand, Captain Lawrence had boarded *Chesapeake* six hours before the engagement and had been met by a raw, untrained crew of which a third
were foreign sailors. Mortally wounded early in the engagement,
Captain Lawrence pleaded with the crew, "Don't give up the ship," but
they could offer little resistance to the Britishers scrambling aboard.
To the dismay of the Americans lining the shores *Chesapeake* struck
her colors and all hands were carried off to Halifax. When Captain
Lawrence's body was returned to Salem, Vice President Gerry led
the funeral procession and the eulogy was delivered by Joseph
Story.

Tension mounted everywhere on the coast as the blockade tightened and the misfortunes of the northern and southern frontiers
were reported. Nervous night watchmen had accidentally killed

two citizens on the streets; those who could spare food contributed it to the "public table" for the fishermen's families. North Shore opposition to the unpopular war hindered loans, supplies and recruiting. Pairs of English cruisers sailed well inside Halfway Rock "hovering like hawks" outside every port, picking up coastal boats and running barges into Beverly to burn vessels at anchor. Marblehead braced itself as three large vessels were reported approaching on Sunday, April 3, 1814. Seasoned mariners then recognized *Constitution* being chased by two British frigates, *Tenedos* and *Junon*, with far superior combined fire power. As the *Tenedos* gained on her, *Constitution* pumped the bilge, threw provisions overboard and sought a refuge. A great number of the crew were from Marblehead and Samuel H. Green offered to pilot the vessel into his home port. Daringly he sailed her between Marblehead Rock and the Neck and scudded into the harbor where *Constitution* dropped anchor at 1:30 p.m. Without charts of the rocks or channels, and observing the fort's cannon, the British stood off while thousands cheered from both the shores. An alarm had rung out and as far away as Salem men began dragging cannon to reinforce the fort and save "Old Ironsides." Saved she was, to return to Boston unmolested and give a good account of herself for the balance of the war.

American naval forces and the privateers made a good showing before the world. Skilled, courageous mariners like the Marbleheaders were capable of initiative, quick action and effective decisions in battle. When Napoleon abdicated and England could concentrate on the United States, American vessels were effectively hemmed in by British convoys. To aid the blockaders a map was published in London of this coast from "Nahaunt" to Egg Rock; especially noted were Marblehead and Salem, "two good ports of the U. S., . . . the grand rendezvous for privateers. . . ."

The extent of the British appreciation of New England's opposition to the war was recorded in a lieutenant's journal aboard HMS *Nymphe* on blockade duty. British orders were to encourage dissension by not molesting local fishermen or pleasure parties, by making agreeable contacts ashore and welcoming visitors aboard. *Nymphe's* crewmen would occupy themselves in gun practice or burning small boats to scare off armed vessels and would then land on Baker's Island or the Salem shore for supplies. A flag of truce was used to purchase food, arrange ransom or release prisoners.

One such deal was arranged with Justice Story, who found no legal barrier to the release of Marblehead's Captain Russell whose wife recently had died leaving five children. A small pilot boat found *Nymphe*, took off Russell and three others in hopes, the

British said, that the "public can estimate the urbanity, humanity and profound skill in the written . . . law. . . ." No such urbanity was afforded a British landing party who reported the people ill clothed and "the ladies on this coast are infinitely more violent than the males—perfect Amazons!"

Only the newly designed clippers from Baltimore had the speed to outsail British frigates. One of those clippers, *Grampus*, brought the British prize brig *Doris* from Senegal into Marblehead. To the astonishment of the town *Doris* carried gifts for the British royal family: Arabian horses, a hyena and jackals. A side show was in store for all—the Arabian horses, though weakened by the long voyage, were handsome to behold in the stagecoach stables; the hyena and jackals were caged in the hold of the ship, which became a popular exhibition place. It was only a momentary respite from the pressure; some mutilated men were arriving home, scores were imprisoned at Dartmoor, England, and others would never return. The young grandson of Gen. John Glover was among the latter. Displaying great courage aboard *Essex* when she had been overwhelmed by a British convoy off Valparaiso, Lieut. John Glover Cowell had remained at his station though wounded. Hit a second time in the leg, amputation was unavoidable; however, young Lieutenant Cowell had lost much blood and failed to rally. His heroism was widely acknowledged and his funeral procession in Valpariso brought together Britishers, Americans and the Chileans to mourn for the brave young Marbleheader.

The grim news of the burning of Washington was somewhat lessened by victories on Lake Champlain and at Baltimore. Much closer to home was the rumor of a British fleet underway to capture and neutralize the ports of Salem and Marblehead. The U.S. Army poured money into the strengthening of the fort; though word was already leaking out about peace negotiations to end the widely scorned "Madison's War." Just before the Peace Treaty of Ghent was signed, one of the administration's loyal supporters, Vice President Elbridge Gerry, died. As an avid correspondent, he was probably well aware of the "secession" movement afoot in New England; nevertheless, Gerry felt obliged to support the president although his letters reveal deep sympathy for the distressed.

The vice president's funeral was formal and quite well attended, though it caused no flurry in Washington. Congress discovered that Gerry himself had been a victim of the embargo and blockade; his business was defunct. No pensions were allowable; however, the government paid for his funeral and, later, for a monument. President Madison appointed Elbridge, Jr. collector of the port of Boston and made opportunities available for two other sons in the armed forces. Forty-three years in political life and government service had left Gerry destitute—unspoken testimony of his scrupulous honesty. His government placed a monument over his grave in 1823 inscribed with Gerry's own words: "It is the duty of every man, though he live but one day, to devote that day to the good of his country." Aside from John Adams, Elbridge Gerry was the only other Massachusetts man ever to serve as vice president.

Within a fortnight of Gerry's death the General Court of Massachusetts called the Hartford Convention. On December 15 twenty-six delegates—none from Marblehead—met "to consult upon measures to restore New England to its ancient position in the Union" and under consideration was an independent New England confederacy with its own defense. They claimed little or no defense was being given the coast, whereas, western and southern interests had fostered the war to open up lands for westward expansion. The arrival of the Hartford Convention leaders in Washington coincided with the news of the peace treaty and the windage joyfully shot out of New England's weakened cannon. A belated New Orleans victory served to hoist Andrew Jackson's house flag and gave a euphoric conclusion to the War of 1812.

The peace settlement was something less than satisfactory. In fact very little was settled about impressment, search and seize or other causes of the war. What had changed was the attitude of Great Britain and the world toward the American experiment; without being spelled out, there would now be a freedom of the seas that America had not known for one hundred years. Nor was any provision made for the immediate release of prisoners from American naval ships, privateers or shore raids, most of whom were being held at Dartmoor Prison, fifteen miles northeast of Plymouth, England. Hundreds of Marblehead men were said to be imprisoned there. As the story goes, an English guard asked a prisoner, "Where do you belong, Jack?" "To Marblehead," was the reply. In amazement the guard said: "Marblehead! I believe nearly every Yankee inside the walls hails from Marblehead. It must be the greatest seaport in America! Where the devil is Marblehead?" "About fourteen miles from Bunker Hill" was the Marbleheader's laconic reply.

Word leaked to the American prisoners of the peace treaty and their restlessness and resentment built to a high pitch. The prison was cold and crowded; the one-mile circular wall forbade escape. When bickering and a baiting incident over a ball in the exercise yard built into a threatened revolt, the British fired into the crowd of unarmed prisoners killing nine and wounding thirty-eight, among them John Peach and Thomas Tindley of Marblehead. Reports of the brutality of the Dartmoor massacre inflamed Marblehead and their demands were pressed by the government and the men eventually released. On the voyage home one group of 'Headers could no longer endure the captain's stinginess of sail and lack of speed, so he found himself a passenger while the elected captain, John Hubbard, with his own Marblehead crew sailed her hell bent for home port. Over one thousand men of Marblehead were involved in that war; many didn't return, but those who did had a new zest for "Free Trade and Sailors' Rights."

9. Marblehead Never Retreats

"Then drink round, my boys, 'tis the first of our joys
　　To relieve the distressed, clothe and feed 'em
A duty we share with the brave and the fair,
　　In this land of Commerce and Freedom."

"COMMERCE AND FREEDOM" sparked Marblehead's recovery from the deleterious effects of the War of 1812. Its fisheries and the fleet had been knocked out again; harbor facilities had deteriorated; financial reverses were felt throughout the town except by some privateers. Nevertheless, circumstances differed from the tedious post-Revolution period which had been plagued by a widespread depression of spirit engendered by national instability and confusion. In 1815 there was a fresh confidence abroad. Having bested Great Britain twice in thirty-five years, the young, scrappy nation that had ridden out the turbulence of dissension and war was ready for growth in industry, trade, and territory. Revival of shipbuilding would soon provide modern designs for swift vessels, not only for the Far East and African trade of Salem, but also for the fisheries of Marblehead.

Meanwhile, the forty-eight vessels of the fleet that survived the war were augmented by British prize vessels purchased by Marbleheaders. These were the brig *Strong*, skippered by Samuel R. Gerry; the 267-ton *Mary*, *Hero* captured by John Gerry, who later drowned on a passage from Gottenburg; the 168-ton *Washington*, owned and skippered by Pedricks and Blacklers. Marblehead made a futile attempt to recapture its foreign trade; however, that was now in the grasp of Salem and Boston. Packets and merchant ships used Marblehead harbor and local skippers commanded some of the finest ships that sailed the China Sea. In 1818 Nicholas Broughton, grandson of the Revolutionary War captain, brought *Java* from China with a cargo of such value that the duty alone was $39,785.

Marblehead turned once more to its fisheries. New markets had opened up as far west as Albany and some "wet fish" was being sailed directly from the Banks to Europe and the West Indies. The vessels were faster; the fares were profitable; privateering and naval experience had sharpened the skills of the seamen and skippers. In fact the availability of trained seamen in time of war was one of the reasons the national government decided to foster and protect the fisheries. In 1818 the Bounty Act was amended to raise the bounty payment for fishing cod on the Banks. The crux of the bounty problem was the restriction to cod fishing (excluding all hake, pollack, halibut and mackerel from the bounty). The fishermen emphasized the training and employment of seamen, food consumption, and extensive use of foreign salt on which the government collected a high duty.

The growth of Marblehead's fisheries was constant, yet not rapid. Late fall fares returning on one December day in 1818 totaled forty-eight fishing vessels plus two coasters and two large brigs from South America and the Mediterranean. The observant Dr. Bentley of Salem wrote: "We cannot refuse our best wishes to Marblehead. No people suffered more exquisitely and yet retained their integrity till the last, unshaken in the greatest events."

The entire country, self-conscious in its new role, seemed to feel the need of self-discipline and reform; the United States must perfect itself in the eyes of the world. Even Marblehead showed signs of taking itself seriously. Energetic organizations were founded to improve and elevate the town.

First mustered together were 125 women who, in 1816, formed the Marblehead Female Humane Society. That year 48 "indigent, sick and infirm" persons benefited from the food, money, linen and clothing distributed. At times the clothing could only be loaned, until the society provided materials for self-employment from spinning, weaving and knitting. Medicines, meat and 2,908 loaves of bread were listed in later annual reports; all purchased from dona-

tions and the ten cents a month dues. Years later, through Everett
Paine's gift of a house and the generous contributions of Dr. Joel
Goldthwaite and others, the Mary E. Harris Home for the Aged
(Harris and Mugford Streets) was established and is still in operation
in 1971 with dues of ten cents per month.

The Marblehead Union Moral Society for the suppression of intemperance and other vices sprang up in 1817. Various vices were
outlined in its "benevolent purposes" and proposals to the town: a
month's jail term for the "lodgers" found at the House of Ill Fame;
apprentice the young and poor to the tradesmen; incarcerate rogues,
brawlers, pilferers, vagabonds of gaming and palmistry and "common pipers and fiddlers"; forbid gaming for money or property
from age twenty up and take away cards, dice and billiards from
those age five to sixty; observe the Lord's Day without sports, travel
or "secular business in the orchards, fields, etc." The Union Moral-
ists zeroed in on Marblehead's wayward ways—profanity (one
dollar to two dollars fine for each offense) or blasphemy (a year in
jail) and intemperance. In condemning debauchery, its effect on the
family, resurrecting old tavern laws, the society was participating in
the mounting resentment toward America's drinking habits.

The old rhumbullion had lost out during the West Indies block-
ades to a potent new kill-devil called whiskey—set up by Scottish
and Irish immigrants. Statistics publicized by the press, showed that
the 1792 annual per capita liquor consumption of two and a half
gallons had, in just over thirty years, overflowed to seven and a half
gallons per person. Excesses caused national and local anxiety, hastening the day of the evangelical "cold water missionaries."

National, state and town temperance societies led the fight; first,
to discourage the moderate, social drinker, then to apply political
pressure and to infuse the campaign with religious preachings. In
Marblehead church members were suspended for intemperance until
a public confession and a temperance pledge readmitted them. They
discountenanced the use of strong drink except for medicinal purposes and communion. Whether communion receptions increased
remains unknown, but there was a sudden mania for potent patent
medicines. These societies at first restrained themselves from demanding prohibition, compromising for temperance, but the fight
had just begun. Marblehead taverns, that from the earliest days had
provided the panorama of the seaport with all of its good and its
bad, continued to flourish; however, they disclaimed any responsibility for the latest phenomenon, that astonishing offshore wonder,
the sea serpent.

From legendary tales of Europe and America it was known that at intervals there arose from the depths an ancient primitive serpent of the sea. In 1817 and 1819 his surfacing was said to have left a greasy film on the water off Pig's Rock and Tinker's Island. *Low's Almanac* gave credence to the serpent's frequent appearances by publishing a sketch of the "Great Marine Serpent" by James Prince. Its dimensions were detailed: 130 feet long, 3 or more feet circumference, flat with 14 protuberances about 10 feet apart, decreasing in size near the tail. The dark brown monster had a white throat and moved slowly horizontally and vertically, except for the swift turns of a snake. Flocks of birds followed the creature. A current parody chanted:

> Let Salem boast her museum and her witches
> Her statues Newb'y; Marblehead her riches—
> We from them all the shining now will take
> The snake and Glo'ster, Glo'ster and the snake.

Marblehead never let Gloucester have the last word; her natives had seen it from the Neck; undaunted fishermen searched the waters with nets and guns. The boat's hands were paid a day's wages, but promised a share in the income resulting from the capture of the sea serpent. On the weekends hundreds of Bostonians came by the new Eastern Stage to scan the horizon for the serpent.

The Eastern Stage Coach Company had been formed in 1818 by a syndicate, offering 425 shares at one hundred dollars each which did double in value before being trampled by the "iron horse." Marblehead was one of the 79 coach lines from Boston and the main stop was at Putnam's Tavern (Washington and Rockaway Streets) where the proprietor offered food, drink, lodging and lore.

The mystery tale going the rounds then was of the old sea captain's treasure and its disappearance. Captain Israel Foster, who had owned *Storm* and skippered several other vessels, must have made many hard-money trades which totaled up to $53,174 in gold pieces, Spanish doubloons, and English sovereigns. All these he hoarded in an old keg from which he drew a gold coin as his needs demanded. After the War of 1812 had been declared Captain Foster had taken his precious keg to a Salem bank which, when British attack seemed imminent, had temporarily moved inland for safety. Foster continued to use the gold pieces from the top of the keg, withdrawing a total of $7,625 by the time he died in 1818. His heirs, who arrived at the bank to examine the keg and divide the captain's loot, were shocked to discover a layer of gold pieces covering small chunks of ballast iron that had been buried in the bottom of the keg—$30,000 in gold was missing. Hiring Daniel Webster for legal counsel, the Foster heirs sued; the court found the bank not liable for the theft, nevertheless public confidence vanished and the bank failed. Marblehead buzzed with speculation—where had Foster gotten all the gold and who had stolen it? There was nothing Marblehead ever loved more than a tale of intrigue and mystery.

The visits of illustrious persons brought some excitement to Marblehead. President James Monroe came on July 8, 1817, accompanied by the governor and was accorded a welcome followed by refreshments at Rea's Tavern, a political conference at the Sewall House and a visit to the flake yards and fort. Some months later, Secretary of the Navy Crowninshield and Joseph Story rode with the hero of the Northern Army, Major General Brown, to Marblehead where the Marblehead infantry met them on the plain and the artillery at the foot of Workhouse Rocks. A few days earlier the same tour of the fisheries had been given to United States senators from Tennessee and Louisiana who openly admired the energy of the town's postwar recovery.

On the day in 1824 that every vessel delayed its sailing and the people filled the muddy, rain-soaked streets the welcome was for an old friend who had come on a sentimental journey. Marquis de Lafayette returned, bringing his son to meet the men of Marblehead and to display for the last time his deep affection for the town. Marbleheaders wanted to show their children a true Revolutionary War hero. Most of the others had gone by now; that year the Revolutionary veterans in Marblehead claiming the war bounty were listed as six between eighty and ninety years old, seventeen between seventy and eighty years old and twenty-four between sixty and seventy years. For those fortunate enough to escape from the clutches of the sea and warfare, longevity was a characteristic reward in Marblehead.

Soldiering was no longer very popular in Marblehead; the array of uniforms and weapons left much to be desired, and during a sham military exercise with Salem the old rivalry got the best of the 'Headers and the small, hard potatoes shot at the "enemy" took their toll. The Salem officer ordering retreat was defiantly told, "Marblehead never retreats," which became the town's watchword for the future.

Years before Isaac Mansfield had written that this was a town that had never excused itself from the politics of its country. Now, to better prepare the townsmen and to promote political knowledge the Columbian Society was formed and its members met weekly to exchange ideas, information, reading material and to participate in ardent debates. "I do firmly believe that man by nature is and ought to be free; that I cherish an ardent attachment to the rights and liberties of our country . . ." was the pledge required of each new member. The "Columbian" influence was apparent for years in the training of town officials and the heated political debates at Town Meeting. Another organization devoted to the dissemination of "useful Knowledge" was the Marblehead Lyceum which had as its first president, John Bartlett, and Isaac Collyer as clerk. The Lyceum brought current political leaders, cultural programs and lecturers to Marblehead for decades; they provided plenty of material for the provocative letters to local newspapers that made their appearance in town after 1830. The *Marblehead Register* was the first published in town and it lasted three years. The *Gazette* and the *People's Advocate* had longer lives than most of the seven. But the *Marblehead Messenger*, published first in 1872, has survived up to the present day. None of the newspapers avoided the current issues and some created them; the myriad of organizations spawned in the "clubby" town received ample coverage and the advertising provided a full panoply of the changing times and ships' cargoes such as rubbers from India, linens from Ireland and porcelain from China. Ships' arrivals and departures, and often their cargoes, were published, plus a list of those "spoken" i.e., vessels met in passage by others who reported the date, location and their condition. Of course, the best source for columns of copy and fervent editorials was Town Meeting.

Town Meetings of the time reflected the widespread interest in self-improvement and also the growth of the population and small business. The 1824 Meeting had accepted a lengthy report from a special committee that recommended formalizing the naming of streets, a charge of twenty dollars per sign and a one-cent fee for numbering each dwelling house. Among the forty street names were the old traditional "Ways," the family names of long-time abutters and others with a strong patriotic flavor, like Mugford, Lee, Union, Washington and Glover Square. Public health ordinances were then voted in order to force the slaughter houses into more sanitary practices, the residents to observe drainage restrictions, and the ships from foreign ports (where cholera or smallpox was present) to drop anchor in a quarantine area between Cat Island and Peach's Point. Only the "health boat," having examined the vessel and its papers, could approve entrance into Marblehead harbor. Some of these vessels were also carrying foreign immigrants whom the captain must indemnify against becoming public charges for three years. The Overseers of the Poor had already erected a new building, but expenses were increasing for food, grain, funerals, candles, horses, soap, hay, wood and a budget item listed as "junk."

For decades school planning and budgets fluctuated according to the monetary condition of the town and its attitude toward education. The more affluent families sent their children to one of the several small, private schools held in a teacher's home or a rented hall. The teachers were usually women or, occasionally, a retired sea captain who could prepare boys and girls for the Academy. Citizens had worried that the establishment of the private schools would alleviate the pressure on the school trustees for educational improvements. That proved true. Another consideration was the number of boys who went to sea at the age of eleven and the high percentage of girls employed in home industries or domestic jobs. School budgets, length and season of the school year, teachers' salaries, and location of the classrooms caused endless debate and no agreement on a firm policy. Three grammar schools followed the primary schools and then Town Meeting, moved by the eloquence of young Franklin Knight who spoke out for higher education and equal opportunity for girls, voted for a high school. The boys and girls would be taught separately. Students had to qualify by examination and then attend regularly—four unaccounted days meant expulsion. Attendance—particularly of the boys—ebbed and flowed like the tide; the girls were more steadfast. Nonetheless, the voters felt that the budget was exorbitant, so the boys' high school was abolished and some years later, the girls' closed. A special room at the Center Grammar was put aside for those who wanted to pursue higher education. Some did; but many boys shipped out as "cut-tails" or cabin boys and others entered the new trade, shoemaking.

Out of necessity Marblehead had long produced heavy boots for its seamen—old town and private documents had recorded tan-yards, tanners, shoemakers and leather sealers—but by the early 1800's cordwaining had caught on as good part-time employment between fishing trips or during the winter. Most of the shoemaking was done at home, as it had been for years. No longer was this a limited trade; now the work was widespread and most of the leather was imported. The women sewed the uppers at home and the men's work was done in an empty store or a tiny building where they shared the expenses of the materials and the wood to heat the ten by twelve by thirteen foot single-room shack. Each man brought his bench and tools and was paid on a piecework basis. Neighbors and schoolboys dropped by and sometimes read the news or argued the town warrant over the incessant hammering. Each Marblehead "ten-footer" was a small public forum. The warm shack had a scent all its own—of men, leather, burning wood, tobacco and, perhaps, just a touch of rum.

Before the War of 1812 interest in, and knowledge of, shoemaking had become widespread on the North Shore. Finished shoes were soon marketed by energetic "salesmen" who carted them around in wheelbarrows or wagons and bartered for merchandise or cash. Men like Ebenezer Martin, Thomas Woolredge, Benjamin Hawkes, Adoniram Orne and Sam Sparhawk began to organize Marblehead production by using a "put-out" system in which a central shop issued the cut uppers to the women by the dozens which, when sewn, were returned for cash payment; just half as much as the men were paid who finished the shoes in the cordwainer's tiny shop. The demand for well-made women's and children's shoes of various colors and with thin soles grew in this country and Europe. The cordwainer now worked fourteen hours a day, but, because of the small sizes, the difficulties of working with wet, fine leather that must be sewn together with waxed threads, he probably produced fewer shoes and earned less money. Young girls of ten and twelve were trained to bind shoes at home and frequently continued in the occupation for years to the detriment of their schooling.

The Marblehead Society for the Encouragement of Domestic Industry had been founded and one of its first innovations was the Braid and Straw Society to manufacture hats and bonnets for males and females of all ages from "straw, grass and other kindred vegetables." These could be manufactured easily (girls of twelve and over could make ten a day), cheaply (two hundred bundles of straw, carted for twenty-one dollars), and successfully (if made to a degree of perfection that would create a demand). The subscribers, such as Messrs. Hooper, Weed, Appleton, Reed, Prince, Hawkes and Mansfield would pay the instructor's salary and board; the person tutored would contribute one dollar or equal amount of work. The hats were sold from two dollars to five dollars and probably distributed in the same manner as the local shoes.

Other small businesses were beginning to thrive, producing candles, tinware, chairs and cabinets, soap and glue, cord and wheels. *The New England Gazeteer* reported that in 1837, Marblehead's population of 5,549 produced manufactured goods worth $398,565, while its fisheries income was $153,487.

The fleet consisted now of ninety-eight vessels, only three of which were under fifty tons; each year the catch was increasing, though the bounty restrictions and high protective tariff were handicaps to the expansion of the fisheries. However, confidence in the future was evidenced by the establishment in 1831 of a new bank, Grand Bank, named for the Banks where Marblehead fishermen had fished since the town began. Local financing for vessels and voyages was now available and captains could take their money from out the keg or false floor for the bank's safe keeping. Many of them never did. The same year the Marblehead Seamen's Charitable Society was formed to assist (and did for the next sixty years) those mariners who ended up high and dry without sufficient friends or funds.

The tumultuous Jacksonian era was shifting alliances throughout the country and intensifying controversy over the role of the state and the federal governments. After the second presidential election in which Marblehead had given its majority to Andrew Jackson, the president came to Marblehead where he was accorded a warm welcome and made a formal address. The display of unity was deceiving, for the Whigs had organized in opposition and the very next year would not join in the July Fourth celebration, but held their own.

Other developments followed swiftly: the telegraph, friction matches, hard coal and the railroad. The Eastern Railroad branch from Marblehead to Salem was opened in 1839 with the station located at Pleasant and Sewall streets. Steam engines had been in use for about four years and the passenger cars were still designed like large stagecoaches. Yet, with rough roadbeds of stones, no springs and hand brakes, the "iron horse" was greeted here with mixed reactions: "You got upset in a coach—and there you were! You get upset in a rail-car—and, damme, where are you?" The trip to Salem took fifteen minutes, cost twelve and a half cents and there were five round trips a day. Fifty cents would buy an additional transfer ticket to Boston. The first locomotive, named Marblehead, was engineered by Joseph E. Glover. The engine house was a short distance away from the depot and every kid wanted to ride the cowcatcher on the turntable near Anderson and Bessom streets. Sometimes the train would roar along at twenty miles an hour, although the track to Salem had been publicly criticized for its many curves. The frequent minor accidents and the wild stories of near-misses kept the town agog. One night in 1848 the last train from Salem collided with the Lynn train killing six Marbleheaders and injuring many others. Nevertheless, that same year there was more pressure for a railroad branch directly to Boston. Marblehead needed extra freight service to haul the annual tonnage which was estimated to be 1,300 tons of cordage and hemp, 1,200 tons general merchandise, 600 tons of shoes and 600 tons of fish. All other merchandise was shipped by sea or by wagon, especially wagonloads of hay for the horses and cows. The town's Hay Scales kept the seller honest by the use of an approved scale at the weighing station where the wagons drove onto the scale, were weighed, and headed straight out into the next street with little or no delay.

Following an act of the legislature establishing an official fire department in Marblehead, the town chose nine fire wards whose responsibilities were to appoint forty-two men and to supervise the cisterns, engines, hoses, hooks and ladders. The penalty for citizens damaging department equipment would be a fine of five hundred dollars or five years in prison. The fire wards had some difficulty sorting out men, engine companies and equipment, especially with two private engines, Torrent and Relief, still in operation. After all, Marblehead had fought fires with its neighbors since the early colonial days. In 1751, when the town was bursting with foreign trade and new importance, wealthy King Hooper had donated the first engine, named Friend. The appointments of fire wards had begun then and in the next century included some of the best known and most famous men of Marblehead. After the Revolution the town purchased Endeavor, housed near the Newtown Bridge (Essex and Washington streets), and then Union stationed in the lower town at Washington and Orne streets. The waterfront fire of 1792 that had started from a child playing with a candle must have had all the drama of any fire in a town where nine tenths of the buildings were wood, the streets winding and narrow, and water available only from nearby wells, cisterns, ponds or the sea, and where strong winds swept the coastline much of the time. At the first sign of smoke or flame the cry of "Fire!" filled the Ways, someone banged and banged the fire gong and the sexton raced to toll the church bells. All business stopped while the men grabbed their shiny, gilt-named leather buckets and headed for the fire. Water-filled buckets moved from hand to hand to splash over the flames that consumed dried-out timbers. Down the "dry line" of young boys the buckets were passed, to be thrown in a pile until filled and sent back up the line. Other men tried to rescue the occupants and bits of their precious belongings. Watch the wind, wet down the nearest house, keep 'em coming—and heaven help the interloper—he got the extra bucketful in the face! In 1792 the well ran dry, the tide was out and four houses and several shops caught fire, and sparks burned vessels tied up to the wharf.

The officially organized fire department set out to be more businesslike—badges for each man, assignments to particular places and equipment, and restrictions on the use of ladders for fixing roofs and such. The fire wards then purchased two other engines, Marblehead and Essex. Each man's loyalty to his company ran deep and loud, from the company's furnished headquarters to fierce competition in arrival and performance at the fire, which now was fought with well-oiled leather hoses that shot the stream from the rhythmically pumped hand tubs. In 1845 the selectmen voted to buy the famous hand tub Gerry, named after Elbridge. Gerry and its company showed its worth very soon after at the big fire at Roundy's Mill commemorated by a stream of verses that only begin with:

> Twelve o'clock when all was still,
> A fire broke out in Roundy's Mill
> Old man Roundy didn't give a damn
> If the damned old thing burned flat as a pan,
> For he was insured in Rotterdam.

It was a November night, so the three-gallon jug kept at each engine house for "pneumonia" must have been drained just as dry as the wells in the drought of 1849. Then the firemen regulated the use of water at the town pumps on Franklin Street, Spring Street, Rope Makers Court, Watson Street and the Training Field.

That drought must have been a real strain, for the temperance societies (as their number grew and their leaders waxed more eloquent) had become more militant. They took it upon themselves to chop down apple trees—that easy source of hard cider—and pressured the legislature into a law forbidding the sale of less than fifteen gallons of liquor at one time—which proved unenforceable, hastening its repeal. One wonders if, in Marblehead, the town crier would, for a fee, have accepted temperance propaganda. He'd probably have cared more for his safety. He was busy, anyway, announcing arrivals of vessels, Lyceum lectures, and merchants' wares.

The mid-nineteenth-century criers like Jonas Bettis, Nathan Homan, Rea Nourse charged for each notice cried and moved around slowly, ringing the big, resonant bell for attention. Then the town crier stood still on particular corners and in loud, rounded tones spoke out the news and notices. The town paid many a charge of fifty cents each for a "Crieing notice" for drawing jurors, cost of a new schoolhouse, and special meetings. Rea Nourse not only rang the bell, but also invented all kinds of household products like ketchup and Nourse's Leather Preservative that guaranteed to penetrate boots and keep feet dry to avoid consumption. But it was Jonas Bettis' unfortunate duty to drag himself around the silent streets with heavy feet and heavier heart to call the women to the wharf that fateful day in 1846.

The first vessel had returned early from the fall fare and her damage foretold the tragic story. On that day of September 19 the Marblehead fishing fleet lay over the Grand Banks of Newfoundland ready to begin hauling in cod. By 9:00 a.m. a storm could be seen in the distance and, as the hours went by, the skies darkened, the winds picked up until by 3:00 p.m. the hurricane-force gale hit with fury, and the seas became mountainous. Suddenly, the wind changed and slammed the vessels from another direction snapping their masts and rigging. The cross seas caused the ships to roll and leap and pitch until it was impossible to steer. Some vessels that had dropped anchor foundered or capsized or seemed to disappear in the waves and then right themselves; others cut loose and drifted; if they could get steerage way and run before it, a vessel could almost be blown to the European coast. At midnight there came a lull and in the darkness no skipper could assess the damage except to his own vessel; yet, the sea was filled with debris that told too much. Daylight gave it away—a demolished fleet and no sign of eleven or more vessels.

When the grim numbers were finally known, 65 men and boys had been lost, leaving 43 widows and 155 fatherless children—gone were men, property and confidence. In Rev. Edward Lawrence's sermon on disasters at sea, given at all the churches, he reviewed the terrible losses of past years and this storm of 1846. For the first time the question was asked aloud: "Is it worth it?"

The question went unanswered; cordwaining did increase, but salt water does not easily evaporate in a breed of men like Marbleheaders, men like the old mariners of the Marblehead Seamen's Charitable Society who collected funds for the bereft families and for a monument to those lost at sea. The usual undercurrent of controversy touched on whether the $350 should all go to the widows and whether the names of the other seamen who died in their beds could be included. On a beautiful afternoon in 1848 strangers from many towns joined the natives at the dedication of the "Fishermen's Monument." The tolling bell did seem to be ringing the death knell of Marblehead's great fisheries.

Manufacturing, the western frontier, the Far East, slavery and expansion caught everyone in its exciting turmoil. The Mexican War (which was generally opposed in New England) tempted few local recruits to the distant Alamo. The next election day brought Marblehead its annual celebration with a military parade, stores full of candy and fruit nectars and special exercises on the Common. Then, in November, the Whig candidate, Zachary Taylor, was elected and announced at a victory rally that there would be no slavery in the new state of California—and all that seemed mighty remote to Marblehead.

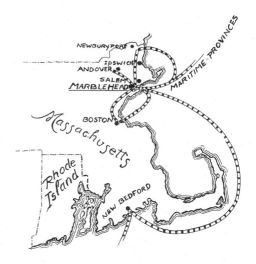

·UNDER GROUND–RAILWAY·

10. Black and Gold

A YOUNG MAN from nearby Newburyport, William Lloyd Garrison, had spoken aloud words that had pricked the consciences of many New Englanders since 1776—freedom, wasn't it meant for everyone? The noble Declaration had promised "life and liberty," although it carefully and deliberately omitted any mention of slavery. That particular moment of crisis demanded a consensus of North and South on the pivotal question of separation from Great Britain; slavery could be faced later when, or if, America emerged victorious. A census ordered in 1776 reported that of the almost half million Negroes living in the thirteen colonies, only 5,249 lived in Massachusetts or ⅛ percent of the state's population. Of that number 1,049 came from Essex County which boasted 50,903 inhabitants along the thriving seacoast. In the spirit of the Declaration of Independence many Marbleheaders, such as Commodore Samuel Tucker and William R. Lee, freed their Negroes immediately, though the rootless souls who had nowhere to go often preferred to stay on as paid employees. The British, to foment further civil strife, offered all Negroes their freedom in a British possession and some took advantage of the enticement, only to discover a new set of problems in Halifax. Some Negroes "owned" by Tories hid, or refused to leave, hoping to become an integral part of America's independence. Still others fought for America's freedom; among them Marblehead's Cato Prince and Joseph Brown who joined the Continental Army, served faithfully and, finally, received recognition and a pension from the government. "Black Joe" Brown's tavern became the focal point for 'Lection Week, usually the last week of May, and a vacation time for all.

The Massachusetts State Constitution had clearly stated in 1780 that all men were free and equal and that there would be no bondage. Interpretation and enforcement were ineffective until 1783 when the Walker–Jennison decision by the State Supreme Court confirmed the legal emancipation of slaves in Massachusetts. Very soon after the problem of relocating the manumitted slaves placed an extra burden on Massachusetts towns' relief funds as unemployed Negroes drifted from place to place searching for a home and occupation. Marblehead's Town Meeting in April, 1788, directed a census to be taken of "Affercins and Negroes" and ordered drifters to leave town or be prosecuted. Some must have moved to Salem, for when that town took similar action two years later among those listed were several Negroes recorded as coming from Marblehead: Judey Clark, Vilot Mirgort, Diner Lord, Susanr Candey; Forteen Lorthrop, James Black, William Jonson and their wives and eight children. These unusual names for persons from West Africa indicated the extent of their loss of identification when they were bartered away by a tribal chief or stolen by slave gangs. Unable to understand their language, owners gave slaves a new name (often a familiar name at the southern port of arrival) and later a freed slave often adopted the last name of the family with whom he had lived. Where these nomadic Negroes eventually settled would be almost impossible to trace, although there are some indications in the referral of the costs of those who became public charges. The town of their first residence was considered to be responsible for their Negroes. Marblehead records pathetic examples in the overseers' bills: a four-dollar charge from Boston for the burial of a former black resident's illegitimate child; a two-dollar-a-week board fee from Ipswich for a "Marblehead black woman in distress and in need of relief," daughter of "Sambo" Orne and Rosanna who, at the time when slavery was abolished, was servant to Richard Harris. The town was advised to pay Ipswich for her support or remove her to Marblehead. Similar relocation problems arose in only a few states, for the national constitution had not freed the slaves. At the convention a few Southerners, like George Mason, had come out openly for abolition while some Northerners, mindful of the New England profits from southern slave importation, relegated the decision to each state, claiming it was a political or economic issue. The harsh expediency of organizing a national government, while any semblance of unity remained alive, resulted in a compromise whereby the southern states had agreed to end the importation of slaves by 1808; when 1808 came, the slave traders evaded prosecution by sailing under another flag.

By 1815 the United States Navy was using swift Baltimore Clippers to pursue swift Baltimore Clippers smuggling slaves. Marblehead skippers and vessels were not found among these slave traders. A few years later the government declared the slave trade to be piracy, punishable by death. Slave trade was the official concern, but what about those who already were slaves?

The Society of Friends and other groups promoted recolonization in Africa by freed Negroes. Not many blacks wanted to go; only a small percentage were ever given the opportunity. Then William Lloyd Garrison declared his nonviolent "war" on slavery demanding immediate abolition, proclaiming, in spite of threats, jail, abuse; "I will be heard." Heard he was—in his newspaper *Liberator* (1831) and in tracts, petitions to Congress, and lectures to antislavery groups. The New England Anti-Slavery Society was organized in 1832 and within five years chapters were established in 118 towns, including Lynn, Salem and Marblehead. Their efforts to awaken the public concern about slavery were supported by their own commitment to conduct any escaped slave to safety and freedom. Southern antislavery sympathizers were informed of the sailing schedule of New England vessels; friendly crewmen made the contact and guarded the wharf while the stowaway was smuggled aboard.

Marblehead's port was used on the inbound route from New York and New Bedford as a connection with Salem and Andover and as an embarkation point where escapees could wipe out a trail by going to Newburyport, Portland or Halifax by water. Because of the bounties on fugitives and some local citizens who disapproved of this lawless practice, the runaways were hidden in secret staircases, false-front ells, unmarked closets, partitioned cellars and attics. Marblehead was not lacking in hideaways; they just needed to dust off the cobwebs from the old smugglers' haunts—perhaps some of the old beach tunnels could still be used.

Those who understood the risk and yet endangered their lives over the years were Simeon Dodge and his wife, Samuel Goodwin, John Purvis, Dr. Samuel L. Young, and other anonymous collaborators who went unrecorded. They used A. C. Orne's house as a cover-up for secret planning meetings; during most clandestine operations friendly neighbors stationed themselves to sound the warning. The Dodges were Marblehead's rescue mission for decades—in their tiny room under a trap door they housed, clothed and fed fugitive slaves, sometimes, for weeks until a safe, carefully timed escape could be arranged along the route. At the Anti-Slavery Convention at Georgetown in 1841 Samuel Goodwin represented the Marblehead group in the formation of the Liberty Party which advocated the end of slavery in Washington, D.C., which Congress itself had the power to abolish in the nation's capitol. In 1844 the Liberty Party was on the ballot in Marblehead, but managed to get only the votes of six abolitionists. A far cry from freeing Washington, D.C., of slavery was congressional action establishing the Fugitive Slave Act of 1850 in exchange for no slavery in California. Federal commissioners were now appointed with full powers to reclaim a fugitive slave anywhere and return him to the claimant and, "At no trial or hearing . . . shall the testimony of such alleged fugitives be admitted as evidence." Citizens were directed to aid in execution of the law and those harboring or obstructing were liable to a fine of one thousand dollars and six months in prison. Cooperative citizens could claim a five-dollar- to ten-dollar bounty, plus expenses, for turning in a fugitive. Antislavery involvement was now dangerous business. Society members went underground; other infuriated citizens formed vigilante committees to warn of the arrival of southern sheriffs, sometimes, by ringing the church bells. The more radical group was the New England Anti-Man Hunting League whose purpose was to kidnap "the slave hunters" and hold them, unharmed, until the fugitive escaped; in Marblehead the league had only seven members. They didn't have many opportunities to function, for the southern sheriffs were being incessantly harassed in Boston. The first year of the Fugitive Act southern sheriffs had appeared in Boston to pick up William Craft and his wife. The Crafts, who had been well educated by the southern Quakers, would have become influential advocates and were particularly sought out by the sheriffs. The "Underground Railway" went into action carrying the Crafts from Boston to Brookline, by wagon to Marblehead, then by boat to Portland where they were put on a vessel bound for England.

Then one night a sheriff showed up unexpectedly in Marblehead, recaptured a fugitive slave, and quickly carried him off. The irate townspeople were loud and fervent in their reactions. *The People's Advocate and Marblehead Mercury*, living its motto: "Independent in Everything—Neutral in Nothing," published the speeches and

flood of letters damning the Fugitive Law as "infamous and unconstitutional" and Negro slavery as "vile and wicked." The clergy
were asked to speak out on the Fugitive Law from their pulpits and
anger swept the town. The less popular rebuttal claimed that it was
wrong to break the law, although it be a bad one, and that such action was affecting the southern orders for northern merchandise, including Marblehead shoes.

The turmoil of the country over slavery in the western territory
and congressional "deals" was felt in microcosm in Marblehead. The
Free-Soilers formed a political party which Garrison had always resisted; their answer to Garrison's plea, "How long will it take such a
propaganda to arouse a sleeping nation?" was "Until doomsday!"
The ticket of the Free-Soilers in Marblehead was promoted by a
rally where free oyster stew was served to all; but in the 1851 election they took only 20 percent of the vote. The "Know-Nothing"
Party whose slogan was "I know" had its advocates in Marblehead
and ran a fairly successful ticket; old party alignments were being
split asunder. Local people listened to the eloquent speeches of
Frederick Douglass of Lynn—a black who could speak of the black
man's plight from his own early experiences.

Marbleheaders, who always loved to sing, applauded the stirring
protest songs of Lynn's Hutchinson Family Singers who sang out
"O Liberate the Bondsman" and "Hope for the Slave." The newspaper regularly carried contemporary poetry of local people, renowned American poets and, occasionally, poems by a writer called
Harriet Beecher Stowe whose book broke across Marblehead like an
enveloping wave and sold like fresh mackerel. *Uncle Tom's Cabin*
brought home to a wide audience the agonizing experiences of slavery, long understood by those active in the antislavery societies.
Now, slavery was on everyone's mind.

The shout of "Gold!" that emanated from California precipitated
one of the most bizarre, adventurous, greedy, glorious, daring and
picturesque decades of American history. That sparkling dust flung
into the eyes of adventuresome Americans brought on the greatest
gold rush ever known. It all began on January 28, 1848, at Sutter's
Mill with one small nugget, well publicized by an enterprising
storekeeper; on May 25 embattled John Sutter wrote in his diary,
"Great hosts continue to the mountains." If the skeptical Easterner
delayed pulling up his stakes, the official confirmation in December
of 1848 by the president of the United States swept away all doubt
and the Midas pilgrimage erupted.

No longer did moving westward mean a steady, slow-moving

wagon train filled with families, furniture and dreams of a new start at a frontier settlement; this was a treasure hunt for men traveling fast and alone, who would dig and pan the mountains of gold and return to live in luxury. Most Easterners were too impatient to face the long, arduous land route and they, quite naturally, turned toward the sea. What they needed was speed and a strong, swift vessel that could round the Horn without running into coastal ports for supplies and repairs. American shipping had been progressing by leaps and bounds since the War of 1812, moving away from the old tubby trader to the fast, competitive coastal and ocean-going packet, then a giant step to the sharp-bowed swift Baltimore Clipper with its tall raking masts and great spread of canvas. The China trade was succumbing to American competition while British designers sat on their hands, confidently protected by their maternal navigation laws. The China Clippers and East Indiamen were the progenitors of the most glorious American sailing ship ever to cut through the waves —the extreme clipper, whose creation was accelerated by the lust for California's gold.

In any era in which the sea was an integral part, Marblehead had to be a part of it. Regardless of the decline of Banks fishing and the growth of landlubbers' shoe business, Marblehead was enabled to take part in America's shipbuilding boom through the investment of Edmund Kimball, one of the incorporators of the Grand Bank. In Red Stone Cove the skilled ship carpenters and craftsmen were busy once more on schooners and small clippers equipped with cotton sails made in Marblehead sail lofts and rigging from the nearby ropewalk. The town was proud of the revival of shipbuilding and turned out in hundreds along the wharves and shoreline to see *Robert Hooper* launched in 1849. Then came another handsome vessel of white oak, *Compromise*, followed by *Anna Kimball, Elizabeth Kimball* and several others including the barque, *Riga* and a brig, *Curlew*. But Marblehead did not have money, men or, especially, yard space to compete with the Boston yards, which, guided by the genius of Donald McKay and backed by wealthy shippers, were building clippers that awed the imagination.

An almost incredible interlocking of circumstances guaranteed the United States this pinnacle in its ascendency on the seas. The timing of that glorious, fleeting era molded together the experience and skill of New England's artisans and builders: the tall timbers of the region, the cotton from the South in the hands of experienced sailmakers, hemp from the east Indiamen for the long established ropewalks. Yet, all this might have remained inert without the brilliant, imaginative men who designed the clippers and the intrepid, daredevil Yankee skippers who sailed them. It was "Up for California" with full speed ahead for one long, continuous voyage around Cape Horn and along the coast of the two Americas to San Francisco and the Golden Gate. The purpose was not to do battle with other nations or compete for trade, but to transport passengers—*fast*. Speed was the singular goal, for these vessels with their slender hulls and sharp lines were never designed for freight capacity. Every person who had hocked his belongings to buy gold-digging tools and a berth on a clipper looked, prayerfully, at the lofty spars, long yards and acres of canvas and instinctively knew that on the treacherous fifteen-thousand-mile voyage the safety of the vessel was only as certain as the daring and skill of her skipper. That reaction was shared by the passengers, crew, designer and the owners.

When naval architect, Donald McKay, was at the zenith of his career, he was asked by his backer, George F. Train, to design and construct the finest clipper ever conceived, weighing as much as two thousand tons, and to christen her *Flying Cloud*. McKay's response was the extreme clipper, *Flying Cloud*, a finely honed racing machine born of his genius and built by Yankee craftsmen in his East Boston shipyard to unheard-of dimensions: 1,783 tons, 229 feet overall, 40-foot beam, 88-foot mainmast and 82-foot mainyard. She was an incredible beauty of a ship and more than ready to accept the challenge to slash the sailing time to the gold fields. McKay and the new owners, Grinnell & Minturn, were out for the record on the maiden voyage. The next decision was crucial. Which Yankee skipper would demand the utmost of the *Flying Cloud* and its crew, carry all the canvas possible, and travel the shortest route? It would take experience, skill, tenacity and daring—and their choice was a Marbleheader, Captain Josiah Perkins Creesy.

The local newspaper columns reported: "The magnificent clipper ship, *Flying Cloud*, was launched on Tuesday last (April 15, 1851) . . . everyone who has a taste for nautical beauty will be well paid by making her a visit at East Boston where she now lives . . . and the longest and largest clipper in the world is to be commanded by Captain Perkins Creesy." The vessel was visited by hundreds of people in Boston and then New York; the bets grew as the gamblers assessed the length, the sail area and the skipper. The race of all the clippers against time to California provoked huge wagers, and so many, that the voyage was split up into several race courses: Sandy Hook to the equator; 50° south in the Atlantic to 50° south in the Pacific, equator to San Francisco, and anchor to anchor time and other segments. The Captain's mate, Eleanor Prentiss Creesy, would sail as his navigator. Even for Marblehead they were an unusual pair.

"Perk" and "Nellie" Creesy were both born in Marblehead in 1814. Creesy went to sea without family fame or fortune, but with plenty of native intelligence and ambition that would carry him through all the grades to skipper by age twenty-three. The loneliness of those thirty-thousand-mile voyages brought Captain Creesy back to Marblehead for his bride, Eleanor Horton Prentiss. The women of the Prentiss family had long watched their men go to sea and then toiled through those many months caring for the children, animals and the household problems, all the while, anxiously, fearfully waiting for word of man or vessel. None of this was lost on Nellie and, when her turn came, she chose to go to sea with her man.

The marriage of Josiah and Eleanor took place in 1841 at the First Congregational Church in Marblehead. Soon after, they sailed to the Orient, never again to be regular residents of their native town. There were no children from the marriage. The Creesys were gone for years at a time on long voyages, for their vessels were in the China and East Indies trade for almost a decade and consistently recorded fast and profitable trips. The captain's prestige grew in New York and Boston, along with genuine respect for the efficiency of his female navigator. Eleanor Creesy learned to use a heavy, bulky sextant, to compute proficiently and to work with the new collection of information on winds and currents that had been systematized by Lt. Matthew F. Maury, U.S.N. In return she supplied Maury with the pertinent and detailed records from the logs of their swift crossings. The most important test of her computation and "Perk's" skill was just ahead.

On June 2, 1851, the race against time began as *Flying Cloud* left Pier 20 and swept out of New York under full sail. Captain Creesy's log carefully verified each day of the great adventure. It was no pleasure cruise. A few days out, *Flying Cloud* lost its main and mizzen and persistent gales and squalls demanded incessant shipboard repairs. The gales slowly diminished; the equatorial calm brought its antagonizing stagnation. But Creesy was never one to retire to his bunk, for he'd been known to shift cargo or mountains of sail to smell out the wind. The heat and the calm ended; the log reported *Flying Cloud* suddenly slammed by "hard gales and harder squalls . . . very turbulent sea . . . ship laboring hard and shipping larger quantities of water. . . ." The rough winter weather of Cape Horn set in with "thick weather, snowsqualls . . . thunder and lightning.

. . ." Captain Creesy stayed on deck all night long, for strong winds and heavy rain were setting *Flying Cloud* to the north where lay the dangerous, rocky tip of the continent. In the cold morning, there was Cape Horn just five miles north and the whole coast covered with snow.

Throughout the roughest night the tough, yet competent crew, including Charlie Bartlett and some other Marbleheaders, had confidence in their "old man." One sailor said, "He was the greatest man for carrying sail ever seen," but, quickly added, "and the smartest shipmaster who ever trod a quarter deck." The tall, stern-looking captain with weathered face and keen eyes carried his great body with dignity, yet moved with the agility of an able seaman in a heavy sea. He was proud, decisive driver with innate Yankee nerve and seamanship. A bold competitor with a lot of luck.

His luck might have been called "Nellie." While her captain was issuing orders to the first mate, his real mate was intently studying *Maury's Sailing Directions* while relying heavily upon her own computations and a decade of navigational experience. Long, tiring hours of holding the sextant or contending with wild seas or a rowdy crew didn't discourage this Marblehead woman; moreover, she was part of the scene in more ways than navigation. Like any demanding racing skipper, "Perk" Creesy was known as a driver, yet he had the enviable ability of a dynamic master to evoke intense loyalty and hard work from disparate groups of men, while his wife exhibited a real concern for the men and their life on shipboard. Mrs. Creesy was the ship's nurse and good provider. She saw to it that plenty of vegetables, chickens, ducks and pigs were taken aboard. Crews reported that the food was good and that they had plenty of sleep. Others repeated the story of her insistence that "the old man" slow down the vessel while dories were lowered to search for a man overboard. She had the racing spirit, too, especially on that July 31. With strong southeast winds pressing every sail, *Flying Cloud* made a (still unmatched) day's sailing record of 374 nautical (433½ statute) miles averaging 15⁶⁄₁₇ knots per hour for twenty-four hours. It was decades before the steamships equaled that day's run.

The tensions of the whole voyage dissolved suddenly at 11:30 a.m. on August 31 when the anchor plunged into San Francisco Bay. The angel figurehead seemed to be blowing a triumphant blast on her golden trumpet, for the sailing time to California had been reduced in one incredible voyage from 120 days to 89 days and 21 hours. That August 31, 1851, was a great day for Captain Josiah P. Creesy and his wife Eleanor, for on that morning all the elements of ship design, seamanship and navigation merged into a triumph that would engrave the Creesy name on the maritime records forever. *Flying Cloud* had ended the fastest voyage ever sailed from New York until two years later when Creesy broke his own record. When praising the crew Captain Creesy said, "They worked as one man—and that man was a hero." Greedy merchants, "outward bound" sailors and lonely eastern prospectors all joined the jubilant celebration—the East and West coasts were that much closer!

Later the exciting news spread to the investors and bettors at the Astor House in New York and to the Merchant's Exchange on Boston's State Street. Exultant newspaper editorials extolled the exploit, "It is a national triumph and points clearly and unmistakably to the preeminence upon the ocean that awaits the U.S.A."

While Boston and New York were still collecting their bets, Captain and Mrs. Creesy with a small crew (most sailors had dashed off to find their gold) produced still another win by reducing the sailing time from San Francisco to China. *Flying Cloud's* docking in New York evoked so much publicity and tumult that the Creesys escaped to Marblehead, undoubtedly for a special family celebration. Moreover, in a town whose love for the sea had never abated, it was a very personal victory.

The rush to California by clipper was like a golden shaft of light for the shipping business, but it faded fast. In the year of 1850 alone, 775 vessels arrived in California bringing 91,405 passengers with the gleam of gold shining in their eyes. Often the officers and crew disembarked with the passengers in the direction of Sutter's Mill or the last big strike; many a vessel never again sailed out of San Francisco harbor. Instead they became floating hotels, storage ships, hospitals, prisons—a floating city 'til their bottoms rotted out. Everyone came and went with the "diggings"; few supplies were manufactured locally, so inflationary prices soared on the "imported" merchandise. Shippers' freight rates soared to sixty dollars per ton, so even the clipper's smaller freight load paid off. Then, suddenly, the market was glutted, prices dived and so did the owners' profits, unless a seasoned captain-trader continued on to China before his return trip.

Grinnell-Minturn's Captain Creesy did that every time— loading up with a cargo of tea, silks, spice, rice or hemp—so, there was fortune at both ends of the voyage. Laden with a rich cargo of tea and silks on one return trip, gale winds and adverse currents forced *Flying Cloud* onto a coral reef, seriously damaging the keel and bottom planking. The skipper floated her off, though she was leaking at the rate of eleven inches an hour. Manning every pump throughout every watch, Creesy's Marblehead cussedness manifested itself, for, without stopping, the vessel limped the whole distance back to New York.

That accomplishment and the profits called for a lavish banquet with testimonials and a silver service for the Creesys. The presentation speaker called Captain Creesy "a skillful commander . . . with talents of a merchant as well as a shipmaster."

Josiah Creesy's brother, William, one of the most outstanding Baltimore Clipper commanders, displayed the same skill with his men and vessel. On the East Indiaman *Oneida* and the Baltimore Clipper *Mary Whittredge* Bill Creesy added his share of renown to the Creesy name.

One of the earliest clippers built in New York was *Houqua*, named after the highly respected Chinese merchant with whom so many traders had excellent business relations. The vessel avoided the opium trade; instead it was instrumental in proving the advantages of other profitable Chinese cargoes. In 1853 *Houqua*, under the command of Captain Richard Dixey of Marblehead, was one of the first ships to enter the newly opened port of Foochow, China, carrying the United States consul to his post. Captain Dixey's wife, Rebecca, was aboard and caused quite a stir as the first white woman to enter the city. The arrival of the consul necessitated the raising of the first American flag which was carried out by Marblehead crew members, William B. Symonds, Frank and John Millett. News of these skippers, their vessels and the excitement at the gold fields was well covered in Marblehead's newspaper.

Marblehead's frontier had always been on the sea, and its gold in quintals of fish or a trading venture, so *The People's Advocate* seemed to refrain from making California glitter too tempting and kept a nice balance of good and bad news. Not long after reporting that *Empire* arrived in New York from San Francisco with one and a half million in gold dust, a letter was published from a local man, already in California, saying that the whole venture was nothing but a lottery for although some good strikes were rumored, hundreds would soon starve unless they were "in trade." By August of 1850 a special column, "From California" appeared in the newspaper, mentioning the dangers of robbery but also adding that "gold appears to be abundant; one man has found a complete gold tree. . . ."

Still the pot of gold overflowed with tales of golden nuggets weighing from four to thirty-two pounds balanced against the gloomy news of the hanging of horse thieves and the severe fire in San Francisco. Marbleheaders in California sent a long letter to the newspaper, requesting that it be published so all their friends would know that Ben Hooper was running one store and Stephen Peach another in Stringtown; George Cloutman and Ben Dixey were in San Francisco, but Ben was leaving to peddle boots to the miners; Lewis Girdler was driving a mule team while Joe Phillips and Gus Gregory had a profitable dance house, but not in the town where the saloon was run by John Gardner with Dan Haskell acting as barkeeper. Oh, yes, and Captain Dan Bruce had "claimed" ten thousand dollars.

A long letter from another Marbleheader, Mrs. Maria L. Homan, was published, describing, with considerable humor, her Horn voyage and the entertainment organized by the ladies, such as, a concert in the cabin-saloon by talented passengers, a dance on deck, a play and Spanish lessons. Unlike her seasick, terrified companions, Mrs. Homan relished the gales, heavy seas, and mountainous waves. "It stormed for a week and I had an opportunity of seeing a storm at sea in all its grandeur." Once while she was in the dining saloon the great wave hit and beans and broken crockery became one, great mass. While other women fainted, Marblehead's offspring did not, and said, ". . . I was not at all afraid and my mirthfulness got just excited enough to enjoy the scene. . . ." Mrs. Homan was thrilled with the San Francisco harbor and was soon visited by her friends with whom she planned to stay until her brother arrived. "I have come to the right place, and I shall like [it]."

Wherever there was fighting the Marbleheaders found themselves in on it so, as the California Indian raids became more vicious, Captain Bartol placed his company, the *Washington Guards* (oh, shades of the Training Field!) at the disposal of the state. Capt. Joseph Wilson commanded the artillery; William Bartlett and Thomas Snow headed the scouting parties.

The names of Marbleheaders deceased far from home were sent back; few were listed as military casualties—more likely, illness or accident. Two unusual news items were an editorial protesting the growing use of opium imported from China—especially its use by women—and an effusive letter from Oregon raving about its beauty and tall timber and requesting Marbleheaders to send some of their best apple seeds to sow in far-off Oregon. The whole thing was too much for the publisher: he closed down the newspaper and went West!

Most Marblehead adventurers chose the sea route; on the other hand, before Captain Creesy and others had reduced the sailing time, the overland route appeared cheaper and quicker than 120 days at sea. At the first cry of "gold" eleven Marblehead men formed *The Marblehead Overland Mining Company* which sold shares to pay for supplies, weapons and transportation. "Overland" did not mean 'rounding the Horn, but rather, starting overland from a port in Mexico, then along the southern route to California by wagon, using native guides. Peter Doliber, Jonathan Chapman, Benjamin Wormstead, William Torrence, A. Cragin and N. R. Blaney (company president), plus several men from other towns, sailed on *Peerless* for Mexico, where they went overland to Brazos and then along the Rio Grande to Brownsville, Texas.

Soon after they were stopped by heavy storms, flash floods and immeasurable mud. Ill with the Mexican "pip" and very discouraged, they huddled in an abandoned farmhouse planning to split up and head for home. One wagon team started for New York, another for Boston, a third for Marblehead—those who were well and impatient rode off on horseback. One Marbleheader joined a passing wagon train and reached California. Doliber and Blaney died on the way and, exhausted and broke, the others finally arrived home.

In 1853 over ten million dollars worth of gold was taken out of California in eight months; however, not long after, prospectors realized that digging gold was backbreaking, spirit-killing work and the placer mines were already well washed out. The 1857 financial panic, war fears, and the repeal of the British Navigation Acts that put the British back in shipping competition blurred the golden glint and ended the glorious era of the "Queen of the Sea," the clipper ship.

Not atypical was the fate of *Flying Cloud*, whose owners now reneged on the expensive repairs necessitated by turbulent voyages, the twisting and extreme leverage of the massive spars. Captain Creesy refused to sail unless the vessel was reconditioned, and so they parted. *Flying Cloud* was laid up at a New York dock and its skipper retired to Salem with his navigator. The retirement was temporary for both, but never again would they race together—there were no more *Flying Cloud* records without Captain Creesy. Her masts and spars were later shortened and the canvas reduced for less strain on the hull and worn rigging. Sold to British merchants, the noble *Flying Cloud* was used ignobly on a North Atlantic run until she went aground on a shoal and was dragged into New Brunswick. There, during repairs, she caught fire and her metal consigned for scrap.

Her captain didn't live to see her disgrace for, after having come out of retirement to skipper in the Civil War and then to sail *Archer* on his last California voyage, Josiah Perkins Creesy suffered a severe stroke. The years of nights and days on deck during equatorial heat or arctic cold had taken their toll and "Perk" Creesy died at fifty-seven.

Alexis de Tocqueville well described the American mariners when he compared them to the Europeans: "The European sailor navigates with prudence; he only sets sail when the weather is favorable; if an unfortunate accident befalls him, he puts into port; at night he furls a portion of his canvas; and when the whitening billows intimate the vicinity of land, he checks his way and takes an observation of the sun.

"But the American neglects these precautions and braves these dangers. He weighs anchor in the midst of tempestuous gales; by night and day he spreads his sheets to the winds; he repairs as he goes along such damage as his vessel may have sustained from the storm; and when he, at last, approaches the term of his voyage, he darts onward to the shore as if he already descried a port. The Americans are often shipwrecked, but no trader crosses the seas so rapidly. And as they perform the same distance in shorter time, they can perform it at a cheaper rate." Then he concluded that Americans have "a sort of heroism" which is a quiet understatement of the courage, skill and initiative of the masters of the clipper ships that opened up the Golden West. Marblehead's involvement was symbolized by a mariner like Creesy of whom it was said, "Captain Creesy typifies the best traditions of his profession, and stands as a noble representative of his class."

11. *Marblehead from Mid-Century*

MARBLEHEAD had other matters than "fool's gold" on its mind, for the town had entered upon a period of business growth, town improvement, and a twenty-year population growth unparalleled until the twentieth century.

The shipbuilders, expanded sail lofts and ropewalks were turning out modern, one-hundred-ton schooners for the fisheries. The vessels and the fishermen were now fewer; yet, the Banks were still fished by a hard core of seafaring men who were mighty upset when the British, aware that the War of 1812 treaty had produced no definite settlement, arbitrarily set limits on American fishing. That old Marblehead fighting spirit flared and fishermen spoke of war—but Britain soon agreed on the premise of "common waters."

Meanwhile, the seeds of a lively new interest in sailing craft already had been planted in Marblehead, though germination would be gradual; however, sailing for pleasure and sport was a promising outgrowth of the recent industrial fortunes and the frustrations of the land-bound sailors. The regatta became part of the summer's entertainment; boats of intermediate tonnage racing for a spyglass or set of colors were allowed thirty seconds per ton and warned to obey racing rules which forbade throwing ballast overboard. Within four years the regatta was called an "imposing spectacle" with crowds on the Neck and Cat Island watching thirteen boats cover the twelve-mile course mentally charted by the professional captains and crews. The Fort Sewall guns discharged their cannon as the 1848 starting signal for the "grand display of nautical skill" at Marblehead.

There was almost as much excitement as on 'Lection Day, when stores and homes were overflowing with gingerbread, pop beer, nuts and India crackers to take along to the "exhibition at the great Hippodrome on the Common" featuring animals, acrobats and loud music. Among the ladies attending were those who were wearing bloomer dresses! Women looked askance; men enjoyed it, as did the local editor who reminded everyone that the present tight-bodiced, long dress compressed the heart, lungs, liver and spine and "checks the free circulation of vital fluid. . . ." Personally, he approved of a lady being able to adorn her person with a graceful, comfortable costume, instead of carrying cloth enough to sail a schooner.

Change was almost frightening: no more Publishment Day when marriage intentions had to be posted on the Town House bulletin board; a woman was principal of the Academy which now urged Marblehead's daughters to continue their education. The Lyceum not only featured the "Juvenile Songsters" who paraded in a Festival of the Roses, but also encouraged local interest in fine arts and membership in the American Art Union.

The mystique of Marblehead had always appealed to literary minds, but most notably to the world-renowned New England poets of the mid nineteenth century. The town's antiquity and legend, its relish for the unsettled score with the sea, the barrenness and beauty, the dance with fate, the loneliness of silent courage, all drew to this relatively isolated spot Whittier, Hawthorne, Holmes, Longfellow, Lowell, Lucy Larcom and many sincere literary hopefuls. The popular John Greenleaf Whittier came from nearby Amesbury to absorb the spirit of Marblehead and to recall his affection for Evelyn Bray (who lived on State Street) in "The Sea Dream" in which he writes of the old gray fort, the lighthouse and the blown sea foam, and then in "The Wishing Bridge":

Among the legends sung or said
  Along our rocky shore
The Wishing Bridge of Marblehead
  May well be sung once more.

In "The Swan Song of Parson Avery" Whittier sadly records the loss of the town's first minister, and in "Skipper Ireson's Ride" dramatically paints (though inaccurately) the fate of "Flud Oirson".

Henry Wadsworth Longfellow, of whom was said, ". . . he touched his world with a magic . . ." was never able to shut out the intriguing sea; so, he often came to Marblehead to camp or stay at a boarding house near the beach. There he wrote "The Ropewalk," and "The Fire of Driftwood":

> The windows, rattling in their frames,
>   The ocean, roaring up the beach,
> The gusty blast, the bickering flames,
>   All mingled vaguely in our speech.

To Oliver Wendell Holmes the romance of Agnes Surriage was most appealing and in a long, sentimental ballad he described her fate.

The peaceful beach, the simplicity and acceptance of the fishermen were sought out by Nathaniel Hawthorne when he came from the gloomy, shadowy house at Salem. He said he walked to Marblehead to make "Footsteps in the Sand" as he strolled along Devereux Beach "from craggy promontory to yonder rampart of broken rocks . . ." and then turned to climb the hill to the harborside where he could talk with fishermen who "know and understand me and my needs."

The women's voices were heard, too, although mostly in song. Lucy Larcom, poetess of the North Shore and dear friend of Whittier's, wrote of women's liberation and the loneliness of a fisherman's wife—both reflected in her famous poem (later put to music), "Hannah Binding Shoes":

> Round the rocks of Marblehead,
> Outward bound, a schooner sped.
>   Silent, lonesome,
> Hannah's at the window binding shoes.

During the Civil War exhausted men in both camps listened to the eternal lament of the lonely soldier, "Do They Miss Me At Home?" written by Caroline Briggs Mason of Marblehead. All the while the amateur poets of the town were producing a wealth of poems and essays that the local newspaper published weekly.

The weekly serial story in the newspaper touchingly narrated the harvest of love reaped from devotion, goodness and temperance. The Washington Division Number 3 of the Sons of Temperance were bent on drying up Marblehead, so they sponsored the Lyceum showing of the *Panorama of the Drunkard*, three thousand feet of moving canvas and two hundred figures illustrating the evils of intemperance.

There were other town activists pleading for faster mail delivery and a uniform, prepaid charge of two cents per letter, the abolishment of capital punishment, the ten-hour-a-day work law, and the annexation of Cuba. One event in which everyone participated was the seventy-fifth anniversary of the Declaration of Independence. It dawned with a salute of fifty guns and pealing church bells, repeated again at noon and at sunset. An impressive procession of over two thousand wound their way through the streets and one editor wrote, "to give a fair view . . . would require a pen larger than St. Mark's and the pencil of a Hogarth."

At the dinner on the Common the traditional Thirteen-Colony toasts and spontaneous sentiments by representatives of the old families hailed Old Marblehead—"Forever renowned for her devotion to the cause of Liberty and Humanity." Nothing could have surpassed the universal joy of the day, except the first fireworks display ever put on in Marblehead—what a glorious Fourth!

A stirring part of every Marblehead parade was the appearance of the military companies then flourishing in town. The three companies, the Lafayette Guards, the Glover Light Guard and the newest Sutton Light Infantry, resplendent in their uniforms and silken banners, were well drilled, though hardly for war, which still seemed remote.

Nor could the town have anticipated the appearance of additional religious sects in the next few years. An unusual development in 1852 was the alliance of several well-known families with the doctrines of the recently founded Spiritualism. Meetings at first were held in private homes; then there were public lectures and, finally, open invitations to "a levee at Bassett Hall." It was not strange that at a seaport already imbued with subtle undertones of superstition and yearning for one more contact with the sailor never seen again, that spiritualism or "manifestations" made quite a penetration. Then, rather suddenly, a third Congregational church called the South Church erupted from a doctrinal and personal schism within the "Old North." Shortly after, in 1859, the Roman Catholics, who had been attending Mass in Salem or in private homes, built a Marblehead church on Prospect Street.

Religious and civil freedom had always been accepted in Marblehead, yet, women's rights seemed no further advanced than in the rest of Massachusetts. Under the old provincial charter a woman owning property was allowed to vote; yet, in spite of tradition, the 1780 State Constitution wiped out that right. Some women who protested were ignored; some men like William Lloyd Garrison fought for women's rights along with blacks' civil rights. Women met throughout the state to put pressure on the legislature; Marblehead women sponsored public lectures to "Vindicate Our Rights." The General Court finally inched along by passing a bill giving a married woman the right to trade and own a business; she could be a witness, though not originate a search warrant; she could own property, yet not vote. The Women's Rights Convention urged that every woman holding property "resist taxation until . . . she is fully represented at the ballot box."

Marblehead women had borne "flocks of children," worked on the fish flakes, tenaciously held homes together while the mariners were gone for months. They were a strong, hardy lot—almost as vocal as their husbands—yet, the cemetery plots were filled with those who, assisted only by a midwife or relative, had died in childbirth. Mothers who survived twelve to fourteen births often lived to inherit the house, fish flakes and, sometimes, a vessel from their seafaring husbands(s). Yet, the town records for centuries are bare of women's names except to list a dole for a poor widow; the only evidence of her participation lies in the deeds and wills where her mark (X) indicated the level of her education. By the middle of the nineteenth century local women were receiving more education, recognition by liberal leaders, and were finding new outlets for their talents. Writer Marcia L. Homan sailed alone on a clipper to California and Caroline Briggs Mason's poetry and songs became nationally recognized. Others, whose names had to be as secret as their underground activities, were involved in the antislavery movement. Women were moving out into the world, just as Marblehead women, who had always sewed shoes at home, were moving out into factories, operating machines, and were being given more rest periods but less money.

General business growth was rapid; in 1851 the county estimated the valuation of Marblehead at $2,033,900. That year a Boston firm published a best seller entitled *Our First Men, or A Catalogue of the Richest Men in Massachusetts*, a book with apt, uninhibited comments on their origins, financial sources and charitable attitudes. It listed thirteen Marblehead residents, some longtime inhabitants like Blackler, Hammond, Haskell, Hooper and Woolredge along with newer residents like Flagg, Briggs, and Chamberlin. The two wealthiest, 'twas said, were Edmund Kimball ($150,000) who began with limited means as a carpenter, moved on to the fisheries and finally to shipbuilding; secondly, Mrs. William Reed, who had inherited $200,000 and was praised as truly understanding the word "benevolent."

The shoe business and the railroad were bringing in people and

trade, and business was expanding in several directions in the manufacturing of oil skins, glue, rope and sails. However, the largest
number of men and women were employed by shoe manufacturers
(most of whom were Marbleheaders) who had built their factories
close to the railroad facilities.

The factory system was accelerated by the initiative and energy
of Joseph M. Bassett who introduced the shoe sewing machine to
Marblehead and then invented many mechanical refinements. Production now necessitated concentrating the workers in a central
shop, though some preparatory steps were still "farmed out" to
homes and "ten-footers." Mr. Bassett was a developer and builder;
his various enterprises opened up much of Mid-Town. When the
1857 financial panic hit the country, of the five large factories Bassett alone kept his factories operating, employing as many men as
possible. There were soon many more unemployed because of the
termination of the fish bounty, the prewar reduction of shoe orders,
and the increased cost of leather.

Early in 1860 a recession hit the shoe business and by mid-Febru-
ary the first labor strike began in Marblehead where there were
more than one thousand shoe employees. The strikers analyzed the
difficulties as unfair wages, competition by price reductions—not
a better product—and a migration wave of untrained workers. Over
80 percent of the workers struck and, though there was some trouble
around the plants, most of the town stood behind the workers, including Mr. Bassett who appeared at the mass meeting and offered
encouragement and financial aid. Almost two months later the factories were able to reopen by agreeing to pay increases; most owners also agreed to a "bill of prices" to support higher-priced quality
shoes. Business conditions had not improved measurably, when the
news that Fort Sumter had been bombarded reached Marblehead
followed quickly by President Abraham Lincoln's call for troops on
April 15, 1861.

Marblehead had been outraged by the Dred Scott decision de-
claring a slave to be property and deeply disturbed by the Harper's
Ferry raids and secession talk. The president's call to arms found the
three Marblehead militia companies alerted, and, as in 1776, Marblehead reacted swiftly and said goodby to its men early the next
morning when the rain-soaked depot was crowded with cheering
yet troubled townspeople. According to the official report of the
adjutant general of Massachusetts, the Marblehead troops pulled into
Boston at 8:00 a.m.—the first troops to arrive—and excited
throngs marched with them to Faneuil Hall to the tune of the vin-
taged "Yankee Doodle." The new Mugford Guards and the four

other companies became part of the Eighth Regiment of Marblehead Volunteers. Recruiting was brisk, then Governor Andrew said, "For Heaven's sake, don't send any more men from Marblehead, for it is imposing on your goodness to take so many as have already come." Town Meeting, which immediately voted five thousand dollars for assistance to the families of volunteers, ended in true Marblehead fashion with three boisterous cheers for the Union.

Marblehead served in many battle areas with the Army of the Potomac and the town's highest ranking officer was Col. Benjamin F. Peach. At Annapolis the Marblehead companies assisted in refloating "the noble old frigate," *Constitution*, from a mud bank and returning her to New York for safekeeping. Young boys falsified their ages to join the action and the tale of fifteen-year-old Albert Mansur of Marblehead was often repeated around town. Albert (against his parents' advice) had enlisted as a drummer boy in the Massachusetts 23rd Regiment and found himself in General Burnside's expedition at Roanoke Island. He participated in the landing then, as the enemy retreated, he drummed the troops along, using broken gun stocks. A noisy and obvious target, he was shot and died on the field, asking, "Which beat?" He had been told, somewhat prematurely, "the field is ours" which, eventually, it was. When the battle ended, Albert's father had been severely wounded and Lt. John Goodwin and Sgt. Gamaliel Morse of Marblehead were dead. The war was longer than ever expected, but was shortened, no doubt, by the successful blockade by the Union navy and privateers.

The North had only a meager navy of twenty vessels, so new gunboats and privateers were, once more, the answer. The gunboat *Marblehead* was launched on the Merrimac River in October of 1861. Marblehead skippers of clippers and fishing schooners signed up for the U. S. Navy to shut off the flow of supplies to the Confederacy. Clipper captains played a major role: Michael B. Gregory was in charge of outfitting vessels; William D. Gregory commanded the U. S. *Bohio* which captured several valuable prize ships and pulled off a trick worthy of a Commodore Tucker or Manley. The *Bohio*, manned by many Marbleheaders, was in pursuit of a large, suspicious vessel which was outsailing her. Captain Gregory had his crew rig up a stovepipe and connect it to barrels in which they burned tar, rope or any smoky material while others threw water on the sails as the winds helped to increase *Bohio's* speed. The Confederate vessel, *Henry Travers*, concluding that it would be hopelessly outclassed by a "steamship," surrendered. At the same time Captain Samuel B. Gregory commanded the steamer, *Western World*, which was used to invade various southern rivers to cut telegraph wires, evacuate black slaves or reinforce coastal troops. Samuel Gregory was so successful as a blockader that the Confederacy put a price on his head.

Captain "Perk" Creesy must have liked the feel of a quarter-deck again, for his *Ino*, with an entire Marblehead crew of Roundy, Pedrick, Doliber, Gale, Graves, Brown, Hooper, Hawkes and others, sailed a new record for the fastest crossing of the Atlantic— twelve days to Cadiz. *Ino* then successfully confined Confederate merchant vessels to port.

By the war's end Marblehead had offered 1,048 men to the Union cause, 827 in the army and 221 in the navy; of those, 110 died, 87 were wounded and others, missing or prisoners. Those who stayed home were supporting the Civil War in whatever way they could. Fort Sewall was remodeled and enlarged; Fort Glover was garrisoned and a Soldiers' Aid Society was organized by Mary W. Graves and Mary A. Alley. Many women went into the shoe factories which were booming with the war orders for army shoes and boots. Mrs. Mary W. Blaney, whose five sons were at war, joined the effort by becoming an army nurse in Virginia—a course rarely taken by women of that period. The town's joy over the surcease of the Civil War tragedy was tempered by the assassination of President Lincoln.

In this postwar period Marblehead did not have to "come about," but held its course to prosperity. The local shoe business boom sustained itself, shipping over five million pairs or 10 percent of the New England total. The workers were buying small homes; the owners were building handsome mansions on Pleasant Street and Elm Street. The fisheries business had gone to Boston and other ports; shipbuilding was disappearing, except for a few pleasure boats. The Neck, Clifton and Devereux were sprouting cottages and summer shacks all full of "summer boarders." As one old fellow put it, "Pretty soon you're gonna go downtown and meet somebody you don't know. . . ." The 1870 census form asked, along with the customary quiz, the value of your estate, real and personal, how many family members under twenty were illiterate, and whether your home was occupied by any one who was deaf, dumb, blind, insane, or a pauper, idiot or convict. Marblehead's census count was 7,703 residents, a 25 percent increase since 1850.

The increase in population added considerable pressure for improvement of town facilities and transportation. The demand for a direct railroad line to Boston was so strong that the 1871 Town Meeting approved a $75,000 bond issue; however, Eastern Railroad stepped in and built the branch within two years. The "Swampscott branch," as it was called, offered frequent and excellent service from the main Pleasant Street station, the high-steepled Devereux depot, and from Beach Bluff and Clifton. The branch depots were paid for through subscription by the abutters who not only enjoyed the personal convenience, but also profited from the faster shipment of farm produce from the large farms on the Neck and in Devereux and Clifton. This branch was principally responsible for spurring the growth of the outlying resort "villages."

Most of the new streets were not lighted at night—just the most traveled ones in the old town where the abutter paid for the installation of the light and the town paid for the lamplighter and fuel which had changed from the smelly camphine fluid to smelly kerosene. Every night about 7:00 (except the long summer's day or in bright moonlight) lamplighters carried their ladders along the streets, lighting each lamp and then returning to extinguish it between ten o'clock and midnight. Lamplighters were paid quarterly (about ten dollars for six lamps) and street lights totaled thirty in 1870 and doubled in number by 1886. It was the use of the same lamp kerosene and candles that caused the many fires, which were admirably contained by the volunteer fire companies.

With every new engine, another engine company came into being to sharpen the competition to keep the old hand tubs and the newer machines in tiptop condition, and to have as much fun as possible. The whole town looked forward to the annual fall fire department parade of the bands—the Gerrys, the Mugfords, the General Glovers, the M. A. Picketts, Liberty Hose, Marblehead Steamer, and Washington Hook and Ladder companies. The prize race between the Liberty Hose and Hook and Ladder companies that "burned up" the track down Pleasant Street only heightened the excitement for the trials when glory covered the company playing the longest stream. As early as 1871 the fire wards gave permission to take hand tubs to out-of-town musters providing other crews covered for them at home. At local fires water was a problem once the nearby well gave out; the main town had pumps, Brick Pond reservoir and then later Red's Pond whose high ground location enabled much of the town to be fed by gravity flow. Considering the ever current anxiety about the water supply and winds, the old town survived because of the day and night effort of the volunteer companies.

There was no paid police force. Constable Bill Sinclair during most of the 1870's managed, with the help of neighbors, to carry off the miscreants to the "lockup." Fish peddlers walked the streets hollering, "Buy a lob—buy a lob (for 5¢)," while an occasional gypsy band roamed around selling baskets. Simeon Dodge and others served as port collectors at the new location near Humphrey and Twisden's Wharf, but there was mighty little business. The prospectus of the *Marblehead Messenger* came out on December 20, 1871, saying "Marblehead's vigorous growth . . . developes an increasing demand for a home journal. . . ." which helped to put the last town crier, Nathaniel Bliss, out of business.

Someone in Boston, no doubt, recorded that in 1850 Marblehead public schools were rated 310 out of 313 schools, not including the academy or private tutoring schools. That situation improved and twenty-five years later the school budget for 1,610 pupils was $16,-427 of which $12,375 was budgeted for teachers' salaries. The students bought their own books until 1875 when Marblehead became the first town in the state to supply its pupils with free books.

For some inexplicable reason one school committee report included a discussion of Marblehead words, particularly four favorites: "froach," bungled needlework; "crimmy," scared to gooseflesh; "kautch," an inedible mess; "clitch" which varied, but usually indicated an adhesive substance. Over all the years Marbleheaders were known for their colorful vocabulary, local idioms and a dialect that hung on, in spite of time, education and invasion by "furriners."

The profitable port of Boston had enticed Marblehead shippers, such as Robert Chamblett Hooper who ended up owning all of Constitution Wharf and part of Union Wharf in Boston. But of far greater importance to the business world was a Marbleheader Andrew Carnegie named in 1912 as one of the twenty men since the world began who could be called a "world maker." That man was Joseph Dixon.

Joe Dixon, prankster, boy tinkerer, young inventor, producer of fireworks, was a hero to his school chums but a trial to his parents. Living on Darling Street so close to the wharf, he was expected to be interested in the sea; not at all—Dixon wanted to experiment with metals and chemicals. His father demanded that Joe "get a regular job." Joseph Dixon did just that and moved restlessly from one occupation to another; however, he left each employer an improved process that was clearly indicative of his inventive genius. When he was a printer, Dixon experimented with flat stone lithography and with printing by solar light which years later developed into photolithography; when in a tannery, he improved color-fast dyes. Yet, it was in the field of graphites that Dixon excelled.

When he needed money for his inventions, Joe Dixon sold graphite products from door to door, especially, stove polish and Dixon's "lead" pencils which had no lead, but a new graphite stick, later rounded and enclosed by grooved cedar wood. Dixon's pencils were well made and cheap; however, the large German company, Faber, had a long established reputation with which it was difficult to compete. The thirty-year-old Dixon, whose loyal wife happily endured the roller-coaster life of an inventor, went to Ceylon to seek out the fine graphite that he had first found in the cargo aboard Marblehead vessels returning from the Far East. From that source he produced graphite crucibles that lasted ten times as long as those previously used by gold and silversmiths. Foundries in Connecticut and New Jersey eventually turned out his strong, high-quality industrial crucible which could be use for alloys, shipbuilding and Civil War armament. On the battlefield soldiers wrote home with the handy, inexpensive Dixon pencil that they could carry in their pocket.

Engrossed in his scientific discoveries, Dixon sometimes neglected to register his patents or delayed until the design was stolen. Restlessly, he moved from one chemical and metallurgical process to another: perfecting lithography and inks to prevent counterfeiting of currency, casting the first steel, then developing a collodian for photography and improving the grinding of optical lens. Patents were issued to Dixon for improvements in galvanic batteries, tunnel construction, planing machines, antirust paints. Thomas Edison admitted his debt to Dixon in the use of his graphite in the incandescent lamp.

Business negotiations for his sole ownership of the crucible company exhausted Dixon and he died suddenly in 1869. He didn't live to see the greatest success of the Dixon pencil or the award of Medal for Progress at the International Exposition in Vienna. He was a rugged individualist from Marblehead with a goodly share of practical common sense, self-educated through intense, extensive reading and experimentation, and ever generous and thoughtful. Money was not Dixon's goal; his motivation was improvement in every process he touched. A noted New York newspaper ended his obituary: "Many prominent men are forgotten in a year, but Mr. Dixon will live in his works and will be best known a half century hence."

Dixon's travels and business had kept him away from Marblehead, though he often had revisited the town and he remembered it in his will by a gift to the Mugford monument and the donation of a valuable library of scientific and historical volumes, as well as his collection of shells.

A "different kettle of fish" was another Marbleheader who always resided in Marblehead, so the world had to come to him. He loved every acre of the town and owned a good part of it; he dug for its artifacts, wrote of its history, and deeply involved himself in church and town developments. He was James John Howard Gregory (1827–1910), known as "James J. H." A graduate of Marblehead Academy, he attended Middlebury College and then earned his degree at Amherst College (1850). Returning to his birthplace, he first taught school and then went into the seed business, developed wide distribution both here and abroad and became known as the "seed king."

In an 1872 biographical inquiry from Amherst, Gregory, tongue in cheek, answered the questions with wry humor. As to whether he had advance degrees or was a member of the bar, he replied, "Have avoided all bars, tavern bars included, and yet await my degrees as a seed grower." Regarding his marriage, he said he'd married Elizabeth Bubier and in spite of Utah (Mormons) he found his wife equal to six of theirs; later, "I aspire to be a useful citizen in my native town and content with being the largest vegetable farmer and seed grower in New England." James J. H. later became a prohibition candidate after being selectman, school committeeman and library trustee. He was married twice more, to Harriet Knight and Sarah Caswell. Without children of his own, he adopted eight children and enabled many others to continue their education.

In business he permitted his employees to draw their own salaries from the cash drawer; he often anonymously assisted needy employees. When the seeds for mailing or propagation were removed from the squash, overflowing boxes of squashes were left in front of the Elm Street seedhouse with a sign, "Help Yourself."

Marblehead had many reasons to be grateful to James J. H. aside from the business he brought to Marblehead, for he served on innumerable town committees and in 1888 gave his Bailey's Headland to Marblehead for a park—Fountain Park—which he hoped would "forever" retain its beauty and meaning to the town. The energetic seed king retired at eighty to devote himself to quiet philanthropy. One of the most unusual aspects was the Marblehead Libraries, a farseeing benefaction crowded into the last two years of his life, and only recently discovered.

Mr. Gregory decided to provide worthwhile, interesting and informative books to southern schools for poor Negroes and mountain white people. Having solicited help from Negro and white educators and won the agreement of Atlanta University to distribute the libraries, Gregory organized the entire project himself. Titles were reviewed, schools chosen and in just over two years James J. H. Gregory supervised the shipment of over 30,000 free volumes to 130 Negro schools and 30 mountain schools, some jails and missions.

Booker T. Washington's *The Negro in Business* and *The Principals of Agriculture*, plus dictionaries, geographies, cookbooks and 40 to 50 fiction titles were included in Gregory's shipments and each book plate carried the name, "Marblehead Library."

The year of the country's centennial, 1876, was one hell of a year for Marblehead. In spite of a recent business recession, disillusionment with government corruption, and a general restlessness in labor, Marblehead's twelve months of '76 were rarely without a booming occasion. The Reform Club with four hundred members and twelve hundred pledges in hand paraded in the dead of winter to a big Lyceum pledge rally. On the birthday of Washington (who had not been a teetotaler) came the Grand Temperance Jubilee with its hope "to redeem Marblehead from previous celebrations which were anything but temperate."

A controversial town meeting kept things boiling, for funds were being raised for two monuments to be dedicated on July Fourth—the Mugford monument and the soldiers' and sailors' obelisk. Town funds were not voted for a Marblehead exhibit at the Philadelphia Centennial Exhibition, so a public subscription of twenty-five cents each purchased a ship's model of a Marblehead "Banker" for the Fair. An old-timer stood up at Town Meeting to complain that the town needed frugal management and "frowny down all fanaticism, and buncombe and gush. Those who furnish such a large amount of chin music . . . a few flashes of silence would greatly improve them. . . ."

Some of the fracas was over the location of Abbot Hall and the lawsuit which was attempting to prevent the use of Common land. The generous bequest of Marbleheader Benjamin Abbot was specifically designated for a town hall for his birthplace, and in July, 1876, the cornerstone was laid with impressive ceremonies. At that very moment crowds in Philadelphia were pressing for a better look at the inspiring Centennial painting, so well publicized by newspaper reports of President Grant's commendation. Archibald Willard's painting, first called *Yankee Doodle*, and then, *The Spirit of '76*, was purchased by Marbleheader Gen. John H. Devereux—it was to hang in the town where the spirit of '76 was a way of life.

That Centennial year offered thrill upon thrill; Murray's Great Railroad Circus arrived with acrobats, vaulters and an "arenic display" of ballet and pantomime and an evening performance of Shakespeare's Richard III, complete with battle action. A week later the regatta of twenty–five boats began near Second Cove in the harbor and raced around Cat Island. Marblehead sailors carried off the prize money. July Fourth began at sunrise with bells ringing everywhere; at 5:00 a.m., the Antiques and Horribles Parade; at 9:00 a.m., the Great Parade; 12:00, Dedication of the Monument followed by a dinner with the Thirteen Colony toasts. Some of the procession went on to a gay picnic on the Neck where the summer campers and yachtsmen were joining in the celebration by scheduling a great regatta sponsored by the Eastern Yacht Club.

The 1876 Centennial year closed with a free–for–all election in which the election parade gathered at the Common and with torches aglow, music and chanting of slogans marched through the town to Barnegat where the paraders rounded the pump at the end of Beacon Street. Members of the parading political party illuminated their houses; members of the opposition darkened theirs and sometimes rocks hummed out of the darkness.

On June 25, 1877, one of the town's most serious disasters struck when at 1:30 a.m. a time of terror began. From an old barn behind the Marblehead Hotel the flames burst forth and the strong wind whipped the sparks down Pleasant Street igniting one wooden building after another. Every fireman dashed to the scene, but were soon driven back from the Brick Pond reservoir and the water shortage became desperate. Men on horseback galloped to Lynn and Salem for help which arrived in time to contain the conflagration to a central business area. The dawn lighted up the sickening, smoking sight—seventy-two buildings, houses, shoe factories, stores, hotels, the newspaper, the railroad depot, the South Church and the central fire station were completely burned out. The news that Marblehead had burned down brought throngs of sightseers and it was estimated that 600 teams had passed the ruins in 35 minutes. The grim holocaust resulted in a $500,000 loss, 90 families homeless and 1,500 jobless with genuine fears that the shoe companies might leave permanently. "Don't Give Up The Ship" and "Marblehead Never Retreats" were the self-assuring slogans of the day. And a typical native remarked, ". . . won't it be a dreary July Fourth?"

And, in spite of the cheery bells, it was. However, most native factory owners agreed to stay and began new construction. Renewed hopes made the formal dedication of Abbot Hall on December 14, 1877, seem a promising augur for the future. The occasion called for inspiring oratory and a stirring ode written by Rev. Marcia Selman, one of the few female ministers in the country and author of "Marblehead Forever." The great bell given by Mr. Gregory was inscribed:

I ring at twelve the joyful rest of noon
   I ring at nine to slumber sweet of night

I call to Free men with my loudest tones
    Come all ye men and vote the noblest right

Abbot Hall in 1882 became the scene for a spontaneous reception
for the twenty-first president of the United States. Chester A. Arthur had no plans to visit Marblehead; however, moored in Marblehead Harbor on a government despatch boat, the president landed
at Dixey's wharf, entered a carriage and took off for Salem. Once
there he was approached by a "sad-faced" man with piercing black
eyes who requested President Arthur to speak to the people of Marblehead. The request was denied because of a pressing schedule. On
the return trip the petitioner was rebuffed again; finally, he jumped
to the driver's box, and soon after brought the carriage to a stop at
Abbot Hall. As the Marblehead fire alarm clanged and the bells
rang out, President Arthur was borne along into an auditorium
packed with citizens who seemed to have expected the coup. President Arthur, greeted with cheers and applause, good-naturedly delivered a brief speech. He was then permitted to leave and was accompanied to the wharf by the delighted crowd. As Chester Arthur
wrote later: "But I can never forget the fact that I was once
kidnapped in Marblehead!"

No effort was made to search out the "kidnapper," but instinctively, the finger of suspicion pointed to the "perpetual patriarch of
that mystic organization . . . the Sea Serpent Club . . . Mr. Samuel
Roads, Jr."

The Sea Serpent Club was a club of journalists and officials who
held an annual outing at Naugus Head. The club's entrepreneur
was known all over Marblehead for his practical jokes, but, Samuel
Roads' real claim to fame in Marblehead was the publication of *The
History and Traditions of Marblehead* in 1880. Mr. Roads represented his town in both houses of the State Legislature where he
earned the reputation of being one of the best orators and debaters.
Samuel Roads was later appointed private secretary to Governor
Russell and chief of the Stationery Division at Washington. His history was revised in several later editions and supplemented by pocket-
size guides. Bachelor Samuel Roads died at fifty leaving an enduring,
tangible heritage for his town.

Like it or not, Marblehead was turning into a summer resort. In
June of 1880 a steam ferry loudly tooted its own maiden voyage
that opened up a new era of harbor transportation for the "Neck-
ers." *Lizzie May* made a dozen trips a day and connected with all
the trains, and Captain Pitman liked to tell about the city slicker

who asked, "Does this train stop in Marblehead?" The conductor replied, "If it don't, there's sure gonna be a helluva splash!" People came from far and near to enjoy the Neck by the day, or set up tents at Camps Lowell or Nashua, or to open up the handsome, new summer homes being built along the shore. The Neck had its own post office, store, meeting hall and newspaper, and soon three yacht clubs. The Eastern Yacht clubhouse was built in 1881 and six years later the Corinthian Yacht Club moved into its headquarters on Sparhawk Point. The first junior yacht club in America, Pleon, was organized on the Neck in 1887. The fascination with pleasure yachting and racing was mounting rapidly and Marblehead's great traditions of the sea would find new expression in the glory its yachtmen would bring to the town.

Summer resort development was soon evident in the other open areas at Peach's Point and Naugus Head and in the Clifton–Devereux "villages." Cottages, boarding houses and hotels greatly increased the summer population of "the farms" and the burgeoning population had expectations of fire and police protection, roads, lighting and other improvements available "over town." Frustrations intensified; a petition led by permanent residents of "the farms" claimed: ". . . there exists no common industry, interest or sympathy . . . time has nourished the discord. . . ." So, in 1884 the issue was secession!

It would have been the first "foreign" inroad since 1649 and Marblehead would have none of it! After a noisy Town Meeting the case went into a state legislative hearing and days of testimony. The town's rebuttal implied speculation plans and presented a detailed survey of Marblehead in 1885 with 7,467 persons (only 1,930 were registered voters of which 61 resided in the proposed "New Town") living within the 2,374 acres blessed with 13 miles of shoreline. It was shown that only 19 children attended the Farms School out of the 1,405 pupils registered in the town. Finally, the total real estate valuation of Marblehead was $3,270,100 of which $1,060,100 was assessed in the seceding area. The proposed march on Boston's State House proved unnecessary, for the petition for a new town was refused.

The culmination of another local crusade was reached the next year with outstanding success; its results would take years to dilute. In 1886 the seventy-year-old campaign of the temperance societies climaxed in victory with a majority vote for the "no liquor license" law. As the satirical new tabloid, *Marblehead Cod*, wrote, "Red's Pond and the harbor are still full and the only parts of town not dried up; thanks to the 'Old Probs' " (Prohibitionists). There was, however, a sudden upturn in the membership of men's "clubs" that often met in the old "ten-footers."

The business district had been rebuilt after the fire and the modern "Rialto" shops were the pride of the central shopping area, only a few steps from the new depot. The beauty of the town had become a matter of concern, so the newly appointed park commissioners urged the planting of shade trees and designated the first official recreation area as Crocker Park (Bartoll's Head), named after a wealthy native, Uriel Crocker, who gave most of the land.

By the fall of 1888 shoe shipments had increased, as well as the competition from Haverhill and Lynn; however, Marblehead was building its business on quality specialty items. Then, suddenly, on an unusually warm Christmas night the town was shaken by a great explosion which blew out the entire front of a building on Pleasant Street. A mass of flames shot up and down the street, and no one could believe it was happening again; yet, with incredible rapidity the fire consumed the same area that had been destroyed in 1877. This time it included the new Allerton block, the Rialto shops, the new fire station, and depot and many new shoe factories. The firemen, even with the assistance of four other towns, could do nothing except contain the fire to the central business district which was soon a mass of smoldering ashes, charred smokestacks, and lost hopes. Fifty buildings were demolished in this fire, two thousand put out of work and, although Marblehead fought despondency, it would not retreat; nevertheless, most of the shoe business did.

Citizens of the town met in Abbot Hall to help one another and thousands of dollars were donated, including a special fund raised by the summer residents of the Neck. The business men formed a cooperative, share-holding association which built factory quarters on Green Street: the town offered inducements to shoe men to stay, however, for years it would not rescind its ordinance that buildings over forty feet must be of stone or brick. The water-supply study was accelerated to connect the system with the Legg's Hill pond; the fire department was reorganized with full-time firemen and with a third Central Fire Station, this time of brick. Despite town efforts the major shoe business drifted away, taking some Marblehead workers with it. Small shoe companies specializing in children's shoes or slippers remained for many years; though the largest factory, Harris Company, that stood outside the twice-burned area, was later demolished by flames. Marblehead's population dropped to a forty-year low and would vary only slightly until 1930. Marblehead had to be content with small business, resort growth, home construction and yachting facilities. It was the turning point in its long history—from fisheries and trade, ships and shoes to a residential town.

Recovery and change at a Victorian pace was what the 1890's held for Marblehead until war dispelled the peaceful decade. On the farms Marblehead's inspector of cattle, Mrs. Amos Alley, reported that 306 cows, 43 yearlings, 4 oxen and 6 bulls were kept in town.

On the docks, the port collector was moving to the foot of State Street for the Customs House was being taken over for coal storage. It wouldn't be long before it would be permanently moved away from the Marblehead waterfront. The old salts had not moved far away from the waterfront—they helped to unload the coastal steamer cargoes of coal, wood or lime. They fished local waters or worked around the ferry or wharf, had their own customs and language, and even names incomprehensible to the outsider. There was Towline, Sinker, Stargazer, Dish Mop, Pepper Leg, Rock Cod, Onion Eye, and well-known titles of which "Eagle-Beak" Weed, "Dog Tray" Cloutman, "Bismark" Bowden, "Down Bucket" Homan, "Tugboat" Stone and "Clambelly" Howard were by far the most complimentary! The rest will wait on the confidence of a Marbleheader. The sea rovers liked action and gang battles were fairly common when the Wharf Rats took on the Barnegaters, or the Shipyarders challenged the Reed's Hillers, yet there was a quick local treaty if they all had a chance to take on the Salem Shags. Visitors had trouble understanding the clipped dialect and the rough "put down" of their best Victorian manners. A buggy drove down State Street and the driver asked if he could get to Beverly by going straight to the shore? "Yes, sorr, if your horse is web–footed and ye have faith in Christ!"

1898 had started out badly with a February 1 gale and snowstorm soon called the Great Storm. Trees and lines were down cutting off outside communication, a ballast lighter and small vessels littered Riverhead Beach and Little Harbor, and a schooner was splintered into bits on Cat Island. Then two news flashes astounded the town: the Klondike gold rush and then, the blowing up of U.S.S. *Maine* in Cuba.

In the war-destined month of April war was declared on the kingdom of Spain and "the eagle screamed and Marblehead flags are flying." Abbot Hall rang its bells to encourage recruiting at a mass meeting that revived the "Spanish pirates" and the need for sailors to protect the coastline. On May 5, amidst flags and songs and bells, Company C, Marblehead Light Infantry marched from the old

Town House to the railroad station and left again. The cruiser, *Marblehead*, was assigned to blockade duty; a torpedo boat purchased from England and named Manley. Fort Sewall was reconsidered and the whole coast was on alert, for the United States Navy could not locate the Spanish fleet that had sailed west from the Azores. Months later two Spanish prize vessels, *Sandoval* and *Alvarado*, were sailed into the harbor under the custody of their captor, the cruiser, *Marblehead*.

The 103-day-Spanish-American War ended and normal activities were resumed. The trustees of the Abbot Library formed the Marblehead Historical Society for the preservation of the town's heritage. Town Meeting of 1898 accepted the Gregory Library Fund, agreed to give the use of the Town House to the G.A.R. and contributed three hundred dollars for heat, and with one unanimous roar voted to celebrate on May 2, 1899, the 250th anniversary of establishment of the town of Marblehead.

12. "Marblehead Forever"

IT WAS AN OLD SAYING that Marblehead reckoned only a year at a time, so emergence into the twentieth century didn't cause much of a stir hereabouts! It was, after all, winter, when the lowering weather meant a heavy snowfall or Nor'easter, as the graying sea was making up into pounding surf and frosty, white spray, and the sea gulls took refuge inland. What trees there were gave lopsided evidence that nothing deterred the cold gusts roaring over the peninsula. Winter seas had always been off limits for the fishermen, but now there weren't even spring fares to look forward to. A man could work in one of the dozen or so small shoe factories, have a trade, run a store, or work for the boatyards or the town. Yet, in Marblehead, to work was to earn a livelihood and not just a deadly way of life. There were sleigh rides, ice skating parties, church socials, and the "clubs." Serious matters must have been settled there, for it was hard to break into the King Solomon Club, Gull Club, All-of-a-Twist or Goo Goo—especially if you were from the "No License" party which claimed some clubs were "rum-holes."

To warm up the place, Town Meeting was still held in the spring. A "Citizen's Party" was now nominating town candidates and despotism was the allegation against the selectmen who "ignored the will of the people." Never had Town Meeting been so crowded, for the gallery overflowed with women who came without suffrage; everyone lustily sang out "Marblehead Forever" just before passing a record $118,500 town budget. Public pressure forced the installation of a Marblehead telephone exchange, which had almost been denied as a result of a demand for free phones at Abbot Hall; however, phones began ringing in Marblehead in 1901. During those resort years the summer houses needed to be opened soon after the yacht yards came alive to launch the entries for the first regatta whose starting gun was the signal for summer. And summer meant sailing, swimming, band concerts, picnicking, hay-rides or a Sunday stroll along Fort Beach where Jack Adams' House served delectable Marblehead lobsters and a fish banquet was called a "shore dinner." Independence Day was still the town's own celebration with new features like the bicycle race and the Grand Tub race at Fort Beach—one hundred yards in any old wash tub paddled with tin plates. August brought the flower show sponsored by the Visiting Nurse Association which was formed in 1896 by twenty-five citizens deeply concerned about the lack of home-nursing care and public health information. The flower show in 1900 had forty classes of flowers, ferns and fruits (if grown on Marblehead trees) and two men carried off blue ribbons: James J. H. Gregory for strawberries and plums and John O. J. Frost for best pears.

It was the newly formed Marblehead Historical Society that urged the collection and preservation of historic objects and documents, though many Marblehead families have unobtrusively, though jealously, protected its heritage of antiques from generation to generation. The town had become chauvinistic over *The Spirit of '76;* all requests to photograph it were steadily refused until one bold stranger "lifted" the painting to photograph it out of doors. When its painter, Willard, was informed of this by author Mary Devereux, he immediately wrote to Marblehead saying that the results of two hours' "exposure to the sun on the painting would be difficult for me to determine. It may dull the varnish or surface without materially affecting the picture." He did fear that the sudden "fierce light and heat" would affect the painting and expressed his regret.

In 1909 "an enterprising fisherman in his dory on the Banks in the morning before sunrise" was accepted as Marblehead's town seal. Another symbol of the town was almost lost forever that year: patriot Jeremiah Lee's handsome 1768 mansion was unexpectedly auctioned off for three thousand dollars to the mayor of Everett who planned to strip its woodwork and appurtenances for future sale to antique hunters. Miss Elizabeth B. Brown raced to Boston to arrange resale and following on her heels was the owner of the New Fountain Inn who purchased the house at a 50 percent markup to keep it for Marblehead. Everyone was asked for a "dime, a nimble quarter or quick dollar" to save Lee's home by July 4, when the rescued mansion was put under the auspices of Marblehead Historical Society of which Hannah Tutt became historian and secretary.

Marblehead wasn't growing in numbers—in ten years the permanent population change was down sixteen—nor had the old town changed much physically. It was the summer influx with its business, land development and location of new town facilities that alerted many citizens to the dwindling of open space. Marblehead had better act to preserve Skinner's Head for the town and the shoreline for public use, they said. Yet, again and again, petitions for these and a scenic drive along the western shore were voted down. The more immediate was real, ". . . horseless carriages are shot like thunderbolts down one hill and up another . . . is Marblehead a race-track . . . ?"; speed limits for autos were set while wistfully hoping for the lasting popularity of the bicycle. The opening years of the twentieth century were marked by a tremendous upsurge in yachting in which Marblehead had captured a preeminent role during the previous century.

Marblehead's involvement in yachting began early in the nineteenth century when the first American yacht club, the Dream Club, visited Marblehead in 1836, in 1845 native Samuel Gregory raced his schooner *Neptune* in regattas off Nahant and Hull, and by 1859 five Marbleheaders were entered in a yacht race along the shores of Cape Ann. Some years later the North Shore yachtsmen, called the Essex County Fleet, raced off Marblehead and among the winners were *Annie* belonging to Franklin Burgess and John Heard's *Rebecca*. It was John Heard, leader of the group, who broke away from the Boston Yacht Club to form the Eastern Yacht Club.

In 1870 the new club moved its fleet to Marblehead, held its first annual regatta, its first cruise, and invited the New York Yacht Club to Marblehead. Outstanding naval designers like Nathaniel G. Herreshoff and Edward Burgess were sailing their new models under the Eastern burgee and a Boston newspaper wrote, "Never has there been so great an interest in yachting matters in New England. . . ." As of old, the billowing white sails coming round Point o'Neck would bring nautical glory and national attention to Marblehead, as had already been predicted in *The New York Times* of 1883.

Marblehead, late in the last century, became internationally recognized when, for three years running (1885–1887), the defenders of the America's Cup sailed out of Marblehead under the sponsorship of Eastern Yacht Club members. The sloops were the first deep-draft centerboarder, *Puritan*, that outsailed the British cutter, *Genesta*, then the *Mayflower* that easily took Britain's *Galatea*. A similar victory came to Marblehead's first steel sloop entry, *Volunteer*, in the Cup race against Scotland's *Thistle*. The return of *Volunteer* to Marblehead was the occasion for one of the town's gayest victory celebrations; on that October night the harbor shoreline was brightly illuminated and all the yachts hung out colored lights. The steamer ferry, *Brunette*, jammed with people singing patriotic tunes with the band on board, towed fifty dories bedecked with Chinese lanterns. As the dories encircled *Volunteer*, a great volley of fireworks brightened the whole sky and the *Brunette's* whistle signal set the church bells ringing and the bonfires blazing on the headlands. At the turn of the century a challenge from Sir Thomas Lipton was accepted and Captain Charles Barr of Marblehead was placed in command of the defender, *Columbia*, which retained the America's Cup under incredibly fluky conditions.

Marbleheaders urged that the America's Cup races be sailed off Marblehead because the trial races had been so successful in these waters; that didn't come about. However, after the Marblehead schooner, *Dervish*, won the Bermuda race from New York in 1907 the next year's Bermuda race was gunned to start in Marblehead. The yachting center's reputation was then enhanced by the international publicity emanating from the "Sonder Klasse" races with Germany which alternated between Kiel, Germany and Marblehead with four out of five trophies being won by Marblehead. There was also a competition with Spain held in San Sebastian in 1907 and Marblehead in 1910 in which the victories were split after a slight grumble over unseaworthy Spanish craft. International competition placed some interesting names on the club rosters which over the years included inventors, designers, governors and Presidents Theodore Roosevelt and William Howard Taft, Kaiser Wilhelm II of Germany, King Alfonso XIII of Spain, and the English earl of Dunraven. These ocean races peaked the season's excitement, yet there were thrills aplenty every week in small-boat racing.

Corinthian Yacht Club had since 1885 encouraged small-boat design and organized racing for yachts under thirty feet. Within a few years its Mid-Summer Series of four races was attracting widespread attention. Aiding Corinthian in its attempt to broaden the base of

The South part of New-England, as it is Planted this yeare, 1634.

Map showing Marble Harbor (1634) in *New England Prospects,* by William Wood.

Joseph Story, Justice of the United States Supreme Court. Portrait by Chester Harding. *Photo George Cushing, courtesy Massachusetts Historical Society.*

Model sailboat racing on Red's Pond. *Courtesy Samuel Chamberlain.*

Fireboard of Capt. Nicholas Bartlett's schooners anchored in Marblehead harbor (c. 1801). *Courtesy Marblehead Historical Society.*

Fish Flakes at Little Harbor (from an illustration in *Harper's Magazine*, July, 1874). *Courtesy Photographic Illustrators Corporation.*

DRYING FISH, LITTLE HARBOR.

ALL male persons from sixteen to sixty-five years of age, belonging to the training-band and alarm lists, living within the limits of the company of militia in this Town, under my command, that is, in the ward called number one are hereby warned to appear and assemble together on the training-field in this Town, on ~~Tuesday~~ next, the twenty-~~first~~ instant, at ~~nine~~ o'clock in the ~~morning~~, for the purpose of chusing one clerk, four serjeants, four corporals, one drummer, and one fifer ; and also that, pursuant to a late resolve of the General Court, one man out of every twenty-five borne on both the aforesaid lists, may be inlisted, or draughted if necessary, into the service of the United Colonies, to serve until the first day of December next, unless sooner duly discharged.

Marblehead, July 18, 1776.   *John Selman*   CAPTAIN.

N. B. Any person who shall neglect to appear agreably to this warning will forfeit ten pounds, to be paid in twenty-four hours afterwards.

Marblehead Call to Arms, 1776. A rare original. Photo Photographic Illustrators Corporation. *Courtesy Essex Institute, Salem, Massachusetts.*

1766 official form for the odious Greenwich-Hospital tax imposed upon seamen. *Courtesy Essex Institute, Salem, Massachusetts.*

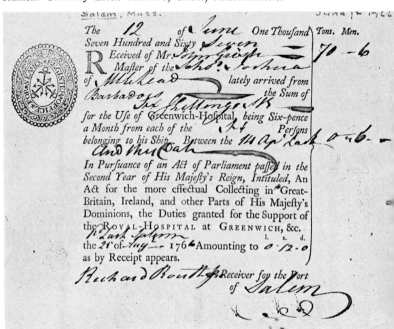

A View of the Landing the New England Forces in y.e Expedition against CAPE BRETON 1745

Marblehead vessels and mariners participated in the Louisburg Expedition (1745). *Courtesy Peabody Museum of Salem.*

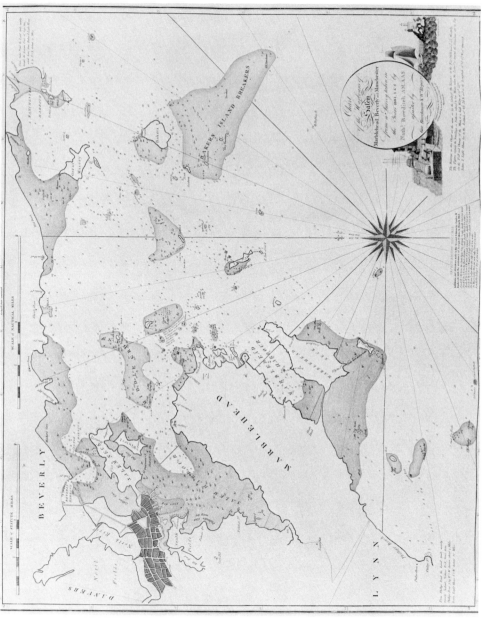

Full-Width Image of map. Nathaniel Bowditch's 1806 chart. Courtesy Peabody Museum

May they be kept from falling quite,
When with fierce wrath they rage.

The LAMENTATION of a bad MARKET.

WEEP, ye men of North, gird ye with fackcloth

Captain John Manley, a woodcut from *Liberties of America*, 1776. *Courtesy Essex Institute, Salem, Massachusetts.*

Ball Gown. General Glover's daughter, Mary, wore this ball gown when she danced the minuet with Marquis de Lafayette at the grand ball at the Lee Mansion in 1784. The gown is of Napoleonic blue brocade with sweeping train over a white, shirred satin petticoat. Jennie Glover Brown, a direct descendant, models the gown. *Courtesy Marblehead Historical Society.*

Colonel Jeremiah Lee, as portrayed by John Singleton Copley. *Courtesy Wadsworth Atheneum, Hartford. The Ella Gallup Sumner and Mary Catlin Sumner Collection.*

"The Spirit of '76," by Archibald Willard. *Permission Marblehead Board of Selectmen.*

Marblehead's *America*, Master Archibald Selman, in January storm, 1803. *Courtesy Peabody Museum of Salem.*

Early lighthouse on Marblehead Neck. *Collection Bowden Osborne.*

James J. H. Gregory Esq., Marblehead seedman and philanthropist. *Courtesy Amherst College Library.*

Looking toward Peach's Point in the late 1800's. *Courtesy William R. Creamer.*

General John Glover. *Courtesy Essex Institute, Salem, Massachusetts.*

Privateer *Concordia* of Marblehead, War of 1812. *Courtesy Peabody Museum of Salem.*

Artist, J. O. J. Frost's primitive: "There Shall be no More War." *Collection Nina Fletcher Little.*

"Peach's Point Marblehead," as depicted by native artist, J. O. J. Frost. *Reproduced through courtesy New York State Historical Association, Cooperstown, New York.*

Old Town winter scene. *Courtesy Samuel Chamberlain.*

"Black Joe's" Tavern, Gingerbread Hill. *Courtesy William A. Slade, Jr.*

Disastrous results of the Christmas fire of 1888. *Collection Bowden Osborne.*

Gerry Handtub Company parades in 1891. *Collection Bowden Osborne.*

Currier print of the record-breaking clipper, Flying Cloud, skippered by fearless Capt. Josiah Perkins Creesy of Marblehead. *Courtesy Peabody Museum of Salem.*

Portrait of Mrs. Jeremiah Lee, by John Singleton Copley. *Courtesy Wadsworth Atheneum, Hartford. The Ella Gallup Sumner and Mary Catlin Sumner Collection.*

Macabre evidence of Massabequash: Indian graves found in Bessom's Pasture. *Courtesy Peabody Museum of Salem.*

Old Burial Hill. *Courtesy Christopher Dierdorff.*

Silver mug made by Thomas Skinner (1713–1761), Marblehead silversmith. *The Metropolitan Museum of Art, Bequest of Charles Allen Munn, 1924.*

Silver caster (for spice) made by Marblehead silversmith, William Jones (1790–1861). In collection of American metalwork-silver, 18th century. *The Metropolitan Museum of Art, Rogers Fund, 1943.*

Marblehead's circular Powder House, 1755, one of the few remaining examples in the United States. *Courtesy Samuel Chamberlain.*

"Front Street, Marblehead, Looking West," 1895. Oil on canvas, by Esther May Barrows. *Collection Nina Fletcher Little.*

Marblehead's signer of the Declaration of Independence, governor and vice president of the United States: Elbridge Gerry. Bust *by Herbert Adams; photo Bob Sinclair; courtesy Town of Marblehead.*

Silhouette of Abbot Hall. *Courtesy Christopher Dierdorff.*

Dame Agnes (Surriage) Frankland (1726–1783), pastel portrait drawn in Chichester, England. *Courtesy Chichester City Council.*

Known as Marblehead's "Cradle of Liberty," the Old
Town House (1727) still stands in Market Square.
Courtesy Samuel Chamberlain.

Jeremiah Lee Mansion (1768), National Registered Historic Landmark. *Courtesy Samuel Chamberlain.*

Close-hauled and beating to windward in Marblehead race. *Photo Bob Crosby*.

Today's version of the Spirit of '76: children in the Horribles Parade (July 4, 1969). *Photo Bob Sinclair*.

yachting had been Eastern, the Beachcomber Dory Club, the Bayview Boat Club and the Burgess Yacht Club.

Then, another yacht club came on the scene in 1902; the Marblehead station of the Boston Yacht Club merged with the Burgess Yacht Club and moved into its headquarters next to the town landing. To celebrate its opening Boston Yacht Club annexed two races to the Corinthian Mid-Summer Series and suddenly it was a week of racing, no longer by invitation, but open to all qualified boats. It wasn't many years before it was dubbed "Marblehead's Mid-Summer Race Week" and broke all records for the number of entries in any racing series in the nation. The Massachusetts Bay eighteen-footer and Herreshoff's twenty-one-foot knockabout flourished for decades amidst keen competition and the introduction of restricted classes, official measurers and more stringent rules attested to the seriousness of small-boat racing.

Nautical activity was not limited to the harbor and open ocean, for since 1894 Red's Pond had been the scene of many a hard-fought race where the designer–owner–builder–skipper stayed on dry land and worried his model boat across the famous, old pond. Though few original records are now extant, it is known that the earliest handmade models were twenty-four inches overall, and there were so many young men who wanted to build sailing models that a model-building school was opened near the pond. The Midget Model Yacht Club lasted through several decades until reorganized into the Marblehead Model Yacht Club. Today, the Sunday morning race and the annual regatta on Red's Pond is where youthful architects can ape the naval architects who have designed fast, sleek yachts to be built by the skilled craftsmen of Marblehead yacht yards.

Two of the earliest yacht yards were Stearns and McKay who built any model from a raceabout to a steel steam yacht at Appleton's Wharf until the wharf went into the hands of another long established yard—the oldest boatyard still in business in Marblehead —Graves Yacht Yard.

James E. Graves (born in Marblehead in 1850) bought a barn in Barnegat where he designed and built his own dories which performed so well that designer Crowninshield urged Graves to expand. Crowninshield then had several of his own design built there, including the nineteen–footer he was taking to Germany to race in 1906. The Graves boatyard has since expanded many times until two large yards now produce a wood or fiberglass design for a dory or an America's Cup defender.

Before World War I one of Graves' competitors was the yard of W. Starling Burgess, son of the internationally acclaimed naval architect, Edward Burgess. However, young Burgess, though he designed and built boats, was then obsessed with air flight. Starling Burgess' inventiveness brought Augustus H. Herring, aviation entrepreneur, to Marblehead where the two built the first Herring–Burgess biplane which was proudly exhibited at the first Aero Show in Boston. It was considered the most impressive plane displayed, although it had never been off the ground. The test flight came two weeks later on February 28, 1910, just seven years after the Kitty Hawk flight. *The Flying Fish* was taken in pieces from Marblehead to Chebacco Lake in Hamilton where the frozen surface acted as a runway for the tiny plane balanced on three skids. Herring was finally ready to take off and did—30 feet into the air for a distance of 120 feet and a near-crash landing. No matter—a man from Kansas bought the plane immediately.

Other more advanced models were flown an average of fifteen feet in height and nearly two miles in distance. Pilot instructions were: avoid wind if possible, don't turn, and land on the slippery marsh grass of Plum Island. Finally, one pilot was able to make a full circle. Despite that, the need for lateral controls attracted the Hungarian inventor, Alexander Pfitzner, to Marblehead where he experimented with a new biplane. Improvements were painfully slow and test flights often unsuccessful; finally, after wrecking the plane in a crash landing, his discouragement led him to suicide in Marblehead Harbor.

Starling Burgess was a restless, eccentric man who continually redesigned his planes with the advice of a stream of now famous aviation buffs who came to the Marblehead plant. In the next aero meet the second-place Burgess plane was praised for the outstanding workmanship of the Marblehead craftsmen. This factor clinched the Burgess franchise to build Wright planes and a British order for the so-called Grahame–White Baby. One of the first recorded parachute jumps was made by Rodman Law (nicknamed in Marblehead "the human fly") from a Burgess plane into Marblehead Harbor. Burgess, the first outside civilian pilot trained by the Wright brothers, opened his own aviation school. He produced at least one extraordinary pupil, Harry Atwood of Swampscott, who gained national headlines for the Burgess–Wright *Moth* by racing trains, swooping over the Harvard–Yale boat race and, ultimately, landing on the White House lawn. The Burgess–built planes profited from the publicity, for the United States Army began to look at the aeroplane seriously.

Naval design was in Starling Burgess' blood and he couldn't resist the idea of a flying boat; his first model flew over the harbor in 1911 and the navy, fascinated by his catamaran type of flotation, later placed a sizable order. Not long after, millionaires were demanding the new flying toy; so Burgess sold his famous Burgess–Dunne aeroplane, which had won the Collier Trophy, to Harry Payne Whitney; then came Vincent Astor, who requested a floating hangar that could be towed well behind the Astor yacht.

Aeroplane manufacture grew rapidly as the war seemed imminent; the United States Army and Navy, the Canadian Aviation Corps placed orders and Great Britain sent a representative who described the plane his country wanted. It was designed, built, tested and sold within twenty-one days by Starling Burgess who called it, simply, Model *O*, or later, the Burgess Gunbus. After a merger with the Curtiss Aeroplane and Motor Corporation, design development was removed from Marblehead.

In December, 1917, Starling Burgess was ordered to the Navy Department in Washington to supervise aeroplane design and construction. His wife, Rosamond Tudor, a recognized portrait painter, went along to work on naval camouflage. Her daughter became the well-known and admired illustrator of children's books, Tasha Tudor. Marblehead was probably the first town to become accustomed to the sounds of aeroplanes flying overhead, and, by peeking into the sheds at Redstone Cove and Little Harbor and watching flight tests, Marbleheaders could observe the fascinating progress of aviation.

There was other fun and fancy in the days when the moving picture business came to Marblehead for location shooting and the local people became extras in *Heart of a Hero* and *Pride of the Clan*, which starred "America's Sweetheart," Mary Pickford. Both films were shown later at the Lyceum.

The youth of Marblehead were recipients of the prewar prosperity with new schools replacing wooden buildings, especially in the large high school built on Workhouse Rocks in 1913. The YMCA, which for a half century had organized outstanding youth programs in town, collected sufficient funds for the brick building on Pleasant Street which has since been expanded. Juliette Low visited Marblehead and so sparked enthusiasm for the Girl Scouts that the town formed one of the country's earliest active Girl Scout troops. A summer resident, Mrs. Charles F. Dennett, saw a need for similar activities for younger girls and supported the innovation of Brownie troops in Marblehead, a branch of scouting that later spread throughout the country. Two decades later Edith Graves initiated the Mariners as a seafaring division of the Girl Scouts and supplied the sailing lessons and vitality while her family yacht yard supplied the Mariners' boats.

When World War I was declared, Marblehead held a "monster" war demonstration at which was read a letter from President Woodrow Wilson thanking Marblehead for its resolutions of confidence in him. The Eastern Yacht Club became the station for seventy-five naval reserves who were to be trained in sub chasing; while Marblehead's own Naval Militia—10th Deck Division—was assigned to the battleship U.S.S. *Nebraska*.

The "red ink" draft numbers were called in July and another contingent of Marbleheaders left for Camp Devens and soon after for France. Over half the number of Marblehead's young men went to war and emotions at home ran high. Townspeople backed the war effort with over 1½ million dollars in Liberty Bonds, and with Live Wire and Public Safety committees. The town felt duty bound to become more internationally minded and planned special gestures of friendship, particularly toward Lafayette's homeland. Local war production at the Burgess Aeroplane Company turned out scores of planes for the British and almost four hundred training seaplanes for the United States Navy. Local boatyards were doing subcontracting for aeroplane parts and, by the end of the war, the Burgess plant was also producing the cab section for dirigibles.

On the night of the "false armistice" on November 7, 1918, a fire erupted at the larger Burgess factory and, fed by combustible materials, soon devoured the entire plant. Four days later at 4:00 a.m. the fire whistles and church bells rang out the real report of peace and the people ran into the streets shouting, "It's over!" Torchlights led the people of Marblehead as of old and it seemed as if they paraded spontaneously all day.

The exuberance of victory, prosperity and reform of the bizarre twenties diffused through the town, opening an era of growth and change that has not yet ended. The population of the country grew 16 percent and that of Marblehead over 18 percent, yet, the spunky, cussed individualism of the town persisted; those who were not immune or in hibernation found themselves, in time, assimilated into its spirit of independence. Just when it was predicted that Marblehead would vote "wet," the national Prohibition Amendment passed and the isolated, dark coves once more found themselves popularized by twentieth-century smugglers, the rumrunners. One of the town characters was soon asked why he had such a red nose. To which he replied, "My nose ain't red, it's just blushing with pride that it ain't been stuck in anybody else's business."

Women's suffrage was the next constitutional amendment and Town Meeting would never again be a male sanctuary, yet few town offices went to women either by election or appointment. The first major Marblehead facility ever named after a woman came into being in 1920 when her Franklin Street property came into possession of the town and was named for the donor, the Mary A. Alley Hospital. It served as the town hospital until 1953 when the larger modern hospital was built.

Action was begun by Senator Lodge in the 67th Congress to convey the Fort Sewall Military Reservation permanently to Marblehead, instead of the mere custody the town had obtained in 1890. In 1922 Senate Bill S.2736 was passed by both houses of Congress and Fort Sewall was returned to Marblehead for its perpetual use as a public park without the right to ever sell that property; if not used for public purposes, the two-and-one-half acre site would revert to the United States. The fort had originally been conveyed by the Marblehead selectmen to the new United States in 1794; and for 128 years its use and maintenance had swung on the pendulum of war and peace, just as it had in the colonial days when it was simply the breastwork on Gale's Head.

Fort Sewall was one of the earliest official colonial forts in America, for in 1644 the General Court's permission to build is recorded with agreement to supply two guns. From then on it appears in the abutters' deeds, as when in 1674 Moses Maverick sold the point of land to Ambrose Gale ". . . except whereon the fort is built. . . ." It was this Gale after whom the headland was named. The town's "Sundry Disbursements" in 1691 listed planks and boards, an ammunition house, carriages for the "grate guns," powder and shot which cost the town one half its annual budget. At the beginning of the next century the Colony sought to recover its additional fort expenses from the British throne, ". . . Marblehead . . . being [an] avenue by which the enemy may make Impression upon us." From then until the Revolution the support of the fort by the town, Colony or throne was dependent on the mounting tension or series of wars with France. The most thorough and professional reconstruction of the fort occurred under Sir Harry Frankland in 1742 when the "good and sufficient breastwork" supported twelve mounted cannon. The captains of the fort were local men who, from Azor Gale to Thomas Gerry, were always outstanding citizens of the town.

Never was the fort rebuilt so rapidly as when Marblehead became a cornerstone in the battle for independence. The British threatened but never attacked the fort which provided a training ground for the militia and acted as a guardian of a vital privateering and naval seaport. Its postwar condition, as reported in 1791 by Dr. Bentley of Salem after reviewing three hundred men in blue and white uniforms and carrying rusty arms, was "disappointing" and may have contributed to its conveyance to outside government hands for the first time in history. Town Meeting on August 25, 1794, ceded the fort to the United States of America. A witness to that release was young Justice of the Peace Samuel Sewall.

A new formality and social life came with the national military installation and parades, reviews, teas, dinner parties and harbor sails were planned for visiting American and foreign celebrities. The entire neck of land was then covered with barracks, officers' quarters, and a parade ground adjoining a well-maintained fort. Yet, the fiercely independent town didn't take kindly to all the soldiers in their midst, as one tragic incident in early 1812 revealed. Two tired soldiers returning from Boston on a wintry night were refused entrance to several homes; next morning their frozen bodies were found a mile from the fort where they had perished in the storm. Their formal funeral service was attended by almost three thousand grieving citizens who formed a procession to accompany the cortege. A commentator observed the public embarrassment, yet added, "Such is our aversion to a standing army and the vulgar fear of soldiers. . . ." Garrisoned during the War of 1812, the fort served nobly during the British naval blockade battles and was very instrumental in protecting the vessel, *Constitution*, but was subsequently abandoned by the military and deteriorated, except when national war emergencies in 1861 and 1898 temporarily restored it.

The fort was given an official name only once in history—Fort Sewall after Samuel Sewall. This longtime town official and state and national representative, who in 1814 became chief justice of the Massachusetts Supreme Court, was so appreciated in Marblehead that the town named its oldest extant public site for him. On September 19, 1898, a national military garrison left Fort Sewall for the last time, for the fort was already in the custody of the town. Finally, in 1922, Fort Sewall, protector of Marblehead for 278 years, was returned to the town "forever."

The 1921 publication of *Assessed Valuations* gave a statistical picture of the changes occurring in Marblehead: within ten years the number of taxable corporations had decreased by 17, whereas resident property owners had increased by 654. The population growth forced Marblehead to conform in 1926 to a ten-year-old state regulation ordering the installation of a sewer system. It entailed dynamiting trenches in the unyielding rock of narrow, winding streets, as it agonizingly inched to modernity. Then gone would be the helter-skelter back-yard privies that for centuries had teetered at every crooked angle; gone would be the "honey-cart" and gone would be the justification for age-old "Shit Hill." Before the town's antiquity totally disappeared, it might be hoped that someone would record it for posterity.

A small, gray-haired artist was trying to do just that and his ingenuous efforts met with a patronizing toleration of an old man's hobby. Marblehead had never seen anything quite like John Orne Johnson Frost. He'd been a Banks fisherman, a carpenter's assistant and a dandy cook at his popular little restaurant which after twenty years burned down in 1888. Knowing he was without insurance, M. A. Pickett Engine Company held a fair and turned the nineteen-hundred-dollar proceeds over to "Jack Frost" but, instead of rebuilding Frost joined his wife in developing her gardening interest into a flower business. At seventy John O. J. Frost found a new outlet in painting the stories of Marblehead, its history, legends and tragedies. Without exception this descendant of an early Marblehead family portrayed his intense pride and intrinsic delight in his town and its heritage. Although the passerby giggled at his primitive paintings for sale in store windows and ignored his home museum, nothing deterred Frost; his prolific brush could hardly keep up with his memories. Collectors, museums, historical societies now own his paintings; yet, perhaps, the greatest recognition to date has been the selection of Marblehead's John O. J. Frost as one of America's most outstanding primitive painters in the "American Primitive Paintings" exhibition that was sent abroad to six European countries in 1954. Among the greats at Parke–Bernet galleries in New York in 1971 were the paintings of John O. J. Frost who had always been delighted to "jaw awhile" about Marblehead and had now spread its fame by his own simple, primitive art.

The 300th anniversary of the founding of Marblehead provoked considerable historic interest and research and climaxed in a three-month, town-wide celebration. On August 19, 1929, President Herbert Hoover wrote,

To the Citizens of Marblehead—
    To have attained three hundred years of age is of itself a distinction amongst American cities; and to have included in those years so much of historical significance as Marblehead can claim, justifies a pride in which, with all other Americans, I warmly share.

Yours faithfully,
Herbert Hoover

The year of 1929 was a gay, happy year of prosperity and tercentenary excitement until the October stock market crash.

It didn't take long to feel its effects, even in Marblehead where there was no banking panic, but not long after some mortgages were foreclosed as unemployment grew. By 1932 Town Meeting had to face the necessity for strict economy; one of the quietest meetings ever held finished the warrant in one night by voting down all highways and sidewalks, police uniforms, a new high school and hospital. The state welfare appropriation was increased based on the outstanding job Marblehead was doing for its unemployed, who were also assisted by community organizations that paid fuel bills, and distributed infant layettes, medicines and food baskets. The bankruptcy of the Sorosis Farms broke up an extensive holding of hundreds of acres which developers bought and, for the first time in history, filled "the Plains Farms" with residences.

Just as things seemed to be improving, on September 21, 1938, after four days of rain the afternoon weather appeared to be lifting when without any warning Marblehead was hit by the full force of a "windstorm" that was not even called a hurricane. All afternoon a dry ninety-mile southeast wind battered the coast; the sea seemed to break from the bottom and build into angry mountainous rollers that were breaking right over Marblehead Rock. The storm's target was, as always, the harbor. The wind, tide and surf vented their force on the scores of boats still at their moorings; within a couple of hours floats broke loose, pilings tilted, many smaller boats had sunk, larger luxury yachts were smashed on the rocks from the Rockmere to Goodwin's Head or were dragging down on the whole fleet. Some owners and professional captains who were aboard trying to save the vessels ended up barely saving themselves, some by climbing from a bowsprit or boom onto the rocky ledge. Many unmanned yachts were carried to sea and never were located. In the pitch dark of evening townspeople and yachtsmen labored to save the remnants of the fleet. Disaster losses were in the millions, many people were hurt but, miraculously, not one life was lost. The destruction defied Marblehead's usually resilient humor, though one old fellow said it was probably the wind left over from the September primary election.

Despite the Depression Marblehead was growing and its beauty and history and yachting were getting national attention. *Life* magazine covered the Marblehead Sea Scouts program and Donald Culross Peattie in *The New York Times* described Marblehead as one of the "Five Great Small Towns in America." The "Yachting Capital of the World" was an accolade often given to Marblehead which had fully participated in the two decades (1920–1940) that yachting writers, designers and builders have called the most illustrious, prolific period of yachting, in view of the creativity in design, the development of ocean and small-boat racing, the broadening of yachting interest.

This period between the two World Wars was conspicuous for the effective innovations evident in several important yachting trends. Herreshoff's "Universal Rating Rule" for yacht measurement was instrumental in the creation and growth of the restricted classes identified by alphabetical letters, such as, the *P, Q* and *R* boats. Many of these were skippered by famous Marblehead skippers: Charles Francis Adams, Charles H. W. Foster, B. Devereux Barker, Frank Paine, Chandler Hovey, Joseph Santry and others who persisted in winning the Astor Cup, the Puritan Cup, Navy Challenge Cup and many renowned trophies, including the Nathaniel Nash Cup which is the last trophy known to have been awarded to the famous yacht, *America.* The 8 Meter Class and the 30-Square Meters (the latter class especially) fostered by Corinthian Yacht Club and by skippers like Arthur Shuman, Chandler Hovey and Alfred Chase, participated in championship races held at Marblehead and in Europe.

The first America's Cup challenge after World War I was successfully met by *Resolute,* commanded by a Marblehead skipper, Charles Francis Adams, later secretary of the navy and commodore of the Eastern Yacht Club. This was the first America's Cup Race in which both the commanding skippers were truly amateur yachtsmen, and it marked the last act of the gaff-rigged sloop and turned all heads toward the Marconi rigging. In 1930 it was hoped that the Cup defender would be *Yankee,* designed by a well-known Marblehead skipper, Frank Paine. Beloved by every yachting buff in Marblehead for her "a Yankee-never-retreats" trials, *Yankee* was never chosen for a Cup defender in spite of setting in 1930 a still unequaled thirty-mile-course record, then losing a final trial race by one second in 1934. *Yankee* tried again in 1937 to outrace *Ranger* designed by Olin Stephens and Starling Burgess. Burgess, having recovered from his love affair with airplanes, had already designed two victorious America's Cup defenders, *Rainbow* and *Enterprise.* Another Marblehead adopted son, L. Francis Herreshoff, had designed the trial contender, *Whirlwind.* The popular 125-foot-overall *J* Class sloops were in competition off Marblehead throughout the entire decade.

A vital contribution to national yachting was occurring in Marblehead during the same period—the development of the first junior yachting and racing programs in America. Pleon Yacht Club's thirty-year sailing experience had already brightened the future of national junior yachting, when the "pot of gold" at the end of the youthful rainbow was offered by Herbert M. Sears. The Sears Trophy, which was first limited to crews from Massachusetts, soon developed into the National Junior Sailing Championship which, according to the well-known yachting author, Leonard M. Fowle, Jr., has been called the most significant competitive development of the twentieth century. The initial Sears Cup competition was held in 1921 and was won by a Marblehead crew under Pleon Commodore Richard S. Thayer, setting the standard for future Pleon crews who, up to the present day, frequently win the National Junior Sailing Championship for Marblehead. The first ten years of the Sears Cup championships were held at Marblehead; since then, the racing has been held at ports from coast to coast under North American Yacht Racing Union auspices. Junior yachting in Marblehead owes a debt to beginners' boats like Starling Burgess' husky Brutal Beast, the encouragement of all the yacht clubs and the creation of the new one-design classes which swiftly replaced the opulent racers of the earlier decades.

The event that made Marblehead the cynosure of all yachting interest was Mid-Summer Race Week which by the 1930's had broken all national records for the numbers of starters entered in any racing series. The first permanent Race Week trophies made their appearance—the Marblehead Challenge Cup and the Leonard Munn Fowle Memorial Trophy for the outstanding performance or noteworthy contribution to Race Week were offered for the first time in 1935. Mr. Fowle, a veteran yachting reporter and member of the Race Committee of all three yacht clubs, had worked unceasingly for the improvement of junior sailing and Marblehead Race Week, along with William L. Carlton and James C. Gray. Yet, the tremendous impetus of yachting in Marblehead came from many sources—leading yachtsmen, enthusiastic young skippers, club officials and local yacht yards and designers.

Boat designers, Starling Burgess, B. B. Crowninshield, John Alden, Frank Paine, Francis Herreshoff, Carl Alberg, K. Aarge Nielsen, and Ray Hunt were closely associated with Marblehead, in fact many of them lived in the town. Along with several classes of small racing boats, they were designing the moderate-size boats to participate in the increasingly popular long-distance ocean racing in which Marblehead yachts were preeminent competitors. The Bermuda Race had been renewed in 1926, the Marblehead–New London was a tricky annual contest and in 1935 the Halifax Race became official as the "off year" ocean race, alternating with the

Bermuda Race. The Boston Yacht Club and the Royal Nova Scotia Yacht Club soon formalized a co-sponsorship of the 330-mile Marblehead to Halifax Race.

Another yacht club burgee was added to the Marblehead gam in 1935 with the introduction of Marblehead Yacht Club which established its headquarters on the town side of the harbor just south of the Boston Yacht Club. The fleets of the five clubs were an unmatched nautical display that brought sightseers from everywhere to be awed by the sight and puzzled by the frequent yachting compliment, "She's a beauty." The local paper explained that a ship is a "lady," even when a man-o'-war, for it is an animated being with a waist, collar, stays, laces, watches, ties, chains, rigging, paint, brass; often has a leg on a race and sometimes doesn't come about easily!

The first staysail rig on *Advance* which crossed the Atlantic from Norway and was greeted in Marblehead with tremendous interest, including that of President Coolidge who watched from the presidential yacht *Mayflower*, anchored for the summer in Marblehead harbor. *Constellation* and *Cleopatra's Barge II* were stars in Marblehead's yachting crown surrounded by brilliant designs and famous winners like *Pleione, Tioga, Yankee, Rainbow*, and many others. But the real wave of the future was seen everywhere in the proliferation of small boats, racing dates and number of participants. War in Europe brought general anxiety that reduced investment in yachting and in Marblehead's one small sail loft, Simmons, and the boatyards were seriously affected even before the entrance of the United States into World War II.

The December 7, 1941, attack stunned the populace but the patriotic spirit of the town sparked immediate plans for a huge public safety committee and a Marblehead home guard. Because of concern over submarine activity and possible saboteurs two camouflaged lookouts and a radar tower were erected on the Neck and guards posted along the shoreline. The Neck blackout was strictly enforced and phones at each end of the Causeway checked out drivers who wished to cross the Causeway after dark. The Coast Guard commandeered many large yachts during early years of the war. The effectiveness of their use was open to question; the neglect of their maintenance was quite evident. Owners were later compensated for damages, but deterioration precluded restoration, as in the case of Crowninshield's *Cleopatra's Barge II*. Still rather bitterly recalled was the day in 1941 when *Constellation*, a noble steel yacht that had raced and cruised over much of the globe, left Marblehead harbor to be cut up into scrap metal. Coast Guard surveillance needs brought into action the Power Squadron which still continues its efforts to improve the use of power boats, primarily by teaching yachtsmen the rudiments of navigation.

Marblehead's heart went out to the men on the World War II cruiser named for the town and reports of the heroic performance of *Marblehead* in the Java Sea and her gallant return to port awakened memories of similar heroic feats of Marblehead's own seafarers who had often sailed the Java Seas. Almost sixteen hundred Marblehead men were in the military service; many bore the names of their ancestors who had been with Washington at the Delaware, among the privateers of 1812 and 1861 and with the army in France in 1918. The deepest roots of Marblehead were still vital and strong in their patriotism. Forty of the town's sons lost their lives, many were wounded or became prisoners of war. *V-E* Day and *V-J* Day in 1945 brought great joy and, once again, the bells at Abbot Hall rang out for peace.

Marblehead now found itself close-hauled beating to windward in a spanking breeze of change unprecedented in its history. In the fifteen years following World War II the town almost doubled in population; fifteen hundred new homes were built filling in the open spaces in Clifton, the West Shore and Marblehead Neck, causing the colorful and articulate local publisher, Eben Weed, to comment that Marblehead was turning into a "damn bedroom town." The twentieth-century settlers were coming from near and far with a fond desire to live in the historic old town by the sea. Their arrival (34.6 percent population increase between 1950 and 1960) put all kinds of strain on facilities and new solutions were needed. Veterans' housing and a new hospital were built; the Abbot Public Library moved to attractive new headquarters in 1954. Several new schools were necessary, for in the intervening postwar years the school enrollment had increased 110 percent and the annual school budget zoomed 784 percent, giving the populace tax tremors and belated recollections of "baby booms." Neither hurricanes, taxes, absence of railroads after 1959 nor crowded conditions seemed to deter the influx of people; yet the rocky peninsula flanked by the sea has obvious land limitations.

The 1971 Marblehead population of 21,183 had tripled the highest population figure of the nineteenth century, giving the town the doubtful honor of being the sixth most densely populated town in Massachusetts. Now only a few small manufacturers remain; local employment is found in wholesale, retail or service business. As in most residential towns, the local problems are intrinsically related to the rapid growth—water pollution, rubbish disposal, zoning and the eternal taxes. The younger generation, their recreation and their schools absorb much of the tax dollar and hours of planning, and controversy. Issues of the decade—political realignment, drugs, peace and manifestations of change and dissent—reach into Marblehead, as has the Vietnam War in which many young Marbleheaders have been involved and some have given their lives. Though annual election of most town officials has persisted for over three hundred years, the increased involvement of all sections of the town is evident now, as is the increased participation of women in government, some by appointment and a few by election to the Board of Health, the School Committee, Town Clerk, and in 1971 the first woman was elected to the Board of Selectmen.

The future citizens of the rapidly filling peninsula should be grateful to the Conservation Commission, the fourteen garden clubs and generous residents who preserve, beautify and enlarge various conservation areas around a pond, a swamp, a beautiful hillside or rocky headland of Marblehead. Playgrounds, beaches, tennis courts, baseball diamonds, a hiking and bike trail along the old railroad bed all offer relaxation and fun to Marbleheaders, even those who don't go near the water, though that's where you'll find thousands every weekend. In fact, most every summer day at Marblehead resembles a yachting regatta anywhere else.

Very recently the official, registered boat moorings numbered 1,811, although the Coast Guard aerial photograph showed at least 2,100 boats. Nowadays the dry sailor augments the fleet, launching his boat at the public boat ramp laid at Riverhead Beach in 1961. From early morning cannon until the evening Twilight Series the harbor seethes with activity as sailing craft and an ever increasing number of power boats seek open water through the maze of moorings. As the sailors head for the starting line, the impact of the basic alteration in the art of modern boat building—fiberglass—is inescapable. The introduction of the fiberglass-molded boats was first met with skepticism, then the idea leaped ahead in the 1960's until there are few classes not feeling this encroachment. Gone are the wooden Brutal Beast and its successor, the Turnabout— replaced by fiberglass beginners' boats that swiftly move the young sailor into other fiberglass one-design boats like the *110*, whose original class was organized in Marblehead. The "midget" sailor of Marblehead is sailing long before the young "cut-tail" of the eighteenth century and, because of the YMCA, Red Cross and yacht clubs, is a far better swimmer. In almost one hundred years of yachting competition Marblehead has the enviable record of never having lost a sailor during a scheduled race, in spite of New England's unpredictable fog and squalls. Winter finds the Marblehead boats, forlornly bare of their stately masts and riggings, protruding from garages, claiming an honored place on the lawn, or nestling closely together in one of the numerous boatyards.

Yet, if anyone doubts the fortitude of the contemporary sailor compared to the fishermen who used to pitch pennies during the blustery winter, let him look to the Frostbiters. From those who complained of winter-sailing hibernation came the idea "Think Summer," bundle up and race in the freezing weather. In 1946 the Marblehead Frostbite Sailing Club was founded by George O'Day, Ray Hunt and other warm-blooded sailors. Since 1961 the 11½-foot fiberglass Interclubs maneuver for position as the Frostbite Club's starting gun echoes around the harbor at 1:00 p.m. Sunday afternoon, November until April. Five races are held near the familiar mid-harbor Frostbite shack which itself is often a winter casualty. Climaxing the season (during which several racers may have been dunked in 20° waters) is the March Regatta which draws competitors from ports along the northeastern seaboard. Most of Marblehead's racing "greats" have been Frostbiters, the polar bears of yachting.

The seaport of Captains Pierce, Mugford, Tucker and Creesy is still producing skilled mariners and victorious skippers. It would be difficult to name a class in which Marblehead sailors have not been champions in New England, or the national or world championships. In ocean racing there are almost as many skippers who have held the forefront like Wells Morss, Brad Noyes, Don McNamara, Charles Stromeyer, and Ted Hood. Hood is the yachtsman whose name brings instant recognition in sailing circles anywhere on the globe, not just because he has won class championships, not because of ocean racing where it has been said that he is "the best upwind sailor in the world," but because of a kind of unique genius of a man who can design his own boat, design and make its sails and race it to victory. The unruffled skipper of several yachts is a self-taught sailmaker who, in 1950, tired of cutting sails on the floors of ballrooms, gyms, or auditoriums, opened his own shop which eventually became known as "the academy of sailmaking." Several of its graduates now operate sail lofts in Marblehead producing outstanding sails that would have awed and pleased Marblehead's colonial sailmaker, Valentine Tedder. In a recent competition of America's Cup candidates Ted Hood had made sails of his own specially woven sailcloth for every competitor, some at the sail lofts he has established in England, Australia, New Zealand and France. The heart of the business is still at Little Harbor where, as one of the two top sailmakers in the United States, Ted Hood has kept the eyes of the sailing world focused on Marblehead.

Hood's experience with the America's Cup as crew, designer, sailmaker and skipper began many years ago. *Nefertiti*, backed by Boston Yacht Club's E. Ross Anderson and Robert W. Purcell, was Hood designed for the America's Cup defense of 1962. *Nefertiti* had been built in ninety-six days at Graves' yard in Marblehead and headed toward the Cup trials with a goodly number of Marbleheaders on the crew and co-commanders "Don" McNamara and Ted Hood who were champion skippers in their own right. Every day of the 1962 trials Marblehead's heart sailed out of Newport aboard *Nefertiti* or *Easterner*, which had been built by Chandler Hovey for the 1958 Cup trials, and the whole town shared the ultimate disappointment when neither boat was chosen as America's Cup defender.

Marblehead Race Week, which *Yachting* magazine called ". . . one of the largest shows afloat . . ." is still a spectacular yachting event. The profusion of races, classes, committees and the number of starting lines brought about in 1969 a new coordinating group for all local racing, the Marblehead Race Association. With the participation of all clubs the *MRA* assists in the coordination of seasonal series, national and world championships, ocean racing and Race Week. The popularity of Race Week is unshaken, averaging 425 legal entries, but the ratio of visiting boats has decreased as the local entries increased. The most constant element is inconstant New England weather which, no matter how the date is shifted, loves to harass the sailors with a range of calm, squalls, wind or fog that has never prevented the completion of the series.

Two other yacht clubs have come on the harbor scene—one formally and one spontaneously. In 1950 a new, white burgee with a blue star chevron came into use with the formation of the Dolphin Yacht Club. Later, among the fishermen around transportation and the town wharf, appeared a red burgee with the yellow letters *CBYC*, or, "Cheap Bastards Yacht Club." The beloved Phil Clark, after whom the town wharf is now named, was made the "commodore" whose great pleasure was to award the *CBYC* stickers. Only about forty small boats fish the local waters now; weather-beaten, rugged men still bring in the haddock and cod and flounder which, far from being cured on fish flakes, are valued in Marblehead or Boston for their freshness. Lobstermen searching the waters for their own personally marked buoys pull up heavy traps of the highly prized crustacean that Marbleheaders love, whether boiled up at home or dressed up in the local restaurants. Most of the fish is still landed where John Codner urged Marblehead to establish a town wharf in 1660.

A widespread appreciation of the old town and its historic sites augmented the fear of its exploitation or wanton destruction as the burgeoning population needed land and housing. The townspeople were urged to create a historic district; but the new bylaw was not readily accepted, even by those who owned Colonial houses because it seemed to dilute another precious Marblehead heritage, individual liberty. "Ain't nobody gonna tell me where ta put my fence" was typical of the cry that first defeated the preservation measure at Town Meeting. Another attempt came after a few more blatant buildings were imposed on a historic street and the Historic District was established in 1968. Few are the early colonial towns in America that have not been rebuilt or restored (Williamsburg, Dearborn, Sturbridge) to imitate the American heritage that Marblehead enjoys as a living reality. No museum with costumed characters, this; Marblehead's historic homes are often lived in by the eighth generation of a family who quietly treasures its Colonial artifacts. Nowhere is history so much an everyday matter.

It is in this Historic District where much of the celebration of Marblehead's most meaningful day takes place on the Fourth of July. The tolling bells still ring out the news of freedom again and again. The Horribles Parade exhibits an innocent Indian holding the hand of a tiny Puritan; witches and sailors mingle with spacemen and, unfailingly, a small family parades proudly as "The Spirit of '76". Historic buildings are open to present rare documents or contemporary art and throughout the town are displayed evidence of the talents of the townspeople in a three-day celebration generated by the Marblehead Arts Festival. Sharing Marblehead's delight in fun and competition are events at the beginning and end of the summer—the hilarious Great Race from Watertown and the historic Firemen's Muster, when the town's ancient hand tubs still perform like winners. But, now, as the "Glorious Fourth" ends, the shoreline and sky are no longer illuminated with flares and the rockets' red glare, for pollution has tainted Marblehead's Fourth.

Marblehead has always attracted artistic people and today's wealth of talent shows tremendous interest in painting, the revival of handicrafts and needlework, along with genuine concern for the accurate restoration of old houses. However, the heart of the matter is the town itself where the spirit of independence lives on, and seldom more effectively than in that "great school of civics," 350-year-old Town Meeting. It's a vital, thriving legislative body with universal membership where any interested citizen can state his individual views on the management, expenditures, laws and plans of his town—one of the last vestiges of truly democratic government with direct questioning of officials, citizen-to-citizen reaction and public voting. Voters recall many recent instances when Marblehead's individualism and nonconformity still rang true. Once when threatened with the influence of the state, a voter's loud reaction was "What the hell's the Commonwealth of Massachusetts got to do with Marblehead?" When Town Meeting denied appropriate funds for token civil defense and was warned that the state law would enforce this, the public answer was, "If they want us to have a civil defense committee, let 'em pay for it!" Federal funds have been refused, army engineers have been told that they don't understand harbor conditions, and the scientific expert must still stand and answer the fisherman's inquiry without losing his "cool." Marblehead Town Meeting is the people's government steeped in tradition, still influenced by descendants of the early colonists who now, as then, warn of the erosion of individual freedoms. If their ancestors crossed the Atlantic in a tiny boat to escape an oppressive king, they are not about to concede their rights to a modern pompous government official.

So Marblehead survives—its Town Meeting and Colonial buildings, its three-hundred-year-old traditions, its spunk and nonconformity, its obsession with the sea, and its natural beauty and ruggedness. Over the centuries the spirit of Marblehead has spread a

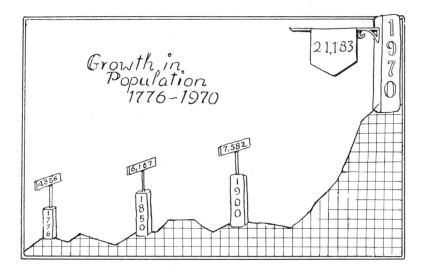

Growth in Population 1776–1970

subtle contagion to which few could be immune. In the past the town has assimilated those who came to Marblehead, rather than being forced to conform to their pattern; the future will judge its present influence. Yet now, as in centuries past, the heritage of the town's hearty spirit and love of freedom and its Colonial landmarks are a public trust of the people of Marblehead.

PART II

Marblehead: *Other Aspects*

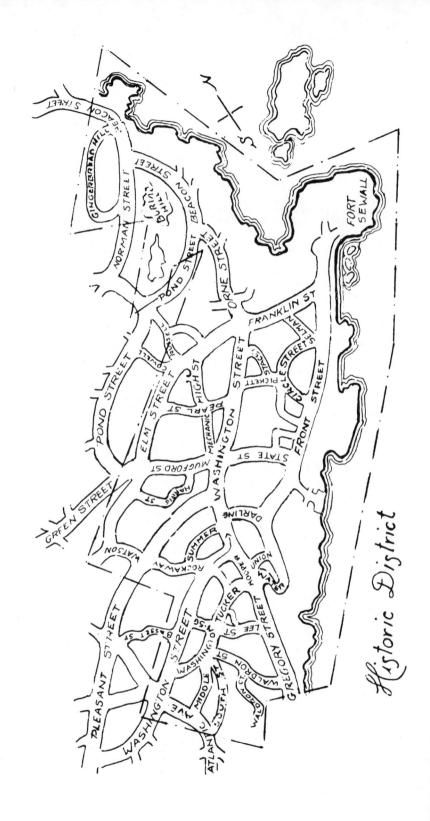

Historic District

1. Historic District

THE HISTORIC DISTRICT ACT, as delineated by the General Court of Massachusetts, was accepted for Marblehead in 1968, and enables Marblehead to continue to preserve its priceless, irreplaceable heritage (an unusual wealth of early houses) not only for itself, but for the Commonwealth of Massachusetts and for the entire country. Marblehead possesses a heritage of magnificent examples of Colonial architecture as well as many smaller, charming old dwellings and other buildings which contribute to the atmosphere of the town so ardently admired that a writer in *The New York Times* declared, "Marblehead is one of the four most attractive towns in America." The narrow streets are a reminder of the past and reveal much of the original town.

Such history could be recorded in books alone, but in fact it is preserved in the very houses where the tough colonial fishermen and daring patriots of the 1600's, 1700's and 1800's lived. The number of houses within the Historic District are a unique and irreplaceable record of the way of life in a quaint New England seaport and a direct link with America's past that may help to retrace, relearn and reassess the meaning of our history as an independent nation. By the time the United States began Marblehead was already rich in his-

tory. The original, narrow streets that twist and wind through the
center of the business section near the waterfront—the streets that
often end in a cul-de-sac—are lined with houses that burgeon
with history. As one native commented, "The houses came first,
then we made the paths."

Travel and transportation were by boat or horseback so in the beginning streets were not necessary, and when they were, the highways were for the most part mere cartways. Following the line of
least resistance, they swung around ledges, rocks and any other obstruction trying to avoid hills and elevations. This crazy pattern accounts for some houses facing the road, some sideways or corner-
wise in all manner of angles, even one in the very middle of a street.
On Gregory, Lee and Front Streets the houses are built on ledges
with the interiors a series of curious ells, and often the main door on
the street side is on the second floor. Older homes have neither
porches nor bays—possibly a weather hood over the doorways.
The buildings are flush with the street, many have common walls
and originally had sixteen- or twenty-four-paned windows. The old
houses have gambrel roofs, hip roofs, pitched roofs and mansard
roofs, and are so close together that there is an existing "drip-rights"
statute in the town laws.

"There is more of the crust of antiquity about Marblehead than
any place of its years in America," wrote M. DeChastellaux, "an air
of smug and substantial comfort in the houses." In the homes the
fireplaces were used for cooking and heating and the fuel univer-
sally used was log wood. A poet once remarked that Marblehead
has more fireplaces than any town in Massachusetts, for some homes
have a fireplace in each room. In other towns any building which
has survived the rigors of a hundred or more winters is regarded
with some reverence; here in Marblehead, a dwelling that has not
reached the two century milestone cannot hope for recognition by
the antiquarian.

The population in Marblehead grew slowly and about 1664 there
were only 44 Commoners, their families and other people living in
the town, and by 1700 there were 125 houses. Some of them are still
standing and of that number two seem to have been changed only a
little, the Norden House on Glover Square and 97 Elm Street. Gone
are most of the earliest dwellings for those first homes were replaced
as soon as any semblance of prosperity came. Those first homes resembled the replicas that one may see in Pioneer Village in Salem,
Massachusetts. These were simple structures, the first floor one large
room with stairs and chimney at one side, or sometimes in the middle, making two rooms. The rooms were used for all the family

activities—sleeping, eating and working—and the large receptacle for chamber lye was by the fireplace. The second-story windows were directly under the eaves of the high-pitched roof. It was the custom to bury the sills of the houses below the ground for warmth.

There is one small fishing shack near Beacon Street, the only remains of the earlier fishing trade. From 1700 to 1790 many people moved into town, attracted by the booming fishing and foreign trade. By 1750 Captain Francis Goelet, wrote, "the Towne of Marblehead, has abt 450 homes all wood and clapboarded," and he might well have added, beautiful, for by this time the Georgian architecture was in full swing and the "codfish aristocracy" had built well and handsomely. The houses were built at every level of affluence from the simple half house to the two-storied box covered with a ridge or hip roof to the luxurious mansion of Jeremiah Lee. Kitchen fireplaces were large, but there were many smaller ones in the various rooms. In the eighteenth century cooking, eating and entertaining were confined to downstairs and the sleeping quarters had been moved upstairs. Decoration of the houses had changed, too. For the well-to-do wallpaper was available; for those not so wealthy there was the stenciled wall. Of the 690 homes in 1790 many have been saved, though of that number many have, of course, been altered. Clapboard was always popular in Marblehead.

The John Hooper Mansion at 187 Washington Street is one fine example of the period known as the Federal Period (1795–1830), represented by the three-storied houses with third-story windows. The Gun House on Elm Street is also Federal in architecture.

Architectural styles in houses changed frequently in the 1800's. The Greek Revival was followed by the Mansard style, both distinctive with the Mansard spelling out Victoriana. Then followed the Queen Anne style with its fish-scale shingles and various materials.

The streets these houses are on are the very byways that the early settlers, the fishermen, the patriots and the children roamed freely. Here the ministers walked and were treated with great respect and politeness, as they occupied the highest status of society in those days. Here the town crier hurried, calling out his news; here is where the sailors hied to and fro; here, too, the "fancy ladies" walked and were recognized. More than that, here was the setting for the vigorous spirit of freedom that was born and where the men of Marblehead played out their roles of destiny.

Human ecology is the study of the relationship of man and his environment, and that series of relationships includes the one between man and his home. In today's society the man-made structures we term houses have been so often abused that our American architectural heritage is all but obliterated, but not in Marblehead. As for the stories of the dwellings themselves, some of the tales, true or fanciful, are as deeply imbedded in the fabric of tradition as are the handmade nails and wooden pegs that support the houses; to remove them would fracture the framework of colorful legend. Almost all the houses commented on are never open to the public; however, if by rare chance a home is open, be sure to look at the pine or walnut cupboard that was popular through the 1700's; this is where the treasures from the Orient are kept, as well as some of the family heirlooms.

Washington Square and Washington Street provide the setting for the fine period houses in Marblehead. Here the "codfish aristocracy" lived and their homes spoke eloquently of their successful trading enterprises; they were the codfish and Bilbao shipping merchants. These homes lend dignity and architectural beauty to the Common.

Abbot Hall on the Common, the training field of long ago, is the most conspicuous building in town as it stands on one of the highest points of land and is sixty feet above the sea level. As an abbot watches over his community, so Abbot Hall seems to assume the role for its town. From every townsman to the homecoming fisherman or sailor returning from a day's sail or several weeks cruising, Abbot Hall, symbol of the beloved town, silhouetted against the blue sky of day or brilliantly illuminated against the blackness of night, spells out "Welcome Home to Marblehead." It stands as a guardian for the arm of land known as Marblehead, which was what its donor, Benjamin Abbot, had intended it to be.

Growing up in Marblehead, Benjamin Abbot harbored an intense love of his birthplace and when he had become a very wealthy man in Boston he wished to express that love and loyalty. In 1872 he willed some $103,000 to the town of Marblehead for the erection of a "building for the benefit of the inhabitants." Typically, some of the citizens had to "look at the bequest from every angle," including the use of the Common land. The objections were overcome and a decision in favor of the Common was finally reached and the cornerstone laid on July 25, 1876. The construction of the building was begun in 1877 and the result was a fine example (perhaps the only good example left, for many such have been razed) of a romantic Romanesque building made of face brick with fine grouting, unusual Caledonia freestone carving and stained-glass windows, and an ample tower of good proportions which has in it a bell and clock, the donation of James J. H. Gregory. The bell is still used to ring the nine o'clock curfew, following an old English custom begun in the town in early 1650; it also booms its sonorous tones on the Fourth of July and other festive, patriotic occasions. The roofs are slated and surmounted with iron crest and gilded finials; the main roof is mansard. At the summit of the spire is a large banneret weather vane topped by a cod and a gilded ball. The foundation is of granite from Rockport. On the second floor the building has an auditorium that seats twelve hundred people and over the years it has seen town meetings, lectures, square dances and dramatics.

During the 1930's the hallways were decorated by the WPA artists and show many phases of Marblehead history. The first floor was originally used for a public library with both adults' and children's rooms; in the 1950's the adults' rooms and stacks were utilized by town offices and the children's room was made into the selectmen's room. In this room is the ancient deed written on parchment and bearing the totem signatures of several Indians for the purchase of that rocky peninsula which comprises the town. In the same room is displayed the flag flown by the cruiser *Marblehead* during the Battle of the Java Sea in February, 1942, and in the hall on a pedestal rests her bell. *Marblehead* is called "the ship that wouldn't die" because after being attacked by twenty-seven planes she was reported sunk by the enemy, but with steering gear shattered and great gaping holes in her sides she limped thirteen thousand miles back to this country. The bell in the tower rang *that* day!

The bust of Elbridge Gerry is in the selectmen's room and there are several valuable marine paintings. The greatest painting is *The Spirit of '76*. In one year more than 150,000 people, foreigners as well as Americans, come to Marblehead to look and draw inspiration from it. It is an integral part of Marblehead's whole fabric, and its donor (Gen. John H. Devereux of Cleveland, Ohio) well recognized that this patriotic painting belonged in the town of Marblehead. Feeling that it was symbolic of the town General Devereux wrote to Marblehead in April, 1880, asking that the painting be "erected in Abbot Hall to the memory of the brave men of Marblehead who have died on sea and land for their country."

The canvas is large; the figures heroic in size. The artist, Archibald Willard, made several sketches before the painting was exactly as he wished. He used his father as the model for the forceful and determined drummer, and the fifer was a friend, Hugh Mosher, an old farmer-soldier who had fifed his way through the wars. The model for the young drummer looking at the old drummer, fearless as he marches proudly, was General Devereux' own son, Harry.

The artist, the son of a Baptist minister, had no formal art training, but he painted with the same house paints he used for decorating peddler wagons with prettily vignetted landscapes and animals' heads. He painted them so well that people began to notice him throughout Ohio. His fame reached its peak in *The Spirit of '76*. It was first displayed at the Centennial Exhibition in Philadelphia where it aroused much attention and people from everywhere came to see it. It was shown in Boston for a number of weeks at the Old South Meeting House, from there it went to the Corcoran Art Gallery in Washington and, finally, when General Devereux purchased it for his birthplace, it came to Marblehead. The donor wrote, "It seems most fitting that this particular painting of Willard's should become permanently identified with the Town of Marblehead, whose history is so interwoven with Colonial and Revolutionary times and whose patriotism shone forth in every epoch of the nation's life."

One critic wrote of *The Spirit of '76*, "All combine to make up that wonderful figure in our history which no rags could degrade nor splendor ennoble . . . Mr. Willard with his powerful but, perhaps less finished touch did more than please the eye of experts; he stirred the heart of a nation."

WASHINGTON STREET

Directly opposite Abbot Hall is 187 Washington Street, the Mansion House. This was built by Captain John Hooper in the eighteenth century; the rear portion of the house was built in 1790 and the front in 1794. His son, John Hooper, Esquire, was one of the wealthiest merchants in town and for many years was president of the Marblehead Bank.

John's son, Samuel, was born here in 1808 and he inherited his father's money sense. He became a member of the Massachusetts Legislature and then a representative to Congress. Here his efforts in behalf of a bill establishing a national banking system won him the plaudits of Secretary of the Treasury Salmon Chase, who attributed the bill's success to "sound judgement, persevering exertion and disinterested patriotism."

The attractive, three-storied mansion has its main entrance on the side, a fine portico approach. The house is topped by an enclosed captain's walk where the first Captain John watched for his ships and where visitors might have a spectacular view.

Among the interesting features of the house is the drawing room with its shuttered windows, the large fireplaces, the graceful stairway and the kitchen with its old-time fireplace.

At 185 is the Col. William Raymond Lee Mansion. An original

deed dated April 25, 1743, states that Justice Samuel Lee of Manchester, Massachusetts, who with his son, Samuel, built many houses in both Manchester and Marblehead, purchased this land. This imposing Georgian home resembles the Jeremiah Lee Mansion in many respects; it was first a small house (now the ell of the home), and then was enlarged. Family papers show that the present large portion facing the street was designed by Charles Bulfinch, the famous architect of that day. It was Col. William Raymond Lee who brought fame to this mansion and it was he who had the house redesigned, moving into it as soon as his first child was born. (His grandfather's widow had been willed the "easterly half" of the house where she continued to live until her death in 1781.) Prior to William Lee's remodeling, the house (known as "The House on the Hill") had a cupola topping its roof, an almost exact replica of the one that is on the Lee Mansion where William Raymond Lee took his bride, Mary Lemmon. Cupolas were not only an added decoration but also were a necessity enabling ship owners to look far out to sea.

Many famous people came to call on the colonel and probably no one more frequently than the Reverend Dr. Bentley from Salem who recorded each such visit meticulously.

The colonel was General Washington's lifelong friend and after one of Washington's visits to 185 the guest sent a likeness of Mount Vernon painted on a rectangular background of glass in gold leaf and sepia. Another family treasure, a fine miniature of the colonel painted by Hancock, is now in the Essex Institute. In the house itself the scenic wallpaper by Dufour was put on the walls about 1829 and has been kept in excellent condition.

In an unpublished manuscript about Colonel Lee his biographer, Mr. Dearborn, wrote: "As did many of his name, Colonel believed that a full stomach was a prevention of evil, and accordingly, annually on Thanksgiving, Christmas, and New Year's Day, he made it a principle to purchase large quantities of fresh beef, pork, mutton and poultry, which, with flour, butter, sugar, tea, spices and fuel were distributed by his benevolent and excellent wife to the poor inhabitants of the town. The most needy and deserving being all known, they were informed at what hour to come and receive their several presents, that they might be enabled to join in the great festivities of those New England holy days. . . ." Lee's sister Annis married Maj. John Pulling, the man who had hung the lantern in Christ Church belfry for Paul Revere.

The Hooper Mansion at 181 Washington Street was built (1740–1745) by Robert Hooper, merchant and cousin of the famed King Hooper, and he lived here until his death in 1814.

There is some similarity to the mansions built in Marblehead during this period because the men who constructed them were all ships' carpenters. The stone of the foundations and terrace was brought back as ballast on ships from Spain and Russia. During this period of sail cargoes were often so light that it was necessary to take on thousands of pounds of ballast to make the ships manageable. Some Spanish marble may be found in the fireplaces throughout the house. This is one of the four or five houses in Marblehead which had an "underground" tunnel for fugitive slaves to use prior to the Civil War and was the secret passage rumored to have been used by merchants for smuggling.

Going east from Washington Square stands the Lee Mansion, built in 1768 by Col. Jeremiah Lee, a Georgian house which a contemporary Boston paper stated was "the most elegant and costly furnished home in the Bay State Colony." The Reverend Manassah Cutler described it as the "most magnificent house in the colonies" though he found nothing else to admire in Marblehead! The building date is outlined in light-colored pebbles in the courtyard. The builder was Jeremiah's brother Samuel, of Manchester, who was a master builder familiar with English architecture and construction. Family records show that it was constructed of big timbers brought from Manchester. The style is Georgian and the wood used on the exterior was grooved in the process known as ashlar construction to imitate cut stone; to enhance this corner quoins were fashioned for the facade. It has always been painted gray with white trim. The Lee Mansion is impressive with its three-storied facade of seven bays and a central pavilion of three bays with an entrance portico supported by Ionic columns. In the 1820's one of the wooden columns which stood at the right of the entrance was discovered to be badly rotted. After considerable search for a piece of well-seasoned pine the bowsprit of the old privateer *America* was finally discovered, and from that was built the column as it stands today. The mansion's cost was £10,000. The hallway is large in its proportions, sixteen feet wide, and the great stairway and the wainscot of the hall are of San Domingo mahogany. The rare Pergolesi wallpapers portraying Roman and Grecian scenes are in tempera and were made in England. Furnishings are connected with Marblehead, such as the four Hepplewhite chairs that belonged to the daughter of Gen. John Glover, the piano stool that was Elbridge Gerry's, the Queen Anne mirror that belonged to the Pedrick family, the paintings of William Bartoll and J. O. J. Frost, the coverlet made by Agnes Surriage and many other fascinating pieces, including fireboards painted by local artists. According to tradition, two of the Hepplewhite chairs belonged to Governor Hancock, and were brought to Marblehead in a trading vessel. These two chairs were found, together with many other antique pieces, in the tottering hovel of two Marblehead characters, "Liz" and "Mopsy" Chambers, when the authorities moved them to the almshouse.

Each room is artistically arranged and the Marblehead Historical Society diligently retains authenticity . . . The entrance hall that runs through the center of the house is baronial in size and the stairway, with shallow treads measuring seven feet in width, leads to a landing that has a high-arch window, on either side of which hang life-sized portraits of Jeremiah Lee and his wife, Martha. They are copies of the John Singleton Copley originals which are now in the Wadsworth Atheneum at Hartford. Copley painted these striking (eight feet by five feet) portraits of Colonel and Mrs. Lee for £25 each. At the time a man's silk stocking could cost more than the coat he wore; a coat might be valued at a guinea, but clocked, silk hose embroidered on the instep cost two guineas. Copley, in 1769, had painted Jeremiah's fine triangular clocks so deftly that they became a hallmark of time and the gentleman. In fact, Copley has captured Lee in his best manner, head well up, scented peruke flowing, hand proudly extended, and he is "making a leg." The etiquette book of that day, *Jauna*, written by one Comenius, instructed, "Rise up, put off thy Hatt, extend thy Hand, make a leg." Mrs. Lee was making her manners, too, for the beautiful, textured gown she is wearing is lifted just high enough to reveal a beautifully slippered foot; she stands easily, simple yet stately, in lines of true grace. The frames of the original portraits were carved by Paul Revere.

Colonel Lee was the son of Justice Samuel and Mary (Tarring) Lee and was born to them in Manchester, Massachusetts, on April 16, 1721. He came to Marblehead sometime prior to 1745 and on June 25, 1745, he married Martha Swett of Marblehead, the daughter of Joseph and Martha A. (Stacey) Swett.

Under his father's able direction young Jeremiah acquired commercial knowledge in his father's counting room. Soon he was managing and dispatching his own vessels, wealth came quickly and he became one of the most influential men of all Marblehead. In the business world Marblehead was no longer a small, struggling fishing village, rather it was the great shipping center of New England— even ahead of Boston, although second to Boston in population. In all there were sixty merchants in Marblehead engaged in the foreign trade and it may safely be said that Jeremiah Lee and King Hooper double-headed the list.

In 1751 Lee was commissioned colonel of the Marblehead regiment. He, Maj. Richard Reed and Col. Jacob Fowle were appointed a committee to build the Powder House, a circular brick magazine on the old Ferry Road. He was moderator at Town Meeting, a member of the Tuesday Evening Club and a zealous patriot. When the difficult days that led to the Revolution came he was generous; we read in the *Concord Yeoman:* "From Colonel Jeremiah Lee of Marblehead, 6 hogshead containing 35 half-barrels of powder. This was received in December and in the accompanying letter Colonel Lee remarks 'don't so much as mention the name of powder lest our enemies should take advantage of it.' 8 hogsheads more were soon after received from Colonel Lee. He also sent to Concord another load—containing tent poles, axes and hatchets and also 318 Barrels of flour which was partly destroyed on the 19th of April." The often repeated story is that Jeremiah Lee joined with Elbridge Gerry and Azor Orne at that famous meeting in April, 1775, at Weatherby's Black Horse Tavern in Arlington—the meeting that was to help our country, but which proved disastrous to Lee for he became ill as the result of exposure there and died at his "retreat" home in Newbury, Massachusetts, a little over a month later.

The Lees had nine children; only six survived to live in the Lee Mansion. (One of the Marblehead legends concerns itself with Mary Lee, one of the beauties of her day: on the day of her marriage to young Nathaniel Tracey of Newburyport she had driven off to her wedding in a coach lined with white satin and drawn by milk-white horses.) However, only two children remained at home with the widowed Mrs. Lee as she struggled against great odds to keep both the home and its priceless furnishings intact against the instability of paper money and decreasing funds. She did entertain George Washington on his first visit, and had the motif of the eagle—the new symbol of the new country—pasted in each of the front windows silhouetted against the flames of the welcoming candles. Finally, keeping the house in order (the slaves had been freed) became a burden for her and she returned to their old home in Newbury where she died in 1791. For a while Samuel Sewall owned the mansion, then the Marblehead Bank bought it and, even though they conducted their business, treated it as the dwelling place it had always been. In 1909 the Marblehead Historical Society purchased the building for its headquarters and with concerted, diligent effort refurbished the home in the elegant manner of the period. The Society has brought countless treasures to it, has sought out manuscripts, records, china, as well as furniture and a horde of other things which tell in their very being what the times were like in a fine Georgian home. Today the Jeremiah Lee Mansion is a Registered National Historic Landmark.

WASHINGTON SQUARE

Washington Square meets 183 Washington Street and 4 Washington Square on the square itself. Number 4 was known as the Shepard House, early nineteenth century; a fine example of Greek Revival, it has a noble aspect despite its small size. When the classical Grecian architecture was introduced into America in the 1820's, it was greeted with great enthusiasm for our country was beginning to feel its strength as a nation and many thought our spirit and system of government embodied that of the ancient Greek republic. Number 4 is a two-and-a-half-storied house with a ridge roof, and the off-centered door is in the gable end.

Number 8 is an excellent example of early nineteenth-century Federal style. The Federal period of architecture (1790–1820) is so called because its birth and that of our nation were almost simultaneous. This house is made elegant by its beautiful portico and doorway.

Number 10 was built in the early 1700's and the earliest deed to be found shows that it was in the possession of William Sandin, a fisherman. He left the home to his daughter, "Deborah Sandin, Singlewoman." This probably was the house known as the Little Jug Inn. Where an arched gateway on the left now stands was originally the ell of the house.

Number 12 (1760–1800) is a mid-Georgian three-storied house. (Georgian describes a long era in which four kings named George ruled England.) George III was reigning when America gained its independence. Houses of Georgian architecture were usually built by master builders and their product showed the builders hallmark. It has been said that the robust Georgian is masculine while the Federal, with its delicate decoration, is feminine. The hall of this home is lighted by a segmented half-circle light over the door.

Number 16 (1880–1900). This house, which has had many different materials used in its construction—clapboards, patterned fish-scale shingles, zippered brick—is nonrectangular with porches, balconies and turrets significant of its style—Queen Anne.

LEE STREET

Lee Street (off Washington Square) parallel to the water's edge of the harbor, was one of the earliest streets. Some claim it was named

for Col. William Raymond Lee, others for Col. Jeremiah Lee—
probably it was named for both.

Number 6, the Nicholson Broughton House (1700–1780), has a
center chimney and wide overhang at the eaves in front. It is of the
Georgian period; it also has a Georgian roof. Nicholson Broughton,
after his reprimand from Washington, left the regular army but
stayed in the local militia and took up privateering.

MIDDLE STREET

Middle Street, which lies south of Washington Square, is particularly important for it is a good example of an old street having all
eighteenth-century houses of early, simple design.

Number 1 stands on the land that belonged to Thomas Nicholson
before 1700. Sometime between 1704 and 1714 the first Caswell
came to Marblehead from the island of Guernsey. Eight generations
of Caswells have been born here, the first of whom was William
who became a private in Company Eight of Glover's Marblehead
regiment, captained by William Bacon.

SOUTH STREET

Leading off Middle Street toward the sea is South Street, and no
story of Marblehead is complete without the tale of a house that is
no longer standing there. Once the gabled-roofed house which
stood on the corner of Washington and South Streets belonged to
Captain John Russell (1728–1811). He was, in 1774, on the Committee of Inspection of British Imports. At his death his "estate" was
found cached under his bed in sea chests:

In guineas and doubloons	$1460.00
6 Bags of $1,000 each	6000.00
1 bag dollars	696.00
Paper money from creditors	2783.12
	10939.12
Ships	1398.00
Real estate & other personal monies	5056.00
He left a total of	$45000.00

WALDRON STREET

Waldron Street, which joins South Street, underwent a variety of
changes. In 1664 it was Waldron Lane (Way to the First, or Waldron's Cove); in 1734 it was known as Way to Fish Fences; twenty
years later, Coney (Cunny) Lane; in the 1800's by two additional
names, Waldron's Court and then in 1872, Waldron Street.

Number 11 was built about 1714 and it is typical of the fishermen's homes of that era. The oak beams and the bricks that are used both in the fireplaces and for insulation between the walls were brought from England. The other timbers used in the structure were cut from nearby Roundy's Hill.

WALDRON COURT

Waldron Court, which leads off Waldron Street, in 1734 was known as Way to rear of Andrews Lot and in 1842 became Waldron Court.

In the rear of 13 Waldron Court there is an extensive, typical Marblehead garden—fruit trees of many varieties, rose bushes, lilacs, wild and cultivated flowers, as well as that which William Bradford listed as the produce of a New England kitchen garden in 1654:

> All sorts of roots and herbs in gardens grow,
> Parsnips, carrots, turnips, or what you'll sow,
> Onions, melons, cucumbers, radishes,
> Skirrets, beets, coleworts, and fair cabbages.

Number 15 is known as the Fettyplace House. Harry Andrews, a farmer, built this house prior to 1750 (the remodeled house at the end of Waldron Court was his barn). Sometime before 1789 William Fettyplace, a Grand Banks fisherman, purchased the property. An old account, dated 1802 and found in a partition of the house, states that the amount of twenty dollars was to be paid to a workman for two months work done on the fish fence, making the amount per hour, ten cents. The room that is now the dining room was originally the kitchen and it has a large fireplace with a dutch oven and crane. The shed beyond the kitchen was originally a cordwainer's shop (shoe shop) as, during the long winter months, many of the townfolk made shoes to be exported to the Orient on Marblehead boats going out after cargo. As the same family owned the house until 1944 it remains essentially the same with very few architectural changes.

GREGORY STREET

Gregory Street lies along the waterfront and Waldron Street leads into it; Gregory Street, in turn, leads into Lee Street.

Number 7 is known as the Gardner Cottage and at one time was the subject of a ceramic wall plaque; this house is very old and is said to have been an early cottage on Great Neck which was floated over the harbor on a raft to its present location. It is definitely seventeenth century and one of the few one-story houses in town.

FRONT STREET

This street was called Fore Street and was once the center of activity. No. 116 is the last of the cordwainers in Marblehead. The fishermen became cobblers during the winter to supplement their incomes, and when the fishing industry, as such, became slack the cobblers' trade was their entire occupation. This accounts for tiny shops like this in the yards of many of the homes in Marblehead.

TUCKER STREET

Tucker Street branches off the northeast corner of Washington Square. Number 5 Tucker Street is the Christopher Bubier Mansion. The records of the Old North Church show that Christopher Bubier, "son of Christopher," was baptized June 16, 1706. He married Marguerite LeVallier on October 30, 1726, and three years later purchased this house, presumably from his grandfather. His mother's name was Margaret Palmer and the original land grant shows it was given to John Palmer on February 11, 1682. In August, 1729, Palmer conveyed the southerly portion of the land-dwelling to Christopher Bubier and there he and his wife lived for seventeen years. In 1746 he purchased the northwesterly portion of land and dwelling from Richard Trevett. Christopher Bubier died in 1789, leaving the house to his daughter, Grace (Mrs. Joshua Prentiss), and then to her children, who finally sold it in 1818.

Mr. and Mrs. Samuel Chamberlain over a period of years, restored the house to its original splendor. Its historical background is no more colorful than the career of its former occupant whose fine etchings, photographs and writings are known the world over. Mrs. Chamberlain is an author of gourmet cookbooks, having collaborated with both her husband and their daughter, Narcisse. Mr. Chamberlain studied at the Royal College of Art in London, and with Edouard Leon in Paris. His etchings are represented in the British Museum and the Bibliotheque Nationale, Paris; the Library of Congress; Boston, Chicago and New York Museums of Art. Mrs. Chamberlain has been a vital force in the Marblehead Arts Association and for the Marblehead Historical Society. She has devoted many years to the Lee Mansion paying particular attention to the documentation and the authenticity of the continual restoration.

Number 10 Tucker Street was once a girl's seminary, (1800–1820), and was built by the Marblehead Free School Association. Originally it contained two school rooms and the large hall was used by the Masonic Lodge.

LOOKOUT COURT

Lookout Court begins at Tucker Street and was known as Prospect Alley. Fish flakes once covered the hill where the townspeople —the women and children, especially—hurried when the town crier alerted them that a vessel was putting in to port. The homes on this small court are fascinating and the view is one of the best in town. In the spring the small gardens sparkle with beauty.

Number 5 is the "Lookout" itself, a three-storied house of Georgian type, adorned with an especially fine fanlight and fluted pilasters in the Colonial doorway. This door was used for a scene in the 1922 film, *Heart of a Hero*. The house was built by Peter Dixey in 1745 when he was a local customs official. The rooms are low studded, and it is one of the few Old Bay State houses to boast a beehive fireplace. The staircases rise at sharp angles, nearly vertical, as they do often in a ship. On mounting three, steep flights one arrives in a small, cozy room through which a giant chimney passes. This is the observation room where once Dixey, the pilot and customs officer (1838–1842), son of the first Peter, watched for incoming vessels. He sometimes worked at his shoes in this room while watching for incoming ships, and when he signaled to the ships he used a "bunch of rags on a pulley." The shipping was not busy in son Peter's time and he alternated working on his shoes with using his telescope. He became more famous for his shoes (handmade throughout and of an excellence unsurpassed) than for his "aloft piloting."

Mr. and Mrs. Waldo Ballard bought the Lookout in 1920 and it was Mr. Ballard's ambition to convert the court into an artists' colony and to have an exhibition of his own, but as one relative said, "He hadn't figured on Mrs. Ballard, for when she said 'No' she meant it, and it was 'No' to that scheme." The Ballards did restore the Lookout and in doing so, when they removed the many layers of yellowed old wallpaper, they came upon the famous Washington Memorial wallpaper that had been struck off by order of Congress at the time of Washington's death. Sets were made for the thirteen states only, one being given to each of the governors. The one for Massachusetts fell into the hands of Mr. Dixey and he used it in his house. The design is an attractive one, representing "Liberty" and "Justice" placing wreaths at the foot of the monument erected to Washington showing the coat of arms of the Washington family. Skilled in copying and designing wallpapers, Mr. Ballard made fifty panels of the historic paper for the house.

LOOKOUT COURT'S OLD STEPS TO LEE STREET

The way down (called Prospect Alley in 1824) to Lee Street was originally wide enough for a horse and shay but has been gradually encroached upon by the property owners. This type of ancient way is typical of the rockbound coastal towns in Devonshire and Cornwall, England, the original home of many of Marblehead's early settlers.

UNION STREET

Union Street meets Lee Street at the junction of Lee and Hooper Streets. Number 2 Union is the "Lafayette House." The Marquis de Lafayette visited Marblehead in his later years, late in August, 1824. He came to the United States at the invitation of Congress; his son, George Washington Lafayette, accompanied him and both gentlemen were welcomed warmly. Marblehead was once again filled with the excitement of anticipation and readied itself for the splendid dinner at which the two distinguished Frenchmen would be guests of honor. A public reception followed and every one who could come did, to welcome the marquis and his son. Before departing, General Lafayette made a call upon Mrs. Mary Glover Hooper, wife of Robert Hooper, Jr., for she was the only surviving daughter of his old friend and companion-in-arms, Gen. John Glover.

The Georgian dwelling, built in 1800, is situated at the junction of five streets—Hooper, Lee, Tucker, Union and Water. A persistent legend grown up around Number 2 Union Street is that the corner of the house was cut away to make room for the beautiful coach and six span of horses of the famous and distinguished visitor from France!

Actually, the house was once a "sweet shop" or tavern which was built originally in that fashion because of the narrow street to make room for the traffic of wagons bearing rum from the harbor for the tavern.

The house, dating from 1731, is the largest, most prominent house in this particular area and is early Georgian in style, having two dormer windows in front and two on the left side. Its interior is unusually fine. Six rooms feature paneling and detail, and a seventh room is unique because of its completely detailed paneling of all four walls. The ownership of this house and the occupancy of the stone house preceding this one on the same site goes back to 1672.

Number 8 Union Street was the birthplace of Benjamin Abbot, Marblehead's benefactor. He was born in Marblehead on September 7, 1795. His mother died when he was very young and his father, a fisherman, remarried. Fortunately for Benjamin, his stepmother was good to him and persuaded his father that he should be allowed to learn the cooper's trade and not become a Grand Banks fisherman. He was apprenticed to a cooper, named Holder, in Marblehead, and when this did not seem to work out well, it was his stepmother who walked to Salem to procure another situation for him.

According to the record of September 1, 1727, Stephen Minot, merchant, transferred to Greenfield Hooper, a tallow chandler, the land on which the "King" Hooper Mansion now stands. The five-storied elevation facing the garden was probably built in the same year, when Robert Hooper, for whom the house is named, was eighteen years old. The three-storied facade was added in 1745. The gracious rooms are filled with rare fireplaces. The upstairs chambers were built to resemble a ship's cabin and an excellent example of hand-carved spiral staircase (which was brought over from England), with the treads serving as boxes for the carved portions, is the most unique feature of the house. The large ballroom on the top floor with its rare bell ceiling was once the setting for elaborate dinners and parties and is now used by the Marblehead Arts Association for exceptional art exhibits, and also for children's art classes. In the basement the old cistern room and wine cellar have been converted into a taproom. Here, in the spacious kitchen with its huge fireplace, luncheons are on occasion served by the Arts Association.

King Hooper, whose name the house perpetuates, had four wives and eleven children. The wealthiest of the merchants in Marblehead, with ships sailing to the West Indies and all European ports, his kindly treatment of his seamen and his innate courtesy earned him the title of "King." He bought the first fire engine and presented it to the town in 1751. A fine Copley portrait of Robert Hooper has been preserved, but the miniature of one of his wives, painted at the same time, was last seen in the 1880's.

His son, Robert Hooper, Jr., married Mary, the daughter of Gen. John Glover, and she inherited the house. At one time there were five Robert Hoopers living—father, son and three cousins—which added continual confusion to the records!

The Marblehead Arts Association purchased the old mansion in 1938 and restored it (even the original colors of the walls, as nearly as possible), and re-created an eighteenth-century garden at the rear of the house.

Bank Square

The National Grand Bank Building, now a professional building, was built in 1831. It is the only bank to have been named for a fishing bank, that of the Grand Bank off Canada and Newfoundland. It is a Georgian Revival building and, being built of granite it gives the feeling of substance and security—most appropriate for that type of institution.

WASHINGTON STREET

Number 147 is The Hooper–Fabens House, a gracious home set back from the street, was built by Nathaniel Hooper (1771–1825) one of the four sons of Robert Hooper, a leading merchant. The wood carving above the beautiful door (which is in the center of the building) is fan shaped, and the door has side lights which enhance it. The door opens into a gracious, broad hallway and the rooms on either side are inviting and appealing in their proportions. The roominess of the hall is repeated on the next two story levels. An air of quiet grace and dignity pervades the house both inside and out.

The house in later years was bought by the Fabens family. The first Fabens were living in Marblehead in 1640 and soon after that they moved to Salem. Squire William Fabens (1810–1883), who bought the house, had an office in a small ell (on the extreme left) for he was a trial justice for many years.

The Robie House at 137 Washington Street, opposite the head of Darling Street, was the home of Thomas Robie, one of the Royalists who fled from the town during the Revolution.

It is one of the most imposing of the few brick houses in Marblehead; its attractive door is away from the street on the left side of the house. This house was also called the Brick Path.

DARLING STREET

One of the oldest thoroughfares, laid out about 1730, is Darling Street which is one way from Washington to Front Street. The houses on this street are all built close together with many a front entrance opening directly onto the street. Almost every house here was built in the 1700's of wooden clapboards, all living up to the charm of the homes built in that area which housed many treasures brought home from the years at sea.

Number 17, which was built in the middle of the eighteenth century, was known originally as the Old Darling Farm House and it was this family that gave the name to the street.

Number 18–22 is the oldest on the street and was built by Ebenezer Martin. At the time he built, the land was called Darling Meadows. Ebenezer, who was a cabinetmaker, it is recorded, was "drowned at the East ward, Sometime Since." (Before June 20, 1806.)

Previous to 1825 the only boots and shoes made in Marblehead were heavy leather boots; after that, manufacturing of misses' and children's shoes was introduced. Ebenezer Martin, the son, was the first manufacturer to engage in this new enterprise, driving from town to town in a cart until he had disposed of them.

Joseph Dixon, who was to give his name to the famous Dixon pencil and invent so many graphite improvements that the scientific community would call him "Graphite Joe," was born in this house in 1799. His father was Captain Joseph Dixon—in 1812 prize master of the privateer *America*—and his mother was Elizabeth Reed. Grandfather Reed had married a member of the Katanak Indian tribe, fought at Bunker Hill, and was killed in a later Revolutionary War battle.

Built of imported English timber with handmade nails, the Dixon house, which Joseph Dixon left as a young man to become a prolific and internationally recognized inventor, has four front doors approached by the stepping stones that once gave the house its name. The rooms contain *H* and *L* door hinges and many window seats. Flowers now cover the top of a well that furnished cool, crystal-clear spring water for the casks of fishermen and mariners from the nearby wharves.

CROCKER PARK LANE

This lane is almost perpendicular to Darling Street. Crocker Park was first called Bartoll's Head, and was used by the Bartolls for fish flaking.

One of the two "castles" in Marblehead stands at 2 Crocker Park Lane. This was built by Mr. and Mrs. Waldo Ballard, natives of Marblehead, in 1926. The ancient castle of Eric the Red in Greenland was the model for Ballard's Castle Brattahlid. The castle lives up to its name, which means "hewn out of rock," as it was built entirely from stone blasted out of the ledge on which it now stands.

Mr. Ballard hired John D. Regan to carry out his plans for, in Mr. Ballard's opinion, "Mr. Regan is an artist in stone." The fireproof building (since it is built of stone) has walls four feet thick at the bottom and battered in to two feet at the top. In the main building is a dungeon and within the walls a secret stairway. The main room is on the second floor and contains a massive fireplace. The building dimensions for that room were 34 x 36 feet, and the ceiling height 12½ feet; 200 could be seated. The floor of the banquet hall is tiled and contains a griffin in its design.

Since 1945, L. Francis Herreshoff, son of the world famous yacht designer, had lived here. Herreshoff was a naval architect in his own right, having many boats to his credit; probably the best known is *Ticonderoga,* a seventy-two-foot clipper-bowed ketch which still holds the sailing-vessel record for the fastest crossing of the Atlantic.

WATSON STREET

Watson crosses Pleasant Street and in doing so becomes Rockaway Street which leads onto Washington Street and borders one side of the Lee Mansion property.

Watson Street was named for Marston Watson, a well-to-do merchant in town in the late 1700's. His house is at the head of Watson Street, its tall central chimney is white with a dubious date painted on it. Benjamin Marston built himself a house with a view (1730–1740). Mr. Marston was a vigorous Loyalist at the outbreak of the Revolution and he was so vocative that he incurred the ire of the zealous patriots. They vented their dislike (for he was suspected of being a spy) by breaking down the doors and entering his home, opening his desks and carrying off his account books. His house was taken by Confiscation Act of the government and eventually turned over to his nephew, Marston Watson.

In February, 1810, twenty-one members of the First Baptist Church of Salem were dismissed so that they might organize a Baptist church in Marblehead. This first Baptist house of worship, known as the "Rock Meeting House," was located on Watson Street. The typical New England church where the Baptists now worship was erected on its present site, Pleasant Street, in 1831.

The Universalist Church, organized in January, 1836, held its services in Franklin Hall until the church on the corner of Watson and Pleasant Streets was completed in 1837. It was here that the Marblehead minister, Rev. Marcia Selman, preached. With the decline in membership in the 1900's the church was up for auction and the only bidder was Marblehead's badminton club, The Gut'n Feathers. This club had been organized in the 1930's and had been playing in Peabody's Garage on Lindsay Street, and also Lyceum Hall, and had been looking for suitable quarters for their organization. They renovated the church edifice by removing the first floor and built one of the best springboard badminton floors in the country. The floor space allows for two double courts and some of the world's greatest badminton players have played here.

ROCKAWAY STREET

Once Rockaway Street was known as the Old Methodist Rocks. The rocks were really a large ledge which extended from Pleasant Street to well below Summer Street. The parishioners of the Methodist Church used them when they attended church service, when their church was on Summer Street. Finally, the ledge was removed by Richard Peach who was the town's principal contractor in building cellar walls and blasting ledges.

SUMMER STREET

Jesse Lee, the pioneer of Methodism in New England, preached the first sermon of that faith in Marblehead in July, 1790. A chapel was built for services in 1801 on the rocks at the head of Rockaway Street. In 1833 the chapel was converted into a dwelling house, and sometimes used as a parsonage. The St. Stephen's Methodist Church was built in 1833 at a cost of five thousand dollars. After serving its members for 125 years, in 1959 it was converted into the Earl Apartments.

It was on Summer Street (once called Frog Lane) that one of the earliest colonial churches in all New England, St. Michael's, was built in 1714. It is the fourth oldest Episcopal church in New England and it is also the second oldest Episcopal church building still standing.

Documentary records show that a subscription list was started on March 31, 1714, with forty names pledging various sums to "build and erect a handsome church . . . and to maintain a minister to carry on the service of God in the ways and methods of the Church of Great Britain or Church of England." (There were many in town who disliked the Puritanism that was continuing its hold upon the Colonies, and the lack of ritual in the Congregational Church made them wish for the Church of England; besides that, the nonconformist attitude of Marbleheaders could always be counted upon for the only thing that they conformed to was nonconformity). Members of the Church of England outside of Marblehead became "benefactors."

For years it was thought that the timber used in the building of the church had been brought from England, but in 1962, through chemical analysis of samples of the original timber, it was found to be good old New England white pine.

Before the church was built (1714), ministers from King's Chapel had conducted occasional Episcopal services in Marblehead, undoubtedly in private homes. The first rector, the Reverend William

Shaw, was followed by the Reverend David Mosson who moved to New Kent, Virginia, where he officiated at the wedding of George Washington and Martha Custis. One of the problems the communicants of the Church of England in New England had to face during a great part of the eighteenth century was the taxation for the support of the Congregational minister. The governor, when appealed to by St. Michael's, censured the selectmen of Marblehead with the result that not only St. Michael's, but also no other church had to support the Congregational minister any longer. Two of St. Michael's rectors had slaves: Mr. Pigot recorded baptizing four of his own slaves, and the Reverend Mr. Bours owned a particularly vicious slave woman. A singing gallery was built in 1732 and was a dangerous innovation, because under Puritan law, churches could not have balconies or music. It is said the prudent warders permitted it to be built, but by parishioners who desired it and at their own expense. Later it was decided to build a lean-to at the back and an invitation was extended to the entire community to assist in a "raising," always the signal for a frolic. The expense record reads, "Paid for rum and charges about fish and wine at raising the lentoo at the meeting house—4pd, 2sh, 6d."

The church was ready with music for the Reverend Alexander Malcolm when he was rector in the 1740's. He, himself, played a flute and was the author of "a very good book on music." A contemporary record of 1748 stated that "Salemites were sailing over to Marblehead to attend the Church of England until it appeared more like a day of frolicking." The Reverend Joshua Wingate Weeks was the rector whose term coincided with the Revolution—he was a firm Loyalist and even in his departure he prayed for the overthrow of the king's enemies. The rector, Mr. Weeks, hurried off to Canada and the church was closed, opening again in 1778.

The St. Michael's silver has two notable pieces used at festivals: a plain silver flagon, given in 1745 by David LeGallais (later anglicized to Gallison), is tall and cylindrical having a domed cover, a scrolled thumb piece and a wide-molded base with a long Latin inscription engraved on it; the paten, of American manufacture, was given in 1764. Unfortunately the 18th century chalice was melted down in 1869 to make two "tulip" chalices.

The twelve-branch brass chandelier hangs in the position in which it was originally placed when it was presented as "the gift of John Elbridge, Esq. of ye city of Bristol, 1732." The inscription of it names the donor, and the maker, an Italian, J. Gallo. The hanger, gilded wrought iron, is contemporary and was probably also made in Bristol. Elbridge's name was to be remembered in Marblehead for this gift and for another pertinent reason—his grandniece became the mother of Elbridge Gerry.

Like all parish churches of the colonial period the burial ground is adjacent to the building. There one may see a raised tomb among the graves:

"Capt. Robert Wormstead
died at Boston Sept. 25, 1809
age 50 and 1 day"

And there is the raised tomb of:

Rev. Peter Bours, church rector
died Feb. 24, 1762 ae 36

There are few churches in this country that also have a sepulcher beneath where, for over a hundred years, it was the privilege of the pew owners to bury their dead in the Sepulchre of St. Michael's.

WASHINGTON STREET

Washington Street is one, if not the most, important street of the town. It starts at the junction of Franklin, Orne and Elm Streets and ends its winding way to Atlantic Avenue.

Number 119, the Holyoke House, is on the corner of Washington and Pleasant Streets. The documentation of many houses is a melange of hearsay, "I remember whens," and deeds. In the case of this house, *The Holyoke Diaries* have recorded the facts for us. It was built by the Reverend Edward Holyoke, first pastor (1716–1737) of the Second Congregational Church. Born in Boston in 1689, the son of Elizur and Mary (Elliot) Holyoke, Edward Holyoke graduated from Harvard in 1711.

A contemporary described him as being of "fine commanding presence and united great dignity with great urbanity in his manners. In conversation, as well as in public discourse, he spoke with fluency and appropriateness, and yet without any appearance of ostentation. In the government of the college he was mild, but yet firm and efficient and in the whole admirably qualified to be its head."

The home he built in Marblehead is still standing on the corner of Pleasant and Washington Streets. In the parlor and library mulberry tiles were placed around the fireplace—each tile representing a book of the Bible. There is fine woodwork throughout the house and on the second story the rooms are paneled to the ceiling over the many fireplaces.

A later owner, William B. Brown, had an artesian well dug

through the solid rock (in back of the house); they found plenty of water and some silver! However, because of expense and the proximity to St. Michael's Church, the project was abandoned.

Under another ownership, plumbers working in the house took up the attic floor and found a room large enough for a man to stand in; this was found between the attic floor and the bathroom. A passageway was also discovered under the attic stairs. In the cellar under the former kitchen another room was found which undoubtedly had served as a smokeroom.

It was in this roomy house that Edward Augustus Holyoke was born on August 1, 1728. Neddy was nine when the family moved to Cambridge; it was a foregone conclusion that he should matriculate at Harvard. After graduation he went to study medicine with Col. Thomas Berry of Ipswich; this training consisted of compounding prescriptions with liberal use of herbs, and riding about with the doctor. When Dr. Edward Holyoke went to Salem in 1749, he charged eight pence each for his first visits. He sat up late in the evening because his patients often called for him during those hours and that occasioned "lying in bed until a late hour in the morning, till seven in summer and eight in winter."

Later, when 119 Washington Street was owned by Miss Gertrude Stewart, the house was put into excellent repair. Joseph Wormstead, who was skilled at graining, grained the hall and the dining room in Old San Domingo mahogany and the parlor in white mahogany; this graining still may be seen. The house today has been divided into five apartments and dormers have been added.

Number 102 Washington Street is a late eighteenth-century Federal—the house that once was the residence of Dr. Elisha Story, eminent physician and surgeon who moved from Boston to Marblehead in 1770 (for generations since Story's occupancy the property has been known as a Goodwin House). His son, Joseph Story, distinguished juror, was born here in 1779. Dr. Story, an ardent patriot, was attached to Colonel Little's regiment as a surgeon. He fought at Lexington and Concord and at the Battle of Bunker Hill he fought beside his friend, Dr. Joseph Warren.

When his first wife, Ruth (Ruddock) the daughter of a prosperous Boston shipbuilder, died she was buried in the Second Congregational Churchyard in Marblehead. His second wife was Mehitable Pedrick, who, by marrying Elisha at the age of nineteen, at once acquired a ready-made family of seven and eventually with her own childbearing, the total brood was eighteen in number! Joseph Story was the first born of the new set of Story children. For a while Dr. Story was unpopular in Marblehead because he was one of the first to believe in and vaccinate for smallpox, but eventually the hysteria over inoculation disappeared. Joseph Story was to become one of Marblehead's most renowned citizens.

An oft-repeated anecdote is told: one day while trying a case in the local court the crier called repeatedly for "Captain Florence of Marblehead." Receiving no response Judge Joseph Story asked to be allowed to call the captain. To his calling "Skipper Flurry of Barnegat," the answer "Ay, ay, sir," was immediately forthcoming as the witness stood up.

When Richard Henry Dana wrote his *Two Years Before the Mast*, Story wrote complimenting him upon his novel and added "some of my nearest relatives began life in the humblest office on shipboard and gradually rose to the highest." It was Story who wrote the bill that became law protecting seamen from harsh treatment.

Number 65, the Captain Trevett House, was deeded in 1716 to Elizabeth Trevett by her brother, Samuel Russell; it was the birthplace of Samuel Russell Trevett (named for his relative) who led a fearless group of young Marblehead men aboard H.M.S. *Lively* when she was anchored off Fort Sewall in February, 1775. Boarding the vessel they made off with the prize of arms (some twenty mounting guns) and concealed them on shore. This same intrepid Captain Trevett later led a Marblehead artillery company in the Battle of Bunker Hill, capturing two British cannon, the only ones to be taken by colonists.

This early eighteenth-century house was paneled by a ship's carpenter and has many rooms resembling those of a ship's, with ceilings sloping at both ends, uneven floors—veritable ship's cabins. It is believed the rooms were built this way to provide a feeling of comfort and familiarity to men while at home from the sea, or probably ship carpenters knew no other method. When the house had only one door there was a tall post at the side of the steps, with a swinging sign gilded to represent the sun at that entrance. Since then the building has been greatly altered. When the Marblehead Arts Association bought the house in 1928, they restored it to its original attractiveness. There are *H* hinges on all the paneled doors and there are seven fireplaces.

Number 54, the Dana House, is architecturally perfect. Built in 1730 by Edward Fettyplace, it has never had any architectural changes and is in perfect condition. The "smoke closet" where the hams were "smoked" is on the third floor. It was the home of the Reverend Samuel Dana, the sixth minister of the Old North Church, who established one of the first Sunday schools in the country in May, 1817.

Number 52, the Pedrick House at the corner of Washington and

Pickett Streets, was the home of Maj. John Pedrick, a fabulously prosperous merchant before the Revolution. Major Pedrick was devoted to the cause of liberty; however, the war proved disastrous to his business, for those of his vessels which were not destroyed by the British cruisers rotted in port, and the depreciation of the Continental money he was paid in for his supplying of naval goods made him almost bankrupt.

His house built in 1756 is Federal both inside and out. The facade is of boards grooved to resemble stone (ashlar), which were brought from England. The interior has spacious rooms with fine woodwork around the fireplaces, wainscoting, dadoes and cornices; there are sleigh window seats. The large central hall is thirty-eight feet long and the stairway is beautifully and gracefully proportioned.

The first Pedrick to come to Marblehead was John Pedrick about whom there is an air of mystery. It is believed that he was a nobleman, probably escaping political prosecution and that, when he arrived in Marblehead (about 1660), "John Pedrick" was his pseudonym. If he wished to live incognito, he chose the best possible site for he purchased land on the Great Neck. From his will many things can be learned about this "nobleman;" for instance, that he could not write; he used a cross (X) for his mark. Miriam Pedrick, his widow, had been one of the First Church organizers in 1684 and two years after her first husband's death, she married Richard Grose. Her progeny numbered 180 children, grandchildren and great-grandchildren when she died in 1717.

Number 44 is a three-storied, eighteenth-century building with handsome stairways and fireplaces throughout its structure. The house at one time belonged to Captain Thomas Gerry and his wife, Elizabeth (Greenleaf). Captain Gerry was a successful business man and was constantly buying property, as well as wharves and ships. The Essex Probate Court has the records of all of these transactions and since the Thomas Gerrys lived in other houses in this vicinity, it may be that Elbridge, the vice president of the United States under James Madison, may not have been born here. It is almost certain that he played in the house when he was a boy and that he and his brothers and sister lived in it when they were young adults.

Elbridge Gerry was a zealous patriot. Faithful to the war and its causes, he helped not only with his speeches and actions but also with his worldly goods as recorded from Concord, Massachusetts: "From Elbridge Gerry of Marblehead, 7 loads of salt fish containing about 1700 lbs. 18 casks of wine—20 casks of raisins and a quantity of oil and 47 hogsheads and 50 barrels of salt. 4 loads of tents —1 bundle of sheet lead seven hogsheads molasses and a quantity of linen."

Writing to Mr. Adams in 1772 Gerry wrote: "I think the friends of the Liberty here will be able to hand you something soon. . . ." And two years later, again to Mr. Adams: ". . . the whole business of life seems involved in one great question, What is best to be done for our country? . . . the bravery of your country men will liberate you. . . ."

In 1783 he was writing his brother "to buy property" and James Austin (who to date is his only biographer, and was one of Gerry's sons-in-law) wrote that Gerry entertained Lafayette in his own home. One must assume that this was his father's home which had been left to his brother, John. He probably brought his bride to this house when he returned briefly to Marblehead. In January, 1786, when he was forty-two, he married Ann Thompson, a beautiful New York socialite. They lived in this seaport town that was recovering from the ravages of war, a very few months, for in May of 1787 Gerry bought a home confiscated from a Loyalist in Cambridge—the same house that eventually would be the residence of James Russell Lowell and would be called Elmwood. (Even when away from Marblehead Gerry continued to buy many pieces of property.) He and Ann had ten children but only seven survived him.

Interesting to note, his grandson E. Thomas Gerry (New York) was legal advisor to the American Society for the Prevention of Cruelty to Animals. He, with others, in 1874 formed the New York Society for the Prevention of Cruelty to Children which, when incorporated in 1875, came to be known as "Gerry's Society."

The churchgoers who later formed the Old North Church "met" before 1638 with William Walton, termed a missionary, who was the unordained minister to those first settlers who came to him with their secular as well as their religious problems. The first meeting house was built c. 1638 on Burial Hill and probably was a barn-like structure; at least it must have been of crude construction as were the dwellings of that time. In 1710 a second and larger structure was built on Franklin Street.

In 1825 the second Congregational church, the present stone church, was erected, the old one on Franklin Street having become dilapidated and unserviceable. Unlike other Massachusetts churches constructed at that time the Old North was made from stone blasted from the rugged ledge upon which it now stands and this is visible to the congregation as they are seated at worship. The church is of particularly good scale and proportion and there is a beautifully executed wooden fanlight over the door. The notable tower, which can be seen throughout the town, is illuminated at night so that its presence is always visible, and it may be seen from the shores of the

Neck and at sea. Atop the tower is a gilded fish weathervane about which Thomas Goodwin wrote, "A fish on a church may seem out of keeping until we realize its religious significance. When Christ's followers were persecuted, hiding from enemies in caves and cellars, a fish, drawn in the sand or dust, or upon the walls, was their sign to other followers. The letters which spelled the word fish, in Greek, when translated into English, read: 'Jesus Christ, of God, the Son, the Saviour.' "

In 1868 a "meadow lot" and two cow leases belonging to the church were sold. This, added to donations from the Ladies Parish Society, enabled the church to purchase land on High Street and to build the parsonage, which is still being used. In October, 1951, the modern parish house was completed, located beside the church edifice.

The Old North's place in the growth and history of Marblehead has been a unique one. Among its most historic treasures is its collection of twenty-five fine pieces of sacramental silver. The silver has been used for generations regularly on each Communion Sunday and for baptismal services.

The service consists of a baptismal bowl, four flagons, four baskets, twelve cups, plates and spoons; all are solid silver except the baskets which are made of Sheffield plate. The Reverend John Barnard, in 1749, gave a flagon (a vessel with a handle and a spout, often with a hinged lip, used to serve liquids) with a dome and molded cover and twined finial, scrolled handle with cherub wings in relief on oval discs. Samuel Burt of Boston (1724–1754) made this and a second one as well. All the flagons are identical in shape and size, each has a Latin inscription and three bear the donor's coat of arms. The second Samuel Burt flagon was donated in 1749 by King Hooper.

The oldest piece of silver in the service, an early beaker (a large, wide-mouthed drinking cup), is English and dates back to Charles II's reign. It bears the inscription, "Belonging to the First Church of Christ in Marblehead 1728." Its height is 5½ inches. There are but two other English beakers in American churches, neither having the embossed decorations of this piece. The maker's mark is a monogram of *CL* or *TC*. The identity is unknown, but authorities on silver consider it to have been made in London, circa 1671.

The outstanding piece of the entire collection is the baptismal bowl designed by Paul Revere and presented to the church in 1773 by Dr. Joseph Lemmon, a Marblehead physician. The inscription around the rim reads, "The Donation of Doc. Joseph Lemmon to the First Church of Christ in Marblehead 1773." The bowl also bears the Lemmon coat of arms. According to his will, dated 1772, he left a bequest of "13 pounds, 6 shillings, 8 pence lawfull money" to purchase "a Baptizing Basin."

This silver is a priceless heritage not only for the Old North and Marblehead (for all the town to treasure) but also for the whole country.

The Old Alley Steps on Washington Street is another of the old rights-of-way. These granite steps, flanked each summer with self-sown hollyhocks, were used by the fishermen to reach the fish fence on the hill nearby. The hills of the old town were dotted with fish flakes; the large wooden frames covered with long narrow strips of wood resting upon posts a few feet from the ground. These same steps were used by the townspeople to reach the road below.

Number 11, the Bessom House. According to the deeds of March, 1720, Thomas Taylor conveyed to James Pearson a certain lot or small tract of land, "ye 16th house lot of the Lower Wind Mill Hill in the town of Marblehead which I bought of the Committee of Commons of said Town"; Number 11 stands on this lot. The earliest mention of the house appears in 1734 when James Pearson conveyed it to Giles Irwin. Eventually, C. Florence Bessom and her brother, Frank L., descendants of the John Patten who fought at Bunker Hill in Captain Grant's company of Gen. John Glover's regiment became owners of the house which has heavy beams, is well built and has ten fireplaces.

Number 6, the Goodwin House, was built in 1698, the third house to be erected on the street. The first floor was, and still is, a store with seven rooms above.

Number 5, the Hooper House, was presumably built by William Hooper about 1780. The house remains the same as it was when first built with the exception of the ell that was built on by William's son, Captain Asa Hooper.

PICKETT STREET

Pickett Street is off Washington Street. Number 2 Pickett, at the corner of both streets, was a tavern long before the Revolution. The house, an eighteenth-century Colonial, was known as the Bunch of Grapes Tavern and a large painted and carved sign hung under the eaves in the front of the house. This might well have been the rendezvous of sailors, pirates, smugglers and patriots, being so close to the wharf and Town House. Under the front stairway, there was a small window through which the liquor (mostly rum) was passed to the front room for the patrons of the tavern. There were many fireplaces in the tavern and narrow halls leading to the various rooms.

It is now occupied by Staceys, descendants of that family for whom Stacey Court and the street are named.

STACEY STREET

Stacey Street (and Stacey Court), off Washington Street, are typical, winding streets distinctive of Marblehead's early pattern.

Number 1 Stacey Street is the Bartlett Garage. When the automobile was first catching on as a mode of transportation, the first gasoline-powered automobile made in Essex County was built in this garage by a man named Goodwin.

The Stacey House at Number 8 and Number 10 is one of the oldest dwelling houses in town; its ridge roof and its peculiar construction, projecting over the street, has long been noticed by passersby. Not only its architecture but also the fact that it is clapboarded in the studs and filled in with brick—without being boarded— testifies to its antiquity. Tradition claims that it was originally a tavern.

MARKET SQUARE

The Old Town House. At Town Meeting held March 15, 1726, it was "Voted that there shall be a Town House Built in said Town this year. And also voted by ye Selectmen shall be a Commite to Treatt with sum worck men. In order for the Building said House & mark Return to the next Town Meeting and also voted that the Town House shall be Built in Ye Land where the Gaol and Cagge now stands on."

Built on the site of the "Old Gaol," this building has often been called "Marblehead's Faneuil Hall" (although it was built in 1721, earlier than Boston's) or "Marblehead's Cradle of Liberty." This is where Lee and Orne fired their fellowmen to great patriotism; this was Elbridge Gerry's first political platform, and where the famous Essex Regiment—the Marblehead regiment—was first organized by General Glover. The Marblehead Light Infantry assembled here with their captain, Knott V. Martin, in answer to Lincoln's call for troops to preserve the nation's unity in 1861. Up through World War I all Marblehead soldiers left from this historic spot. The open-air market, sometimes on the first floor and basement, was supervised by a clerk of market appointed by the town. He checked the scales to prevent cheating, and kept strict account of the hours the market was open.

The hall itself is attractive—its quoins set it off dramatically —and it has a circular window just under the apex of the roof. Its windows are small paned, the steps leading to the front door are large pieces of granite and the rise of each stair is high.

Number 1 Market Square. On the corner of Mugford Street (also known as Market Square), north of the Town House stands a house originally built before 1695 by William Walters, cordwainer and inn keeper, when the trustees of the Commoners granted the land to him. Before that date the town pound stood on the lot and it was on this spot that straying cattle were confined. On May 4, 1732, the dwelling house, slaughter house and land—at that time appraised at £350—was conveyed to "Nathan Bowen of Marblehead, scrivener."

This house, one of the oldest in town, has an overhang between the first and second stories, and a narrow, arched gambrel roof and is one of the unusual ones in Marblehead.

MUGFORD STREET

Mugford Street is to the west of the Town House on Market Square. In 1667 it was called Way to the Woods, (Ancient Way to the Ferry to Salem). In 1684 it was the Highway and in the 1700's it was called first Way to New Meeting House, then Queen Street and in 1757, Way to the Ferry (Salem). In 1824 it acquired its present name Mugford Street, being named for the war hero, Capt. James Mugford.

Many knowledgeable antiquarians state that the house at Number 23, built in 1720, has one of the most outstanding doorways in all Marblehead.

Number 32 is the Captain Mugford House. This gambrel Colonial home was built in 1758 by John Griste, for whom a local architect designed it. He, his wife and daughter Sally lived there and when Sally married Captain James Mugford her parents gave her the home. Shortly after his marriage he was impressed into the British service and was confined on board a gunboat lying in Marblehead Harbor. Brave Sally could not stand this. She rowed out to the gunboat, boarded it and "demanded" that her husband be returned to her as she needed him to support her. Amazingly enough her demands were granted and, as promised, her James was delivered at Gerry's Wharf when the curfew bell rang.

Mugford was one of the first to be killed in the Revolution. He, supposedly, was buried in the Unitarian Churchyard; however, the grave was never found. There is a monument to him and his brave companions in the Old Burial Ground. Sally married again—a man named Martin, and their great-great-great-granddaughter, Miss Madeline Orne, lives in the house. It was her privilege to christen U.S.S. *Mugford* a few years ago.

The Second Congregational Church—Unitarian. The Meeting House on Burying Hill had been in existence many decades, when an assistant to the aging Reverend Mr. Samuel Cheever was to be chosen, and in December, 1714, John Barnard was selected. The choice prompted many persons to withdraw from membership in the society, pledging funds for a new meeting house under the ministry of the other candidate, Edward Holyoke. The new meeting house was immediately erected and on April 25, 1716, twenty-seven persons formed the Second Congregational Church and on the same day Edward Holyoke was ordained as its first minister.

The "New Meeting House" was built on the same site that the present one occupies and a tall tower rose above it which served as a beacon to home-coming seamen. The only visible clock in the town at that time was located in its steeple. Diagonally down the street was the Bowen house and it was natural that to Nathan Bowen should fall the task of keeping the clock in perfect running order. In the 1740 town records is the notation, "to pay to Nathan Bowen £5 to look after the clock per year."

One of the prized possessions of this church is its Colonial communion silver considered by Yale University to be one of the most "exquisitely lovely" of all the Colonial silver in existence. This is particularly pertinent to Marblehead for three of the pieces were wrought by a native, Thomas Grant, the other eleven pieces were made by John Coney, John Burt and Jacob Hurd, all eighteenth-century silversmiths of Boston. One of the tankards has the maker's mark of Thomas Grant of Marblehead (1731–1804).

In January, 1832, a new addition was built upon the foundation of the old one that had been razed earlier in the year. The new church had a square belfry and a bell to call its members to worship; however, in 1877, during the town's great fire, the church roof was ablaze but the quick action of Thomas J. LeCraw saved the church from burning. It was consumed in the fire that swept through it on October 1, 1910; the only piece remaining was the bell. The church, as it is today, was built in 1911 and one of its ministers of this twentieth century was the Reverend William Stanley Nichols, a direct descendant of Rev. Edward Holyoke. Dr. Nichols was minister from 1943 to 1946 and was then made minister emeritus, a title he enjoyed until his death in 1958.

In 1950 several classrooms were added and the most recent improvement came in May, 1961, when a larger new church school wing was dedicated. In order that the wing might be built it was necessary for the church's old graveyard to be relocated. An act of the Massachusetts General Court gave permission for this to transpire with the result that Marblehead's illustrious colonial citizen, the famed leader Jeremiah Lee, lies in a tomb *beneath* the church's recreation room! Before the graves in the church graveyard adjacent to the edifice were changed, Miss Gertrude Neilson and Mrs. E. Lewis Holman took careful notes of the stones in their original positions, the earliest stone having been laid in 1715; 12 Revolutionary officers and men are at rest here and among the 230 and more graves there are many names important in the annals of Marblehead's history.

Number 37 Mugford Street is known as the Jayne–Prentiss–Story House. Peter Jayne, who for many years was a noted schoolmaster in Marblehead, built it in 1724. In 1790 Joshua Prentiss married the widow Dorothy Jayne. By buying the Jayne children's half of the house Prentiss became the second owner. The Prentiss family continued to entertain the Methodist ministers just as Mrs. Jayne had when her first husband was living. At this time in 1791 the Methodist Church was organized in Marblehead in the upper small hall. In remembrance of the occasion eleven tiles (Biblical subjects) were placed over the fireplace. The Story family later owned it.

During the years preceding the Revolution the Committee of Safety—John and Samuel Adams, John Hancock, Elbridge Gerry and Azor Orne—held its meetings in one of the chambers of this house and it has been called "the breeding place of the American Revolution." In order to keep their sessions very private these men came over the road from Boston at separate, stated intervals. When the Revolution was over George Washington visited the house.

Here, too, the Tuesday Evening Club held its meetings—General Glover, Elbridge Gerry, Dr. Story, Colonel Lee, Azor Orne and other well-known citizens were members.

One of the oldest Philanthropic Lodges of Freemasons held its first meetings in this house—the charter was given in 1778.

ELM STREET

Elm Street is long, from Spring Street to Orne. Originally (in 1667) it was "ye lane or highway that leads to ye common or woods"; in 1711, "ye highway on ye back side of ye town." Then, by 1727, it had become Back Street, and much later (1831) was known by its current name, Elm Street.

On this street the poorhouse was built by the town near the head of Pearl Street and some eight rods away from where the first smallpox hospital was built in the 1700's.

The first portion of Elm Street at the junction of Washington, Orne and Franklin Streets, from Number 1 on, are examples of typical "1700" clapboard homes, although some have been covered with shingles. Number 8 Elm Street is supposedly the only house on the

North Shore that has a three-quarter gambrel roof—it has three gables. The floorboards are very wide, there are six fireplaces, and more than half of the kitchen wall is of old brick. The house has a "borning room" (usually a small room with a fireplace where the mother could be confined, taken care of and the baby kept warm and out of drafts). At one time there was a shoe shop in the building. In 1872 it served as an office for the *Marblehead Messenger*. It backs up to the smallest private way in Marblehead, a tiny alley that runs from High to Elm Street. Built high on a grassy, rock mound it commands a fine view of the ocean and Baker's Light. The first record of Number 8 changing hands is dated 1730.

Number 19, the Squash House, was originally a fish house located on Gerry Island. Such a house was used to store salt fish during the night, after it has been removed from the drying yards of fish flakes. When James J. H. Gregory, the seedsman, owned Gerry Island, he had the house moved to its present location and used it as a place to store his squashes—thus the name. When the squashes ripened, he removed the seeds and sent them to every part of the United States. In the early 1930's the Squash House was leased by Parker Kemble for the purpose of establishing a permanent little theater in Marblehead. Its unusual shape establishes its place among the landmarks of the place.

Number 39 is a modified Federal dwelling, built in 1832, with a ridge roof. When the Unitarian Church was razed in 1832, the old pews of the church (built in April, 1716) were used for paneling the rooms in this dwelling. The four rooms on the first floor were paneled from the floor to the ceiling and held together by wooden pegs. The hand-carved mantels came from another Beacon Street house that was razed.

Number 45 Elm is the Gun Artillery House. On September 26, 1808, Marblehead ceded to the United States government as much land on the southerly side of workhouse lot "as may be necessary to the erection of a brick gun house thereon." The old Gun House was built soon after 1808.

Number 97 Elm, one of the oldest houses on the street, is a Colonial clapboard built sometime after 1692; it was constructed of lumber cut in the forest that covered a part of the town in the early days. The beams of the house are of heavy oak. On the first floor are the living room, dining room, and kitchen; both the living room and dining room have fireplaces. There is a Bible closet over the mantel in the dining room, where in the colonial days the family's Bibles were kept. The floors throughout are made of wide boards. The rooms on the first floor are handsomely paneled and old *H*-hinges are on all the doors of the house.

MECHANIC STREET

Mechanic connects Pearl Street with Mugford Street. Unquestionably the oldest summer residence in Marblehead is that house built by John B. Brimblecom of England. In the early 1700's, long before Marblehead was a summer resort, Mr. Brimblecom would come to Marblehead to spend the summer fishing and would then sail back to England for the winter. He finally tired of this commuting, made his summer dwelling into a year-round house and became a successful merchant.

Where the house stands used to be called Cow Lane, as the cows were driven to pasture through the nearby lane. The hill behind this house is known as Brimblecom Hill—the Gerry School stands on it.

The Bradstreet–Brown House, Number 1 Mechanic, is on the corner of Mechanic and Pearl streets. The Reverend Mr. Simon Bradstreet, second minister of the Second Congregational Church, built the fine home in 1738 when he succeeded Rev. Edward Holyoke. His daughter married the Reverend Isaac Story, and she inherited the house.

Here, William Story, Esquire, the father of the Reverend Mr. Story, came to live; he was the clerk of the Admiralty Court before the Revolution. (His office was on State Street in Boston and, on the night in 1765 when the citizens, infuriated over the passage of the Stamp Act, ransacked the house of Governor Hutchinson, they destroyed many of the documents, papers and books that were in Mr. Story's office.) Story thus having moved to Marblehead to be with his sons, lived with Isaac, and in 1799, died in the house on Mechanic Street.

PEARL STREET

Pearl Street is perpendicular to Washington Street, west. Number 7 is one of the few brick houses in Marblehead. This one belonged to Capt. William Blackler who figured prominently in Glover's regiment at the Delaware crossing. The captain had formerly owned Number 44 Washington Street. This house at Number 7 has a fine courtyard with the main entrance, and the house itself stands sideways to the street. It is probably the only house in Marblehead that can boast a Samuel McIntire-designed interior, with all the wonder-

ful scrolls, baskets, and so forth, that were carved out of wood by
that superb, noted craftsman.

HIGH STREET

Number 13, a Federal-type home (*circa* 1800) was the childhood
home of Captain Josiah Perkins Creesy whose sailing record as captain of the *Flying Cloud* (fastest ship from New York to San Francisco in 1851) was not soon equaled by steamers. If it is true that sur-
roundings shape the destiny of men, this could be said of the house
in which Captain Creesy grew up. It was built by his father with
curved door frames and a narrow companionway to the kitchen.
The father's skill as a builder is visible in the spiral staircase and the
wooden beams and joints in the attic. On the wall beside the attic
stairway a sloop is carved "A.C. 1827." Josiah's younger brother,
William Andrew Creesy, also became famous as a Baltimore Clipper
captain.

Number 19 was build in 1860 and was the old Gerry School. It
was here that Miss Mary Alley taught. In 1910 it was converted into
a dwelling and the center entrance which had been the school entrance was moved to the side. Over the door is a beautiful carving
with the word "Liberty" inscribed in a banner.

STATE STREET

State Street leads from Town House or Market Square to the
water. It was once nothing more than a narrow lane made into a
corduroy road, then New Wharf Lane. It was called King Street
and Old Way, and finally, by its present name.

Isaac Mansfield, a wealthy man by colonial standards, owned a
number of parcels of land in the vicinity of Abbot Hall: the lots the
old North Church now stands on, some of Peach's Point and a great
deal of land around the State Street area. Part of the land he owned
on State Street was beach property, "clear to the water," which was
then called Codner's Cove. In 1720 he had a large portion of this
land filled in with rock and stone and built a home on it (Number
23 State Street) with timber which was brought from England. By
law he owned ten feet of the road at the time he was building. He
had the garden paved with cobblestones and built a "summer house"
on what was marsh land.

Number 17, the "Old Gallison House" was built in 1732. As late
as 1919 Gallisons were living here. The house itself has very heavy,
enclosed beams. There are many fireplaces, in fact every room in
the attic area has one. The chimney is a large one, typical of the
kind that were built into Colonial houses.

Number 9 State, a gambrel-roofed, eighteenth-century clapboard house was the home of Captain Edmund Bray, the father of Evelyn Bray. Miss Bray met John Greenleaf Whittier, the Quaker poet, when they were classmates at Haverhill Academy. It has been reported that she was in love with him, as much as he with her, but he was a poor farmer's son and Miss Bray's parents objected strongly to the match. It is believed that she was Whittier's only sweetheart and that the disappointment over her marriage to another was the reason he remained single. Evelyn became a teacher, went south to teach, and married William S. Downey, an evangelist. They soon moved to New York City, and rumor had it that theirs was a stormy marriage. At the death of her husband Mrs. Downey moved back to Washington Street, Marblehead, where she lived two years with her brother, Captain Knott Bray. After that she moved to a "rest home" in West Newbury, ironically, next door to Whittier's home. In fact, the room she occupied the rest of her life had been furnished by Whittier himself in memory of his beloved sister —and neither Whittier nor Mrs. Downey knew of their proximity to each other!

GLOVER SQUARE, #11

Glover Square swings off Front Street and into State Street. The General John Glover House was built for him in 1762. George Ethan Billias, in his *General John Glover and his Marblehead Marines*, states that "Glover cannot be ranked in importance with Washington, Greene or Gates. Yet, of all the American generals, Glover alone by virtue of his seafaring experience was able to render to the patriot cause a military contribution as significant as it was unique."

This man who played such a sustaining role in the American Revolution was the son of a house carpenter (whose father also had pursued the same trade) and Tabitha Bacon Glover. He was born in 1732 in a double house which his father had built in a gloomy section of Salem near the prison.

On October 30, 1754, Glover married Hannah Gale in the Second Congregational Church of Marblehead and, as was the custom of the time, Hannah Glover stood before the entire congregation along with other church members who "ownd their faults." The one she "ownd," John, arrived five months after marriage. When he was in his forties Gen. John Glover wrote to a friend, Horatio Gates, "Love is in some measure so involuntary a passion, it cannot, It ought not be Controlled."

By the time Glover was twenty-seven he was a self-made man and could be counted among the "ruling aristocracy." Established as a gentleman, he built a large, two-storied house on what is now Glover Square, real proof of his belonging to the privileged class.

The door of this house opens onto a central hallway at the end of which is a large kitchen. In the front of the house on either side off the hallway are rooms whose windows look out on Glover Square. The front hall stairway leads up to the second-floor bedrooms which have ample fireplaces.

When Glover returned from the war he was not well. He managed to accrue some wealth and bought the farm and land near the border of Lynn, Marblehead and Salem where he spent his last days. He outlived his second wife and most of his children, which saddened him greatly because he was such a family man.

Number 13 Glover Square was Captain James Mugford's birthplace. James Mugford, Jr. was born in this house in 1749. In the short span of life allotted to him he was to become a beloved figure. He was a sea captain, was active as a town official, and became a gallant hero in the Revolution as well as one of the first casualties. His childhood home is a gambrel-roofed, two-storied house, typical of the 1700's with its three dormer windows.

Number 15 Glover Square is the Norden House. In 1637 all the land around Glover Square was owned by John Coit, whose first dwelling was a wigwam. Later he built a house on the hill that is now Merritt Street. In 1647 Coit sold to William Pyt "all the houses and his third part of the stages where were fish flakes with the land adjoining"—the tract of land that the Norden House was built on sometime between 1657 and 1686. The land itself, through several generations, passed to the wife of Col. Nathaniel Norden, a Loyalist.

The very low-studded house has a mammoth fireplace with an oven in the living room. The stairway in the front hall is hand carved, in fact, every piece of wood in the house was hand cut, and the nails, windows and window-fastenings are all handmade.

There is a secret stairway at the side of the front entry which leads directly to the spacious attic where, when John Mahoney was the owner of the house, Masses were said for the Catholics who had no church of their own at the time.

Number 17, a gambrel-roofed house, was built in 1700 by Thomas LeCraw who willed it to his son, Eben. Eben in turn willed it to his twin sons, Thomas and John; Thomas was willed the upper part of the house and John, the lower. Both brothers were shore fishermen, and both made shoes in the winter. Having these same interests, it would seem that life would be easy for them; however, it wasn't, for both possessed vile tempers and so after one terrific altercation they ceased speaking to each other. If they wanted to communicate, a third party would act as the emissary of the message or query! They died two years apart, and they remained silent to the very end.

The house was built of heavy oak timbers, entirely handmade. It has twelve rooms and six fireplaces.

FRONT STREET

The large dwelling standing on the corner of Glover and Front Streets, Number 82, was known as the Old Tavern. In the early years it was called Three Cods Tavern. In the early days of New England the tavern, inn or ordinary, as it was variously called, was second only in importance to the colonial meeting house in the settlement.

The property the Three Cods was built on was part of Lot 38 of the original Marblehead grants, which had been owned by John Coit prior to 1635. In 1800 the property was owned by a man whose name had come down through generations of Marbleheaders, Samuel Sewall. Probably the date of the tavern itself was 1680. During 1775 when the British frigate *Lively* was lying in the harbor several shots were fired from her. One of them struck the tavern and became deeply imbedded in the wall. When it was necessary to replace the clapboards the oft-told bullet tale proved to be a true one for the shot was found.

Another legend grew out of the tavern, this around *Merlin* that was sent as a replacement of *Lively*. The petty officers and some of the marines from *Merlin* imbibing in the tavern shouted abusive, contemptuous remarks about the Yankees, and claimed that the Yanks were cowards. Present and hearing these unprovoked remarks was Marblehead's young Robert Wormstead. Quickly breaking a broomstick across his knees, Wormstead brandished it in the air, saying loudly: "Enough of this boasting, I have no weapon but this, but I'll take you singly or collectively." The challenge when accepted resulted in swords flying in all directions, for Wormstead was a powerful fencer and the braggarts were defeated.

Before the war with England the tavern was patronized by officers and crews alike from British ships as well as American sailors off merchant vessels, for the tavern was the spot to get hot toddy and rum.

The Eagle House is a three-storied house situated on 96 Front Street some distance back from the street, for there are now houses standing in front of it. They in turn are built on the land that was once Col. Jonathan Glover's famous large garden. The house was called Eagle House because at the gate to the entrance of the garden were two posts upon which stood a gilded eagle with outspread wings. The eagle had just become the adopted symbol of the new United States and was appearing in many places. By building this house, this brother of Gen. John Glover established himself as a recognized member of the "codfish aristocracy." He was a shrewd business man and accumulated wealth with adroitness. He was also one of the proprietors of the smallpox hospital on Cat Island and when he learned of the anger of the people and the resentment many of the alarmists had over inoculation and treatment, it is said he placed two small artillery pieces in one of the rooms of his house fronting the street intending to give the crowd warm welcome if need be.

A man of means, and one who seemed to enjoy spending his money, he afforded himself the services of John Singleton Copley to whom Jonathan's portrait is generally attributed. He also rode to church in a conspicuous yellow coach drawn by two white horses, driven by a colored servant with two more Negro coachman behind; these were undoubtedly servants. Jonathan was a self-made man who served his town well and "in style."

In the beginning the inhabitants of the towns—Marblehead in particular—were riddled with superstition, and all natural phenomena such as excessive lightning, eclipses, and the like filled them with fear of the supernatural. Coupled with the fact that the population was mostly seamen, tales of the sea and its toll added to the already high level of emotions. Many were the tales that were told. The seamen told of phantom ships seen in storms and the shrieks of witches and roaring gales that were heard on the sea in the dark of night. Then, too, there is the story about one eccentric sea captain who, just before his one hundreth birthday, being reminded of the uncertainty of life, bluntly retorted that he needed no advice, adding: "I have had my clearance papers for sometime, and am only waiting sailing orders."

The women, too, had their superstitions and customs. During the light of a new moon the young ladies would gather around to drop nails into a big pot of tallow on the fire, wishing hard as they did this, for a girl knew that the next man walking toward her after this ritual would be her future husband.

And while knitting a maid might take a ball of yarn she was using and hurl it out of the window into the street. Whoever (male, of course) retrieved and returned it would be sure to be her future husband. Swinging an apple peeling three times around one's head and letting it fall into position would spell out the initial of the future husband's last name. If one could find a four-leaf clover and place it over the front door, the next male entering the door would be the one destined for matrimony.

When a Marblehead ship sighted another out on the fishing grounds, the cry "Bodgo" was answered by "Molly Waldo" from local crews. This was at once a signal for the long boats to be lowered, whereupon the seamen swapped yarns and messages to be carried back into home port by whichever ship made Marblehead first.

At home nearly every house boasted a "scuttle" from which one could look far out to sea from the rooftop, watching for the returning ship as well as the departing vessel—but never watch a vessel completely out of sight, for that would bring it bad luck! Diaries reveal that the women used to "gossip from the scuttles at about the same time of an evening, and if one knew of a girl bearing a child out of wedlock it was quickly noted as a "Marblehead situation." Some women had real widow's walks atop their roofs where they could pace the four "corners of the earth"—too often the widow's walk was called a "widow's weep" for often her husband's ship came home without him, the sea having demanded its toll.

But there were times of frivolity, too. 'Lection Week was an annual affair, but those events which came unexpectedly were the best kind, such as a "raising" of a house or lean-to. Everyone helped for both wine and other liquors flowed freely. There was the good old potent Medford rum, hot and buttered in winter time, and the less strong "beverige," a summer drink that was water flavored with molasses and ginger. Also, "switchel" was a similar "beverige" but when served out to sailors was strengthened by a little, very little, vinegar and rum. Ebulum was made of the juices of the elder and juniper berries mixed with ale and spices, and there were plenty of elderberry bushes around, both "natural" and those that had to be planted, for they were a "necessary" to keep off "spirits" and their fruits made excellent wine and the berries had "real medicinal value."

The colonists married early and often widowers and widows hastened to join their fortunes and sorrows. A wedding was a whole week of unrestrained merrymaking. Everyone in town could attend the wedding (and usually did), and when the guests at last were ready to depart they would put the bridegroom in his nightshirt, put him in bed beside his bride and the entire company— regardless of the protests of the bride—would march around the nuptial bed throwing old stockings, shoes and other missiles of "established potency" at the newly wedded pair by way of bringing them good luck.

The boy of ten or twelve years of age learned to be a skilled fisherman. He was called a cut-tail for he cut a wedge-shaped bit from the tail of every fish he caught, and when the fish were sorted out the tails proved each man's share of the profit. The young girls were never idle for there was always knitting to be done and the use of the niddy noddy was a constant task; that handy device for winding yarn was pickup work to do at odd moments so that Satan could not find "idle hands." Some of the better-off folks had a swift, which was less complicated and accomplished the same thing. The women had plenty to do: bear and take care of the children, care for the house; make all the garments from scratch, such as shear the sheep, card the wool and dye it (having first planted the seeds and raised the plants to get the dye); tend out on the men folk and help with the fish flakes. And too, too often, help out with the extra tasks of war, which meant more knitting and more bandages. There was little time for feeling sorry for one's self and work was the order of every day except Sunday.

By the nineteenth century woman's work load had eased up some and the sewing circles and church groups had been established. One such group met every Friday afternoon and their nimble fingers sewed, stitched and knit whatever was in current demand. They were often called on to make layettes for, as one local doctor said, "You never could predict the exact arrival time of the first child, but the second time round the baby always took nine months agrowing." This group called themselves "The Hardy Ables" and they exchanged recipes and local gossip as they worked. They were fond of peach brandy: "So easy to make, fill the stone crock almost full of brandy, just barely peel the peach, then throw the whole thing in stone and all—and wait a good while." Yes, on a Friday afternoon it was the thing to serve (first straining it) and appropriately the stitch that they were using on the receiving blankets was called the "feather" stitch, for it was just that after refreshments were served. This group continued for years with weekly meetings. When they were much older they called themselves "The Hardly Ables."

OAKUM BAY

Oakum Bay is the locality immediately south of Lovis Cove where Selman Street meets Front Street. The storms roll in against the small beach and spend their fury on the shore, thus playing their role in perpetuating a legend that has been a part of Marblehead lore since the latter part of the seventeenth century. Chief Justice Story averred that he "had heard those ill-omened Shrieks again and again in the still hours of the night!'"

Oakum Bay was not only associated with "the screeching woman" but this locality was the place where the infamous Quelch was apprehended and where Captain Kidd himself came.

CIRCLE STREET

Circle Street, off Front Street, is one of the narrowest, winding streets, a semicircle, in the old section of town.

The most renowned house on the street is Number 19, the Skipper Ireson House. Although the skipper was called Floyd, his real name was Benjamin. He had come from Lynn to live in Marblehead. One of the earliest settlers in the area was Benjamin Ireson, and the skipper was not a native. A short while before the crisis of his life in Marblehead he was called into the federal court on the charge of violating the controversial Embargo Act of Congress, which forbade Americans to engage in foreign commerce (actually, smuggling was an accepted practice, and Ireson was held in esteem by his fellow fishermen). His brigantine *William* in Lynn Harbor transhipped freight to *Mary* to be carried to a foreign port. As a result, *William* was confiscated by the federal government.

In the late fall of 1808, the schooner *Betty* was returning to port with her hold filled with fish and sailed by the schooner *Active*, out of Portland, Maine, although she was in distress off the Highlands of Cape Cod. Headed for Marblehead, *Betty* was sailing right into a tremendous gale and on that particular midnight came upon *Active*, drifting at the mercy of the late October storm. The skipper hailed *Betty* and asked to be taken aboard. Such a tremendous sea was running that Skipper Ireson did not command his unwilling crew to go to the rescue; he and his ship sailed on, not even "lying" by the wreck until daylight. *Betty* continued on her course and when she reached Marblehead her timorous crew lost no time in running about the town filling the taverns with the tale about their captain's deplorable behavior. The townspeople accepted the crew's distorted version and immediately commanded a vessel to go in search of *Active*. It was found that a few men aboard her had already been saved only a few hours after *Betty* sailed by.

Naturally, the story of Skipper Ireson's dastardly decision was noised abroad, and on the next bright moonlight night, Ireson heard a knock on his Circle Street door. Outside stood a ruthless, exasperated band of men who grabbed, tarred and feathered him, placed him in a dilapidated dory and dragged him through the streets of

Marblehead. The town reveled in this ignominious punishment. Fortunately for Ireson, the mob was halted at the border of Salem by the magistrates who forbade them to go further. The bottom of the dory dropped out and the mob hastily transferred Ireson and the remains of the dory atop a cart and retraced the ride home. When at last he was released, exhausted, it is claimed he quietly said to them, "I thank you, gentlemen, for my ride; but you will live to regret it." The slander was a tragic blow to his mariner's career. His declining years were spent in peddling fish which he caught from a small dory, and in gardening. He tended his garden despite increasing blindness, and it was not until after his death that the true blame was accurately placed upon his crew.

Some years later, this deplorable incident was elaborated upon, and when it reached the ears of John Greenleaf Whittier, the Quaker poet, it sang itself into an epic ballad which was to immortalize the skipper. Whittier had visited Marblehead so he knew the fierce, independent spirit of its townspeople and their forthrightness. However, he garbled the facts and with the aid of James Russell Lowell he made the dialect of the people a queer mixture of sounds. As editor, Mr. Lowell first published "Skipper Ireson's Ride" in the *Atlantic Monthly* in 1857, where it reached many readers who were delighted with the scandal of the seacoast town and especially the role that the women played. Samuel Roads, Jr., the town historian, partially cleared up the facts in his *History and Traditions of Marblehead*, and presented them to the poet. In return, he received a letter of apology from Mr. Whittier. The controversy over the accuracy of the presentation has long since quieted down, but the story itself lives on in this modest clapboard home.

SELMAN STREET

Selman Street runs from Franklin Street to Front Street; in fact, in 1824 it was called Franklin Place. As early as 1720, it was the Way to Ingall's Cove (now called Lovis Cove) and by 1851 it became Selman Street, named for Archibald Selman, who was the master of the ship *America*. He built Number 3 Selman Street, *circa* 1738. The floorboards in it are very wide, the ceilings are low, and throughout the house there is fine paneling. A full cellar is under the house with the original old cistern still working well. There are six fireplaces, one of them so tremendous that it could accommodate two men standing with both pairs of arms outstretched. In this fireplace a strong metal piece is extended across the width, presumably used in smoking meat. There are dutch ovens in the dining room and upper hall indicating that the house could have been used by two parts of the family.

Number 9, the Hooper–Johnson House, supposedly the oldest house in the street, was built by John Hooper in the early 1700's. This house is built with heavy beams, has large fireplaces and hand-made doors and hinges. One of the fireplaces is so mammoth that a side of beef or two sheep might be roasted in it. Tradition has it they often were.

Selman Street has only one sidewalk, probably because the trolley cars from Salem and Boston needed to squeeze down this street.

FRANKLIN STREET

Franklin Street from 1663 through 1750 was called a "Way:" Way to Harbor or Waterside, Way to Fort, Way to Ingall's Cove, Way to Great Harbor, Way to Meeting House to Fort, then Franklin Place and, in 1851, Franklin Street—one which is truly paved with history—and named for Ben Franklin.

One of the finest of the eighteenth-century houses on it is Number 7. It was the home of Parson Barnard. It was built for Barnard in 1716, has a gambrel roof and authentically Georgian features.

He was quoted throughout the Colonies for he was an outstanding leader. There is no doubt that he had a real influence on the life and thought of the Colonies as well as his great impact on Marblehead. The house at Number 7 still seems to bear his imprint.

Number 6 Franklin Street was the Mary A. Alley Hospital before it was converted into the present apartment house. Miss Alley had inherited the home from her uncle and willed it in 1904 to the town for an emergency hospital (after serving as a home for her niece, Miss Lizzie Knight, and her cousin, Miss Marion Parker) together with thirty thousand dollars, the interest on which was to be used for repairs. On October 19, 1920, the town took possession of this generous gift and a board of trustees was established. The house itself had been erected on the site of the second Congregational Church building.

Mary A. Alley, a native of Marblehead, and the daughter of Andrew Alley and Elizabeth Hawkes Alley, was a dedicated school-teacher who attended state educational meetings for introduction of new ideas for Marblehead. Devoted to the town where she taught, she was also secretary of the Soldiers' Aid during the Civil War, on the board of the Marblehead Female Humane Society, and was co-founder, with Mrs. Grace Oliver, of the Marblehead Visiting Nurse Association. From her diary we learn of her sympathy and generosity to her neighbors and ailing townspeople, for she was continually delivering jars of jelly and bowls of soup to sick friends, and flowers for shut-ins. She was fond of driving a horse and buggy—the horse "must have exercise"—and frequently she took neighbors on her daily rides and drove her uncle to his business appointments or to view real estate. She displayed rare business acumen and kept ledgers and account books. With a keen interest in nature and the moods of the day, she observed and recorded her delight, such as, "a snow scud came 'cross the harbor today." When the new streetcars clanged their way down Franklin Street past their home, her concern prompted her to will the house as a hospital, knowing that there were no other facilities for treating people injured in streetcar accidents.

Number 10, the home of Moses Allen Pickett, a penurious shopkeeper, was built in 1779; it is an example of Colonial gambrel architecture. He had another role, that of an artist. He painted on glass and his pictures joyfully depicted green cows and horses eating red or blue grass. His patrons were children who were excited with wonder at and admiration for the queer man who dared paint in vibrant colors. When Moses Pickett died on March 31, 1853, it was learned that after a few small legacies, he had bequeathed the entire residue of his estate to be used as a fund of $13,400 "to comfort the widow and the fatherless, the aged, and the sick and the unhappy." His house, he directed at his death, should be kept in repair and "let to widows at a moderate rent," providing that those to whom his house gave shelter were natives of the town of Marblehead.

Number 16, a later John Devereux House (sometimes called Burrill–Devereux) was built in 1727, the same year as the Hearth and The Eagle House and the Town House. This Georgian house shows a fine bit of Colonial workmanship of the early builders with magnificent doorways that are in fine condition.

Number 17, one of Marblehead's few seventeenth-century homes (*circa* 1685) is known as the Ambrose Gale house. Mr. Gale owned a great deal of property, not only on Franklin Street but also in other sections of the town. In the area of Franklin Street, he owned out to the sea, including the land that Fort Sewall was built on and extended around the shoreline over Walton's Marsh to Little Harbor Boat Yard.

Number 18 Franklin, a Georgian home with gambrel roof, was built between 1720 and 1750 by Thomas White. In Savage's *Genealogical Dictionary of New England* the first Thomas White in Marblehead settled in the town in 1668. Captain John and Captain Philip H. White, brothers, lived in the White house for many years;

Captain John lived upstairs and Captain Philip on the lower floor. The house has eight rooms and five fireplaces. The Captains White were joint owners of a fishing vessel that used to fish off Labrador and, by coincidence, they were the first to have carried a missionary, Frank Carpenter of Andover, to Labrador years before Dr. Grenfell went there.

Number 29 Franklin, called by some the "Old Mansion House," has been kept in a fine state of repair. It belonged to Capt. Glover Broughton, a veteran of the War of 1812, who was the venerable town clerk in 1861, when the call for troops for the Civil War came.

Number 30 is known as the "Hearth and The Eagle" house. This lovely 1727 home was built by Elbridge Gerry's father, Thomas, later sold to Captain Conklin, who had married Sarah Gerry. He was in command of Fort Sewall during the War of 1812 and the officers attached to his regiment were billeted in this house. The soldiers of that regiment made the blinds, which are still being used and are in splendid condition. Marian Martin Brown, who long owned the house, traced her lineage to the settlers of Marblehead, is one of the town's recognized artists, and for many years was the town's art supervisor for Marblehead's school system. More than that she was steeped in the lore and history of Marblehead and possessed that almost lost art of story telling. Her home was chosen by Anya Seton as a setting for her novel, *The Hearth and The Eagle.* Miss Seton had been hunting for a New England town to weave an historical novel around and none suited her until she stood in Fountain Inn Park in spring and looked down on Franklin Street abloom with plum blossoms. Enchanted, she walked along the street and stopped in front of Number 30, attracted by the gilded eagle over the doorway, although she did not know that an eagle on a doorway meant "Welcome, come in for a cup of grog" to any captain coming into port.

ORNE STREET

Orne Street, as well as State Street, was once a corduroy road. The land was so swampy and muddy that to get to the fishing wharves on the fort it was necessary to build a road (formed by laying logs transversely) so that the wagon loads of fish could be taken from the wharves to the fish flakes along the shore and to the storage houses.

Number 14 was built prior to 1785 and a contemporary historic survey commented: "A noteworthy example of architectural style, this structure should be preserved along with many similar in order to maintain an historic old fishing village or seaport." At one time the house was owned by Mr. William Chamberlain who, in sheds behind the house, built the well-known Chamberlain dories.

The house at Number 31, the John Trevett Pearce House, was probably a fishing shack prior to 1728.

Number 32 is a Colonial salt box. Built around 1730, it was the homestead of Captain John Dixey, a descendant of Thomas Dixey, who ran the first ferry from Naugus Head to Salem.

The house has had few additions. The interior is simple and there are four Colonial fireplaces with swinging cranes and a "bundling door" with a small window set into one of its upper panels so the chaperone could observe how the courtship was progressing! At one time there was a cobbler's shop in the rear which is now used as a garage.

Number 39, built prior to 1650 and known as the Old Spite House, has a beautiful view of the sea, as it is right over Gas House Beach. The house received its name because the three Graves brothers, all fishermen, lived in the house completely independent of one another. Each brother built his own part of the home; the wealthiest brother had an old coffin maker's shop moved from Pond Street for his part. Each section was partitioned off and there were three entrances and three stairways inside the home; one could go from one part to another, but didn't! It has many historic features, and, of course, three fireplaces.

Number 18, the Azor Orne House, was owned by the man for whom the street was named. He was born in Marblehead in 1731, the son of Joshua Orne, a prominent merchant, who had served the town in many capacities.

The land on which the house stands was purchased in 1762 and the house—more modest than the Lee Mansion, but a fine home of that era—was built immediately. Originally L-shaped, the north ell was added in the 1800's. The paneling of the library (the built-in bookcase spans the entire back wall) is fairly recent and is made from boards out of the slaves' quarters in the attic. The interior, Georgian in design, has been restored to colors close to the original shades and hues. The exterior was "modernized" in 1838 in Greek Revival style. Like so many of the houses in Marblehead—in the Historic District in particular—the gardens are placed in the rear of the house. At Number 18 one finds a terraced yard with beautiful garden beds and trees. As recently as 1958 one might see the famous Lafayette pear tree, reputedly given to Mr. Orne by the marquis when he visited town.

The front of Number 28 Orne Street, which is plain and only

two stories high, gives no indication of the age of the house. Diligent searching of deeds has revealed that it was originally built by Samuel Walton, the son of the Reverend William Walton, the first minister in Marblehead, between 1661 and 1671. The original house was a two-storied, pitched-roof structure which has been added to and changed. The Ornes, who were the second owners, added a lean-to, and the Bowdens had the central chimney removed and exposed a "summer beam"—a great oak beam, eighteen inches square, which ran from the chimney to the front of each room between the two plastered ceilings. This type of beam (a horizontal beam resting upon the walls or frame of a building and supporting the ends of joists) is written about in many books on New England, but is not often seen. The house has been modernized but much of its old construction has been untouched. A beautiful yard and garden in back add charm to this home.

Fountain Inn Well—Agnes Surriage's Well

In the early part of the eighteenth century Nathaniel Bartlett built an inn on the brow of Bailey's Head. He named it the Fountain Inn, since there was a spring of exceptionally good water, covered by a wellhead, in the middle of the garden adjoining the inn. This inn not only accommodated travelers who came to Marblehead, but also provided the setting for the most talked of romance of the eighteenth century in New England—that of pretty, young Agnes Surriage, the tavern maid of Marblehead, and Sir Harry Frankland. The only remaining vestige of the romance that was "the talk of the land" is the Agnes Surriage Well, now surrounded by private homes on Fountain Inn Lane.

Charles Henry Frankland came to Marblehead frequently as a collector of the port of Boston and as superintendent of the construction of Fort Sewall in 1742. Frankland, who was then a young gallant of twenty-six, belonged to an influential English family and had been sent to Boston two years earlier, probably not by choice, but to avoid scandal at home. When he first met barefoot, comely Agnes, she was but a sixteen-year-old servant at the inn. Noting her beauty, he gave her money for a pair of shoes. Captivated by Agnes, he returned again and again and it was not long before he had convinced her parents (Edward and Mary Surriage) and her minister, Dr. Edward Holyoke, that he would like to educate her and take her to Boston as his ward. In the fashion of the day, she was tutored in manners and deportment and those domestic arts proper to an eighteenth-century lady.

In 1747, Henry Frankland succeeded his uncle, Sir Thomas

Frankland, to the baronetcy of Frankland of Thirkleby in Yorkshire and from then on used his rightful title. Agnes had become his mistress, and to escape Boston gossip Sir Harry purchased 480 acres in Hopkinton, Massachusetts, where he built a fine mansion and cultivated a great garden. He was an ardent horticulturist and sought out new plants and seeds, bushes and trees wherever he went. Agnes shared his love of flowers and became a truly cultured gentlewoman.

Sir Harry's "scandal" finally caught up with him for, in 1752, a boy named Henry Cromwell arrived in Hopkinton and Agnes treated him as a son. He had been born in 1741, but the name of his natural mother was never revealed. The Franklands, being proud of their blood connections with the Oliver Cromwell family, gave that surname to the boy.

Later Henry Cromwell became a lieutenant in His Majesty's Navy. In 1805 he changed his surname to Frankland since he was bequeathed a country mansion and a great fortune by his father's bachelor brother, William Frankland. According to the terms of the will, Henry Cromwell and his son were to adopt the "name and arms of Frankland before they received their bequests."

In 1753, when Sir Harry was called to England to settle a lawsuit, he took Agnes but she was not accepted by the Frankland family. In fact she was rebuffed by everyone. Sir Harry took her on a continental tour which terminated in Lisbon where they lived for a while and were there in March, 1755, at the time of a great earthquake. Sir Harry, who was in the heart of the city when the earthquake struck, was buried in the ruins. After the tremors had subsided, Agnes hurried out in search of her lover-companion and miraculously discovered him as he lay under piles of rubble. Alone and unaided, she rescued him. In gratitude for saving his life, Frankland at last rewarded her with his name. His *Diary* records that he wrote back to the Second Congregational Church in Marblehead for a copy of her birth record, and sometime between May and August, 1755, they were married by a Catholic priest in Spain. Immediately after they returned to England and en route, the marriage was resolemnized by a clergyman of the Church of England aboard the ship. Agnes Surriage was now legally Lady Agnes Frankland and everyone accepted her for what she was and always had been— constant, devoted, generous and good. In 1757 Frankland's health began to fail and from then until his death in 1768 they spent some time in Hopkinton and in Boston, but for the most part in Europe. Frankland's journal reveals his preoccupation with his health during this period and almost every entry contains a remedy for his ailment, a "bad throat."

Besides frequent health reports, Frankland recorded numerous tips on flower raising and preservation. He noted, too, many purchases for Agnes and kept track of their tendency to obesity, suggested eating habits, and was continually noting style changes. "When a fashion is become all most universal, tho it may appear ridiculous to you—it is best to comply and not to appear too singular in your own opinion." Two revealing comments from his journal seem to bear directly on his own personal life, "Put a Bridle on thy Tongue, Set a Guard upon thy Lips, least the words of thine own mouth destroy thy peace." And, "No Lady of Distinction will marry any man unless he authentically makes it appear that His ancestors have been Gentlemen and equally married for a succession of 16 generations."

Upon his death, Lady Agnes returned to Hopkinton where she entertained Henry Cromwell and her own Marblehead family. As the tension of the colonists mounted (and the eve of the Revolution approached), Lady Agnes received permission from the governor to return to the Frankland home in the north end of Boston on Garden Court Street. True to her husband's beliefs Agnes was a Tory and at the Battle of Bunker Hill she took the British soldiers into her home and nursed them. Almost immediately after, she sailed for England and settled in Chichester, where she was befriended and beloved by all her husband's relatives and those who came to call her friend. In 1781 she married a banker named John Drew (a Chichester man who took an active part in all the affairs of the city) but the marriage lasted less than two years for Dame Agnes died of "an inflammation of the lungs" at the age of fifty-seven.

Her portrait and her gravestone, "Dame Agnes Frankland, Relick of Sir Charles Frankland, Bart. and late Wife of John Drew" are in Chichester. The only remaining relic of Agnes Surriage to be found in Marblehead is a green quilted coverlet which she made. It rests on one of the beds at the Lee Mansion. Sir Harry's *Diary* is in the archives of the Massachusetts Historical Society in Boston.

THE OLD BRIG

Moll Pitcher, a celebrated fortuneteller, was born in 1738 and grew up in Lynn, Mass. Her granduncle, old Edward Dimond, a very strange character, was credited with great power of second sight with control over good and evil spirits. Many people came to him to be told the whereabouts of lost money and stolen goods. So it is told that his advice was sought by many, but any evil doer who came to him was immediately punished. At one time when a sum of money had been stolen from an aged couple, Dimond told where it could be found and the very name of the thief. Still another time when a culprit who had stolen wood from a poor widow came for advice the wizard "charmed" him and made him walk all night with a heavy log of wood on his back. Marshall Putnam Thompson wrote a long poem about his abilities in *The Unhanged Wizard: A Legend of Marblehead*.

This was the heritage that Moll (Mary Dimond) Pitcher was born into. Her father was John and her granduncle, Edward, the "Wizard." In 1700 she married Robert Pitcher, a shoemaker, and went to live in Lynn. However, she always remembered the seaport and helped many a Marbleheader while the Revolution was going on. Merchants, sailors and people in every walk of life came to consult her and placed great confidence in her predictions. She could tell the fate of missing friends, and how to recover lost valuables, how to discern the future, and what would be the most important event in their lives. Her prop was a teacup and tea leaves, but she used this only for effect, for she "saw" long before the question was posed. It is said that "her name went abroad to the farthest region, and has everywhere become the generic title of fortune tellers, occupying a conspicuous place in the ballads and legends of popular superstition." The German-born science writer, Willy Ley, once asked, "Aren't there any other women except those bit players, Betsy Ross and Moll Pitcher who had a part in your country's development?" Moll foresaw a glorious future for the United States, but said there also would be periods of darkness. Her forecasts of the outcome of the War of Independence were as accurate as though she were directing the developments and the causes and effects of the battles.

She predicted and described many future inventions—the wireless, the skyscraper, and the telephone.

Judge Newhall of Lynn wrote concerning Moll: "Her countenance was intellectual, she had that contour of face and expression, which if not positively beautiful, was decidedly interesting, a thoughtful, pensive and sometimes downcast or far off expression. . . . She became celebrated not only throughout America, but throughout the world for her skill." Whatever her secret power was, she was successful and was called a pythoness by Whittier, the poet.

The home that old Edward Dimond owned, and where Mary Dimond (Moll Pitcher) visited, is called the Old Brig. It was built prior to 1700 from timbers of an old brig which had been wrecked on the shore. The house is one of the oldest in the town and is located on Orne Street (across from the Agnes Surriage Well sign) and is near the corner of Pond Street, directly opposite Old Burial Hill.

OLD BURIAL HILL

Following the English custom of burying their dead in the churchyard, the early settlers chose their first burial ground on the site of their first meeting house. This hill, commanding a full view of the shore and surrounding country, would have discouraged a surprise attack upon the inhabitants when at church. It was on this hill that the first settlers came to listen to William Walton, who, although he had obtained his degree in the field of religion from Emmanuel College in England and had had a parish there, was never ordained by the people of Marblehead. In spite of the fact that he was their pastor and the one they listened to as he administered to their wants and ways for over thirty years, there is not a marker for this man who cared so greatly for his fellow townsmen, nor is there any record of where he was buried.

Ledge exists everywhere in this old burial ground and soil is only inches deep yet this spot is hallowed ground to many of the great of early Marblehead. Early in the history of Marblehead it was considered "old," for Town Meeting minutes of 1736 record a "committee appointed to survey ancient Burying Ground and to make some computation of ye cost that would arise in Financing same." The men appointed to the committee were John Oulton, Richard Reith and Samuel Stacey. They were mainly concerned with the boundaries and if it were possible to adjust the boundaries, to fence them off.

Today, people visit this spot to note its view of the town, the coastal islands and the sea beyond and to indulge in the latest current hobby of gravestone rubbings, for here many interesting, historic stones offer material for this art work. It is in the carvings on the gravestones, often distinctive in their simplicity and design, that we find the most characteristic expression of the colonist as an artist. Symbolism and simple imagery appeared, familiar at the time to both the educated and the unlettered, when skilled stonecutters chiseled out varied ornamental patterns. Graphically, in one form or another, they became the gravestone art of New England.

Despite early neglect and the erosion of time the gravestones in Old Burial Hill stand shoulder to shoulder, the one unchanging record of the first settlers and the pre-Revolutionaries' reverence for death.

The oldest stone which is located near Red's Pond is that of Mary Lattimer:

> "Here Lyes Buried
> Ye Body of Mary
> Wife to Christo
> Pher Lattimer
> Age 49 Years
> Decd Ye 8 of May
> 1681"

Close by is the second oldest stone:

> "Here Lyes Buried
> Ye Body of
> Mr. Christopher Lattimer
> Aged about 70 years
> Decd October Ye 5th
> 1690"

A short distance away from these two is the tomb of General Glover:

> "Erected with Filial Respect
> to
> The Memory
> of
> The Hon. John Glover, Esq.
> Brigadier General
> in the Late Continental Army
> Died January 30, 1797
> Aged 64

On the brow of the hill nearby is "Ministers' Row," the gravestones of Samuel Cheever, John Barnard, William Whitwell and Ebenezer Hubbard, all of whom were ministers of the First Congregational Church.

One of the headstones has an eagle, wings spread wide, with a star over its head. Its beak holds a banner which reads: "Victory—Peace." Beneath is the legend:

> "Joseph Brown
> 1750   1834
> Marblehead's "Black Joe"
> A Revolutionary Soldier
> A Respected Citizen"

Small, but unusual in the fact that it was erected for a slave, is the tablet:

"Agnis Negro
Woman Servant
to Samuel
Russell Aged About
43 years Decd
July Ye 12 1718"

Many of the stones that were on the hill a century ago have either deteriorated or have been stolen. One of the often quoted stones that is missing is:

"Here Lyes Ye Body
of Mrs. Miriam Grose
Who Decd in the
81st year of her
age & Left 180 children
Grand Children &
Great Grand Children"

Near the gate on Pond Street is a monument marking the grave of Captain James Mugford, Jr., the first of Marblehead's Revolutionary soldiers to lose his life for his country.

To the hero of the War of 1812:

"In memory of
James Dennis
Hammond
He was one of the Heroes of
the Frigate Constitution and
having been wounded in the
capture of the Java he
received a pension from his
Grateful Country untill
his decease, which happened
Oct. 24, 1840 at the age of
54 years 10 mos. & 14 days

Immortal honor to all those
Who bled in Freedoms Naval Fights
And vanished all their Country's foes
To gain Free Trade and Sailor's Rights."

The largest monument of white granite which stands on the top of the hill commemorates an unforgotten event in the history of the town and the time in 1846 when eleven vessels from Marblehead with their entire crews, consisting of sixty-five men and boys, were lost in a storm on the Grand Banks.

There are many, many graves—women such as Elizabeth Brown Holyoke, the Reverend Edward Holyoke's wife, and numerous children's graves, for the rate of infant and child mortality was high.

Walking around Burial Hill one notices many family plots, some completely fenced; there are a few twentieth-century graves. One is greatly impressed with how short the span of life was for many, the number of short-lived babies and children and the death toll of women, their mothers. One contemplates, too, the patriotism that was the force of the men here interred, for in this crowded place history speaks silently, but eloquently, of Marblehead's citizenry.

GINGERBREAD LANE

Before 1682 this was an ancient way, then a county road, and finally in 1824, Gingerbread Lane. It is off Beacon Street, winding its way back to Norman Street.

Gingerbread Lane is very crooked, very ledgy and very narrow, but this has never deterred anyone from traveling it to "take in the view" it offers of Barnegat, the coastline and sea, and to enjoy the woods, pond and Colonial houses. The hillside itself provided a place for the soldiers to practice their annual drills, bakers from town to cut firewood for their ovens, and it was dotted with shoe shops during the 1800's. People came, as they still do, to look at the red Colonial salt box house which was formerly a tavern.

It is thought that this tavern was built in 1690 by ship's carpenters. It is a typical Colonial salt box, complete with bulls-eye glass in the light in the front door and the carved pineapple of hospitality over the door itself. There is one central chimney in the house and four fireplaces (without mantels) from which the trammel iron extends to hold pots. The floor in the central room has deep nicks in the wide original floorboards made by the dancing boots of yesteryear. It is said that the wood throughout the two-storied house was taken from an old ship. There are hand-hewn, rough, vertical beams and wide, worn floorboards and wooden pegs throughout. Two unusual features are a borning room opposite the kitchen and a nearby trap door beside the door leading to the cellar. A spiral, nautical-style staircase winds with narrow treads to the second-story attic. It was here that the present owner, William Henry Barry, found "Black Joe's" own fiddle, his Revolutionary War gun and a cradle made from a wine cask. On the property is a tiny shoe shop by the side of the pond.

In 1796 Joseph Brown bought half of the same dwelling and in 1798 he purchased the "other ½ from Mary Seawood, widow." "Black Joe" (Joseph Brown) was born to a Gay Head Indian and a Negress; he endeared himself to all, having been a Revolutionary soldier and at all times a respected citizen. His wife, Lucretia, was known to all as "Aunt Crese." In the 1800's when May was the month for merrymaking, and the last week of it 'Lection Week, the townfolk wended their way to Black Joe's, for it was a week of holiday: work ceased, there was no school, and Black Joe was host and Aunt Crese hostess. May days were fair and bright and the hillside was readying itself with new leaflets. The early wild flowers of spring were in bloom and the first buds were on the numerous berry bushes. Children came with coppers clenched in their fists to buy Joe Froggers, those wonderful large ginger cookies made by Aunt Crese and named for the big fat frogs in Black Joe's pond that were croaking their welcome of spring, too. The pennies would also purchase foaming, homemade root beer, and roasted peanuts whose shells, as well as pennies, could be pitched in the pond. The older folk came, too, with eagerness. The men could play pitch-penny and try their luck at the Wheel of Fortune; the women folk could exchange bits of gossip, enjoy the day to the full as they ate gingerbread and the election cakes filled with both currants and raisins. As the sun set, and the fires were lit, inside they would go, some to watch but more to dance on the well-sanded floor. Joe played his fiddle and neither he nor the dancers wearied of the continuous round of jigs and reels, for both music and dance steps were infectious.

After Black Joe's death Aunt Crese continued to run the tavern and to bake her goodies. It was her practice, on early summer mornings, to pluck the wild rose petals that grew abundantly all over the hill. Gathering them early assured that they would be dew covered and thus receptive to the salt process she was to put them through. At the end of the season her firkins and crocks bulged with them; she knew the art of distilling the essence of roses and when the process was completed she bottled her rosewater to be used as a fragrance or a flavoring. Both were sought after for brides wanted to be sweet on their wedding day, "smelling like a rose," and housewives wanted their cakes and cookies to have the subtle, delicate flavor that rose flavoring adds to desserts. Aunt Crese baked many a wedding cake (that was another specialty of hers), and the bride who ordered one received a bottle of rosewater as a gift from Aunt Crese!

Neither folklore nor history has recorded the death of Aunt

Crese. The last trace of the family recorded was when the Brown's adopted daughter, Lucy A. R. Brown Fontaine, sold the house for $1,175 to Henry Barry in 1867. It has remained in the Barry family ever since.

The Doliber House nearby, made of clapboard and shingle (*circa* 1650), is located in the middle of a large lot surrounded on three sides by the street. The present garage was once a shoemaker's shop called Ten Footer. The land on which the house is built was purchased from the Indians, who never bothered the dwellers.

From a deed search and land court title we read: "The Dermody house is built on land which John Norman sold to Robert Knight September 28, 1651."

At one time, in the late 1800's, Miss Marcia Selman, who was the niece of Captain Knott V. Martin of Civil War fame, lived here. She is best remembered for her song dedicated to the town, "Marblehead Forever," sung by all down through the years.

The floorboards are wide (over twenty inches), but not twenty-one or twenty-two, for boards of that width had to be sent back to England and anyone found possessing such was heavily fined. The beams, heavy ones, are put together with wooden pegs and the few nails that are in the house are handmade. The ceilings are low studded and the adze's marks are visible in many places. Some of the best-known Marblehead families at one time owned halves of the house: Norden, Girdler, Doliber, Brown, Fettyplace, Hine.

Down the road from Black Joe's tavern was a rival inn run by Aunty Bowen, also known as "Ma'am Sociable," for she was a kindly soul and a terrific talker. It was she who called Gingerbread Hill "Mount Pleasant." But often, when the young people who had purchased the apples she sold would hurl them back at her, yelling "Sour" and other epithets, her reply would be pithy and unladylike!

Aunty Bowen's inn, built in the eighteenth century, was known as the Bessom House and it was frequented by Marbleheaders. It is in excellent condition and continues to lend charm to the landscape.

Partially hidden by the brush and rocks, steps lead to Number 56 Norman Street, Captain John Manley's home, which looks as it did when he owned it in the 1700's. Snuggled in under the brow of Gingerbread Hill, it is still a two-storied dwelling; in 1834 it had a barn and a shoemaker's shop. The interior has had few major changes.

Captain Manley achieved what so many men of fame wish for— perfect secrecy as to his private life. Little, if anything, is known about that. He was probably born in England in 1734, but why did he use the surname of Russell in Marblehead? What was he doing in Boston? Where did he disappear to? Some future findings may unravel the enigma of those threads of his life's pattern. His wife, Martha Hickman Russell, owned the home and after his death she divided it among the children.

The streets in the Historic District have scores of other historic homes and sites, such as Jonathan Proctor's on Hooper Street, the Deacon Doliber house on Beacon Street, and another one of the older houses in town, the Sweet-Carroll house at 59 Washington Street. These are only some of the seventeenth-, eighteenth- and nineteenth-century houses in a town where the historic landmarks are interwoven with the lives of the people who live here. As important as the houses to the preservation of our town's and the country's heritage are the narrow and winding streets on which the houses are located—for these very streets are a Colonial hallmark.

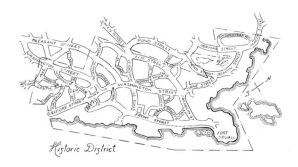

Historic District

2. Arts and Crafts

A KEEN AWARENESS of the achievements of early Marblehead pervades all levels of this generation as it too emulates the skills involved in the many facets of the art world. The accomplishments of every era are revealed in the artifacts that have been preserved, and the rich heritage of the preceding three centuries which is ours exists primarily because of the talents of our ancestors. In colonial times, and well into the nineteenth century, many men lived and attained whatever measure of success was theirs by virtue of one or several skills, making useful and decorative objects. Of the limners who came to Marblehead to capture on canvas the likenesses of their contemporaries little has been written. The colonists were captivated and had their portraits painted by such outstanding artists as John Singleton Copley, who came often to Marblehead and finally embarked for England from this very port. Gilbert Stuart and Chester Harding came here, too.

Marblehead lured many famous artists over the years, and continues to do so. A hundred years ago N. A. Lindsey, while walking along the beach at Devereux, found Childe Hassam contemplating the seascape and quickly persuaded him to design the masthead of his newspaper, *The Marblehead Messenger*. That masthead—for which the now famous artist received five dollars—is still in use. It was recoppered once, but what a collector's item it is, for current art authorities quote that the least of Childe Hassam's works in to-day's market brings many thousands of dollars. To name but three artists who drew inspiration from Marblehead: Maurice Prendergast, whose water colors of Marblehead may be seen at the Museum of Fine Arts in Boston, and two portrait painters, Ethel Colver who worked in pastels and who loved to make children her subjects, and Orlando Rouland, whose medium was oil and who was elected to the American Academy of Artists.

There were native born Marblehead men who achieved recognition in the field of painting: William Thompson Bartoll was born in Marblehead in 1817 (one of twin sons of John and Rebecca Thompson Bartoll) and he lived here all of his forty-two years, dying in 1859. He descended from an old Marblehead family and, like so many other artists of his day, he first started as a house painter, doing murals and decoration. Most of his work of this type has been lost or remains hidden under layers of wallpaper and paint in the old Marblehead houses. However, one example of his skill at wood graining may be seen on the paneling in the great room of the Lee Mansion; this work was done in 1852 and has lasted remarkably well. Many of his portraits also may be found in this mansion and in Abbot Hall. The clarity of his style and use of colors make the portraits come alive.

Another Marbleheader, John Orne Johnson Frost, was seven years old when William Bartoll died. Frost, too, could trace his ancestry back to the early 1600's. In 1868, when he was sixteen, he shipped out on a fishing schooner headed for the Banks. He was to complete only one more such voyage, for when he fell in love with Annie Lillibridge he was more than willing to quit the sea. J. O. J. ran a restaurant for many years.

Having grown up in a family that told Marblehead stories of war and history, it was natural that Frost should entertain his own son with the same tales. When his wife died, and there was no one at home to talk to and to retell the stories he loved so well, Frost took to illustrating those favorite old narratives. He was nearly seventy and had had no training in art, but undaunted, using brilliant colors and the theme closest to his heart, the story of Marblehead, he recorded in primitive fashion his pride of his hometown. Two years before he died he distributed handbills announcing his first exhibition, though he did not call it that. The handbill read that he "has opened his new art building containing about eighty paintings depicting his life on the Grand Banks and in the town of Marblehead.

There will be a charge of twenty-five cents to see these paintings.
. . ." Few came, and slight interest was shown in the paintings that
are today sought after and have been auctioned at Parke–Bernet
Galleries in New York. He left behind him in 1928 approximately
one hundred paintings, some even found tucked behind the eaves in
the attic. The Marblehead Historical Society owns many of his
paintings and they are displayed in the Lee Mansion, a few are at
the Smithsonian Institution and the rest, collector's items, are in private collections in Marblehead and throughout the country. His medium? Ordinary house paint!

Arthur William Heintzelman was not a native of Marblehead for
he was born in Newark, New Jersey, in 1891. However, he brought
distinction to his adopted town for he had accrued honors before
moving here, and continued to do so. He fell in love with Marblehead and was a leading citizen. He received his training at the
Rhode Island School of Design and when awarded their Alumni
Traveling Scholarship he went to the capitals of Europe and lived in
France from 1921 to 1935. It was after this that he and his wife
came to Marblehead to live. His list of prizes and honors was a long
one when he accepted the post of Keeper of the Prints at the Boston
Public Library. Many examples from Mr. Heintzelman's brush, cra-
yon and needle are in the museums and private collections here and
abroad and several of his etchings are of Marblehead's waterfront.

On June 17, 1968, a rare honor was bestowed on a Marblehead
resident, a reception at the Boston Public Library, for the trustees
of that library were saluting Samuel Chamberlain, who had written,
illustrated and helped produce the book that the library published
—another rare honor in itself. In *Etched in Sunlight* Mr. Chamberlain told of his love affair with the world, narrowing it down to
New England—in particular, Marblehead. One reporter wrote,
"fellow townsmen who read the fullsome account will know how
renowned an artist and man they have amongst them."

Of all the artists who have glimpsed the charm of Marblehead
none have recorded it in so diverse a manner as "Sam" Chamberlain
with his photographs and etchings. Residing in the Christopher
Bubier house on Tucker Street he looked from his windows onto
the harbor below and the sea beyond. He has walked the town in all
its weather.

His awareness of sunlight and shadow has made him an inter-
preter of mood, of seasonal changes, of the elemental beauty of
sturdy New England architecture. His photographs give us a feeling
of imaginative selectivity and composition.

So keen has been the interest in art (one art dealer in town estimated that in 1970 there were probably three hundred artists in town) that in 1922 a group of artists, including Francis T. Flanagan, J. Selma Larsen, S. B. Duffield, Philip Von Saltza, James Keysella, W. C. Hunter, Charles P. Snow and Miss Louise Snow formed the Marblehead Arts Association, electing Orlando Rouland as their first president. Their first exhibit was held in the American Legion Hall in the summer of 1923. By 1927 the Honorable Frank G. Allen, governor of Massachusetts, and Frank Butler (watercolorist) had become officers and the association had decided to offer its membership to craftsmen.

In 1925 a great exhibit of *Ship and Sea* was held, the choirboys from St. Michael's sang sea chanties, many veteran captains gave lectures, and the attendance soared to 3,182. By 1926 the association's membership had grown to 188: 26 were artists, 40 were craftsmen, and 122 were "interested" in art. In 1937 Arthur W. Heintzelman became president and things began to take on a new complexion under his nine years of vigorous leadership. In 1927 the "Arts" purchased the Captain Trevett House on Washington Street for a mere $5,500 and restored it, successfully using it as their headquarters.

The association felt it had outgrown its headquarters in 1937 and as the King Hooper Mansion was on the market Mrs. Heintzelman and Mrs. Samuel Chamberlain headed the committee which was successful in purchasing it for eight thousand dollars. Thousands of hours of labor have gone into restoring the building as it is today, the chief exponent of the love of arts and the dedication to that facet of life in Marblehead.

In 1940 Marblehead became the print center of America, for a day at least, for the Marblehead Arts Association was honoring Frank W. Benson, the dean of American etchers by arranging an exhibit of ninety of his famous prints, mostly of wild fowl. Five other graphic artists participated in this Frank Benson Day: John Taylor Arms of Greenfield brought his press and demonstrated his art of etching; Arthur W. Heintzelman made a drypoint; Thomas Nason of Connecticut, a copper engraving; Samuel Chamberlain made a soft-ground etching of the King Hooper Mansion where the program was held; and Kerr Eby, the renowned plate printer pulled the prints from all four demonstration plates.

The Arts Association still has exhibits, art classes for adults and children, holding high the standards of the art world. Marblehead with its beauty and unique "backdrop" continues to attract not only painters, etchers, and print makers but also illustrators, book-jacket designers and cartoonists who chronicle the times in another perspective.

Of the two dozen or so cabinetmakers who lived and created in Marblehead the only one whose work received national attention was that of Deacon Nathan Bowen. This man was born in Marblehead in 1752 and one of his pieces can be seen at the Detroit Institute of Arts. It is a bonnet-top chest-on-chest and it is attributed to Bowen from the marking on the back, "NB 1774." This mahogany chest was made for the wedding linen of Mary Ann Hiddin. The Museum of Fine Arts in Boston also possesses an unattributed chest-on-chest almost identical to that of the one in the Detroit Institute of Arts. Some of the other craftsmen were: James Aborn, Thomas Appleton, Jonathan C. Blaney, Moses Briggs, Thomas Brimblecome, David Flint, Nathaniel Fowler, Henry Grant, John L. Harris, William Jones, Benjamin Laskey, Thomas Laskey, George Lemastor, Joseph Lindsay, Ebenezer Martin, George Whitefield Martin, Thomas Martin, Samuel Parker, Robert Phillips, Joseph Potter, Jeremiah Francis Smith and Nathaniel Swett.

Prior to the establishment of the colonial banking system, silverware was considered the safest, soundest kind of investment. From the West Indies and other trade routes Spanish and Dutch coin flooded the seaports of New England, and Marblehead was one of those seaports. The surest way to protect money was to take it to a local silversmith to be transformed into tankards and teapots, candlesticks and casters, platters and porringers, salts and spoons.

In addition to their own trades, silversmiths—who, of necessity, had to be versatile—functioned as clockmakers, dentists, bell founders and repairers, cabinetmakers, blacksmiths, and decorators of painted tin. Sometimes they were referred to as whitesmiths because they worked in a light metal whereas the blacksmiths used iron which was dark or black. The silversmith could wield an anvil and knew the handling of metals; he was well equipped for the task of blacksmith and bell founder as well, although the reverse was not true for the blacksmith for he was not skilled to handle delicate materials.

The exciting life associated with a master craftsman like Paul Revere hardly could be matched by a silversmith in the small town of Marblehead. Surprisingly enough, Marblehead had a number of silversmiths whose work proved them to be top craftsmen and whose pieces now are displayed in museums in our largest cities.

The first of the silversmiths to reside here was William Jones (1694–1730). Details of his life are not recorded but he evidently was very successful at his craft and one of his pieces is in the Metropolitan Museum of Art in New York City. He left an estate valued at £3000, a considerable sum for a craftsman who was only thirty-six when he died.

Thomas Skinner (1713–1761) was another Marblehead silver-smith whose work is displayed at the Metropolitan Museum of Art. Thomas was born in Boston on March 8, 1713. Dana, in his *Richard Skinner of Marblehead and His Bible,* states that there were also stone buttons, rings, buckles and spoons among the gold and silver on hand in his shop, where there was also a glass showcase valued at ten shillings.

John Jagger was born in Marblehead in 1713 and in 1735 he mar-ried Isabella Jones, the widow of goldsmith William Jones of Mar-blehead. The Museum of Fine Arts in Boston has a tankard made in 1738 for Rev. Simon Bradstreet and Mary Bradstreet bearing his mark and it is the only known example of his work to be in exis-tence. He must have died prior to 1764 as Lynn's vital records list the death of Mrs. Sibella Jagger, widow of John Jagger, on Decem-ber 24, 1764.

Many pieces of Thomas Grant's work (1731–1804) exist. Some are still in private collections and some are on exhibition in the Lee Mansion and the Essex Institute. Two tankards and two communion cups wrought by him are in the Unitarian Church on Mugford Street. During the Revolution he was a captain in Col. John Glov-er's regiment. He also owned the seventy-two-ton schooner, *Han-cock,* which was one of Glover's vessels chartered by authority of General Washington. An Essex deed of 1767 establishes his gold-smith's shop on the corner of "Welds Land"—"S. 14 Feet upon Ye Cart Road of 15' wide and E. 11' upon Highway." A pair of beakers and a tankard made by Thomas Grant were given to the Second Congregational Church in Marblehead in 1772 and 1773.

William Bubier (1737–1792) was born in Marblehead. His sister Margaret was the wife of goldsmith Thomas Grant with whom William Bubier served as first lieutenant in Col. John Glover's regi-ment during the Revolution. He died intestate and no inventory was filed at the probate court, but he was called a goldsmith at the time of his death even though no maker's mark had been ascribed to him.

The son of Thomas Grant and Margaret (Bubier) Grant was named Thomas J. Grant (1761–1815). He married Lydia Stacey in 1786. Prior to that he was in the Marblehead Regiment in the sec-ond year of the Revolution, as a fifer in his father's company. Al-though his father, brother and uncle were all silversmiths he was not listed as one until February 16, 1810; he was called a silversmith in a deed of land registered on that date. A mark (touchmark) similar to his father's has been found on a spoon at the Marblehead Historical

Society's collection in the Lee Mansion. This has been attributed to him since it is made in a style too late to have been made by his father.

William Grant (1766–1809) was also a son of Thomas and Margaret (Bubier) Grant. Although he is listed as a silversmith by Belknap in *Artists and Craftsmen of Essex County*, and called a goldsmith in the Essex County Probate Court records, April 20, 1809, he had no mark ascribed to him and died intestate, and neither tools nor silver are listed in his inventory.

David Northey (Northee) was born in 1778 the son of John Northey of Marblehead. A goldsmith with silver mark attributed to him, he was also listed as David I Northee. A funeral ring made by him in 1752 is in the Essex Institute.

Teaspoons made by James Appleton (1785–1862) are often used in one home on Franklin Street. He was known as the "Father of Prohibition." He engaged in the jewelry and silver business for ten years (1823 to 1833), and then moved to Portland, Maine.

The greatest collection of silver in Marblehead is the silver sacramental service belonging to the First Church of Christ in Marblehead, mentioned elsewhere in this book.

A pre–Revolutionary clock of native manufacture is a rare, exciting acquisition. The Marblehead clock that is in the old parlor of the Crowninshield–Bentley House, owned by the Essex Institute, is one of these rarities. Engraved on the round nameplate at the top of the dial is the name of the maker—"Henry Harmson—Marblehead." This clock was made for John Cogswell in 1730.

There is a tall clock with a walnut-veneered case in the Lee Mansion. The dial is signed "Henry Harrison, Marblehead." Dean A. Fales, Jr., authority on antique furniture and furnishings, states that the names Harmson and Harrison are so much alike there is a strong possibility that Harmson could have made these works also, the vagaries of the engraver of the dial accounting for the discrepancy in the spelling of the name. Unfortunately, there is no further information concerning the Lee Mansion clock.

What were the women contributing to the arts? The needle was their constant companion for ever since time out of mind the woman, the mother and homemaker, had as her intimate companion the needle. Here in Marblehead, as everywhere throughout the world, needle decoration is an art, and as an art it is closely bound with daily life; thus needlework has been the woman's medium, just as the pen and paintbrush are for recording history. The dye pot was necessary for those first woolen threads and Marblehead was among the first to receive shipments of indigo and fustic. Through John Foster's orders the sloop *Good Luck* came often to Marblehead with these two necessaries. Probably indigo reached here quicker than it arrived in most of the other towns for Eliza Lucas Pinckney, the horticulturist, who first raised indigo in our country, sent her first indigo to her cousin, the wife of the Reverend Mr. Fayerweather of Boston. These early samplers, pieces of crewelwork and needlepoint still remain for the most part in private homes; the beautiful Sparhawk sampler is still on the bedroom wall in "The Hearth and the Eagle" house on Franklin Street.

Many other womanly pursuits were carried on—tin painting, and many others. Just as busy, creative fingers today produce beautiful crewel pieces and needlepoint creations, so does the tray painting continue, and a cooperative group of artisans under the name of "Rusty Rudder" are interested in promoting and performing in the field of handicrafts, as the Art Guild does for the artists.

Pottery, the oldest of the handicrafts still practiced in New England, dates back to the beginning of time. Marblehead pottery, now treasured as a collector's choice item, had its origin in a therapeutic program launched by Dr. Herbert J. Hall, a Marblehead physician, in 1904. He established a workshop in his Devereux mansion where his patients were taught to mend overwrought nerves by means of carefully guided work in certain crafts. As a result, pottery making was encouraged under trained direction and from the very beginning harmonious colors and simple lines were characteristic of the pieces produced.

Later, the direction of the pottery shop was taken over by Arthur E. Baggs, who developed his own formula for mixing clay—a blend of white, western clay and common red clay from the nearby city of Peabody. Some of the pieces were molded, while some were thrown and turned. After the first firing the pieces were smoothed with great care and glazed with the soft colors: a beautiful old blue which came to be known as Marblehead blue, a warm gray, wisteria, yellow, green and tobacco brown. The attractive hallmark for Marblehead pottery was a ship under full sail with an *M* on one side and a *P* on the other. The mark was always impressed except for experimental or exhibition pieces in which instances the mark was painted on the surface. The glaze was exceptionally smooth, silky matt or dull finish, and each piece was lined with a glossy enamel of a color harmonizing with the outer glaze. Designs were carried out in simple style, emulating seaweed, fish and marine animals. Since the demand for this pottery made it necessary to move to larger quarters, Mr. Baggs established the Pottery Shop at 111 Front Street and became owner and proprietor. He maintained his shop until 1936, while continuing to teach at Ohio State University, but he spent his summers in Marblehead. One of the chief designers of this sought-after pottery was John Selmer–Larsen, and Benjamin Tutt was one of the best-known workers. The shop with its sign advertising Marblehead pottery faced on Front Street. In the rear were two kilns described as "six or eight feet across" and behind these were the workshops. At the present time, a complex of town houses occupies this area.

From its earliest days Marblehead's streets have had an unusual number of children. The earliest visitors, as well as the visitors of today, have commented on the "large numbers of children." Down through the ages toys have attracted youngsters as well as the adult who purchases them, and they have especial appeal to the collector. The gift of a toy is bound to create a common bond of friendship and to see the toy maker himself is boundless joy. The annals of Marblehead records no toy maker, as such, until 1921 when Daddy Scott came onto the scene. A sign on 4 Stacey Street bore the legend, "Scott Novelty Co. Toys (Walter B., Harold J. and Hugh D. Scott)." Hugh David Scott was Daddy Scott, the toy maker.

In 1929 the shop was located on 97 Front Street and the Scotts' reputation for excellent toys had spread far beyond this old New England seaport across the United States. Here ingenious toys were skillfully and enduringly fashioned. All the Daddy Scott toys were made from clear pine except where metal was necessary. Wheels and similar parts needing extra strength were made from a high-grade birch veneer; where necessary, toys were skillfully painted. An ordinary rubber band was used for propelling the mechanical toys; without the band the toy was "free" and could be used as a pull toy. If you were lucky enough to have bought one of these toys you now possess a real collector's item.

Orlando Rouland, the eminent portrait painter who lived in Marblehead at 1 Lookout Court, painted a large, fine portrait of Daddy Scott designing a toy in his shop on Front Street. Mr. Rouland went on to New York City to win further acclaim there but this painting has recently been acquired by Mrs. Rupert W. Jaques of Marblehead, an authority on dolls and toys. In 1930 Daddy Scott's Toy Shop moved to 18 Sewall Street and for many years now it has been known as the Scott Wood Company and no longer makes the toys for which it was famous.

To girls of yesteryear the perfect gift was that of a doll. In the middle of the nineteenth century the most sought-after doll (which could be of any size) was a wooden doll made of pine or maple, sometimes with pegged joints which allowed the arms and legs to move. "Penny-woodens" is an endearing name to doll collectors, for it refers to this simple wooden-jointed doll that was so popular. Rachel Field, in *Hitty*, the story about one such doll, set the stage for a renewed interest in a wooden doll for the girls of this century. Designing with great imagination, Alice Wainwright gave to a new generation of doll "mothers" a wooden doll she named Polly Shorrock. From her studio home on Tucker Street hundreds of these lovely Polly Shorrock dolls went to their new homes in the 1950's and 1960's. Polly was a slender twelve-inch doll, beautifully dressed and she was soon followed by a smaller model, Araminta. Little girls (and their mothers, too) wanted both. Their creator has moved from the town, but Polly Shorrock and Araminta are still sought after.

Prescott W. Baston has proved himself a master of miniatures, for he has created historic figures of Lilliputian stature. This graduate of the Vesper George Art School in Boston tried many avenues of art until he finally found his forte. In 1938, as a sculptor of miniatures, he established his own studio, the Sebastian Studios, Inc., in Marblehead. After extensive research on the subject, Mr. Baston uses clay for sculpting each of his miniatures. Then a plaster mold is made which enables the studio to cast its "molding piece" from gypsum cement. Each figurine is hand painted and there are over four hundred different subjects, colonial pairs, historic persons, regional couples, Dickens characters and many others. There are three figurines that are truly Marblehead: "*The Spirit of '76*," *The Lobsterman* (with an exact replica of the lobster trap the native lobsterman uses here) and *The Skipper*. The model for this was Captain Dolliber, as Mr. Baston often models from life. Mr. Baston says, "Here in Marblehead, which is one of the chief art centers of the country, there are many artist-employees who have the skill necessary to work in the artistic production of the collection."

3. Salemside, Upper Division and Mid-Town

AEONS AGO when the ice claimed New England, it carved out the arm of Salem's harbor and Forest River, thus creating a barrier for those who wished to go from Salem to the rocky peninsula of Marblehead. Some of the ice floated out to sea, other ice chunks remained, becoming buried in sand and silt carried along under the glacier. Finally, when all was melted, the sand which had clung to the icebergs seeped down leaving large depressions, or kettle holes. They look exactly like a kettle, deep and dark, and locally were, and still are, called dungeons. It was necessary to travel around them. They provided a wonderful, "scary" place to play—a place for everyone to shun at night. These strange circular depressions were barriers to Marblehead's entrance from Salem. The way to reach Marblehead quickly was by ferry; the other way, on land, was by a path that was to be called Old Salem Road. That first road, opened in April, 1660, followed a path over the bridge, passing over Stony Beach (called Webb's), between the river and Legg's Hill and beside the dungeons.

In the early settlements each town was fenced and at the highway gates in the fence were maintained. Marblehead Gate was such a gate and was there as late as the 1770's. The records show that, in

1692, Thomas Darling was paid "1 cow lease for work," for hanging the gate at Forest River bridge and looking after it. In 1706 the town was still ordering the Forest River gates "kept up." In 1666 another road from Salem to Marblehead came into use—the old Lynn Road into Marblehead, the road that is now known as Tedesco Street. Still another road in use today was laid out in 1737; this was called the Old Road to Forest River and now is Lafayette Street.

John Humphrey had already arrived in New England when Salem Town decreed "that there shall be a plantacion at Marblehead." In 1635 the court decreed "that Mr. Humphrey's land should begin at the Clifte in the way to Marblehead which is the bound between Salem and Linn, and also along the line between the said townes to the rocks, one mile, by estimation, to a greate red oake, from wch he said marked tree, all under & over theis rocks upon a straight line to the running brooke by Thomas Smyth's house. . . ." Not only all these lands, but also still farther west into what is now Lynnfield and including Suntaug Lake; Mr. Humphrey was land rich! His lands in Marblehead that stretched to the sea (the Atlantic Ocean) were known then as the Plain Farmes, and Mr. Humphrey was instructed to allow the "Commoners" the privilege of eventually buying the same. All that part of the territory easterly of the line running from Forest River to the sea was Mr. Humphrey's land of 350 acres—but Salem had other plans for it. The town worried about this land grant to Humphrey for there was agitation for a college to be built for the Colony. Having it near Salem seemed plausible, if 300 acres of this same tract of land (a portion reassigned to Humphrey) had been granted to Thomas Scruggs in the year 1635. Quickly, Salem appointed Rev. Hugh Peter and John Humphrey and others to offer to survey or choose the land for the college. The board of advisors decided that the college should be in Newtown (Cambridge) near the seat of government.

At this time he conveyed to Emanuel Downing the two ponds known henceforth as Coy Ponds and a hill, later called Legg's Hill, which overlooked them. On the same day that Downing was "given" the land, the court granted him the right to maintain this as a shooting ground. Naturally, the ponds were named "Coy" for the duck coys. American Indians had made decoys out of rushes many centuries ago and the white men were quick to copy them. Did Mr. Downing use these? No—he had brought his own from England.

John Humphrey was important to the growth of New England and to this special sector of it, Marblehead. He was treasurer of the

120 persons who formed the Dorchester Company of Adventurers, a wealthy company of joint stock owners. Prestige and dignity were theirs and when they met they called themselves the New England Planters' Parliament. Their purpose was "to establish a fishing and trading colony with a minister."

One of the outstanding solicitors of this group was Mr. Humphrey. As treasurer he should have migrated to New England to become deputy governor with Governor Winthrop, but stayed behind and Thomas Dudley came in his place. Scheduled to arrive in New England in 1630 and then again in 1632, he was still in Dorchester. This angered Governor Winthrop, who apparently had not been informed that Humphrey's second wife had died and that he was now busy wooing Lady Susan Fiennes, the earl of Lincoln's daughter and sister of Lady Arbella Fiennes, who, having married Isaac Johnson, was already in Salem. He continued to raise funds for the company and in 1634, he, Lady Susan, and their children arrived in Salem in June with money for the company, a good supply of munition and sixteen heifers. Although his very good friend was the Reverend Hugh Peter, Humphrey did not join a church during the years he was here.

From the moment he arrived Humphrey continuously reported the disapproval of many who had come with him (his own dissent included) of the selection of Massachusetts for the settlement of the Colony. He wanted to relocate south, observing "that snow even at Narraganset lies less," and to go "to the Hudson River at least." Trying to make his wife and himself happier, he built a "manorial" home in the "bleak wilderness," having brought timber and brick for that very purpose. That house is standing today on Paradise Road in Swampscott, having been moved from its original setting on Elmwood Road. The house is clapboarded and the interior wall is of large bricks, the huge fireplace burns six-foot logs and there are fireplaces in the four large rooms and in the two smaller chambers. Before Humphrey left, his name was entered as "debted" with a cabalistic sign, and his barn was maliciously burned. Winthrop made note of this in his *Journal* and the more dreadful fact that Humphrey had left his children behind; actually the only one left behind was Joseph, who remained to care for whatever property he could. Misfortune dogged Humphrey back in England: he did not receive the appointment to Providence Island, nor did he add to his personal estate.

Humphrey died at fifty-seven, and was not accorded the credit for accomplishment in establishing the Colony of Massachusetts Bay.

On the Salemside shore of Marblehead at the bridge where the Forest River empties into the sea stood the Lead Mills, originally known as the Chadwick Lead Mills. A wharf was here in 1900 where sailing vessels could unload the pig lead which was put to soak in large crocks shaped like bean pots. In 1967 the Lead Mill houses were razed.

Along the shore from the Lead Mills site is a cove that was known as Throgmorton Cove. This is where John Throgmorton had a home and a hog house on the land that had been granted him by Salem in 1635 but in the following year he fled to Rhode Island.

William Beale built a grist mill in 1649 on the cove which was in use until 1674. This site, it was later discovered, had been a workshop where tools were made and outlines of wigwams and fire holes were visible.

During Prohibition rumrunners used Wyman's Cove, which had been called Pirate's Cove or Smuggler's Cove, to land their cargoes and at one time a pitched battle took place between the rumrunners and local police. In one raid, in 1930, Patrolman Kelley died as the result of having a gas bomb thrown in his face. The case did not come up for trial until 1932; each of six men was fined two hundred dollars and no one was prosecuted for Kelley's death, "for only Kelley could identify the bomb thrower, and he was not alive." To the west of the cove is an area known as Legg's Hill.

John Legg was one of the earliest settlers in Marblehead and in 1659 he was one of the five who worked on "seating" the meeting house. He probably owned Legg's Hill as an investment. On the Indian campsite behind the hill a number of artifacts have been found. Two centuries later the Legg's Hill water reservoir and a standpipe, which was for the "exclusive use of Marblehead" (because of the serious fires in Mid-Town in 1877, 1888 an additional water supply was needed). A dam had to be built to keep the salt water out of the wells in that area.

Nearby is the site of the Gen. John Glover farm homestead. In 1781 he was allowed to purchase the confiscated Loyalist estate located on the main road running from Marblehead to Boston, practically at the junction of the boundary lines of Salem, Marblehead and Lynn (now Swampscott).

In the 1900's Gen. John Glover's farm was opened to the public. The same house was remodeled and added to in the 1950's and is now known as General Glover's Inn, a nationally famous restaurant on the North Shore.

General Glover's name is perpetuated in another building in this end of town, for the Glover School, which stands on the corner of Humphrey and Maple Streets, was built in 1928 and was added onto in 1949. This same site was originally an Indian palisade and then the Farm School where James J. H. Gregory taught.

Lafayette Street (named that in 1900) is the continuation of Pleasant Street. Acres of land on this western end belonged to the Wymans by the nineteenth century. When Isaac Wyman, a descendant, died in 1910, he left lands and money for the construction of the Wyman Memorial Church of St. Andrew (Episcopal). The beautiful stone church was erected in 1924 on the very location of the private Wyman graveyard. Recently a campanile has been placed on the same ground, the Board of Selectmen "loaning" the bell that was placed in it; the bell was one left from the fires of the nineteenth century.

The very first settlers used the Upper Division of Marblehead as pasture lands for their cows and feeding grounds for their hogs. There were many obstacles to this use of common lands: the territory itself was frequented by Indians and packs of wolves; the distance from the settlement was another factor; those who had land grants in that particular area often did not erect fences, nor did they keep them in repair if they had marked off the land. Consequently, very early the town employed shepherds to lead the cattle to their grazing grounds. It was a common sight to see a young lad, a shepherd, leading several cows, and the task of herding pigs was even harder. Because of careless practice two types of town officers were established; hogreeves, officers whose duty it was to impound stray hogs, and fence viewers who surveyed the property lines and noted when the fences needed repair. As both cows and hogs were necessary for food, these were important duties.

The land west of the junction of today's Lafayette Street and West Shore Drive (part of the old Upper Division) bears the name of the man who long ago owned it, John Gatchell. On his property, which was part of the Plain Farms, an Indian fort once stood. This same land, known as Gatchell's Pit, is now a municipal playground with a baseball diamond and a tennis court. On the hill and in the woods beyond, on town-owned land, stands the Marblehead Girl Scout camp, Camp Shorelea. The town fathers gave permission to the Scouts to use this spot, and the shore beyond, for swimming, to further the unusually active program for both Boy and Girl Scouts in town.

In March, 1690, the General Council granted Marblehead the privilege of having more taverns. In 1723 John Edgecomb opened an inn situated close to Gatchell's Pit and near the stagecoach line. His boundaries were from "ye sign post . . . through the centre of the stack of chimneys." Back in 1641, when John Humphrey had returned to England, his property subsequently had been divided into numerous parts; some parts were sometimes called "Upper Division" but more frequently "farms."

In 1884 the owners of the farms were meeting not for the purpose of cooperation but were petitioning to secede and were joined by Clifton and the Neck. The smouldering was of short duration and Marblehead continued to be Marblehead.

The Hathaway property became part of the Little's Sorosis farm which not only had a piggery, but also a sheep and poultry farm, and during World War I provided employment for many and supplied an incredible amount of corn and vegetables for the army. A typical farmhouse of that period is still standing on Widger Road. Nearby is the town's only hospital, Mary A. Alley (1954).

There are several schools in this area, including the Malcolm Bell, named for the former Representative, and the Tower School, a private school. Centrally located are: Roads School (1904), honoring Samuel Roads, Jr.; the High School (1913) with its several additions on old Workhouse Rocks; the Junior High (1955). St. Stephen's Methodist Church moved in 1954 from "downtown" into its modern place of worship at Lafayette and Humphrey Streets.

By 1724 the Commoners had divided the land of Marblehead into three divisions: Upper (near Salem), Middle and Lower (toward Little Harbor). As it grew more crowded in Barnegat and the older section, the people moved to Mid-Town, calling it Newtown. But the real development in Mid-Town surged forward in the mid–1800's, propelled by industrial activity. Edmund Kimball had reactivated the shipbuilding and had built homes for his workers; Mr. Bassett was employing more people for his shoe factory and as more homes were needed, he developed housing units.

There were sheds all along Redstone Lane that had three different kinds of builders' sand in them; the "boom" had begun. And on Barnard Street, the ropewalk was active with its buildings being used for the spinning of rope yarn, the largest being 675 feet long. There were two: the Marblehead Cordage Company and the Lackey ropewalk. The fire of 1871 ended that activity. Besides this, the town business was spreading in several directions, from the stores and stables to mills and manufacturers of shoes, glue and oilskins. New streets were laid out, street names were changed and the railroad helped in the activities. Bowdenville was along the rail line and on to the west, "a development village," for shoe workers. Mid-Town, when started, developed quickly. In this new industrial part of town there were some older homes, and they still stand.

On Prospect Street, Number 70, Commodore Samuel Tucker's house, is one of these. In excellent condition, this house of simple design, made of unpainted clapboard, has a bronze plaque on its side, designating it as the former home of the daring naval commander of the Revolutionary War. The story is told that when an officer rode up to deliver the commission, he noticed a man busily engaged in chopping wood in the backyard, and seeing that the laborer had his sleeves rolled up and his face partially covered by a tarpaulin hat, he inquired, "Can you tell me where the Honorable Samuel Tucker lives?" Tucker paused and reiterated, " 'Honorable'? 'Honorable'? There's not any man of that name in Marblehead. He must be one of the family of Tuckers in Salem. I'm the only Samuel Tucker there is here." The officer immediately handed this unassuming Marbleheader his commission.

As a boy, Sam Tucker had served on an English sloop-of-war and a merchant ship. When he was commodore it was his duty to safely land John Adams in France. Neither one knew that John Adams would one day be president; nor could they foresee that they were responsible for another future president, for accompanying his father was eleven-year-old John Quincy Adams. Flown from Tucker's vessel was the Pine Tree flag of Massachusetts made by Mrs. Tucker.

Ambrose Gale, descendant of the early selectman, owned Number 45, where he made shoes in the tiny factory in the rear.

On this street a church once stood. Freedom of worship had always been a part of Marblehead and when, at first, there was no Roman Catholic church in Marblehead, the small band of Catholics walked or rode to Salem in fair or foul weather to attend Mass. Within a few decades, private homes within the town were used for this service: the first home to be used for this was that of Dennis Donovan on Commercial Street; the year was 1851. The first established place of worship, built in 1859, was at the junction of Prospect and Rowland Streets—opposite the house that Commodore Tucker had lived in. In 1872 a new church edifice was built on Gregory Street, but it was struck by lightning and burned to the ground before it could be used.

In August, 1927, a tract of land from Prospect Street to Atlantic was available for purchase and was ideal for a group of parish buildings. In 1928 the handsome, granite cruciform, Gothic church, Our Lady, Star of the Sea, became an actuality. Next to it was the rectory and later the convent and the parochial school were built across the street. The school was adjacent to Seaside Park which was town owned and had been part of the Bubier Plains.

One of the oldest farm houses in Mid-Town is the one on Number 1 Vine Street that once belonged to "Aunt Sally" Goodwin. It was built by Philip Goodwin at the end of Girdler's Lane, known now as Village Street, then hardly more than a cow path. There are fireplaces in every room, wide floorboards, and all the doors have *H* and *L* hinges with hand-wrought iron latches.

On Green Street a cemetery is directly across from the Story School on the corner of Elm and Creesy Streets. The story is that Thomas Brown, owning the land where the cemetery is located, built upon it as many good-sized tombs as his land would permit. These he sold at auction to the highest bidder. The newspaper for November 24, 1824, carried this: "Capt. Nicholas Tucker for a tomb in new Burial Ground being no. 3 in NE tomb of the three which I built $75." Many of the graves are mounded, and some are fashioned like root cellars with their brick arches, slate doors and wooden blocks. The mound itself is grass covered.

The row on row of tombs are shared by many, the legend on one such metal door:

> John Ingalls ½
> and
> Peter S. Powers ¼
> 1858
> Benjamin Selman ¼

One of the oldest mounded vaults is that of

> Azor Orne
> June 6th 1796

On one weathered stone:

> "His little feet
> on the golden street
> will never go astray."

Whose? Time has obliterated the name and date.

A fine monument was erected by the town benefactor, the man who presented the town with the building bearing his name:

> Erected by
> Benjamin Abbot
> of
> Boston

In memory of his Family
Benjamin Abbot Sen'r.
Died on Mon. Oct. 24, 1844
Ae 77

The Woodfin plot has a fine piece of granite, a small replica of
Bunker Hill Monument. And Josiah Creesy, father of the famous
clipper captain after whom Creesy Street was named, is buried in
this cemetery.

First Church of Christ Scientist, diagonally across from Green
Street Cemetery on Elm Street, is an early American design to conform to the traditional architecture of Marblehead.

The Powder House on Green Street is one of the rare buildings
in Marblehead. The town has three unusual, thoroughly unique at-
tractions for the tourist; the Lee Mansion, *The Spirit of '76* painting,
by Archibald Willard, and the old Powder House. There are only
three pre-Revolutionary powder houses still standing in the United
States, each different in structure. The one on Green Street is a curious, completely circular building, the same inside as out; it was
built from brick, in 1755, shortly after the outbreak of hostilities in
the French and Indian War. Col. Jeremiah Lee served on the committee in charge of its construction. It was used as a storehouse for
muskets and ammunition not only during the French and Indian
War, but also the Revolution and the War of 1812. Time has not
marred or changed but has only seemed to make the handmade
bricks more lustrous.

There was a great deal of repair work done at the Powder House
for war preparation and current munitions in 1812. Previous work
had been done in 1802; the town records state "Painting ball of
Powder House .50." In the eighteenth century, a "Keeper of the
Powder House" was appointed annually.

Waterside Cemetery is off West Shore Drive located on a commanding height and is one of the most beautiful cemetery locations
on the North Shore. Beautifully cared for in its excellent setting, it
fulfilled the need in 1859 to accommodate the population growth.
The site, one mile from the center of town, was known as the Bessom Pasture, and had been the general location of an Indian palisaded village. Originally called Water Side, it is the burying place
of many of Marblehead's nineteenth- and twentieth-centuries' well-
known figures: Samuel Roads, Jr., the town historian; James J. H.
Gregory, the seedsman, and, marked by a small monument, the
grave of primitive painter, John O. J. Frost, with a stone which is
surrounded, in season, by lilies of the valley and in back of the stone
there are three of the "singing rocks" that came from Frost's back

yard and attracted many visitors. When Henry Ford had heard of Frost's singing rocks he had written, inquiring about them. Mr. Frost had replied by sending him a box of the boulders. It was discovered that the musical quality of these stones, when compared with that of other known musical stones, was not extremely high. However, considering that Mr. Frost's stones never had been cut to any definite pitch and that all of them were large, the range of notes was said to be rather remarkable.

To the east of the entrance of Waterside Cemetery are three glacial boulders named "The Three Sisters." The surrounding pasture was known by the same name. Adjacent to Waterside is Harborside Cemetery which is private but cared for by the Marblehead Cemetery Commission; it, too, has modern grave sites.

Changes in architecture were occurring every decade or so in the 1800's and one innovation was Octagon House. This type of home had been designed by Orson Squire Fowler, a New York farmboy, who, when a student at Amherst College, was ebullient about all that related to the pseudoscience, phrenology. He became a lecturer upon the subject and in the zenith of that career he conceived the revolutionary kind of place to live in. Octagon House was to be a simple and direct building, utilizing all the benefits that mathematics, nature and physics gave the octagon. This eight-sided house in its classic form had Doric pillars and pilasters, and in 1850 and 1853 there was a veritable boom in this type of building. When Thomas J. Bowden of Marblehead was in the Civil War, he saw one of these new houses for the first time in Virginia. As soon as he returned home he had one built for himself at Number 12 Mount Vernon Street. The house in its unusual shape has a cupola on top of the mansard roof and two bay windows on the first floor. Despite the odd shape of the house, all of its rooms are square. It is one of two octagonal houses in Essex County.

The Abbot Public Library, built on the corner of Pleasant and Maverick Streets is a fine, modern library building, designed by Marblehead's well-known architect, Arland A. Dirlam. Its doors were opened in 1954 and it has served the citizens of Marblehead well. There are many attractive features: excellent reading rooms, the children's room, the auditorium, and specially designed lights with nautical motifs that proclaim it to be a seacoast building. Other artifacts (besides shelves of books pertaining to Marblehead) include the model of a brigantine which was made by Walter C. Leavitt and hanging directly over it a watercolor of the same vessel under full sail painted by his son, John F. Leavitt. The Leavitts descended from John Swett, one of the early collectors of customs of the port.

On one of the walls is a wood-carved head of Gen. John Glover in bas-relief, by Carl A. Goddard.

On Hewitt Street, once called Maverick Place, stands one of the oldest houses in town, and the oldest in this section of the town. Age of a house is determined by copies of deeds and wills and even then the construction may predate the first recording. Such seems the case in the early house at 11 Hewitt Street.

The house itself indicates that one part is older than the other. The original house probably consisted of one large room with its huge fireplace and an Indian closet in back of it, which in turn may have been used for the underground railway in later years. This room is low studded with big beams and wide floorboards. The lean-to (part of the original house) is now the kitchen; a gracious, wide hall extends through the house from one portal to the other. From one side of the hall a stairway leads to the second floor; the two rooms off the other side attest to later building (not too many years later). The rooms are spacious and attractive; both have large fireplaces. In a registered deed transfer of property we learn that Moses Maverick, town father and Isaac Allerton's son-in-law, sold this house and an area estimated at about forty acres to William Hewitt in 1680.

Mr. Maverick had been granted ten acres on the Main near Little Harbor in 1638. In 1640 he acquired the acres around and including the land on which he built the 11 Hewitt Street house. In 1637 he had been appointed a juryman, an important position, six years later he was made a constable and for years he was a selectman. In 1648 he was awarded three cows. No one else was assigned as many; two were allotted to the other important men, so Moses Maverick was *the* man of the town. His first wife, Sarah Allerton (daughter of Isaac), died in 1658, and six years later he married the widow of Thomas Roberts. He died in 1685 and she survived him by twelve years.

In 1680 they both conveyed the house that had been occupied by Philip Welch to William Hewitt, for whom the street was named. He in turn willed it to Mary Boober, "doe for and in consideration of the love good will and affection which I have and doe beare towards my loving maid Mary Boober of said Marblehead County and province aforesaid singlewoman whom I brought up have given and granted and by these presents I the said William Hewitt doe freely clearly and absolutely give and grant unto the said Mary Boober her heires executors administrators and assignes forever all and singular that my dwelling house which I now live in scittuate in Marblehead aforesaid with all my out houses barns and orchards with all my farme and land which I bought of Mr. Maverick. . . ." Mary Boober was the youngest daughter of Joseph Boober, a deceased friend of Mr. Hewitt. Hewitt personally appeared to sign his will and Stephen Sewall was the recorder.

Mid-Town is a combination of all the phases of Marblehead and continues to be the barometer of the town for it changes frequently with new businesses. Mid-Town is active and spirited.

4. Barnegat, Peach's Point and Naugus Head

"FOR MARBLEHEAD is Marblehead, has been, and always will." Barnegat is Marblehead—for real, with all its yesterdays. The barricaded little harbor of the hardy, venturesome colonists has changed as little as any part of Marblehead. The geography is unspoiled; the houses with their ells and added rooms masquerade as eighteenth- and nineteenth-century dwellings, and the descendants of the colonists are fiercely protective of their heritage and their town. Barnegat is positively possessive about Marblehead, whose failures and foibles are known and understood and affectionately laughed off. Sensitive to a stranger, wary of his reaction, resistant to expediency, Barnegat—by its surrounding hills, the sea and the islands—seems insulated from modernization. Alive and well is the spirited individualism and personal independence that was anchored there by the nonconforming founders who sailed into the snug harbor and built their first settlement on its protected shores.

The cove of Little Harbor was enclosed by peninsular arms which, with two islands, broke the force of the sea; the boats could be moored well inside where the fish could be unloaded and split for drying on the nearby hills and headlands. The forest gave its trees for houses and ships, the ponds and brooks were clear and fresh, and pastures could be cleared in the land over the hill. Name the found-ers of Marblehead—Allerton, Maverick and their first companions like Joseph Doliber, Ambrose Gale, John Peach, Nicholas Merritt, Robert Knight, Thomas Pitman and William Walton; history rec-ords place them around Little Harbor. There the earliest fishing station with its flake yards and warehouses was set up; there was the first anchorage for the pinnaces and shallops that dared the un-known seas for cod and mackerel; there was the launching place for *Desire*, the third vessel built in the Colonies. Little Harbor was the home of the first two preachers and was where men began to set up shops. They were not tempted by the size and shoreline of Great Bay or the land which a few settlers were granted in isolated areas, like John Gatchell on the Neck, Devereux on the beach, and Cod-ner on the bay. Official documents, grants, and deeds conceded that Little Harbor was "the Main."

Little Harbor was a friendly berth tucked in between the fort and Peach's grant. A makeshift corduroy road went around the ir-regular, semicircular cove bumbling over ledges, through marshes, and crossed a shaky little bridge over the swift-running brook that poured down from the highland. It was this bridge (near Doak's Lane) that seemed to have been called "first bridge" and that was eventually, a demarcation line for Barnegat. The road led to Old Burying Ground and the meeting house; those landmarks of colonial life and death huddled together on the high lookout over the Little Harbor settlement and the sea.

Just as the vigor and struggle centered there at Little Harbor, so did the superstition and fears. Wizard Dimond's house was tucked below the hill and the "witch," Mammy Redd's, not far from the pond. And if they and the Burial Ground didn't give a man a "crimmey" feeling, the pirates using the dark, well-protected cove would. The smugglers, who followed them, knew that the rocks and shoals would prevent pursuit into the cove and that the people could mind their own business. Barnegat on the New Jersey coast was known as a pirates' rendezvous where their bonfires, acting as false beacons, wrecked innocent ships which were then plundered. That is given as one unsavory source of the local name, though no records hint of local pirate lures. A more likely source is the Barne-gat of England or the possible possession by a Jacob Barney of Salem of land bordering on the gat; Barnegat is a name not found in early documents.

As Marblehead and its shipping and fisheries expanded, the Great Bay was used as another anchorage; nevertheless, Little Harbor was still active and men like Captain Thomas Peach were buying property on which he built his house (16 Beacon Street) with a right-of-way to his wharf. In 1726 the selectmen sold him a strip of land lying between the highway and Peach's marsh where there is a well and "said Peach is to keep from being ever Damnified by reason of said Peach barne standing by ye well." Other houses were built or added on to during the prosperous days of the fisheries and foreign trade. On the hill was Nathaniel Bartlett's Fountain Inn frequented by fishermen, smugglers and the collector of the Boston port, Sir Harry Frankland. By 1750 widow Mary Bartlett had named the "Tavern," its gardens and orchard as part of her dowry; it then passed into several different owners' hands and seems to have disappeared by the time of the Revolution.

Dropping off from the Inn on the sides of Ram's Hill or Idner's (sometime Idler's) Hill were the fish flakes on hillsides long barren of timber. The great harbor with its large schooners and prize ships had not so diminished the use of Little Harbor that a group of business men was discouraged from planning a new enterprise called the Little Harbor Corporation. In 1805 the corporation, which included men like Thomas Elkins, Stephen Swett, William Story, William Read, Joseph Brown, Joseph Dennis and Robert and Nathaniel Hooper, presented a petition to the General Court saying, "Common harbor is very dangerous and vessels insecure from its exposure to violent easterly winds . . . Little Harbor might be a very safe, convenient harbor for docking. . . ." The object was to improve Little Harbor by widening the channel entrances and dredging the flats from which the sand and gravel would be given to the town for highways. At a meeting at Rea's Tavern the members planned for boat repairs, plus winter storage of vessels which would pass through an entrance gate and pay a toll—under fifty ton charged thirty cents per day and sliding scale up to two hundred- to three hundred-ton vessels for seventy cents per day. This business conducted in the area from Doliber's Point to Gerry's Island to the town highway would be expected to return a 12 percent profit or revert to the town.

Captain Selman led the opposition which doubted the motives, found the scheme ill-defined and a great risk and expense to the town. The General Court refused the petition and within six months the interest in the Marblehead Dry Dock had faded. Thirty-five years later a breakwater was proposed—a 39-foot-long wall from the eastern rocky ledge of Ephraim Brown's island to Gerry Island. It would be 21 feet high, 10 feet thick at the base narrowing to 6 on the top and would protect a 100-foot pier to the west. This commercializing venture was also denied. Nature took a hand in 1851 when a violent storm swept wharves away, lifted shore shops from their foundations and drove fishing boats and two large schooners up on the shores.

The heeltappers' ten-footers must have been shaken by the high winds, for, by now, the home shoe shops were scattered like tiny blocks around the cove and perched on the ledges where the fish once dried. Bessoms, LeFavour and John Wadden were all involved in the shoe business. "Daddy" Wadden had a shop next to his house where, it's told, he was hammering away in 1861 when Town Crier Ray Nourse made his rounds. When heads popped out of windows and doors, Nourse was crying out, "All good citizens are to meet at the Town House tonight—except traitor Daddy Wadden." Wadden picked up his shoemaking stirrup and tore to the street where he beat up Nourse for questioning his pacificism. Direct action was the answer to many neighborhood feuds, like the time one neighbor shot another in the shoulder over building a disputed fence—even though a police officer was present.

Property lines drawn to vanished stumps and stones have often kept things at a high pitch in Barnegat. One owner, wanting to banish all doubt, kept her deed posted in her window. As if there wasn't enough excitement over the years, the Spiritualists used to hold meetings over the store in Swett's old house behind which mischievous boys would rig up lines full of pans; at the crucial moment the culprits would clang every pan and scare the wits out of those inside the meeting and out. Up and down Orne and Beacon Streets would come torchlight parades for elections or victory celebrations or for temperance, and as lights burned in every window in Barnegat, the marchers and band would go 'round the pump and back again. At one point someone even started a paper, "Punch Jr. of Barnegat, Mass.," devoted to fun and frolic and temperance. It was a short-lived publication.

The fisheries had been replaced by the shoe shops which were then replaced by the factories in town. Little Harbor has seen the Gas House which gave the beach its name, the Burgess Aeroplane Company, and the yacht yards and sail lofts. The fishing dories and lobster boats were plentiful over the years but now the fishermen are few—though Barnegaters still drop a line near Jack's Rocks for luck, or they talk a good fish story like the time "Bucket" Barclay and "Poppy" Stevens and "Tuffin" Russell made the Boston papers tellin' about lookin' out over Little Harbor toward Cat Island where they saw the sea serpent, the one named Marblehead Minnie. She was about seventy-five feet long, pretty and about five hundred years old and seemed to be moanin' and groanin' for her boy friend.

She'd be back for the Fourth and, meanwhile, the kids shouldn't stay out of the water, for "she wouldn't scare one of Mother Carey's chickens"—and Poppy swore he was a stickler for the truth.

Though James J. H. Gregory wrote a paper many years ago about the ocean waging a "victorious battle over the land" and the seawater moving in and covering tree stumps and old pilings, residents now notice the shallowness of the water, the silt, and point out a tree well inland where a grandfather tied his boat. The filling in of nearby wetlands, brooks and springs may be responsible along with tidal shoreline changes. The home construction in the old pasture behind Barnegat have robbed the residents of the wild strawberries and blueberries that grew there in abundance; pollution has made suspect the seaweed long collected for favorite "Irish moss." Those are physical changes but, as long as the old Marbleheaders at Barnegat can hold out, nothing will break down that priceless spirit of independence.

If you're going 'round the ferry, you could go by Sadie's Sweet Shop, so long a sweet-smelling paradise of penny candy for the neighborhood children; then past Grace Oliver's old house on Doliber's Point, leading to the beach that bears her name. Or use the steps cut into the hill next to Captain Manley's (John Russell's) house that once led to Gingerbread Hill and Black Joe's and Aunt Crese's tavern; then down the other side of Mount Pleasant where competitor Auntie Bowen ran her tavern and penny shop. The hearty, talkative "Ma'am Sociable" was one of the often quoted characters in Marblehead; for example, "It would take a meeting house to hold my acquaintances, but a pulpit would hold all my friends."

The cartway that cut through to the ferry road was right through the point of land named for the first John Peach and his relatives who owned so much of the northwestern part of the peninsula. John Peach should rightly be called a town founder for he swore in a deposition that he had come to New England in 1630. His name appears in local official records in 1636 and thereafter, he is mentioned in town records over one hundred times from the time he was elected to the first Board of Selectmen (then Townsmen) and held other town offices. Although he is called "Senior" family genealogy finds no heir, but a cousin, John Junior, who was an important and outstanding citizen of Marblehead. When John Peach, Sr. died, his will named relatives in Swinsborough, England, and in Barbados and Marblehead, especially William Peach, son of his cousin. In a 1700 map William Peach, married to Emme Devereux, is shown as owning several parcels of real estate near Doliber's Cove. His descendants often appear in historical records and in military accounts of the Revolution, especially in the Rhode Island campaign where a "William" was under fire while transporting bread to the troops. He was not injured, but the bullets had to be dug out of the soldiers' bread. William owned the house sold later to Joseph Brown and Aunt Crese because in the postwar depression William and his wife left to live in Vermont on 128 acres of land that had been bought for £60. From Marblehead to Newbury, Vermont, William Peach walked next to the horse which carried his wife and two-year-old son, Twisden. He carried a willow stick and whip in his hand and in great joy planted them in the ground when he finally stepped on his own land. It's told in Newbury that they took root and are still alive today. Most of the Peaches stayed right in Marblehead and held on to some of the land of their forebears whose name clings to the Point. It hadn't been many years since Indians had departed from their nearby summer camp sites where, while the children roamed the beaches, the men fished the waters and hunted porpoise whose meat, particularly the livers, the tribe enjoyed. By 1637 Salem declared, "All the land on the Darby Fort side up to the Hogsties and so to run along toward Marblehead 20 pole into the land shall be reserved for the comons of the towne to serve it for wood and timber. . . ." It was suggested that the land be divided into ten-acre lots until everyone was supplied. There is no indication that Marblehead did this until after it escaped Salem's rule in 1649 when the Commoners divided up the lands and cow commonages. Three decades later this exclusive ownership was challenged by non-Commoners and parts of the land had to be shared with these later colonists. By the close of the seventeenth century Peach's Point was shared by Reith, Codner, Bartoll, Bartlett, John Conant, minister Samuel Cheever and others who had inherited various parcels. Pasturage, farms and orchards made the land desirable, but lonely; so houses were rare, for the owners preferred to live at Little Harbor or on the Great Bay.

The 1724 Town Meeting edict divided up the town and Little Harbor was assigned to the Lower Division where a gate was hung by Thomas Doliber's property; the Middle Division cut across the peninsula to include land leading to the ferry. In assigning new lots boulders, cherry trees and stone piles marked boundaries for owners like Ebenezer Hawkes, Girdler, Orne, Swett, Hooper and Thomas Gerry. It was in 1755 that a Richard Rindge was granted a liquor license in a house on the cove, "where this season of the year [vessels] can only unload with safety." That year French neutrals or prisoners in the Colonies were placed in the few houses on Peach's Point, so they would not be in a position to spy on Marblehead harbor activities. Yet, the danger of lighted beacons to guide the French fleet to the Darby Fort area forced the transfer of the French families to inland towns. The decades between then and the Revolutionary War brought few changes to the western shoreline.

Some of the shoreline points retain their colonial names; most have been forgotten. In the old days a Marbleheader rowing his dory from the ferry wharf to Little Harbor would have first passed Bass Rock, where old Bartoll swore he caught the largest bass, even larger than those at the next point called Peaked Rock. Then to the eastward was Lap-stone Cove, where the home shoemakers could find a cove full of rounded, flat stones that would just fit a man's lap and furnish a hard surface on which to hammer. And just around the bend from Lap-stone were the timbers of an old wharf and a rusted out ringbolt that willed its name to Ring-Bolt Point where, it was said, anything from a cunner to a sturgeon might take the bait.

A far easier way to reach the ferry was by the old cartway that passed the high Beacon Hill which gave the later road its name. The old mill pond and swamp that had been dammed up by the miller, Robert Knight, and which was later called Flag Pond, was on the left. Nothing remains of those early buildings, yet on the opposite side is a 1715 three-storied farmhouse (built by Mark Pitman) with Doric columns and a captain's walk. It once was used by the town as a smallpox hospital whose contaminated dead were buried on the property. A century later another owner, Captain Freeto, leased it to James J. H. Gregory who was growing vegetables on much of the open land on the Point. The soil must have always been fertile thereabouts, for the earliest deeds mention cornfields, probably inherited from the Indians. For two centuries Peach's Point was primarily used for farming.

It was in 1871 that an abrupt change in its use and growth was brought about by the purchase of a major portion of Peach's Point by Francis W. Crowninshield of the Salem shipping family. He built a home there in 1872 which is still used by his descendants; three years later his son, Benjamin, bought seventeen more parcels from the Appleton family. Somewhat later a home was built for his daughter, Mrs. Josiah Bradlee, for whom Bradlee Road is named. Following the Crowninshield purchases the character of Peach's Point developed from pastoral farms into a summer colony. Relatives and friends lived as a closely knit community that had its own traditions, especially, the July Fourth picnic and the still lively

Labor Day Croquet Tournament. Summer houses were built at intervals, usually, on Crowninshield land. Then one day out of the north appeared a scow on which rested President Taft's former summer home that had been moved from Beverly. It was placed at an ideal shorefront site, but all that remains now is the smaller house made from the kitchen ell.

The Rindge house which had been built in 1880 remains an enigma. Mrs. Rindge had come as a bride into the handsome mansion with its magnificent view and the family enjoyed it for years until they moved to California, leaving the house as if they were merely going out to tea. Children would sneak in to play and imaginatively concoct tales of the sudden departure and the emptiness. In California the Rindges bought up land that was to become part of Los Angeles and on their huge, coastal land grant built a castle-like seashore home. The well-known Adohr (Rhoda spelled backwards) dairies in California were named after a Rindge daughter. Why the Peach's Point estate was left empty and why it was allowed to be taken for taxes by the town of Marblehead in 1940 remains obscure.

The residents have long had a community float and have moored their boats, including a certain tooting old steamboat, nearby. The seafaring Crowninshields, whose Marblehead family branch had been known in contracted Cornish as "Groundsel," owned several famous yachts including designer Edward Burgess' *Tomahawk* and Nathaniel Herreshoff's *Cleopatra's Barge II*. The latter yacht belonged to Francis B. Crowninshield and his wife, formerly Louise duPont, who had been raised at Winterthur. Mrs. Crowninshield, the "grande dame" of Peach's Point, brought to Marblehead an avid interest in historic restoration and collections. She aided Children's Island, gave Crowninshield Island (Brown's Island) to the Trustees of Reservations for conservation and helped immeasurably to restore the Jeremiah Lee Mansion for the Marblehead Historical Society. By the time of Mrs. Crowninshield's death the summer colony had evolved into year-around residents who, undoubtedly because of the Crowninshield's century-old land holdings, now enjoy more open space than can be found anywhere else in Marblehead. The Point, once bared to its rocky boulders and wild bushes, has again been planted with trees and shrubs that must resemble the verdant forest first seen by John Peach.

To the south the area remained open land for centuries until recent development laid out streets and private residences in the section now called Peach Highlands. Once pastures joined Steer Swamp which has now become a conservation area. At the western side of the Lower Division pasture stood Tilting Rock, which appears throughout history as a puzzling boulder left by the glacial retreat or placed there for some long-lost reason.

If Peach's Point seemed quiet, pastoral and unnoticed, Fort Darby and Naugus Head were not. Documents prove this headland to be one of the earliest recorded in the history of Marblehead. Fort Darby (Derby) on Naugus Head was probably erected soon after 1629 by Acting Governor Endicott's men as a protective measure for the Salem colony, and possibly, the fishermen living at Little Harbor. The name seems to have been adopted from a similar headland at Derby in Dorsetshire, England. William Wood, in his 1634 *New England Prospects*, writes "It [Salem] hath . . . the other Summer harbour which lyeth within Derbies Fort, which place if it were well fortified, might keepe shippes from landing of forces. . . ." The fort is named as a demarcation point in the 1636 timber ordinance and also in the first grants which went to John Pride, Edward Beauchamp, Christopher Young, Samuel More, Thomas More, and Massy, Palfrey, and a 30-acre grant to William Stephens with the stipulation that he will remove from Salem and stay in Marblehead. As few of these names appear in early Marblehead records, it may be assumed they were Salem colonists who may not have established or improved their claims on that far-removed peninsula. However, communication with the settlement at Marble Harbor was improved in 1637 by the first ferry of this entire colonial area. It was called the Fort Darby ferry and left from a wharf just west of the fort. Nicholas Liston is mentioned as having a brief term as ferryman, but he was soon replaced by George Wright who was granted five acres on the "forestside for planting." For a tuppence he rowed or sailed passengers to the Salem wharf at the foot of Turner Street (House of Seven Gables), known as Butt Point. The busy operation was leased to Marblehead ferrymen; the income, however, was used for Salem schools. Then in 1644 the lease went to the person most often associated with the ferry, Thomas Dixey, who was later succeeded by his son. Their land was abutting the ferry wharf on what became known as Nogg's Head, the description of a headland at an angle to a stream (Forest River) which, in England, was then called a "nog." It took two hundred years for it to become Naugus Head.

The delay of standing in line for the ferry (which complaint was aired at Marblehead Town Meeting) shouldn't have seemed too long for, quite naturally, a jolly tavern developed at each end. In Salem the Blue Anchor served up whatever was coming off the vessels or was made locally; at the Marblehead end was a tippling place just a few steps away from the wharf. Because of its reputation as a Sabbath churchgoers "escape" Marbleheaders had christened the grog spot, "Tom Bowen's Church." For over thirty years the fact that irreverent Tom Bowen was in and out of trouble didn't seem to close down the handy stopover. It didn't take long for the ferry traffic to open up that end of the West Shore, for as early as 1686 the new land grants specify keeping the "ferry path" clear to allow Thomas Dixey to ". . . pass on foot or with a cart down to the cove and peaceably ingress or egress. . . ." In setting up the Middle Division the old ferry road was used as the dividing line for the "ferry lots" which specify free access, "open forever for ye use of the wharf". By 1737, petitioners Joseph Swett, Thomas Peach and others requested a more convenient ferry route to run north along the Middle Division line which was then laid out along what is roughly Green Street and eventually led to the Town House.

By the time of the Revolution Marblehead had several "hyways" leading out of the town and its activities were concentrated on the great harbor; so Naugus Head and its ferry became far less important than in earlier days when it spared the colonists a long hike or horseback ride through the winding Indian trails to Salem. In 1805 Dr. William Bentley and other Salemites often came by private boat to picnic and fish off the Point. He called this a "water party." Tom Bowen was long gone, yet Aunt Morse with her good cakes and ale wasn't far away. Dr. Bentley credited Colonel Orne with clearing the overgrown bushes and making Naugus Head fit for "grass ground." He also remarked, in 1805, that the Salem Crowninshields were going to take land there, but that owner Micah Haskell pleaded poor "health and situation."

The War of 1812 caused Naugus Head's old fort to be repaired as a coastal lookout and as drill area for Fort Sewall troops who could practice firing more safely there. Again in the Civil War it was activated as Fort Miller. By then the place was having a rebirth of farming which James Gregory had developed extensively; he built a fine seaside home just off Cloutman's Lane in 1876 (which was irreverently tagged as "carpenter Gothic") and beautifully landscaped his own estate with flowered walks and unusual shrubbery. In 1881 the house was offered to President Garfield for the summer, but the president reluctantly declined Mr. Gregory's invitation. Somewhere near Mr. Gregory's property was a great stand of old sassafras trees that were so valuable to the early colonists. Some still remain and one or two residents can still make "balm of Gilead" tea.

Not far away the Naugus Head Grove became a well-known resort spot where the Salem and Magnolia Boat Company had stationed a large barge and offered picnics, a band, dancing, and evening illumination and fireworks. It was near this grove that Samuel Roads often held the chowder meetings of the Sea Serpent Club. Nothing more was ever heard of an earlier proposal to build a bridge from Naugus Head (foot, carriage or even railroad) to Derby Wharf in Salem. Instead, that part of the peninsula was soon clustered with small summer cottages. The Cove cottages, each with its unique name, were rented for all or part of the summer season and not far away were the campers with their tents. The number of people now living on the whole peninsula caused Beacon Street to be widened in 1888 and the first fire-alarm box to be installed.

This century's development of Naugus Head was tied in with the long discussed, often postponed West Shore road. Since West Shore Drive became a reality, most summer cottages have been replaced by permanent homes until, like much of modern Marblehead, land is far more valuable and open space diminishes. The recently acquired conservation lands assure the children and the townspeople of the future enjoyment of Marblehead's scenic western coastline. And it's possible that the new town boating facilities there will bring more nautical activity than the West Shore has seen since the days of the Fort Darby ferry.

5. Clifton and Devereux

THE MASSACHUSETTS BAY COMPANY had from the beginning promised its shareholders quality grants of land in the New World; so two eminent shareholders, who were later arrivals, were given land grants abutting one another and including all of what is now Clifton, Clifton Heights and Devereux sections of Marblehead. The first grantee, who had previously been offered the second most important colonial appointment, came in 1634 and several months later, coincidentally with the General Court's decision to make Marblehead a separate "plantacion," was awarded a strip of land of 350 acres "betwixt the Clifte and Forest River." John Humphrey, Esq. was given this land to improve and sell to approved inhabitants of Marblehead. As the plantation status was brief, the acreage undoubtedly remained in Humphrey's possession. The use of word "Clifte" is repeated in historical documents and is surely the derivation of the present name "Clifton"; its first English owner is immortalized by having one of the heavily traveled streets cutting through the section bear his name, Humphrey Street. His abutter and fellow Massachusetts Bay Company shareholder, Hugh Peter, spent seven years in the Colony with notable effectiveness, yet in the irony of history nothing in Marblehead calls him to mind, for even his property carries the name of the second owner, Devereux.

Both Humphrey's and Peter's grants ran east and west and contained frontage on the fresh water river to the west and the sea on the east, and in between were swift-running brooks, spring-fed ponds, rich meadowland and thick woods. Much of the area must have been very desirable, for years before the Indians had selected it for camp sites. The Naumkeag tribe, whose lands Humphrey and Peter were granted, had been severely reduced in number by Indian wars and disease; those few who remained around Marblehead were friendly to the possessive colonists. But the Naumkeags within two generations were only an echo of a civilization, leaving the relics of their fort at the site of the Glover School and of their large encampment at the Goldthwaite Reservation and Devereux Beach. It's not strange that legend tells of the Marblehead superstition that a person walking through the old Indian Burial Ground with tingling goose flesh could ask aloud, "Indian Chief, Indian Chief, what have you done to deserve to be here?" and the breeze would whisper the chief's reply, "Nothing at all, nothing at all." Neither owner, John Humphrey nor Hugh Peter was personally involved in any known form of Indian exploitation or restriction, though both expressed the need for additional farm labor; on the other hand, neither the nomadic Indian nor seafaring fisherman fitted into that constricting mold.

John Humphrey came to the Salem colony although he was obsessed by the advantages of Caribbean settlements. This "gentleman of special parts of learning and activity" who had labored hard in promoting the plantation was now being brought low in his estate by financial losses, a serious fire, the expense of many children (from local records thought to be seven in number) and the rigorous climate. By 1640 a boatload of colonists led by John Humphrey sailed from his waterfront near the cliffs (Clifton) to England for advice and supplies before moving south. In response to Humphrey's Massachusetts claim, the General Court in a gesture of appeasement or Christian kindness remitted £250 to John Humphrey which many people, realizing the Colony's financial strain, highly resented. Yet, the Humphrey Farm had admittedly developed into more valuable, productive property for the Colony; by 1665 Moses Maverick, John Peach and other early inhabitants had bought out the Humphrey claim "adjoining Mr. Peter being 400 acres more or less except 50 acres and 2 ponds granted to Mr. Downing" (Governor Winthrop's brother-in-law). From then on that grant became known as the "Playne Farm" and for generations to come was "put out to pasture."

Hugh Peter had been granted the adjoining property two years after his arrival in Salem; however, he had been so occupied traveling around with words of inspiration and encouragement that in 1636 the Fort Darby (Naugus Head) land grants were postponed until Hugh Peter's land could be laid out. Without question the enterprising Hugh Peter had exciting plans for his land although his own natural interest was unquestionably in ships and fishing. As a public-spirited, capable and energetic man, Peter's life was constantly activated by public circumstances and official demands. During his first years of ownership, widower Peter was also active in the private venture of courting a new wife, Deborah Sheffield— moreover, officialdom was in on that, too. John Endicott wrote the governor that Mrs. Sheffield's affections seem to be abating since she disliked to come to Salem on the terms he (Peter) had written; then, Endicott wisely added, "I find that she begins now to play her parte, and if I mistake not, you will see him as greatly in love with her (if shee will hold a little) as ever shee was with him. . . ." The governor also heard from Hugh Peter that he didn't know whether Mrs. Sheffield would have him, adding that "if I cannot make an honorable retreat than I shall desire to advance." As predicted, Mrs. Sheffield married Peter but their married life was brief and tragic, for the year after the birth of their first child, Elizabeth, Mrs. Peter became "of unsound mind, which deprived him of her society. . . ."

Hugh Peter led a busy life as a minister and colonial advisor. The first colonial press in Cambridge presented new possibilities which Hugh Peter did not want overlooked, so in 1638 he wrote a fellow minister in Bermuda, "Wee have a printery here and thinke to goe to worke with some speciall things" and urged that any new offerings be returned by Captain William Pierce, master of *Desire*. Peter was later ordered to the mother country to observe Parliament's colonial attitude and expedite shipment of West Indies cotton. Once back in England, Hugh Peter's friends, including Oliver Cromwell, used his talents, sending him on the Irish expedition where he could talk reform to the soldiers, just as he did later to the country people crowding English churches and marketplaces to hear his witty sermons. His theme, brightened by jest, was reform in the English Church and State, and, as he told the women, they might have "to hug their Husbands into this Rebellion." He returned to his former Holland parish for "reform" funds and was so effective that precious jewels were dropped into the collection. In the ensuing Civil War that tore England apart Peter pressed for more religious tolerance

and reform in the army, law, Parliament and education, which resulted in his appointment to the awesome responsibility of Commissioner for Amending the Laws.

By the time of the Restoration Hugh Peter had enemies in both
camps, some jealous of his advancement, others offended by his
witty barbs which had been published and relished by all of London. Accused of involvement in the regicide plot Peter's defense
was based on his New England residence at that time and his sincere
efforts for bloodless reform. Condemned to be hanged, his execution
was a vicious, gory retribution as he was forced to watch a friend
hanged and disemboweled. When asked by the executioner how he
liked that, Hugh Peter's bold courage didn't desert him, for as he
climbed the ladder, he replied that God had permitted it to give him
support to face the same. Even while Hugh Peter's head rotted on
London Bridge, his oratory was posthumously published in *The
Tales and Jests of Hugh Peter* in which his sermons were misinter-
preted and spiced with lewd, Chaucerian material. It's unknown
whether copies of this libelous book were ever brought into this
Colony, where the sense of loss of the man and his colonial dream
was genuine. About the time of his incarceration Hugh Peter's
agent and one of his former Salem deacons, Charles Gott, sold his
Marblehead property of three hundred acres, listing the boundaries
as: the Forest River on the west, Throgmorton's Cove northwest
and Tinker's Island to the east. The entire Hugh Peter grant was
purchased for £100 by John Devereux.

It was said that John Devereux was the son of nobility and a descendant of Robert Devereux, son of the earl of Essex, beloved and
beheaded by Queen Elizabeth I. His first grants were for twenty
acres and a house lot but, in spite of being called a mariner and fisherman, John Devereux could afford to lease Hugh Peter's large
grant which he then bought in 1659. The deed specifies a "Raccoon
Lot" adjoining the marsh; yet the value or purpose of the Raccoon
Lot (except for the obvious possibility of valuable pelts) is puzzling,
for during the next 150 years it is often held out of the will as a specific bequest. The southwesterly side of the grant was sold off after
a portion was taken for Commons land. John Devereux quickly established his acreage by a long, stone-wall boundary. The land on
the eastern side along "ye sea" was his preference, for its soil was
rich and brooks and ponds sparkled in many places above the beach.
The fishing and clamming were excellent, the small animals and
birds plentiful, and the apple trees found the soil and moisture to
their liking. John Devereux' love for his land, removed though it
was from the town and its close-knit security, was so deep that in

his will he asked that it "remain in the family and the name of Devereux from generation to generation . . . forever and ever."

For fifty-nine years John Devereux deeply involved himself in Marblehead town affairs including the honor of election to the first Board of Townsmen (selectmen), regardless of the fact that he was one of the few colonists whose home lay outside the harbor settlement. Distance from town didn't affect Devereux' participation; at the age of seventy-seven he was still showing up to give depositions regarding land claims by the Indians, some of whom he must have known from their former camp site on his land.

In his will, signed only by a "mark," John Devereux remembered his "dear and loving wife, Ann," and divided the cattle, horses and land among his male heirs, and gave cash to his daughters, Emme, married to William Peach, and to Hannah, wife of Joseph Swett. Hannah and Joseph Swett bore the three girls that married into the Lee, Hooper and Marston families and along with Peach family intermarriage, John Devereux became grandfather to five of the best-known Marblehead families of the eighteenth century.

Upon John Devereux' death in 1695 the grant was suddenly contested by Elizabeth Barker of London, only daughter of Hugh Peter, who claimed Charles Gott had "insufficient authority to execute the deed." Widow Ann and son Robert Devereux were advised not to contest; John Legg later revealed in a sworn deposition to the superior court that he had witnessed in 1705 that Mrs. Devereux and her son Robert had treated with Major Stephen Sewall of Salem and Daniel Zachary of Boston about the farm. The agreed price was £400 of which £100 was a down payment. That payment was made up by an old £50 receipt from Governor Winthrop to John Devereux, £20 cash and £30 borrowed from John Legg. The deed was properly signed over to "Robert Devorix" with the ancient stipulation that one black peppercorn be submitted every six months, come St. Michael's Day (September 29), ancient symbolic tribute of occupancy.

By the turn of the century the Humphrey–Plain Farms had been sliced up by the trustees of Marblehead lands—and "sliced" is the term—for just as in the later layout for Marblehead Neck, the property lines were drawn strictly parallel and horizontal across the peninsula from the Salem border to the ocean, running northwest to southeast. The eastern half that is Clifton had been sold or passed down by some of the original grantees so that Samuel Reed had received his lot in 1685 as a dowry from his father-in-law, Richard Rowland; Mrs. Mary Woods' land came in 1687 from her father, John Peach; the same year, Jonathan Norman's from his father,

Richard. The largest section had originally been the property of the early settler, John Parnell Bartoll, whose eldest son, William, sold off portions to Robert Bartlett and in 1689 transferred the strip abutting John Devereux to Benjamin Ireson, "Lyn" planter, for £33.

The deed to that particular tract is an interesting document that was witnessed and attested to by the signature of the minister, Samuel Cheever, and the marks of William Furnace and Thomas Rumney. The town of Marblehead had "purchased" its town property from the Indians only five years before and land owners were justifying their own claims by attempting to obtain an Indian signature; on this deed that person was Thomas Rumney (the surname given to the leading Indian family in the area). The Benjamin Iresons went through distressing times during that decade, for in 1692 the witchcraft panic had invaded Lynn and Ireson's wife had been arrested as a witch. She had been imprisoned and held for months until released by the governor's decree. By strange coincidence, another Clifton plot belonged to Constable James Smith who was responsible for bringing the witchcraft witnesses and Mammy Redd to court.

Legend says that an earlier witchcraft incident at Devereux Beach sobered the townspeople's attitude toward such accusations. Desire Perkins, a popular eighteen-year-old, was whispered about by a former girl friend until the witchcraft gossip raised some outspoken suspicions. In her anxiety and fear Desire Perkins ran away to the loneliness of the shore and, as a group of searchers appeared, the imaginative young girl, fearing their intentions, jumped into the surf and was drowned just off John Devereux' beach.

The extensive Devereux property was soon to become a hindrance to the building of public roads, especially the complicated route to the Neck. When the Marblehead Neck grants were being bought up, a better route for "cattle drift" became a necessity, yet all the approaches were owned by John Devereux. In 1670 he permitted a "highway" to be laid out starting through his high dry ground to the beach where it turned sharply northeast along the shore and across the rocky isthmus. There was no noticeable change in that route until 1720 when a more direct route (Beach Street), closer to the highland but requiring two small bridges over the brooks, was approved. The new Way to the Neck, while still on Devereux property, did not partition it as before.

During the eighteenth century the property stayed quite unchanged in the hands of the Devereux family who worked as shipwrights, joiners, or mostly, husbandmen in their orchards and farms. Later, Humphrey Devereux becoming a well-known town physician and Benjamin Devereux marched out with Glover's regiment in 1776 and then switched to privateering on *True Blue*. In the next century Burrill Devereux, Latin scholar and schoolmaster, helped establish the Marblehead Academy and, as selectman, was on hand to greet President Washington in 1789.

By 1800 pieces of the Devereux farm had begun to be sold off, and in the 1837 financial panic the federal "Surplus Revenue" funds contributed thirteen thousand dollars to Marblehead and everyone had ideas about how to spend it. After several Town Meetings, resignations and parliamentary maneuvers, the proposition to build a new alms house on the Devereux Farm squeaked through and Humphrey Devereux was paid thirteen thousand dollars for the land. Town opposition was unabated until two years later when the tract was sold to Ephraim Brown at a loss of two thousand dollars. The disintegration of the original grant had taken place, but John Devereux' name lives on in the Devereux section of Marblehead.

John Humphrey's Clifton grant had no strong, enduring family to carry on a traditional ownership, so various owners cleared the land and farmed it. Almost a century saw only a scattering of farm houses and barns and almost no interest in further development. Then, about the same time that Longfellow was sitting before a warm hearth in a Devereux boardinghouse composing "The Fire of Driftwood," Horace Ware was building his own fire under the town by petitioning for a new town, which was subsequently refused. The feeling of neglect and inattention persevered; ten years later a town remonstrance was circulated to prevent further consideration of the annexation of the "Farms" to Swampscott. An admirer wrote of the beautiful farm and delicious, perfect vegetables grown by "Father Ware"; on the other hand, the town, noting the activity stirring in the southern plains, was anxious over other kinds of growth which Father Ware and others were cultivating.

The first effort in 1847 to have a railroad from town, through the farms and Swampscott, to Lynn and Boston failed because of lack of capital subscription; yet, in 1866 when most of the town favored the idea, the capital still needed to be raised and the land acquired. The opponents (placidity and acceptance were never part of Marblehead's nature) proposed, instead, the new avenue, commenting that the population was increasing (more than 482 voters), valuation was up (over $28,000) and the railroad prospects looked dim; so, why not open up two miles of unproductive land for new summer residents? Call it Marblehead Avenue, they wrote, in a widely distributed pamphlet, "It will become the favorite centre of the healthful, joyous and inspiring influences of summer by the sea." The local railroad "lobby" held off the appropriation; shortly after, the county built part, forced Marblehead to contribute about $10,000 and by 1870 everyone enjoyed Atlantic Avenue, a ready access to both Clifton and Devereux. The railroaders had their turn when Town Meeting agreed to a $75,000 bond issue which was never used because the Eastern Railroad Company went ahead with its own construction. When in operation, a lady who spoke French and the conductor engaged in a running pronunciation skirmish, but, being the conductor, he always won as he bellowed out, "Dever-rocks."

The avenue and the train speeded up the trip for the friendly vacationers coming to "delightful, beautiful" Devereux and Clifton. There were carriages, horses and bikes to carry the visitors to the comfortable boardinghouses or hotels or to their own camp, of which the best known was the "Peabody Camp" near Clifton Heights, where Peabody residents set up a tent colony similar to those on the Neck. And, later, when some tiny summer cottages were moved there from the Neck, Clifton was called "the daughter of the Neck."

Its neighbor, Devereux, was still owned by only a few residents, primarily George A. Smith, whose farm was best described in an 1870 Boston advertisement: "Best seashore farm for sale, containing 110 acres with fruits of all kinds and one of the highest cultivated and valuable farms in New England. . . ." Three days later the Smith farm belonged to John and William Goldthwait and Henry F. Pitman who soon after divided most of it into house lots, except the open area next to Devereux Beach. Shoe manufacturers built along the avenues, such as, on Lot 78 purchased by Mr. Otis Roberts who, the following year, built 264 Pleasant Street, a large splendid house for the period with great fireplaces with special marble mantels. Three floors of high-studded rooms were topped with a tall-windowed cupola which had seats on three sides. This excellent observatory provided a fine view of the harbor and the ocean and at one time held a valuable telescope. Other handsome, well-built houses went up along the main road for the Graves, Goldthwaites and other permanent residents; and somewhat later the largest, best-known, the Devereux Mansion, was erected on Beach Street. The whole section was now frequently referred to as "Devereux Village," just as Clifton was called "The Farms."

The shoe business, boatyards, fishing and trade absorbed the town's interests, while the more "remote" areas felt isolated and ignored. The relaxed summer campers loved the casual combination of rural and seashore life, but the permanent residents' resentment had decades of practice. The blossoming of Devereux and Clifton with a main highway, train service and increased property values created the moment to be declared a legitimate child of Marblehead or leave home. A group led by Caleb Childs and Benjamin P. Ware cast the die: secede! In 1884 a formal petition was presented to the state legislature for the formation of a new town which would embrace the parts of the town to be amputated from the original grant: the whole Humphrey Farm, the Hugh Peter land, part of the Upper Division Commons and the Neck. If the separation were legalized, Marblehead would then contain 1,015 acres and the new "Farms–Great Neck" town would be larger with 1,359 acres; the estimated seashore line of Marblehead would decrease from 13 miles to 6 miles. No native worth his salt would stomach any mutilation of *his* town by pixilated petitioners—and the civil war of words began.

The petitioners' formal statement reviewed the historical differences in the pursuits of the two "towns." The grounds for divorce were complaints of Marblehead's treatment of the district: an absence of town improvements, proper fire protection, road repairs and constabulary surveillance of the marauders who ruined or robbed their fields and orchards. They claimed that to add "wanton oppression" to "gratuitous insult" Marblehead placed excessive valuation "double its selling value" on "The Farms and Neck" and so collected 23.87 percent of the whole tax and in return, allegedly spent $9/10$ of 1 percent on sectional expenditures. And, finally, an excessive number of liquor licenses and resort permits had been granted, so that "the roads and shores are infested with disorderly persons, who frighten ladies, children and the timid with unrestrained ribaldry." The petition concluded that the proposal for the new town had, instead of redressing local wrongs, elicited "a volley of invective." A barrage of bombast or a cannonade of calumny exploded. You'd have to be breathing your last to miss Town Meeting *that* year!

Surrounded by signs of "Be-Ware," the voters mustered everything but their grandfathers' muskets until cooler heads proposed a businesslike statistical study to be presented at the legislature's committee hearing. Town Meeting would approve, if all papers and documents were kept in the town safe! The hearing took place on February 10, 1885, with legal counsel and agitated witnesses appearing for both sides. The din of the "ruffle" continued until the legislative committee refused the petition, and so secession efforts ended. Before long Devereux and the Neck saw the end of the farms in the proliferation of private residences and resorts.

Clifton Village grew rapidly as a summer resort for the railroad now brought travelers from Boston in just over forty minutes. Mr. Swazey and his barges, *Atlantic* and *Anna May* (hacks with rows of benches, drawn by a team of horses) met all trains and carted the vacationers off to the Clifton House, or the Hotels Crowninshield or Beach Bluff or Bellevue. Road's 1887 guidebook called Ware's Clifton House one of the finest hotels in Essex County and listed the official address as Beach Bluff, Massachusetts. The Clifton hotels were known for their table. There was a wide choice of resort activities: fishing, swimming, boating and golf and tennis which climaxed with interhotel tennis matches. A few minutes away was the Clifton Golf Club (south of Community Road) with 125 members who claimed to enjoy the "sporty" rocky 9-hole course along Atlantic Avenue and east of the Hathaway and Alley Farms. It also housed the "Don't-Lend-A-Hand" Card Club which was said to have something to do with "draw" and had club branches in Boston, Cambridge and Newton.

The final stop for Swazey's barges was Clifton Heights Square (Ticehurst and Casino Lane area) which was surrounded by summer cottages built on three major tracts of land. Very little of the land was sold for cottages; "ground rent" was charged by the year at an annual cost of $50 to $250. The Clifton Heights Association ran a casino with a full program for the enjoyment of summer residents. There were "Casino Hops," stage productions called *The Casino Gaieties*, tennis, croquet and preaching services. Two annual traditions were established very early—the children's July Fourth Horribles Parade and the fund-raising Labor Day Auction. Highline fishermen caught tautog and sea perch from the rocks and one just might sneak over the hilltop pond to tempt the German carp said to live there. The increasing number of visitors and summer residents necessitated a Clifton post office branch whose first postmaster was Fred Chapman.

The Spanish–American War inspired "Patriotic Whists" and an entertainment known as a "Dove German," a dance performed just by the ladies. All the proceeds of the Clifton benefits were given to the Eighth Regiment. Old "Cow Fort" was upgraded to Fort Glover for coastal defense and Devereux was the army headquarters for the whole area. With the 1898 Alaska Gold Rush on everyone's mind *The Messenger* reported a Clifton "Klondike," when the excavation for C. H. Isburg's new well brought up quartz containing small flecks of gold. As the well was already at 175 feet and "innocent of water," it was thought to be more marketable as a mine, than a well!

Affluent families from nearby towns were now buying land and building impressive summer residences and stables. Many, though remodeled, are still in use and the stables serve as separate dwellings.

Mr. Shuman and Mr. Dreyfus built homes in the area of what is now Shuman Road; Charles Eaton's beautiful home was listed as a show place in the *North Shore Directory of Houses;* and Mr. Dunbar erected the white house on the Atlantic Avenue hill that was later used by the Irish consul from Boston. One of the most palatial was the B. F. Keith estate which overlooked the shore from Devereux Rocks where the theater-chain owner entertained luxuriously. Mr. Keith often took his guests by carriage to the harbor dock where they boarded his steam yacht *Courier* to commute to Boston. Twenty years later the residence of Cardinal O'Connell inspired the entry road to be christened "Cardinal's Alley." In the interest of privacy the cardinal fenced off the high rocks used by the public for years; the next morning he found a sign reading, "The earth is the Lord's and the fullness thereof, but the rocks belong to the Cardinal." His Eminence apologized publicly and had a gate opened on Cardinal's Rocks.

The next to the last stop on the Eastern Railroad's line was Devereux Station where Station Master William Trasker helped sort out the passengers going by Nelson Burpee's barge to the various boardinghouses. The best known was the Devereux Farm, or Mansion, that featured croquet, bathing and boating. The boats would sometimes be rowed to or sailed to Ram Island on which was a house owned by Eugene Damon, a fisherman who paid twelve dollars annual "ground rent." The Devereux Mansion was advertised as being near "roads and driveways . . . among the best in Essex County"; when all the carriages had their driving hour along the shore and around the Neck, it was locally called the "coaching parade."

The Devereux Mansion was later remodeled into a country club named the New Cliff Club which proved unsuccessful, so in 1912 the house was converted into a sanitarium under the direction of Dr. Herbert J. Hall. The recuperative treatment called for handicrafts like weaving or pottery making, recreational study of languages and music, and rest. The Mansion's unusual therapeutic program of creative pottery design and production was taught by Arthur E. Baggs. He later opened his own business on Front Street where he sold Marblehead pottery which is now a collector's item. The sanitarium was later headed by Dr. Joel E. Goldthwait of Boston, who specialized in orthopedic therapy. After the town had turned it down for a hospital, the Devereux Mansion was razed in 1933 to make way for the building boom that had begun in the mid-1920's and has not yet ended.

The depression years, and especially the bankruptcy auction of the Sorosis Farms, spelled the end of the open farm areas which were quickly bought up by developers and sectioned into formal streets. When the farms were gone, most of the open space vanished and house lots were filled with private, single residence homes except for the schools, Veterans' Housing, churches and temples, conservation areas, and a few limited business sections. The Glover School (1928) expanded in 1949 to take care of the growing school population, yet in 1957 an entirely new school was built on land that had once been the Hotel Crowninshield. The school was named after Dr. Samuel C. Eveleth who had been chairman of the Marblehead School Committee for eighteen years. The Hobbs Community Club developed as a result of a gift from Lina E. Hobbs to the town in 1930 of 80,000 feet of land and a fifteen-room house, as a memorial to her late husband, Samuel Hobbs. It has since served as a meeting place for the Boy and Girl Scouts and various clubs, for a while as a branch of the Abbot Library and more recently, the Community Counseling Center. The club is still an active, self-supporting organization working for the benefit of the community.

The Veterans' Housing on Broughton Road, named for the Revolutionary War Commodore Nicholson Broughton, was built in 1949. The Clifton Lutheran Church, designed by local architect, Dr. Arland A. Dirlam, was built in 1954 and shortly after two temples were erected on Atlantic Avenue. The first, the Temple Emanu-El at 393 Atlantic Avenue, evolved from the congregation of the reform Temple that had started in 1954 with fourteen families and by the following year numbered seventy families and shared the facilities of Marblehead's earliest church, the Old North. The modern sanctuary and religious school were dedicated in September, 1959. The more conservative synagogue and religious school of Temple Sinai was built high on a hill at 1 Community Road and was dedicated on May 13, 1962, thirteen years after the congregation had been established in Lynn. The Jewish Community Center was built on adjoining land as an educational and recreational facility for all ages, from kindergarten tots to senior citizens.

With the density of the population and home construction, the ecology of Clifton and Devereux has altered with the loss of marshy wetlands and by underground drains; the disappearance of the Devereux pond and its tributary brooks, and the recession of the waters of Oliver and Ware ponds which Town Meeting voted to preserve as a conservation area recently.

The shoreline of the old Devereux property has been saved for the use of the townspeople through Joel E. Goldthwait's generous gift of the Goldthwait Reservation and the taking by eminent domain of the cabin colony at Usher's Beach in 1962. The landmark on the beach that is most missed is Timmie's—the stand run for forty-one years by friendly Timothy S. Cahill, who refused to succumb to storm or wind or drag racers. When his stand closed, a lot of beachcombers, parkers, picnickers and town talkers must have gone hungry, for no place could ever replace "Timmie's."

Throughout the Clifton and Devereux sections few of the street names reflect their history except for the former owners like Devereux, Humphrey, Smith, Goldthwait, Hathaway, Rose, Shuman, Ware, Bartlett; there are names for trees, presidents, developers, poets and some historic colonists like Conant and Winthrop. Where once John Humphrey, Hugh Peter and John Devereux could follow only Indian trails through the forest to the "Clifte" and the shore, thousands of people have homes and children, animals and the problems that population and Marblehead's popularity have wrought. The still lingering sense of separation dwindles as they participate as modern Commoners in town government and planning. Marblehead's beauty, the sea, the harbor and its history ever retain their fascination and deserve the lavish praise of a Whittier or a Hawthorne and recall the description of Henry Wadsworth Longfellow, written at Devereux Farm in 1846:

> Not far away we saw the port,
> The strange, old fashioned town,
> The lighthouse, the deserted fort
> The wooden houses, quaint and brown.

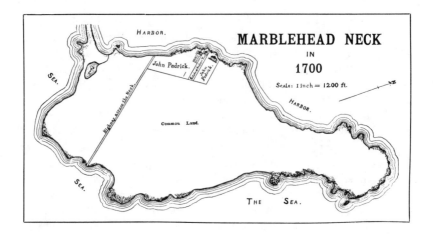

HARBOR.

MARBLEHEAD NECK
IN
1700

SCALE: 1 inch = 12.00 ft.

John Pedrick.

SEA.

Common Land.

SEA.

HARBOR.

THE   SEA.

6. *Marblehead Neck*

AN ISLAND of shade trees, ornamental shrubbery and gardens encircling residences—large and small, old and new—some on formally delineated streets, others on the old serpentine roads of yesterday—this is what the sightseer observes as he drives 'round the Neck; yet, all he sees is the shore-to-shore modern carpeting over the storied centuries of Indian, colonial and early American life on Marblehead Neck. As far back as 1614 Captain John Smith called it "a goodly headland separated from ye shore by a marvellous deep bay. . . ."

The three hundred acres of Marblehead that protrude eastward into the Atlantic Ocean are, in the first place, not an island at all, but rather a tombolo or peninsula extending into the sea connected to the mainland by an isthmus. This isthmus has determined the development and uses of the Marblehead Neck for centuries. Its most elementary function, together with the Neck, is to enclose the harbor which, deep and almost landlocked, was equally attractive to the Indians and to the colonizing fishermen. Few clues of the Naumkeag tribe can now be found on the Neck; in the nineteenth century arrowheads and other relics were uncovered at many sites and an experienced eye could discover the hand-chiseled conchoidal cuts in the Indian quarry above Ballast Beach.

The Naumkeags must have had small summer encampments on the Neck while manufacturing their tools and weapons from the hard hornblende, for there were the obvious advantages of fresh springs, fishing, hunting and beautiful locations for the feasts that followed canoe races or other contests. The Indian custom of burning underbrush strengthened the tall trees that flourished in an open, park-like grove. The tribe is said to have had a burial ground on the northeastern side and town records imply that some unfortunate victims of the 1777 smallpox epidemic were also laid to rest on the sparsely populated Neck.

Until the nineteenth century very few people were interested in living on the windswept, protective arm of the Great Bay. Its name seemed as unstable as its population, as it fluctuated between Marble Necke, Great Necke, Marble Head Necke, Nanepashemet or Manataug; moreover, a visiting geologist, later viewing its jumble of metamorphic and sedimentary rock, called it "the glory hole of Essex County."

Porphyry, syenite, greenstone form the outthrust ledges and jagged cliffs of hard rock, while the sedimentary rock and limestone inevitably succumb to erosion and wave power; the geological combination has produced a few good beaches, within the incredibly zigzag shoreline. The churns and spouts gouged out of the softer stone still throw the salt spray high in the air, unceasingly continuing the eroding process and slowly remodeling the configurations. And amidst the "jumble" might be still found baffling specimens of unrelated rocks destined to drive to distraction the amateur geologist ignorant of the fact that ballast stones from many parts of the world were hove into the shoreline waters.

Vessels lay just off the Neck to take on casks of its renowned spring water or to cut timber for ship stoves and repairs. The colonists had inherited a beautifully wooded "island," which was soon denuded of trees in spite of a series of ordinances. It was too late to save the woods on the Neck.

The Neck played an inconspicuous role in Marblehead's earliest history. Like the rest of the town, it belonged to Salem which granted the first few "ackers" to John Gatchell and his brother, Samuel, along with other Marbleheaders: John Coit, Thomas James, Will Keene, Nicholas Liston, Ralph Warren, George Chinn and Widow Blancher. Records of the first buildings are scarce, except for the deeds filed in sales and wills, such as, the 1655 purchase from John Coit of land, beach, and salt marshes by William Pitt, whose guarantor was Moses Maverick. On Pitt's Beach (the southwest corner of the Neck) there was a natural salt deposit which two centuries of owners tried to develop in hopes of creating a local source of salt used in curing fish. They experimented first with a primitive method of running sea water over shallow tubs and allowing for sedimentation and sun evaporation; much later, a more extensive salt works was built using a windmill and pumps to bring in sea water. Evaporation was assisted by sun reflectors; however, the minimal production at Pitt's Beach could not reduce the large importations of salt.

William Pitt married Susannah Alley whose daughter Mary became the wife of a town official, Christopher Lattimore. In 1668 Susannah Pitt's will requested that her husband give her daughter Mary half of the Neck land and arrange two other personal bequests: twenty shillings to a fatherless boy, Geo. Porter, and her green petticoat to her friend, J. Williams. Lattimore's deed had listed a house, fish stage and "marsh and land by a little pond or ye beach and cutting over a little neck of land and straig to the swamp East." Gravestones, dated 1681 and 1690, for those two early Neck owners, Mary and Christopher Lattimore, are the oldest markers known at the Old Burying Ground.

Christopher Lattimore had sold off a parcel of land to John Pedrick who soon built a house and barn; later, another piece went to John Searl and Andrew Tucker, who in "Jenewarie 1692" had a "parsell on the Neck" and leased additional land to be fenced for one hundred years and a day at a charge of one shilling per year. By then, the 1670 two-pole-wide (thirty-three feet) cartway across the Great Harbor beach had stimulated the town's interest in the Neck for pasturage.

In 1684 Captain Samuel Ward was given sole "herbage" for £5 in silver, annually, with the provision that any person from town had first refusal of any cow commonage before any strangers, "they paying as a stranger will do for the same." Marblehead had grown in population and prosperity; the additional cattle and horses needed the Neck pasture land, so Town Meeting set up rules for "the drift of the cattle" to the Neck and forbade its use by strangers. The Great Pasture was the name given the central and southern grazing areas, watched over by a herdsman.

In 1706 Nathan Bowen, Esq. recorded the layout of "a particular way" close to the western shore which was later called the Farm Road, and for decades it was the only Neck road except for a narrow cartway west to east across the pasture to the ocean. Early grants soon began to change hands and additional land was leased for fish fences which now decorated both sides of the harbor.

A 1720 petition signed by eighteen Neck property owners told the General Sessions Court that "there being much business done at ye said Neck," Robert Devereux' action in closing the road over his property was obstructive; the road should be opened, or lay out a "common hiway in some other place forever." A Court-appointed committee reported a new way would be less prejudicial and the gate at each end should be paid for by the petitioners, plus the Court's fees. This decision was ordered despite the opposition of the selectmen who felt that there was no need for the highway; nor had they been asked in due manner to agree to the proposal or layout. The new route reduced the distance and roughness and, undoubtedly, advanced land values on the Neck.

In 1724, the town of Marblehead officially decided to divide the remaining town land into several divisions which would be represented at Town Meeting; one of these separate divisions was the Neck. The thirty-two Neck landowners organized themselves as the Proprietors of Great Neck and appointed a committee to trace old grants and subdivide all the rest of the Neck. The surveyor drew in three pasture areas and a commons. Each ran east to west and recognized the quality as well as quantity of the parcels. The Neck Proprietors, with Azor Gale presiding and John Stacey, Jr. acting as clerk, agreed ". . . that every proprietors name as written upon a peas of paper and so put under a Hatt and one man to be chosen to draw for ye whole of ye proprietors. . . ." Of the twenty-six men whose names were in the hat, many were well-known, prosperous citizens, such as first pasture owners Richard Skinner, Nathaniel Norden, Francis Bowden and John Legg's family. The second pasture hat drawers included Rev. Mr. Cheever's successors, John Conant, William Peach's heirs and Samuel Russell, while the third pasture strips were drawn by townsmen like Robert Devereux, Eleazor Ingalls, John Roads, Christopher Bubier, and Samuel Reed. The surveyor, Joseph Burnap, Jr., also recommended that the same landing be used and that there be a new highway from the northern end.

The Proprietors voted that everyone could bring cattle to drink at the Great Pond; later, the cattle, horses and swine increased, yet sheep were discriminated against and excluded from the Neck. It was then arranged that someone pay cash to hire a bull to be brought to the Neck. The Proprietors held regular meetings for a hundred years first at Sarah Ingalls' Inn, then at the Sign of the Three Cods and later at Stacey's Inn. After the Revolution the business meetings were formally held at the Town House.

The surveyor's 1724 map identifies various shoreline points, such as, on the western shore Pitt's Beach, Homan's Marsh, Boden's Point, Black Jack's Point and on the eastern side Great Head (Castle

Rock); Swallow Bank (west of Flying Point) and nearby a spring and two sizeable ponds. The land sales committee for the Proprietors supervised the rapid turnover of property to well-to-do men like Joseph Swett, Robert Hooper, William Blackler, Philip Bessom, Isaac Mansfield, Samuel Sewall, Thomas Gerry and Jeremiah Lee. In Jeremiah Lee's will the Neck inventory lists a fish fence, three fish houses bought of Andrew Tucker's successors for £180, with a cook room thereon; plus a strip of land in the third pasture.

When Marblehead was in the zenith of its foreign trade, the Neck was a quiet, secret rendezvous for the smugglers' underground, those same secluded coves having long since been discovered by the pirates. In the middle of the eighteenth century land prices on the Neck reflected affluence and inflation; whereas, in 1746 four acres brought £20, and by 1763 two acres went for £60. In this latter period John Andrews (Andrews Lane) bought land near Boden's Point where he built his residence, and by 1794 Andrews owned twenty-seven acres, "the best house on the Neck, . . . outhouses . . . and excellent stone walls." Mr. Andrews' excellent walls and house are still in existence, though his house was remodeled several times and, finally, enlarged by the Eastern Yacht Club, was called Samoset House.

Perhaps the reason the Andrews home is still standing was that, unlike many Neck owners, he resided there year around and just may have held his ground when the few other permanent residents fled into the town for safety at the onset of the Revolution. In 1774 a British regiment was stationed on the Neck; however, neither the location nor the atmosphere was tolerable in this rebellious seaport, so the "redcoats" departed. As desperation deepened during the cold winters of the Revolutionary War, the fuel shortage caused the people to burn whatever was not in use at the time. By 1780 a town committee was asked to estimate the value of warehouses, fish fences and even houses which were "unnecessarily used as fuel by the inhabitants." By the end of the eighteenth century the Neck was found to have only the Andrews farm, three two-storied farm houses with pitched roofs, and the cellar foundations of a dozen or so earlier buildings. The Neck had lain dormant during the War of Independence, and in the postwar period any hope of reviving its use would depend on the improvement of Great Harbor Beach which by 1790 was called the Causeway.

From the earliest colonial times this isthmus had been a storm target and a governmental headache. The first cartway was frequently torn up by gales and surf; the next road was temporarily repaired by the Neck petitioners, and by 1727 the town went to the General

Court for help. Destructive seasonal storms and flood tides the previous year had broken through the western end of the beach and the town feared its port would be destroyed if the sea made its way between the Neck and the mainland. The Provincial Legislature agreed and contributed £350 to repair "the fortifications" of the isthmus and build a sea wall, which was soon after declared to be too low. Then, in 1790, when Marblehead was trying to rebuild its shattered town, there, as always, was the causeway awaiting attention. The now state of Massachusetts considered "the preservation of the harbor to be a matter of public concern" and granted four thousand dollars for the repair of the causeway, to be repaid by a local lottery. Salem's Dr. William Bentley wrote in his diary that on April 1, 1790, "a Gazette extraordinary [*Essex Gazette* "extra"] was printed this day . . . to announce the fortunate members in the First Class of Marblehead Lottery." He reported the sale had been amazingly rapid; hundreds were sold for speculation and "there is hardly a person who is not an adventurer." Those adventurers helped, perhaps unwittingly, to preserve the causeway and Riverhead Beach Commissioners were appointed to prevent obstruction and encroachments.

The threat of war with France or England over freedom of the seas preyed on their minds, so Marbleheaders weren't interested in "colonizing" the Neck, but, they did enjoy an outing there. One visitor tells of going to the Neck—ladies by carriage and men by water—where they fished and then feasted on their catch while sitting on the great rocks. The picnickers then walked across the "island" and feasted on the July sunset that silhouetted their town against the fiery glow. But it wasn't that calm and peaceful for long. The "Dogs of War" growled anew, Britain and the United States were at war again. Some of the naval battles were being fought in the offshore waters of Vice President Gerry's hometown. In 1813 Marbleheaders raced by every kind of conveyance to the Neck only to see their United States frigate *Chesapeake* defeated in a bloody battle with the British *Shannon;* fearfully, they waited for a follow-up attack on the town, so guards and guns were quickly stationed at the far end of the Neck. None came, yet the alert remained. Bombardment seemed inevitable again on a July Sunday in 1814 when *Constitution* escaped capture by slipping by Point o' Neck into the Marblehead harbor. Cheers from the Point resounded across the harbor joining the shouts from Fort Sewall. Not long after the British drove an American coaster upon the Neck's eastern shore and fired several rounds at her without causing serious damage. At the close of the 1812 war Marblehead rushed to ship out and fish again. However, for the Neck, the days of fish flakes were gone forever and its bucolic agricultural age was dawning.

It was a good time to buy on the Neck and Ephraim Brown did, the first purchase being Lot 12 sold by Sarah Doliber for $200. Mr. Brown attended the auction of Jesse Blanchard's (Blanchard Street) farm that included the former Andrews' dwelling, two large barns, an icehouse, warehouse and fish fence, 130 acres and Ballast Beach, which he bought as one parcel at a total cost of $6,475. By 1839 Ephraim Brown owned two thirds of all the Neck, so the Proprietors of Great Neck dissolved their organization after 105 years.

Ephraim Brown wasted no time in making the best of his farm: a wharf (Pleon pier) 150 feet from high-water mark was approved to enable vessels to dock on three sides; the soil proved very "susceptible" and squash, onions, corn and cabbage grew abundantly; the fields produced 100 tons of hay a year; and Brown's own schooners carried his produce to Boston and New York.

The town's desire for more sophisticated navigation aids stimulated petitioners' demands for a lighthouse now that it would not guide the omnipresent British into their port. Despite a hassle with the government over its location, the local committee flatly stated they weren't about to bargain about "the point of Neck," for their wish was "to make it easy of access to the careworn and weather beaten mariner." It took four years to obtain approval, acquire the land for $375, and to complete the white stone tower. This 1835 light was a primitive arrangement that probably burned the piggery's lard oil or whale oil. When the lighthouse was later improved, Keeper Goodwin said that it was eighty feet above sea level and, as a "white light of the sixth order," could be seen for twelve miles.

The first keeper was Ezekiel Darling, a former quarter gunner on *Constitution*. During the War of 1812 Darling had been wounded and held prisoner; yet, when offered a pension, he had refused it because he said he was "disfigured, but not disabled."

Miss Jane C. Martin, the only woman lighthouse keeper on the coast, was experienced in the care of the light from ￫ssisting her father at the Baker's Island Light and she was succeeded by John Goodwin and Captain James Bailey. One keeper used to tell of the vessels pouring oil on rough waters to reduce the wave action in dangerous areas. 'Twas said to be Ben Franklin's theory that a teaspoon of oil smoothed a half acre of water.

The lighthouse keeper's family now lived on "government grounds" in a cozy house connected by a covered walkway to the tower base where the circular staircase climbed skyward. Carrying a night's supply of kerosene oil, the keeper mounted the 134 steps every morning to fill the well, then polished the lens and pulled down the curtains that prevented the sun from discoloring the lens. Before 7:00 p.m. the ascent was made again to fire the light that guided mariners until morning.

By late in the century the government's annual stipend to a lighthouse keeper was five hundred dollars. In 1895 the picturesque old light was torn down and replaced by a higher, steel tower whose light could be seen at greater distances; by 1920 the only steady green light on the coast was electrically controlled in the main town.

The road to the lighthouse was often interwoven in the political scramble for an improved causeway. An 1846 petition was refused but the agitation continued until 1869, when the State Legislature finally authorized Marblehead "to construct a Sea-Wall and Road over River Head Beach and Marblehead Neck . . . said Sea-wall to be not more than 50 feet from, and not higher than the present break-water. . . ." Marblehead built the Causeway and life and business on the Neck took on a new complexion.

Marblehead Neck blossomed during the next half century into what the guidebooks characterized "a beautiful seaside village." As early as midcentury the old Swallow Bank farm (230 Ocean Avenue) had been opened up to summer boarders. People from the town had long used the Neck for picnics, parties or a camping weekend; now "strangers" with their tents and fishing poles stayed on for weeks. In 1867 a piece of land came on the market and was purchased by residents of Nashua, New Hampshire, some of whom were to be long associated with the Neck: Messrs. Kimball, Barr, and McQuesten. The first four summer houses (Nashua Street and Ocean Avenue) were the only buildings between the lighthouse and "Samoset" house. In Nashua Village, as it was later called, separate tents were used for cooking and the tiny shanties were "Rube Goldberg" creations—sides hooked together, so one wall could be raised to serve as a door, full-size picture window or an awning to shade the family enjoying fresh clams, Neck blueberries or a glass of Frank Graves' "Creole Nectar." With "temperance" rampant in town Graves advertised: "How to tell a Gentlemen from a mere fellow. A good way is find out if he drinks Frank Graves' *Creole Nectar*. It is hard for anyone to take that beverage and be other than a gentleman!"

Two ingenious families moved two railroad cars to the Neck for summer homes, which eliminated the cottage rental of $75 to $700 per season. Not to be outdone, a summer migration moved in from

Lowell and on leased land set up Camp Lowell on the southeast side of the Neck. Both camps loved to fish and swim and moored their dories in the harbor not far from the first Neck ferry. Boston's *Commercial Bulletin* reported as follows: "The booths and cozy little shanties are in full bloom, dainty city damsels may be seen bereft of fashions folly and conducting themselves in a manner that would shock the sensitive nerves of a sojourner at Newport or Saratoga; and stiff and stern pater familias frees himself entirely from the meshes of his ledger and bank account, and roams about the Neck revelling in the freedom he encounters at every step." Things were going swimmingly until the Brown heirs decided to sell their Neck property at an auction to be held on January 11, 1872, at the Town House.

On that day 230 acres with two miles of waterfront plus the farm, hotel, outbuildings and Ballast Beach were knocked off by the auctioneer for $255,000 to the Marblehead Great Neck Land Company. In anticipation of a railroad line to Boston this company laid out 250 lots, built Ocean Avenue, threw out the Lowell campers (many of whom went to Clifton and Cat Island) and waited for the steam engine—which didn't materialize soon enough. Their mortgage was foreclosed in 1878 and the property reverted to the administrators of the Brown estate; parcels were sold off and within two years the permanent homes on the Neck totaled sixty-eight.

Nashua Village residents owned their own land and built a meeting hall, which was turned over in 1870 to the Marblehead Neck Hall Association. Two other signs of growth were a grocery store and post office where Post Mistress Mary B. Bailey handed out the mail. The post office branch name was Nanepashemet, even though there was movement on foot to change the Neck's name to Manataug.

On July 2, 1881, a Neck newspaper, *Manataug Pebbles*, published by Charles D. Howard, appeared with a Shakespearean quotation on its masthead: "The murmuring surge that on the unnumbered pebbles chafe." There was little "murmuring" except that, contrary to the law, ballast was still being taken from Ballast Beach by men wading waist deep through the cold water to carry stones to the dories that transferred the ballast to the waiting droghers. Other ballast thieves were being chased from harbor coves. Aside from that heavy note, the surge of summer resort excitement was evident in theatricals, "Germans" (dances for an audience by twelve to fifteen couples doing the waltz and quadrilles), moonlight straw rides, dory racing, picnics and more picnics. (Intimate note: For picnics there had been designed in ladies' apparel special picnic panties: long, light undergarments with lace and with a convenient aperture.) The guest lists of the Ham House, Atlantic Hotel, Old Orchard House and Samoset House were published in the newspaper along with the coming events: fireworks, mackerel fishing parties, "candy scrape" at Sky-High and a cooking club to which young gentlemen would be invited as taste testers. The big news was three major developments: the Eastern Railroad had scheduled nine trips a day from Boston, every one of them met by Captain E. A. Pitman's new steam ferry, *Lizzie May*, which carried seventy-five passengers at ten cents each, or fourteen commuter trips for one dollar. *Lizzie May* made at least thirteen round trips a day, and Captain Pitman had a locker full of Marblehead sea stories and his own adventures with pirates in the China Seas. Pitman's tales were particularly appreciated by the yachtsmen—and there were plenty of them now that the Eastern Yacht Club had opened its new clubhouse.

Amidst fireworks, illumination of the harbor, and bands blaring, the Eastern Yacht Club Clubhouse's gala opening had taken place June 9, 1881, followed the next day by a club regatta that was blown right off the calendar by a Nor'easter. The chiding of those members who had wanted headquarters built in less vulnerable Manchester or Beverly began that day, but without noticeable effect on the yachting enthusiasm that had been engendered in Eastern's first decade. In March, 1870, the founders had broken away from the Boston Yacht Club to form their own Eastern Yacht Club. A Boston newspaper said: ". . . the yachting club foremost in rank . . . although the youngest in date . . . was the Eastern Yacht Club." The new official burgee was flying for the 1870 regatta when the clubhouse was still a locker room on Boston's India Wharf. The Eastern's clubhouse on Marblehead Neck was the culmination of tremendous interest in the new club and yachting.

Marblehead Neck was fast becoming a favorite resort and the casual camping days were almost at an end. Houses and hotels were being constructed; the most notable was the large Nanepashemet Hotel (Nanepashemet Street and Ocean Avenue) overlooking the ocean, described in Kimball's 1882 *Handbook of Marblehead Neck* as the "most modern hostelry in town." Built in Colonial style it featured the view from all of its eighty rooms and from the balcony on the roof and the porch that swept around three sides. The Nanepashemet retained its top position until destroyed by fire in 1914. To provide for carriages and teams, a group of men formed the Marblehead Neck Club Stable Company, which continued for twenty-six years.

If the Clifton agitation for secession from the town in 1885 had succeeded, the Neck's connections with Marblehead would have been ended and it would have become part of the new town. Although the petitioners went through a wild state legislative hearing, the legislature denied the formation of a new town. There had been little outward support of the petition from the Neck, undoubtedly, because most Neck people were nonvoting summer residents. Nonetheless, the "summer boarders" had known the sting of some town resentment, despite the fact that the decline of the shoe business made Marblehead heavily reliant on the summer trade and the expansion of yacht yards, sail lofts and waterfront business.

The founding of a second yacht club on the Neck enlivened greater yachting interest. The Corinthian Yacht was organized in 1885 under the aegis of William S. Eaton, Charles H. W. Foster, and Benjamin W. Crowninshield who became its first commodore. Eastern Yacht Club seemed to ignore any craft under thirty feet; so Corinthian's purpose was to foster interest in and sponsor racing for boats from sixteen to thirty feet. The idea caught on quickly and the first of hundreds of important races for new small classes was held the year that the famous Knockabout Class was introduced. Having purchased the Sparhawk property, Corinthian Yacht Club built its first clubhouse in 1888 and set the dues at $5.00 per member. The club expanded rapidly and ten years later constructed a larger headquarters on the same location. Corinthian's emblem was the Flying Pegasus of Corinth; its motto reflected the current classical influence in the Roman quotation, "All is ready to contend and prepared to answer back."

Another group of yachting enthusiasts was prepared to answer back to the senior yachtsmen, their large boats and expensive clubs. In 1887 the boys and young men formed the Pleon Yacht Club, the first junior yacht club in America. The first commodore, Arthur G. Wood, helped choose the name from the Greek word *pleon* ("sailing") which the young people of Marblehead have been, and still are, encouraged to do by the Pleon Yacht Club. With the advent of three new yacht clubs the local paper spoke glowingly of the new yachting center of America.

From then to the end of the century the Marblehead Neck history was positively idyllic. The townspeople of Marblehead continued to enjoy the beauty and relaxation of the Neck as they had for many decades. Families would row over for a picnic on the beach where the fresh-caught cunners were quickly fried in butter in a creeper (Marblehead for fry pan). Or clam chowder would be made on the spot, and afterwards they would sing or dance on the beach.

If father brought the wagon over the causeway, the family might camp a day or two in the tent. There was not yet any problem with public ways!

The "beautiful island" season for the summer people ran from May 1 to November 1 and the wild flowers grew in profusion, though the trees were few. Mr. Charles Parker, who owned Red Gate, made it his personal responsibility to restore the Neck to its early colonial beauty when many varieties of trees flourished here. He not only experimented with seeds, but, as president of The Massachusetts Horticultural Society, he also planted a wide variety of saplings and encouraged others to do the same. By way of freakish accident Mr. Parker planted the first English oak on the Neck—the acorn seed having been found in the crop of a smoked pheasant sent to Mr. Parker from England. The Neck was also a natural flyway where bird watchers spotted many rare species. The ponds had been stocked with fish, even goldfish, and the so-called Stratton's spring water was preferred for the best tea. The ocean fish were abundant; so were the skunks. To reduce the number of *Mephitis Americana* a bounty of fifty cents to four dollars, per skin, was offered with the reminder that the skunk fat made good liniment! Seaweed, full of iodine, was recommended for Irish moss pudding, or, well dried and bleached, for beer. And if one kept a sharp lookout on the beach, good fortune might wash up the peculiar substance that Mr. Zachariah T. Wiley had found; that 14½ pounds of whale ambergris earned him $3,200.

There were wildly exciting days, too, when the sea serpent was seen off the eastern shore of the Neck. Bloodcurdling descriptions went from piazza to piazza; Castle Rock spectators were sure they glimpsed the primeval, spiny fins emerging from the sunlit seas. One night the British steamship *Norseman* went up on Tom Moore's Rocks at 3:00 a.m. in a howling southeast gale. Fighting high surf the Massachusetts Humane Society boat took off thirteen men and eighty-eight more were carried in a breeches buoy to safety. The weather in 1898 set all kinds of records—the harbor had been frozen over that winter and a severe November storm with seventy-mile winds all night ruined the Causeway.

Marblehead had petitioned the federal government for a lifesaving station to be located on Flying Point; on the other hand, Senator Lodge preferred Nahant and with his congressional influence the station was located there in 1898. When the Spanish–American War was declared that spring, the effect was noticeable on the Neck because the summer residents were involved in the war effort at home or worried about the Neck being bombed. The scuttlebutt was that Abbot Hall made too good a target for the elusive Spanish fleet that might be steaming toward the northeast coast.

The Neck's tranquil summer beauty was unbroken by bombardment, so rentals and building continued to pick up.

Somewhat later town departments had installed some street lights, improved roads and police protection; gradually, large impressive homes made their appearance for summer and year-round use. In 1897 Captain John Ward, the peppery skipper of a coastal schooner, had built his dream house (400 Ocean Avenue) which, it was said, resembled a house he had admired in Maine. The handsome three-storied, symmetrical house was placed on a granite foundation and laid out in the style of the 90's with large, square, high-ceilinged rooms around a spacious central hall. The remarkable feature of Capt. Ward's central hall was the staircase which copied in half dimension the stairway in the Jeremiah Lee Mansion. The fine, clapboard home with its broad summer veranda set with pilastered corners and Ionic capitals was the joy of the captain until he died.

Soon after, Robert Bridge, who owned a large portion of the Neck, built his house (204 Ocean Avenue) in the triangle at the end of the Causeway; later, Governor Frank Allen resided there. Few houses caused more comment than that of Charles Sanborn of the Chase & Sanborn Coffee Company. Set back from Ocean Avenue at the top of the S curve the Sanborn estate (no longer standing) overlooked the sea from the high, rocky bluff and the view was magnificent from the piazza that almost encircled the house. It contained 1,300 electric lights, 50 of which lighted the oval dining room, though the fixtures were hidden behind a wide cornice. An unusual feature was the bicycle room with bikes enough for all guests, who occupied the seashore guest house. A large number of townspeople were employed in the construction of this and other large homes being built early in the twentieth century.

Probably the most unique was the house that Isabella Stewart Gardner built for her protege, George Proctor, of whom her biographer, Louise Hall Tharp, wrote, "George Proctor appeared on the scene at this point to become Mrs. Jack's most troublesome protege." Isabella Gardner fostered Proctor's talent as a pianist, introduced him to notables in the music world, sent him abroad to study, and arranged for him to play before Paderewski. In spite of "Mrs. Jack's" efforts Proctor seemed unwilling to devote the time and effort required of a concert pianist. Mrs. Gardner, now a widow, began building the miniature replica of an old world Spanish villa at 246 Ocean Avenue about 1910, and the influence of her imaginativeness, her travels and her charismatic personality are everywhere in evidence in the design and unusual features of "Twelve Lanterns." It sits high on huge rock outcroppings and boulders, one of which Mrs. Gardner had moved there to hide the underpinnings of the house. A Spanish archway and winding stone steps lead to the stucco house roofed with grooved tiles brought from Italy. Ancient Chinese tiles were decorously placed on the balconies. Inside the house there are no two rooms the same size or shape; even the ceilings and windows differ. The entrances to the main room are from behind a huge chimney whose great fireplace with its hewn rock mantel outlined by matched floral tiles opens into a high-vaulted studio room. Hand-hewn beams and three circular sun windows add interest, but the focal point is the far end designed for the grand piano. In that room are the first of the twelve lanterns that give the house its name. One of the most unusual features is the twelve-foot-square tower room entered by a steep, narrow companionway and lighted by twelve windows with magnificent views of the sea and Marblehead. Mrs. Jack never resided at "Twelve Lanterns," but gave the house to George Proctor when he married. Nor did the Proctors live here, so it was later sold without ever having the great music issue from the piano studio as Isabella Gardner undoubtedly hoped, when she frequented Marblehead to supervise every detail of the construction of the small villa on the Neck.

House construction increased rapidly; nevertheless, very few were occupied during the winter. America's entrance into World War I closed many homes and Eastern Yacht Club, but Corinthian offered its hospitality.

The titillating twenties brought a tremendous growth of yachting that kept all the yacht clubs on their toes and social calendars well filled. It was too tempting for a developer to resist, so in the mid twenties an office went up on Ocean Avenue to sell about sixty lots at prices from $750 to $1,500 which could be paid for on the installment plan for as little as $13.50 per month. The advertisement read: "The very idea of Marblehead brings to one's mind pictures of beautiful surroundings, incomparable summer pleasures and the picturesque quaintness . . . combined with fashionable gaiety to be found at a watering place patronized by our best people."

On September 8, 1920, a number of Neck residents had gathered at the Marblehead Neck Hall and had agreed "to preserve and maintain the distinctive characteristics of this beautiful spot." Their new organization was called the Marblehead Neck Improvement Association and its first president was Henry A. Morss, who with ninety-two Neck residents realistically tackled the problems of growth and change. The minutes of the Improvement Association are the key to Neck problems and growth of the next half century, just as the minutes of the Proprietors of Great Neck were in the 1700's.

The 1924 assessed valuations revealed that Neck, which made up $\frac{1}{10}$ of the town area, had a real estate valuation of $3,567,100 or $\frac{1}{5}$ of the total, so Neck residents pressed the town fathers for more fire and police protection and influenced the choice of location for a new firehouse. When the 1926 sewer installation began in town, it was hoped it would soon reach the Neck—almost forty years later it did; meanwhile, the Neck was zoned for single-family dwellings in 1928 and a growing public awareness of water pollution put pressure on residents and yachtsmen to refrain from dumping waste in the harbor.

The depression years caused a necessary decrease in most town improvements, except federal projects. The public works programs to create employment renewed interest in building a breakwater which, it was proposed in 1933, would extend four hundred feet across the entrance at a cost of $480,000 paid by the federal government. The breakwater issue has surfaced at intervals, but each time it has been defeated by Town Meeting. The last business on the Neck closed in 1937 when after fifty years the post office and store closed and became a home (103 Harbor Avenue). The summer resort had turned the corner.

In the mid thirties one of the landmarks of the Neck had reached completion; Carcassonne, or the Castle, as it is known, was built by Lydia Pinkham Gove at a cost of $500,000. Plans specified the use of as many local unemployed as possible; when finished, the Gothic French castle with its central tower quickly became a showplace. The stone house has a complex, yet symmetrical, facade with a ridge roof and cross gables and four tall chimneys. Enclosed in the iron spear fence punctuated by stone columns is Carcassonne itself, the tennis court and swimming pool all taking every advantage of the magnificent view from the high waterfront site. The elegant interior contains glass staircases, an elevator and a small number of large rooms. Its first owner was as unusual as the castle. The granddaughter of Lydia Pinkham, Miss Gove was an officer of the medicine company and later of an advertising agency which backed Howard Johnson in his first famous restaurant at the 1939 New York World's Fair. Lydia Gove was a lavish hostess who purchased "Sky High" for the use of her friends and for entertainment, adding to it formal gardens and steps to the sea. Active in civic affairs Miss Gove became a trustee of the Mary A. Alley Hospital, which after her death in 1948, considered buying the estate for a town hospital. Town Meeting turned down the option because of its location and conversion costs; the half-million dollar house was then sold for a reported $50,000 and since has had a succession of owners; however, it still remains the Neck's "castle."

The same New York World's Fair inspired another unusual home on the Neck, the Block House, which was copied from an early Colonial structure. Bachelor Arthur Stevens built the full-size replica in 1939 at 253 Ocean Ave and in later years raised the house one story higher. The square lookout topping the house can capture miles of scenery in any direction.

Rocky, sandy Marblehead Neck which had long since been denuded of trees owes its beautification to individual residents, the Improvement Association, the Club of Small Gardens organized in 1931. The Winter Garden Club came into being in 1947 to beautify and preserve the Neck and to learn what indigenous plants would grow there. Shortly after the club, with the cooperation of Tree Warden Loring Clark, began a long term program of planting the Neck with the flowering salt-resistant hopa crab trees which line the roads with pink blossoms in the spring.

Damage to the Neck from the 1938 hurricane was very extensive to houses, trees and power lines; yet the longstanding plea for underground wires was again denied, so later severe storms and the 1954 and 1955 hurricanes again left the roads littered with wires and broken poles. Building had come to a halt during World War II except those buildings erected for security purposes: the radar tower above Ballast Beach (Fuller's Beach) and two camouflaged observation tower houses built for Battery 206 of the artillery engineers. One at 291 Ocean Avenue was built to the height of five stories, each attached by pull-down iron stairways with trap doors to close off each section. Each floor housed telescopes and detection instruments. Fake windows were topped with real observation slits set in the thick, one-foot walls. A second tower was built inside a Colonial-style house topped by a widow's walk at 310 Ocean Avenue. A coastal blackout had been imposed and only Neck residents were allowed to cross the Causeway at night. Although submarine activity was reported, no one ever presented evidence of saboteurs. By the time World War II ended, the character of Marblehead Neck had clearly changed to its current residential year-round pattern of living.

The government placed the land at Point o' Neck, which was an historic landmark long before the lighthouse was built, on the market. That headland of history and sentiment was purchased by Neck resident, Chandler Hovey, and given in 1948 to the people of Marblehead for their pleasure forever. Named for him, a park is now enjoyed by the solitary sea gazer, the artist, the frogman, the sightseer, but mostly by lovers of the sea, its vessels and its sailors. From that rocky headland spreads the wide panorama of the Neck, the Causeway, the town and the irregular shoreline that ends on the opposite headland, Fort Sewall.

Not far from Chandler Hovey Park is Point o' Rocks Lane where in 1948 America's most renowned playwright lived in virtual isolation. Eugene O'Neill and his third wife, Carlotta, moved into what he wrote Charlie Chaplin was "a small house by the sea." He described later how he had, for $85,000, turned "a dinky summer cottage . . . [into] a beautiful little house." On the glassed-in porch the tormented playwright stood scanning "dat ole devil sea" with his binoculars. A victim of Parkinson's disease, Eugene O'Neill could not write, but he could dream, and remember, and watch the restless sea that for so long had captured his fertile imagination. Lonely, depressed and ill, the O'Neills had few guests and made no friends on the Neck. Their neurotic, isolated existence after a flamboyant career and international acclaim closely resembled the tragic finale of an O'Neill play. Overcome by desperation, on a winter night in 1951, Eugene O'Neill fled into a swirling snowstorm and broke his leg in an icy fall. He and Carlotta were both hospitalized and never again returned to the Marblehead Neck house.

There was in the 1950's only one sizeable wild area left on the Neck and that was partially laid out by a developer. The Improvement Association and bird lovers from the whole town joined to save the area with its fresh-water ponds, tall trees, high grass, berry bushes, and other food that served the natural migration station. Bird watchers submitted a total of 118 species of birds seen there. In the 1920s to preserve pheasants and other species of birds which frequented the Atlantic flyway, no shooting was allowed on the Neck, except when the night herons became a nuisance and were killed off within two years.

Mutual cooperation and voluntary contributions saved seventeen acres in the center of the Neck for an official sanctuary accepted by the Massachusetts Audubon Society and it was opened in 1954 for the pleasure of the public and as a "rescue" stopover for migratory birds. At that time a bird watcher could easily sight fifty species a day during a migratory period; half the number would now be a lucky day. The decline is laid to the increased use of the sanctuary as a playground, and to pesticides, noise or airplane traffic.

The street names on the Neck for the most part originated from former abutters like Foster, Follett and Blanchard, or from names (like Ocean Avenue), given by early developers. Only a few historic names survived, such as Nashua Street and Cove Lane. Harbor Avenue at the Causeway end was once Broadway and led into the best-known Farm Road. However, the shoreline and headlands' names have not changed in centuries.

Predominant and quite unchanged are the nineteenth-century clubhouses which have added facilities for swimming and increasingly popular tennis. The newest clubhouse, Pleon, is maintained by the officers of Pleon with a senior advisory group, and Ephraim Brown's old Stone Wharf is now crowded with small boats and young people preparing for sailing classes or racing or just enjoying their own clubhouse. After May 30 the traffic and excitement mount as fast as the keen competition in Summer Series, Race Week, ocean racing or national championships. Cruising crews build small mountains of equipment and supplies on the club floats; club launches look as if they might be headed for a year's voyage. The yachting talk is of wind and weather, starts and spinnakers, courses and crews in a language not unlike Esperanto to the land-lubber or inland visitor—a roach is not a bug, a cradle is as unrelated to an infant as a sheet is to a bed, and coffee grinder and stays and coaming and boom have a meaning all their own—even the harbor scene is incredible. The Eastern Yacht Club has celebrated its 100th anniversary; yet, the debate of the old Piazza Committee regarding rigging and design goes on endlessly. When the yachting season closes in the fall, the dinghies and yachts are hauled ashore to become an accepted adjunct to the house or garage until time to scrape and paint and rig for the next season of wind and weather, starts and spinnakers, courses and crews. The clubs have given continuity to yachting, just as some of the old families have given to the "island" for over a century; yet change is constant, too.

Still, the sharp chilling winds of winter whistle through the shutters carrying along the deep thud of the bell buoy; the snow and sleet pass horizontally on their way to the mainland; the branches snap from the trees and the surf sweeps against or over the Causeway making it unsafe to cross. The sea has not given up its age-old fight to cut a passage through and isolate the island. Nature succeeds in that when thick, damp fog even isolates neighbor from neighbor and the "groaner" reminds them they live on the arm into the sea. Indians, Commoners, farmers, campers, vacationers and resi-

dents have had one reaction—wishing the all-too-brief summer
were endless. Strictly summer residents could now be counted on
your fingers; the seasonal "beautiful seaside village" has become a
full year-round participant in the life of the town, its government
and its future history.

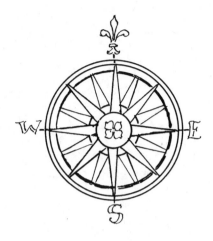

7. Offshore Islands

FROM THE VANTAGE POINTS of the Great Head (Castle Rock) of Marblehead Neck, or the rocky jutland that supports Fort Sewall, or the headland of Fountain Inn Park, one may see the offshore islands that make a charm string of beauty in sea-girdled Marblehead. (There are about a dozen islands, only half of which are habitable.) Louis Agassiz, when he visited the North Shore for the first time, ventured the conjecture that the line of islands had been a continuous promontory in prehistoric ages, extending from the shore and that from time to time the sea had broken through. Gazing toward the coast as it stretches out to Cape Ann, it is hard to imagine that not only the distant shore but also the islands, the small as well as the larger ones, were once entirely covered with pines and woods. Now only a few gnarled trees and some pine bear witness to the once lush growth, for these islands and much of the shore were denuded long since of timber for ships, houses and fuel, and few trees were replanted. It is also difficult to imagine sailing by these islands and waters without any aids to navigation, but such was the case in the seventeenth and eighteenth centuries—no horrendous fog warnings, no bells or flashing buoys and no lighthouses.

In 1713 the legislature voted to erect a small lighthouse at the entrance of Boston Harbor and it was to be paid for by charging fees to the vessels which passed it. With that exception, the coast of New England was entirely unbuoyed and unlighted. The twin lighthouses on Thacher's Island were not lighted till 1771, over a half century after the lighthouse in Boston Harbor, and those (for there were two, originally) on Baker's, not until 1798. The Reverend William Bentley of Salem was instrumental in getting the lighthouses on Baker's. Marblehead's lighthouse on Lighthouse Point was placed there on the Neck in 1831. All of the offshore islands originally belonged to Salem and most of them still do. However, they are claimed by all Marblehead sailors, and many of them are frequented by Marbleheaders. Identifying the islands from southeast to northeast, the first is Ram Island, which is really a large rock off Marblehead Beach and south of Flying Point on the Neck. Ram Island, supposedly, was once the home of an old sea captain. A freshwater spring on this island provided him with good, clear drinking water. Today, it is the home of only thousands of seagulls.

Tinker's Island is six hundred yards from Flying Point—really two small islands connected by a narrow strip of land—bare at low water. The island is a short distance from the Neck and a very deep, irregular channel runs between it and the shore—Blockhouse Beach (known as Brown's Beach in the early days). In the middle of the nineteenth century, the lighthouse board supplied wood and candles, which were kept in a small hut to be used as a refuge in case of shipwreck. A Boston vessel from Spain, loaded with iron, was wrecked on this island during a snowstorm on April 2, 1786. The whole crew perished; the bodies were recovered and buried in the town. In the early nineteenth century sheep were pastured here and occasionally camping parties stayed on the island, for fishing was good. Today there are several cottages or camps where squatters stay. They paid taxes to no town or city until 1969. They must, of course, furnish their own transportation to and from the island, provide their own lights and carry their own water, for there are no springs on the island. The origin of the name "Tinker's" is from the abundance of tinker mackerel that run close to its shores.

An attempt was made to have the islands, Tinker's and Ram's, become part of Marblehead. An original document found reads (in parts): "At a meeting of the town of Salem, January 28, 1807, voted that a committee of 3 be chosen to collect and furnish documents relative to title of Rams Island and Tinker's Island." And, "Voted that the town give instruction to their Rep(s) in the General Court and request them to show the town's right to Ram's Island, Tinker's

Island and the rocks prayed for by the Marblehead Marine Society and to use their influence to present the prayer of said petition being granted. . . . That the said inhabitants have claimed, held and occupied Ram I, Tinker's Is and have leased the same and received rents thereto from the Inhabitants of Marblehead and others since 1759 to the present day and now claim the right of property in the same and also in the rocks aforesaid at their late meeting unanimously voted to request their Representatives to speak—their rights and show title to the islands—rocks aforesaid the jurisdature of which is prayed for by the Marblehead Marine Society and to use all their influence to present the prayer of their petition being granted.— L. Punchard, Town Clerk"

Prior to the 1807 petition, Isaac Mansfield, clerk of the Marblehead Marine Society, petitioned Salem on April 1, 1802, and the General Court of the Commonwealth of Massachusetts on Jan. 7, 1807, "to place suitable monuments and marks on Ram Island, Tinker's Island, Marblehead Rock and Cat Island Rocks"—also, to "plant trees." A week later the House passed the request favorably, and the following week the Senate "read and concurred." In February the legislature added to the bill two more sections saying, "if any Person or Persons shall on said Islands or Rocks mar, Injure or *Deface* any of the trees or buildings. . . . Pay for each & every offense the sum of Twelve Dollars." Section 3, ". . . if any Person or Persons shall take away from the Islands and Rocks aforesaid any earth, stones, or gravel, each & every Person so offending, shall . . . the sum of Twelve Dollars for each ton of Earth, Stones or gravel. . . ."

By March 2, 1818, a petition came from Captain John Wooldredge seeking the renewal of monuments, and so on, "as the same are now in a state of decay and destruction." This petition continued until 1882, and by that time the Marblehead Marine Society had gone out of existence.

September 5, 1889, Captain John Murphy of East Boston leased Tinker's Island for ballast, and in 1913 Albert Prince leased the island for the establishment of a boy's camp, but no records of the camp are available. In 1917 the Reverend Mr. Edward Small, minister of the Methodist church, lived in a cottage he called Driftwood Fortress. He loved the island, so he often offered his cottage to young couples he had married for their honeymoons. The first rock they stepped on when coming ashore was the "Bride's Rock." He made paths, named the rocks for some of the couples, and noted the weather and tides. Known as a strong man physically, the Reverend Mr. Small did all the manual labor of moving boulders and rocks to make foundations, and edged the many paths he had made with rocks of considerable size. He found the island a good growing place and soon his vineyard was flourishing, as well as a large raspberry patch. His parishioners enjoyed telling the tale about him when he proved he really was a strong man. His reputation had preceded him and when he arrived in Rockport, Massachusetts, he was finally badgered into a "strong man" contest. A crowd of husky Finnish workmen, seeing Mr. Small standing on one of the quarries, persuaded the strongest of their number to challenge the minister. Picking out two extremely large rocks, the Finn carefully carried first one and then the second and bowed when the crowd cheered. Mr. Small estimated the size of the two great rocks. Then, choosing one that was heavier in weight than the two put together, he effortlessly carried it the same distance. Having completed the task, he patted his challenger on the shoulder and quietly said, "There, Son, you return it from whence I got it." Carrying two twenty-gallon milk cans filled with water (which he had to have while living on Tinker's), he never set the cans down but would stand holding them with great ease while he continued a long conversation with a neighbor on the island. In 1923 William Finch and George Doherty fought a running battle, each claiming the island as his own. The dispute was never resolved.

This island, which is dotted with pheasant and laced and perfumed with wild roses, where striped bass and lobster are the order of the day, where there is no tax collector and no municipal services provided, has its own protective Tinker Island Association. Fred ("Gar") MacFadden was the island historian and the first president of the Tinker Island Association and he always stated that the federal government owned the island and those on it were squatters. He also recorded that one year a young boy, visiting one of the islanders (about twelve cottages were on the island), became ill. There are no telephones on Tinker's, and on that particular day there was no one to row a boat but, fortunately, a resident of Marblehead Neck noted a distress signal, the American flag being flown upside down, and notified the harbor police who evacuated the youngster. Mr. MacFadden, too, could recall the days of rumrunners landing in the dead of night on the northern point of the island. Although the City of Salem claimed the island in 1969, and now cottage owners pay taxes to Salem, it still is a great place to get away from the demands of civilization.

Tom Moore's Rocks form a long ledge, bare at one-third ebb tide, about one-fifth of a mile off Long Beach (Ballast or Fuller's). A spindle identifies these rocks. In the 1600's a Tom Moore of Salem had fish-flake rights on the Neck, and, inasmuch as his boat sank and he went down with it, these rocks were probably named for him. Salem records show that his widow was granted the right to keep his fish rights on the Neck.

A quarter of a mile southeast of the Neck lighthouse lies Marblehead Rock. It is really two islets, connected at low water. A granite marker surrounding a spar buoy five feet long is on the eastern islet as a navigation aid. In the 1800's a part of the church pulpit was supposed to have been located on it. It now provides nesting grounds for countless sea birds.

Moving east, Half-way Rock is so-called because it is half way between Cape Ann and Boston. The defiant-looking, precipitous rock is three miles out into the Atlantic. It is almost forty feet high and in a raging storm the sea seems to spout up over it like a fountain. It was for many years the custom of outward-bound fishermen and mariners to throw coppers on this rock for luck. It also followed that the younger, adventurous boys would row out and try to retrieve these "good-luck" coins! One enterprising seaman sailed out to gather in the pennies thrown on the rock. He was caught in the act and heavily fined.

Cat Island, or Lowell Island, or Children's Island, is one-half mile long north northeast of Half-way Rock. In 1635 Robert Cotta, a tailor who lived in Salem and owned a home there, kept sheep on the island that was to bear his name. Most small islands during those years were used for the purpose of keeping sheep; furthermore, Catta Island up to 1665 was free to anyone and owned by no one. In 1664 Robert Cotta sold his dwelling house and land in Salem and no further trace is found of him; the only thing remaining was in the name—Cotta Island. The following year the General Court granted the island to Governor Endicott and, in 1684, it was bequeathed by Zerubbabel Endicott to his daughters under the name of Cotta (or Catta) Island. Three years after that, the girls' brother, Samuel Endicott, sold the property for them, thus closing the first proprietorship of Catta Island. Unlike Misery and Baker's, "Cat" Island has been privately owned.

On March 4, 1687, Richard Reade of Marblehead bought Cat Island for sixteen pounds. Mr. Reade had enjoyed a lasting friendship with Governor John Endicott and it was natural that Endicott should sell the land to his friend. Thus the Reade family were the first purchasers and possessed the island for nearly half a century until Samuel Reade forfeited it on an unsatisfied mortgage in 1761. The first mention of any house on the island comes from Samuel Reade on February 20, 1738, when he wrote of "the house and woods thereon." The Waite family from Marblehead assumed ownership from 1761 until just before the Revolutionary War.

The continuing increase in foreign trade into Marblehead brought with it the dread disease, smallpox, and in 1773 John and Jonathan Glover, Elbridge Gerry and Azor Orne took immediate steps toward the construction of an inoculation center at Cat Island. As the General Court was not in session, the petition to combat the disease by establishing a hospital was signed by the principal gentlemen of Salem, Marblehead and Beverly. When asking for permission to open a hospital, the petition stated that fifty-nine persons in town (Marblehead) already had the distemper and "fourteen out of twenty-one died." The petition was granted and the four organizers —the two Glovers, Azor Orne and Elbridge Gerry—privately purchased Cat Island from William Waite on September 2, 1773. By October the construction of the Essex Hospital had begun. Rules and regulations were set up and soon Dr. Hall Jackson of Portsmouth, New Hampshire, was the doctor in residence. The patients had to get themselves to the island, and upon their return patients could not come ashore without certification from the hospital and permission to land from the selectmen. The Proprietors paid not only for the construction of the hospital but also the salaries of Dr. Jackson and his colleague, Dr. Ananias Randall of Long Island.

The first of January, 1774, the hospital's accomplishment could be recounted. At this period the common preventative measure against smallpox was inoculation with material from human cases of the disease. Despite the Proprietors' efforts and generosity in helping to wipe out the disease, a resentful attitude developed because of the fear of inoculation among some of the Marbleheaders.

In January 18, 1774, the *Essex Gazette* carried the following advertisement: "Wanted—A quantity of damaged feathers also an old one-horse cart. Enquire of the Printers." Dr. Edward A. Holyoke recorded in his *Diary*, "Two days after, 4 Marblehead men, suspected of attempting to steal clothing from the Hospital on Cat Island, were tarred and feathered, placed in a cart and hauled from the town house in Marblehead to Salem and return escorted by a procession of over a thousand people, many of whom were in uniform." In his entry for January 26, 1774, Dr. Holyoke wrote, "The small pox hospital on Cat Island, off Marblehead was destroyed by incendiaries. 2 men suspected of being concerned in the affair were arrested Fe. 25th following, on a fishing vessel in Marblehead harbor, and taken to Salem jail." That evening, a mob from Marblehead assembled, burst open the doors of the jail and carried off the prisoners in triumph. The two rescued prisoners were John Watts and

John Guillard. General and Colonel Glover, four years after the destruction of the hospital were still hopeful of recovering their loss through the services of Benjamin Hichborn, lawyer of Boston. This did not come to fruition and finally, after the Revolution, the proprietors of Cat Island gave the island to Deacon William Williams. His claim was sold at auction and bought by Edward Fettyplace. The Fettyplaces sold the island in 1848 to David Blaney of Marblehead.

The Salem and Lowell Rail Road Company was formed in August, 1850, with Stephen C. Phillips as president, and, wishing to expand, they looked over Cat Island and consequently purchased it, forming the Salem Steamboat Company. They also decided to build a hotel, The Island House. So many Lowell people visited the hotel, it became known as the Lowell House, and the island, Lowell Island. The steamship called for people at Marblehead, as well as Salem, and there were day trips, "excursions," from Marblehead at the cost of 12½¢ a trip! A gay, happy life was enjoyed in the summer at the Lowell House and the season ended in September with an annual regatta. However, later under a new hotel manager, the Island House became unpopular, and in 1878 the trustees sold Cat Island to Samuel B. Rindge for forty-five hundred dollars. It was he who converted the hotel into a new hospital, calling it Children's Island Sanitarium. Mr. Rindge gave the island to the West End Nursery on Blossom Street and the Infants' Hospital of Boston, both of which were run by the Sisters of St. Margaret of the Episcopal Church, and they also managed the sanitarium until 1900, after which time the Boston Community Fund supported it until 1946.

Later, the island was taken over by the Marblehead YMCA, which continues to conduct a successful summer camp for children on it. About five hundred children attend the camp in four sessions —some for two weeks, some for three and some for the full summer; they range from eight to fourteen years of age and come from Marblehead and nearby communities. The program offers the following sports and activities: baseball, softball, volley ball, archery, riflery, swimming, arts and crafts, nature lore and, naturally, a sailing camp for the older children.

Eagle Island, three quarters of a mile northeast of Cat (Children's) Island, is high and covered with shrubbery, surrounded by shoals and is about two hundred yards long. Reverend William Bentley wrote of the abundance of wild parsnips growing there in the late eighteenth century; today there is only a lush growth of small shrubs and many varieties of goldenrod.

The Gooseberries are two small islands located southeast of Baker's Island. In the days of the China trade, schooners leaving the harbor for trips to the Orient would stop first at the Gooseberries. Here the large stones were gathered from the island and placed as ballast in the holds of the ship. When the schooners reached their destination, the stones were thrown overboard and the cargo taken on the ships maintained the same weight.

In 1966 the Massachusetts Audubon Society initiated an experiment in which seagulls living on the islands near Marblehead were dyed pink. The study was to discover the location of the nesting and feeding grounds of these birds. As the different colors indicated various locations, it was easy to spot the birds and their "native homes." For once the air was gay with psychedelic wings!

Baker's, the largest of the islands that lies outside Marblehead, dominates the scene with its sixty acres and massive outcroppings of rock. Governor Winthrop, in his early writings in 1630, called the island Baker's Island, with no other source of identification than that. It lies right in the path of all shipping and was the skipper's home landmark for the port when returning from the Banks. At the instigation of the Reverend William Bentley of Salem, the island was "marked" by the erection of two lighthouses, one much larger than the other, familiarly nicknamed "Mr. and Mrs." In 1631 the island belonged to the Commonwealth and in 1660 Salem was granted ownership. By 1670 so much of the timber had been cut from it, an injunction was placed by Salem that wood could not be hewn without special permission from the town. In 1700 the island was mortgaged for £450. At a much later date the island was purchased for the price of $1,833.33. In 1731 Mr. J. Turner II (of House of Seven Gables fame) bought the island and eleven years later transferred the title to J. Turner III, and from then on Baker's Island remained in private hands. In 1835 Ephraim Brown of Marblehead purchased it, selling it to Jeremiah Sullivan of Boston in 1849. He, in turn, sold it in the same year to another Marbleheader, Jane Courtis. She remained in possession of it until 1887 when she sold it to Dr. Nathan A. Morse, a professor at Boston University. Now there are sixty-one cottages and some other buildings on the island.

It is again the Reverend Mr. Bentley who supplied the most interesting facts about the island. Frequently sailing there to picnic, he wrote that the island was a haven for countless rabbits, and that, although the winter depleted their numbers greatly—to say nothing of the hunters who caught them for food—summertime seemed to replenish the supply. Off the island were excellent fishing grounds. Many squatters brought over cows, for the grass was excellent for summer grazing. Geese, hens, ducks, and cheese and corn, too, could be purchased from those living there during the summer season. At one time there was a hotel, Winne-Egans, on the island. Kerosene, water, ice, and food had to be imported by the island ferry.

Bentley also records the storms off Baker's. In July, 1814, "Five men perished from a Boat belonging to Marblehead upon Baker's Island breakers in the gust of 23 of June which threw down the Spire of our steeple." Three winters later, the schooner, *Arnold Sears*, carrying wood from Maine, was shipwrecked on the outer side of Baker's Island. The men escaped but the vessel and cargo were lost. She belonged to Captain Thomas Martin of Marblehead.

In 1854, the three-masted ship, *Favorite*, went ashore on the southern breakers about three miles below Baker's Island. She was loaded with merchandise of all kinds and, bound for Boston, she got off course and was wrecked on the breakers. On the wintry Sunday following the storm, Mr. George Tucker of Marblehead (who had a shoemaker's shop on family property on Front Street near Tucker's Wharf) made a trip to *Favorite* as she lay on her side in the waters. He and his companions rode the breakers in a dory and, spotting the cathead of *Favorite*, he climbed on the bow of the ill-fated vessel and succeeded in salvaging the cathead, which is a protecting piece of timber or iron near the bow of a vessel to which the anchor is hoisted and secured. It was an extremely cold day and they were forced to walk on the ice in the harbor almost to the Point and haul their dory with them, a dangerous way of rescuing a cathead. *Favorite* was finally freed of part of the cargo and then a strong wind broke her up, and various parts of her were washed ashore on the islands about the inner bay. The precious cathead is now in the Lee Mansion's collection. Formerly painted black, it is now gray with its eyes painted green-yellow with black pupils—eyes that must have gazed on many parts of the globe.

Great Misery has eighty-six and a half acres, and on both Great and Little Misery cattle grazed in the summer, for a century or more ago the herd could pass from Great to Little Island at low tide. The islands received their name of Misery from Moulton's boat which was shipwrecked there, and for a while they were called Moulton's Misery. His name, however, was eventually dropped.

Francis Higginson, in June, 1629, entered in the journal of his voyage an account of his arrival in "the harbor of Naumkeag— every island full of gay woods and high trees. So many islands replenished with thick woods and high trees and many fair, green pastures." The green "pastures" are noticeable still on the Miseries, Great and Little. These two islands connected by a bar have been the property of the Trustees of Public Reservations under the act of the legislature in 1891. Earlier, they were densely wooded and provided revenue for the settlement of Salem prior to 1640, when cutting the woods was prohibited.

It appears in the records that these islands were conveyed to one Bartholomew Gale in 1662 (Gale's Rocks are marked on the charts on Manchester Shore). And four years later, Mr. Gale described himself as "of Marblehead and twenty-five years of age". It is to be regretted that Tyler, from whom Gale received the deed to the island, neglected to perpetuate in his deed either his Indian name or the Indian designation of the island. Captain George Corwin became lessee of the island in 1678 and built a truly elegant house which was to set the tone of the island for the future. In the 1770's Marblehead's Benjamin Marston enjoyed a beautiful summer residence here, and the island continued to be popular during the next century and more.

Great Misery, the mecca for many a memory-making Harvard reunion, was once the setting for a never-to-be-forgotten turtle feast.

Salem's merchants in the late 1700's were prosperous and enjoyed spending their wealth. Catering to this particular clientele was Prince Hall of Boston, a tall, lean, dignified Negro who was a chef *par excellence*. In 1803, at Antigua, West Indies, some natives captured a hooked-beak great turtle; this huge leviathan was four feet long and three feet wide. Placing him in a dugout canoe, they paddled to a Salem-bound ship at anchor there in the harbor. Bartering was hardly necessary, for all aboard knew that here was a prize to be taken home to be enjoyed at a great turtle feast. Weeks later, when the lines of the vessel had been made secure in Salem Harbor, word came immediately from the owner of the ship to sell the turtle to the highest bidder. The East India Marine Society had not had a celebration for a long time, so now all appointments were ready— the turtle, the purchaser and the caterer, Prince Hall. The members of the East India Marine Society were all deep-water mariners; only those who had rounded either Cape Horn or the Cape of Good Hope were eligible. The only setting appropriate for this proposed turtle feast was Misery Island. A hundred invitations were sent out and there were a hundred acceptances. Prince Hall and a couple of dozen of his black men sailed to Salem and ported the turtle to the island. Cooking utensils, vegetables (carrots and potatoes) and Madeira wine—tables, too, as well as boxes of silver—had to be taken to the island for this was no ordinary celebration for any ordinary club!

All was accomplished with efficiency and as soon as Prince Hall had his equipment assembled in working order he asked to have the turtle released from its box. Using a large bunch of parsley to entice it to push its head out of its enormous shell, a cutlass held in his other hand, as the turtle reached for its chlorophyl treat, he severed its neck. Then came the exacting art of cutting up the turtle meat for, if the gall bladder broke as the bottom shell of the turtle was removed, the flesh would be ruined for human consumption as the taste would be unpalatable and intolerable.

The surgeon's skill was his, and soon Prince Hall had pies that would serve one hundred, done to perfection for the assembled guests. So the East India Marine Society toasted all the ships at sea, their country, their islands and the women who waited for them at home. And who recounted this glorious occasion? None other than the Pepys of Salem, the eminent, lovable Reverend William Bentley, who enjoyed life to its fullest, especially on the islands off Marblehead and Salem.

The 1900's brought a real period of social activity to Great Misery. The Misery Island Club House was built (the Casino that was to be the setting of many a gala Harvard Class Reunion), the Bleak House that belonged to the Harwoods, many other houses, with tennis courts and even an airplane landing strip! A steam launch brought the summer residents and their guests and the days were filled with the pleasure of a successful summer vacation. In the early 1920's the summer colony began to dwindle, and in 1926 a mysterious fire swept across the island, demolishing all of the cottages. Just prior to that, Mr. Joseph Henderson had his home cut in two and successfully floated on a barge across to Marblehead where it stands as a house on Flint Street on Marblehead Neck. Today, picnickers enjoy the island and note the foundations, all that remain of the summer houses.

Coming closer to Marblehead Harbor, one sails past Coney Island, which consists of about one and one-half acres of coarse grass and stony soil. In the outer confines of Marblehead Harbor, one sees on the town side and near Peach's Point, Brown's Island in Little Harbor. This is connected with a narrow strip of land to the mainland, passable at low tide. This island has had many names—Brown, Maverick, Charles, Crowninshield, and the Coast Guard charts call it Orne. In April, 1709, when the island was called Charles, the Commoners granted all that great head of land on the northeast side of Charles Island to Edward Dimond, "shoreman," for the sum of thirteen shillings. He was probably the famous "old Dimond." Tradition has it that in the vicinity of where the bar between the island

and the mainland now is, and which is uncovered at low tide, there was once fine farming land. Brown's Island had a clubhouse on it —a men's social club known as the Heliotrope Club, in the early 1900's. Many fish dinners were prepared and enjoyed by the members of this club. The island was given to the Trustees of Public Reservation by Mrs. Louise Crowninshield. It has been the site of a Girl Scout camp and is used by many for bird watching.

Gerry's Island, named for the Gerry family, is smaller and closer to the mainland in Little Harbor. When the Reverend Samuel Cheever first lived in Marblehead, his home was on this island. At one time cows were pastured here, after being led over at low tide. A small fish house was removed to the mainland, and it became the Squash House of J. J. H. Gregory. It is still standing today on Elm Street. Gerry's Island was also known as Priest's Island, for priests from New York had a small house there. The island is now owned by the Hood Sailmakers.

Parson Barnard had a Negro servant named Jack, who used to fish from a well-known rock off the east end of Gerry's Island. This rock became known as Jack's Rock.

8. Flora and Fauna

SOIL IN COASTAL New England towns is light and sandy and rocks are so abundant that gardening becomes a thoroughgoing challenge to seashore dwellers. Marblehead is no exception. In fact, sometimes it seems that the glacier left us more than our share of granite, schist and mica. Yet, nature has a way of balancing her deficiencies. Mists and fogs supply abundant moisture and the sun radiates a rare, diaphanous quality of light which makes the blues bluer, the pinks pinker, and the yellows more golden in seaside gardens. Even the commonest wildflower blooming in a rocky crevice takes on a jewel-like quality. Ocean spray and relentless winds contort and twist branches and twigs so that they assume curious, twisted shapes, not unlike those of Japanese bonsai. Birds scatter seed as do mists and air currents, with the result that both native and exotic flowers often appear in the most unlikely places.

The wild seaside roses described by such mid-seventeenth-century writers as Josselyn and Wood flourish today, sprawling over great boulders and ledges, adding their sweet perfume to the salt in the air as in the 1630's. More than two centuries later, the great, single, rose-pink and white flowers of the rugosa rose appeared to mingle their fragrance with the indigenous eglantine. This rugged and thorny rose (which came from China) is noted for its luxuriant foliage and showy red fruits, and was first planted in the great gardens on the Neck in the late 1880's. The birds scattered the seed everywhere and the rugosa rose took root all along the Marblehead coast and, by the same process, elsewhere along the entire seaboard. The brilliant red fruits or hips, which are a prime source of concentrated vitamin C, are known in the Orient as sea tomatoes. Both the wild "damask" and the rugosa rose send forth a few blooms even into late November, and no bit of living color is more welcome at this time of year.

Every fishing town welcomes the fragrance of flowers to offset the omnipresent, pungent fishy smell that fills the air, especially in spring. When, in May, as Whittier so aptly described it, "blossoms of apple and lilac showed," the air in Marblehead all the way to Salem Road was filled with fragrance. The lilacs still bloom in the dooryards. Roses, peonies and climbing honeysuckle come in June; beds and borders, pots and tubs, all bright with color, make midsummer memorable everywhere one glances. The brilliant red of sumac leaves and the misty purple of sea lavender and fall aster skirting the town announce now, as in bygone days, the coming of winter. When snow falls, here and there among the rocks the gray clusters of bayberry are still in evidence, together with what remains of shriveled rose hips along the shore.

The flower that has become synonymous with Marblehead was one that grew first, ages ago, in China where it flourished around beehives. It reached the western world close on the heels of the silk trade caravans. The first blooms of the hollyhock, *Althea rosea*, were welcomed warmly by English gardeners in 1543. Then, the early settlers brought the seeds to America, for John Josselyn, in his *New England Rarities Discovered*, recorded its appearance in dooryard gardens prior to 1650. Hollyhocks soon made themselves at home in Marblehead. They grew like weeds, springing up along the narrow edges of the crooked sidewalks, behind fence posts, in the crevices of walls, among loose rocks. In fact, wherever the disc-like seeds fell, great rosettes of soft, round leaves made the rocky ground lush with green. As the warm days of June lengthened, the sturdy stems of the hollyhocks—four, five and six feet tall—reached for the sun. By the fourth of July, there was hardly a picket fence or gateway or dooryard that did not have its share of hollyhocks in bloom—behind it, around it or near it. After the turn of the nineteenth century, some poetic soul christened this old fishing community "Hollyhock Town." Later, when amateur and professional painters "discovered" Marblehead, they lavished their attention on these stately flowers. Sarah Symonds, ceramicist of Salem, made them famous in her plaster models of Marblehead doorways and gateposts, and hundreds of painters transferred their bright colors to paper and canvas. Yet, the native Marbleheaders took them for granted—they had been here always. Tourists gathered seeds as they roamed about, put them in their purses and carried them home to Ashtabula, Sioux City, Independence, and elsewhere. These were no common flowers—these hollyhocks that grew like weeds in Marblehead! On the other hand, Marblehead children used them to make hollyhock ladies or dolls, as they called them—the fully opened bloom makes a beautiful skirt; two buds of the right proportion placed correctly make the body and the head; toothpicks provide arms—what more could any little girl want? Even the letter carriers knew how to make them and would teach a child if mother had neglected to do so. Hollyhock colors, except for blue and purple, run the gamut of the rainbow—white, pink, rose, red, blackish-red, yellow and orange. Some are single or semidouble, others are as full-petaled as roses, and a few show fringed petals. The double-flowered forms were known in the seventeenth century as were the fig leaf variety.

In the latter part of the eighteenth century when the Chinn family of Marblehead kept diaries, they mentioned that among the earliest hollyhocks in America sown from seed were those planted by John Fisher of Marblehead, who lived on Prospect Street at the head of Commercial Street. Mr. Fisher apparently had an unusually keen interest in growing things—fauna as well as flora. He probably was among the first home owners to introduce picture windows. On his terraced lawns he kept two peacocks. For his own and his family's amusement, he installed two exceptionally large windows which protruded from the above-ground basement on the front of his house so that the birds themselves might strut and spread their tails to their own reflected vainglory.

Those first mariners, who were also the earliest commentators, were greatly impressed with the abundant vegetation which they saw. William Wood, Francis Higginson, John Josselyn and Governor Winthrop have left vivid impressions of the "new-land" as they found it. In two books John Josselyn paid special attention to "Marblehead-Orchards and Gardens." In *New England Rarities Discovered*, published in 1672, he mentioned such native plants as cattail, watercresses, wild sorrel, spurge which "growes upon sandy Sea Bankes," speedwell, chickweed and wild mint. Among the many flowers, he noted three kinds of violets, loosestrife, the daisy (that was to become known as the New England, or oxeye, daisy, said to have escaped from Governor Endicott's garden at Salem), Solomon's-seal, yarrow, St. Johnswort, and many others.

Berries were numerous—the bearberry that grew near the salt marsh (a prehistoric ground cover along the entire Atlantic coast, stretching even to California), the bayberry (called candleberry on the Cape), blackberries, huckleberries, gooseberries and dewberries (no doubt, wild raspberries) and quantities, in fact fields, of strawberries and blueberry bushes. "Turnips, parsnips, and carrots seemed sweeter and bigger than those found in England." As for the trees, there was an abundance of "pine, sumacke, oak, sassafras, chestnuts and maples." Of all the flowering bushes he saw, he preferred the cherry and the shad.

Seeds of many exotics had traveled to this shore with the settlers in the ships they arrived on and in the packing around their furnishings. The settlers brought barberry, Scottish broom and the oxeye daisy that is still called "bulls-eye" by Marbleheaders. Josselyn wrote that wild marjoram, caraway, Queen Anne's lace, cat mint, and dyer's woad were happily naturalized on these shores. Countless others found welcoming soil and the region around the Dungeons and St. Andrew's church bear testimony today to the part *Genista tinctoria* played in our forebears' dye pots, for these tracts are sunny with the lovely yellow bloom of the woad, whose blossoms flourish gaily in July. As for the indigenous vegetables found here, there were beans, maize and pumpkins.

There is no mention of the plant pests that bother man when he touches or breathes them. Rampant in growth, probably then as now, are great patches and stands of poison ivy, poison sumac, chokeberry, ragweed, nettle and stickle burrs. The carriers of the seed of these undesirable plants are the feathered folk, since Marblehead is a natural flyway.

Legend has it that Sir Harry Frankland brought the first lilacs to Marblehead. This may have real foundation, for in Sir Harry's *Diary* he records time and again his keen interest in botany. His Marblehead sponsor, the Reverend Edward Holyoke, had an avid interest in "growing things" and it is very probable that these two men exchanged plants. Frankland went everywhere to find seeds of unusual plants and countless cuttings of shrubs and bushes. Azaleas, in particular, flourished at his Hopkinton, Massachusetts, home.

Dr. Manasseh Cutler of Ipswich began to study the botany of Essex County at the close of the eighteenth century and his work was continued a century later by John Robinson of Salem. Mr. Robinson organized a team of amateur botanists who observed plants in Marblehead. Later, he wrote that "along the seashore is found an abundance of plants peculiar to the region of salt water marshes and beaches." One rare discovery was the cinquefoil, *Potentilla tridentata*, previously recorded only at the Isles of Shoals and on Mt. Washington, which was found growing on the Neck. An abundance of wild flowers flourished both in the marshes and the meadows on Marblehead. Robinson also observed that there were about one hundred and fifty species of algae to be noted in the ocean and inlets. For more than fifty years, classes in seaside botany have been conducted by Harvard University and Boston University along the shores of Marblehead.

One of the first garden clubs in the Northeast, the Marblehead Garden Club, was founded in 1926 by Mrs. William Chisholm and promoted by Mrs. Everett Paine. Since its inception, it has pioneered in many civic projects. Long before it was a recognized word in everyman's vocabulary, *conservation* was of special concern to this club. Civic beautification, care of parks, public ways and plantings, suppression of billboards, cultivation of plants in one's own garden and the establishment of scholarships in the field of horticulture have motivated the membership from the beginning. This club was the forerunner of a dozen clubs in the same town that followed in its footsteps to make Marblehead garden conscious. The tree department of the town has been cited frequently for its planting program and Marblehead is noted for its unusually healthy trees—both for the hundreds that make the streets colorful in spring and summer and those that give shade. The town is noted also for its countless private gardens, large and small, many hidden from public view. The plantings at the Lee Mansion, charmingly authentic in the best Colonial tradition, are maintained by the Marblehead Garden Club.

Mrs. Arthur Teele, a member of the Marblehead Garden Club, became so interested in the art of flower arranging that she succeeded in launching "The Arrangers of Marblehead." Somewhat later, in 1946, she wrote a book on her favorite interest, *Facts About Flower Arrangement*, which is still in use, and which made her a recognized authority. The members of the Arrangers of Marblehead, under her leadership, took up the challenge and many have become expert in the field, not only becoming judges (some of them life judges) but also capturing many first prizes and the coveted John Taylor Arms award at the annual spring flower show of the Massachusetts Horticultural Society.

The Fruit and Flower Mission, organized in Boston to bring joy to city shut-ins, was championed by Marbleheaders at the turn of the twentieth century. On Sunday nights, each week, Miss Emma

Martin placed buckets of water on the front porch of her home near the railroad station on Pleasant Street (now the site of the National Grand Bank). There flower lovers took their cut blooms which were then packed in hampers to ride the rails to Boston on the early Monday morning train. For a number of years until he died, J. O. J. Frost, who dabbled in paints and became famous as a truly remarkable painter of primitives only after his death, used to bring neat little bunches of sweet peas from his Pond Street garden for this flower-sharing program. Unfortunately, times have changed and the Fruit and Flower project was discontinued in 1970.

Rose growers, amateur and professional all across the nation, held Harriet R. Foote in high esteem for nearly fifty years. As the wife of a retired minister, she started by growing roses in a modest way in her garden on Beach Street, and they flourished. Soon she began to collect all the types of roses that she could locate, in the manner of Empress Josephine at Malmaison a century earlier. It was not long before she had a thousand varieties, including hybrid teas, hybrid perpetuals, climbers and ramblers, noisettes and Bourbons as well as the various old-fashioned roses, and visitors came by the hundreds to see the marvelous rose garden adjoining her modest house. Her advice on culture and collecting varieties was sought far and wide. She wrote, lectured and acted as consultant to estate owners and landscape architects. She was the envy and admiration of the American Rose Society and all its members. Mr. and Mrs. Henry Ford called her to Dearborn, Michigan, to supervise the planning and planting of a three-acre rose garden in the mid-1920's. Finally, in 1948, she was persuaded to write a book entitled *Mrs. Foote's Rose Book*. Even in her declining years, and until her death in 1951, this remarkable woman maintained her garden with notable enthusiasm and skill. She was a perfectionist in methods of planting, pruning and maintenance and laid down her principles with the preciseness of a country schoolmarm. For several decades the Massachusetts Horticultural Society sent its visiting committee to Marblehead frequently to inspect and admire the work of this distinguished woman rosarian who outshone all the men in her chosen field. More than once she lectured at the Society's hall in Boston.

In a much more modest way Miss Mary Sullivan, who lived on Lincoln Avenue, kept the name of Marblehead green in rose-growing circles with her prize roses for many years. Presently, Mrs. Eva Tatterfield of 24 Taft Street carries on the rose-growing tradition in an even more remarkable way by preserving and drying the prize roses that thrive in her garden, and creating permanent arrangements.

James J. H. Gregory, whose life span was from 1827 to 1910, promoted great interest in gardening both in his native town of Marblehead, across the nation and, in fact, to the growers the world over. A keen man, dedicated to helping others to enjoy a better life, he looked to the good earth to help him. His most avid interest was in producing seed of superior quality, but to do that he realized that he must grow stock that was exceptional. Despite the lack of soil and the abundance of rock, he was able to accomplish his ambition right in Marblehead. He owned and leased tracts of land on Peach's Point, Green Street, and other sites in Marblehead, as well as extensive acreage in Danvers and Middleton—over four hundred acres. His venture with the seed business was purely by accident. Though an accomplished grower, he had only handled the produce until a man wrote to him asking advice about a nice winter squash. Gregory wrote, "I heard of his request and we happened to have one. My father called it 'Marm Hubbard's squash,' so I sent him the seed." The recipient was so pleased with the squash that he wrote a lengthy paper about it and gave Gregory's name, so simultaneously the seed business was established as well as the name—"Mother Hubbard Squash." Gregory was to develop another well-known squash which he named for one of his adopted sons, Warren. The Warren Squash is another fine winter squash. During his life he wrote and published many articles and books on agriculture, such as *Onion Raising; Cabbages: How to Grow Them,* and so on. In fact, he perfected one of the best onions on the market and eventually branched out to include flowers. For half a century or more, he annually sent out an *Annual Circular and Retail Catalogue.* The catalogues started with the listing of cabbages and in 1870 he added zinnias. Most of the seeds he had grown himself, but occasionally he imported seeds from France and Germany. Each packet had instructions for growing. He was Marblehead's Luther Burbank.

The terrain has had its influx of gypsy moths, Japanese beetles and the continual annoyance of earwigs that plague all and everything. One record of a similar situation was noted in Nathan Bowen's *Diary* in "1743" and again, "on June 26, 1762 the fields along Cross Street are devastated by meadow-worms."

The earliest settlers kept numerous cows, goats and pigs which were allowed to roam at will throughout the town and it is said that they made many of the paths used by the townspeople. As for the wild animals then, as now, there were, and are, numerous skunks, some wild rabbits, raccoons, countless squirrels and too many other rodents.

The famous John James Audubon paid a visit to Marblehead in

1840 to solicit funds for his proposed portfolio of bird portraits.
Whom he asked for financial help is not recorded, but in his diary
he reveals he left without the aid he sought: "Salem Masstts Sepr
18th 1840. . . . Docr Wheatland I called on at ½ past 7 and asked
him to accompany me to Marblehead which he did. We were taken
to Marblehead 4 miles in 10 minutes for 12½¢ each, passing amid
Salt marshes and rocky grounds almost deprived of trees. —At
Carrs going to Boston, we met with Docr Pierson who gave me 2 of
his Cards for 2 Persons, of wealth at Marblehead and on whom we
called, but it was no go! We sauntered about this unique Village for
a while, viewing the Harbour and aridity of the rock prospect
around us and indeed beneath us for about an hour. All here indicated strongly the fact that all Marbleheaders have to depend on the
products of the sea for their livelyhood, and I was glad after all that
I had seen this place."

A century later another naturalist, Donald Culross Peattie, walked
the hills and dales of Marblehead since he was courting a young
woman, Louise Redfield, a resident during her undergraduate years.
During this time he fell in love with Marblehead itself and wrote
about its beauty glowingly in his *Journey Into America*.

Sea birds here are numerous—the herring gull, the great black-
backed gull, the cormorant, the Atlantic kittiwake and several other
water species. Marblehead can boast of sandpipers, too, especially
the purple species that add color to the autumn shore. Common
birds abound—a host of sparrows, a murder of crows, a murmura-
tion of starlings—to name but three families. Since Marblehead is a
natural aerial flyway, many, many flocks of birds stop on the shores
on their journey north and south. While a century and a half ago
the bald eagle frequented Swampscott, none of the Marbleheaders
seemed to have noted its appearance here. However, in recent years
the snowy owl has been a visitor and countless "southern" birds
spend the year round in various places about the town, particularly
the mockingbird, cardinal and tufted titmouse. An eager and dedicated group of Auduboners records these winged creatures and enjoys the seventeen-acre Audubon Sanctuary on the Neck. The
ring-necked pheasants that may be found in Marblehead have always been protected, and the nye of these birds make Peach's Point
and the Neck colorful; their strident call is often heard and wakes
many a resident. In late September the migrating monarch butter-
flies drop down by the hundreds to visit the gardens and fields momentarily.

Often in winter the seals from farther north play about the harbor
waters and the sea produces many fishes, including pollock, cod,

flounder, haddock, mackerel, clams, and lobsters, as well as those that are not edible, some whales and sharks.

Marblehead proves itself to be a mecca for the naturalist and the ecologist.

In 1971 a new rose bush was named "Spirit of '76." Hybridized by an industry in Monticello, Florida, it was inspired by Archibald Willard's painting of the same name. The new rose embodies "the glowing spirited red that the painter used in the flag in the painting and it is hoped that the rose will inspire the nation's resurgence of love and appreciation of our beautiful country and heritage." Appropriately, specimens of this rose will be planted around Abbot Hall.

Bibliography

Abbott, Katherine M. *Old Paths and Legends of New England*. New York: Knickerbocker Press, 1904.

Adams, James Truslow. *The Founding of New England*. Boston: The Atlantic Monthly Press, c. 1921.

Alden, John R. *The History of the American Revolution*. New York: Alfred A. Knopf, Inc., 1969.

Alderman, Clifford Lindsey. *Stormy Knight: The Life of Sir William Phips*. Philadelphia: Chilton Book Company, c. 1964.

Austin, James T. *The Life of Elbridge Gerry, Vol. I & II*. Boston: Wells & Lilly, 1829, 1829.

Bacon, Edwin M. *Historic Pilgrimage in New England*. New York: Silver, Burdett & Co., 1898.

Banks, Charles Edward. *The Planters of the Commonwealth*. Boston: Houghton Mifflin, 1930.

Banks, Charles Edward. *The Winthrop Fleet of 1630*. Boston: Houghton Mifflin Company, 1930.

Bartlet, Sarah S. *What to See in Marblehead*. Salem: Salem Press, c. 1907.

Belknap, Henry Wyckoff. *Artists and Craftsmen of Essex County, Mass.* Salem: Essex Institute, 1927.

Bentley, William, D.D. *The Diary of William Bentley, D. D. (Pastor of the East Church, Salem) in 4 Vol.* Gloucester: Peter Smith, reprint edition, 1962.

Billias, George Athan. *General John Glover and his Marblehead Marines*. New York: Henry Holt Co., c. 1960.

Bowen, Catherine Drinker. *Miracle at Philadelphia*. Boston: Little, Brown and Company, 1966.

Bradford, William. *History of Plymouth Plantation*. Boston: Massachusetts Historical Society, 1912.

Brewington, M. V. and Dorothy. *Marine Paintings and Drawings in the Peabody Museum*. Salem: 1968.

Bridenbaugh, Carl. *Gentlemen's Progress—Dr. Alexander Hamilton—1744*. Chapel Hill: University of North Carolina Press, 1948.

Brooks, Charles. *History of Town of Medford* (Revised 1866 by James Usher). Boston: Rand, Avery & Co., 1866.

Brooks, Van Wyck. *The Flowering of New England: 1815–1865.* New York: E. P. Dutton & Co., Inc., 1936.

Brown, John Hull. *Early American Beverages.* New York: Bonanza Books, 1966.

Bullard, F. L. *Historic Summer Haunts from Newport to Portland.* Boston: Little, Brown and Company, 1912.

Burr, George L., editor. *Narratives of the Witchcraft Cases.* New York: Charles Scribner's Sons, 1914.

Bynner, Edwin L. *Agnes Surriage.* Boston: Houghton Mifflin Company, 1886.

Chadwick, John. *Captain Chadwick.* Boston: American Unitarian Association, 1896.

Chase, Mary Ellen. *The Fishing Fleets of New England.* Boston: Houghton Mifflin Company, 1961.

Clark, Arthur H. *Clipper Ship Era.* New York: The Knickerbocker Press, 1911.

Clark, Charles E. *The Eastern Frontier: the Settlement of Northern New England, 1610–1763.* New York: Alfred A. Knopf, 1970.

Coffin, Charles Carleton. *Daughters of the Revolution and Their Times, 1769–1776.* Boston: Houghton Mifflin Company, 1895.

Colonials and Patriots. Washington, D.C.: U. S. Department of Interior, 1964.

Colver, Anne. *Yankee Doodle Painter.* New York: Alfred A. Knopf, Inc., 1955.

Comer, William R. *Landmarks: In the Old Bay State.* Norwood: Norwood Press, 1911.

Crawford, Mary Caroline. *Social Life in Old New England.* Boston: Little, Brown and Company, 1914.

Crosby, Irving B. *Boston Through the Ages: The Geological Story of Greater Boston.* Boston: Marshall Jones Co., 1928.

Crowninshield, F. B. *Log Book of Cleopatra's Barge II.* Boston: The Merrymount Press, 1948.

Cutler, Carl C. *Greyhounds of the Sea.* New York: G. P. Putnam's Sons, 1930.

Dictionary of American Biography. New York: Charles Scribner's Sons, 1933.

Dodges, The. *Puritan Paths.* Newberryport: Newburyport Press Inc., 1963.

Dole, Frederick H. *A History of Windham, Maine.* Westbrook: Henry S. Cobb, 1932.

Dole, Samuel Thomas. *Windham in the Past by Samuel Thomas Dole, edited by Frederick Howard Dole.* Auburn: Merrill-Webber, 1886.

Drake, Samuel Adams. *New England Legends and Folk-lore.* Boston: Little Brown and Company, 1906.

Drake, Samuel Adams. *Nooks and Corners of the New England Coast.* New York: Harper Bros., 1875.

Earle, Alice Morse. *Customs and Fashions in Old New England.* New York: Charles Scribner's Sons, 1898.

Earle, Alice Morse. *Home Life in Colonial Days.* New York: Grosset & Dunlap, Inc., 1898.

Earle, Alice Morse. *The Sabbath in Puritan New England.* New York: Charles Scribner's Sons, 1891.

Earle, Alice Morse. *Stage Coach and Tavern Days.* New York: The Macmillan Company, 1905.

Evans, Charles. *American Bibliography, Vol. 1, 1639–1729.* Privately printed by the author. Chicago: The Blakely Press, 1903.

Fairchild, Byron. *Messrs. William Pepperrell: Merchants at Piscataqua.* Ithaca: Cornell University Press, c. 1954.

Fairhaven, William A. *Merchant Sail, Vol. 1 & 11.* Center Lovell: Marine Educational Foundation, 1945–1955.

Fales, Martha Gandy. *Early American Silver for the Cautious Collector.* New York: Funk & Wagnalls, 1970.

Federal Writers' Project of New Jersey. *Colonel Knox and George Washington.* New York: The Viking Press, Inc., 1939.

Fiske, John. *Beginnings of New England.* Boston: Houghton Mifflin Company, 1889.

Fitzgerald, John C., editor. *Writings of George Washington.* Washington, D.C.: U. S. Government, n.d.

Flynt, Henry N. and Martha Gandy Fales. *The Heritage Foundation Collection of Silver, with Biographical Sketches of New England Silversmiths, 1625–1825.* Old Deerfield: Heritage Foundation, 1968.

Foley, Daniel J. *Gardening by the Sea: From Coast to Coast.* Philadelphia: Chilton Book Company, c. 1965.

Forbes, Esther. *The Running of the Tide.* Boston: Houghton Mifflin Company, 1948.

Foster, Charles H. W. *The Eastern Yacht Club Ditty Bag: 1870–1900.* Norwood: Plimpton Press, 1932.

Greene, Lorenzo Johnston. *The Negro in Colonial New England (1620–1776).* New York: Atheneum Publishers, 1969.

Hansen, Chadwick. *Witchcraft at Salem.* New York: George Brazillier, Inc., 1969.

Hawthorne, Hildegarde. *Old Seaport Towns of New England.* New York: Dodd, Mead & Co., 1916.

Hay, John, Library. *Yankee Doodle.* Providence: Brown University Press, 1939.

Haywood, Charles. *Yankee Dictionary.* Lynn: Jackson & Phillips, 1963.

Haywood, Charles F. *Minutemen and Marines.* New York: Dodd, Mead & Co., 1963.

Higginson, Francis. *A True Relation of the Last Voyage to New England, written from New England, July 24, 1629.* London.

Hinsdale, Harriet. *Be My Love.* New York: Creative Age Press, 1950.

History of Essex County. C. F. Jowett & Co., Boston: 1878.

Hofstadter, Richard. *Great Issues in American History, 1765–1865.* New York: Random House, Inc., 1958.

Holyoke Diaries, The, 1709—1856, with introduction by George Francis Dow. Salem: Essex Institute, 1911.

Hornby, Lester C. and Sylvester Baxter. *An Artist's Sketchbook of Old Marblehead.* A. W. Elson & Co., Belmont: 1906.

Howe, O. T. *Argonauts of '49.* Cambridge: Harvard University Press, 1923.

Hutchinson, Thomas. *History of Massachusetts.* Salem: Essex Institute, 1795.

Hutchinson, Thomas. *History of Massachusetts Bay.* Cambridge Harvard Edition, 1936.

Jackson, Shirley. *The Witchcraft of Salem Village.* New York: Random House, Inc., 1956.

Josselyn, John. *Account of Two Voyages to New England.* Lord, 1673. Boston: Reprint, William Veazie, 1865.

Josselyn, John. *New England Rarities Discovered.* London: Published, 1672.

Kimball, George. *Witchcraft.* George Kimball, 1892.

Knight, Sarah. *A Journal of Madame Knight on a Journey from Boston to New York in the Year 1704.* New York: Wilder and Campbell, 1825.

Lacock, John Kennedy. *Marblehead: The Historic Landmarks and Points of Interest and How to See Them.* Boston: J. Miller, Jr., c. 1929.

Leighton, Ann (Mrs. A. W. Smith). *Early American Gardens.* Boston: Houghton Mifflin Company, 1970.

Levin, David. *What Happened in Salem?* New York: Harcourt, Brace, Inc., 1951.

Lindsey, Benjamin J. *Old Marblehead Sea Captains and the Ships in which They Sailed.* Marblehead: Lindsey, 1915.

Ludwig, Allan I. *Graven Images.* Middletown: Wesleyan University Press, 1966.

Mannix, Daniel. *Black Cargoes.* New York: The Viking Press, 1962.

Marlowe, George Francis. *Churches of Old New England.* New York: The Macmillan Company, 1947.

Mason, Caroline Atherton Briggs. *Utterance, or Private Voices to a Public Heart.* Boston: Phillips, Sampson & Co., 1852.

Matloff, Maurice, editor. *American Military History.* Washington, D.C.: U. S. Army, 1969.

McKay, Richard C. *Some Famous Sailing Ships and Their Builder, Donald McKay.* New York: The Knickerbocker Press, 1928.

Miller, John C. *The First Frontier: Life in Colonial America.* New York: Dell Publishing Co., Inc., 1966.

Morison, Samuel Eliot. *Builders of the Bay Colony.* Winchester: University Press of Cambridge, Inc., 1936.

Morison, Samuel Eliot. *By Land and By Sea*. New York: Alfred A. Knopf, Inc., 1953.

Morison, Samuel Eliot. *The Intellectual Life of Colonial New England*. Winchester: University Press of Cambridge, Inc., 1956.

National Gallery of Art, Smithsonian Institution, *John Singleton Copley, 1738–1815*. Washington, D.C.: National Gallery of Art, c. 1965.

Newhall, James R. *History of Lynn, Essex County, Mass. including Lynnfield, Saugus, Swampscott and Nahant*. Lynn: 1883.

Palfrey, Eleanor. *The Lady and The Painter*. New York: Coward–McCann, Inc., 1951.

Peattie, Donald Culross. *Journey Into America*. Boston: Houghton Mifflin Company, 1943.

Perley, Sidney. *History of Salem, 3 Vol*. Salem: Essex Institute, 1924.

Perley, Sidney. *Marblehead in the Year 1700*. Salem: Essex Institute, 1910.

Perley, Sidney. *The Facts of Essex County, Mass*. Salem: 1889.

Phillips, James Duncan. *Salem and The Indies*. Boston: Houghton Mifflin Company, 1937.

Phillips, James Duncan. *Salem in The Seventeenth Century*. Boston: Houghton Mifflin Company, 1933.

Phillips, James Duncan. *Salem in the Eighteenth Century*. Boston: Houghton Mifflin Company, 1936.

Rettig, Robert Bell. *Guide to Cambridge Architecture. Ten Walking Tours*. Cambridge: Massachusetts Institute of Technology Press, 1969.

Roads, Samuel, Jr. *The History and Traditions of Marblehead*. Boston: Houghton Mifflin Company, 1880.

Robinson, Joseph S. *The Story of Marblehead*. Salem: Privately printed, 1936.

Roosevelt, Theodore. *The Naval War of 1812*. New York: G. P. Putnam's Sons, 1900.

Sagendorph, Robb. *America and Her Almanacs*. Boston: Little, Brown and Company, 1970.

Sarles, Frank B., Jr. and Charles E. Shedd. *Colonials and Patriots: Historic Places Commemorating our Forbears: 1700–1783*. Washington, D.C.: U. S. Dept. of the Interior, 1964.

Schlesinger, Arthur M. *The Colonial Merchants and the American Revolution*. New York: Frederick Ungar Publishing Co., Inc., 1966.

Seton, Anya. *The Hearth and The Eagle*. Boston: Houghton Mifflin Company, 1948.

Sewall, Samuel. *Diary of Samuel Sewall, 1674–1729, 3 Vol*. Boston: Massachusetts Historical Society Collections, 1878.

Shipton, Clifford E. *New England Life in the 18th Century: Representative Biographies from Sibley's Harvard Graduates*. Cambridge: Belknap Press of Harvard University Press, 1963.

Shipton, Clifford K. *Roger Conant: A Founder of Massachusetts*. Cambridge: Harvard University, 1944.

Skinner, Charles M. *Myths and Legends of Our Own Land*. Philadelphia: J. B. Lippincott Co., 1896.

Snow, Edward Rowe. *Romance of Boston Bay*. Boston: Yankee Publishing Co., 1944.

Starkey, Marion L. *The Devil in Massachusetts*. New York: Alfred A. Knopf, Inc., 1949.

Story, Isaac. *The Parnassian Shop (pseud: "Peter Quinn")*. Boston, 1801.

The Strange Adventures of a Castaway Philip Ashton . . . a real Diary. Marblehead: N. A. Lindsey Co., n.d.

Stryker, William S. *Battles of Trenton and Princeton*. Boston: Houghton Mifflin Company, 1898.

Stryker, William S. *Battle of Trenton*. Trenton: Noor Day & Noor, 1894.

Sweet, Frank H. *Grandmamma's Tales of Colonial Days*. Boston: McLoughlin Bros., c. 1907.

Tharp, Louise Hall. *"Mrs. Jack."* Boston: Little, Brown and Company, 1965.

Upham, Charles W. *Salem Witchcraft, Vol. I & II*. New York: Frederick Ungar Publishing Co., Inc., 1831.

Vaughan, Alden T. *New England Frontier: Puritans and Indians 1620–1675*. Boston: Little Brown and Company, 1970.

Warden, G. B. *Boston 1689–1776*. Boston: Little Brown and Company, 1970.

Weston, George F., Jr. *Boston Ways: High, By and Folk*. Boston: Beacon Press, c. 1967.

Whitehill, Walter Muir. *A Handful of New England Portraits*. Brattleboro: Stephen Green Press, 1969.

Willison, George E. *Saints and Strangers*. New York: Reynal & Hitchcock, 1945.

Winslow, Ola Elizabeth. *Meetinghouse Hill, 1630–1783*. New York: The Macmillan Company, 1952.

Winslow, Ola Elizabeth. *Samuel Sewall of Boston*. New York: The Macmillan Company, 1964.

Wise, DeWitt D. *Now, Then Baker's Island*. Salem: Baker's Island Associations Inc., 1964.

Wood, William. *New England Prospects, edited by E. M. Boynton*. Boston: Prince Society, 1898.

NEWSPAPERS

Essex Gazette, Lynn Daily Item, Manataug Pebbles, The Marblehead Chronicle, Marblehead Ledger, The Marblehead Messenger, Marblehead Register, The People's Advocate and Marblehead Mercury, Salem News, Salem Register.

PAMPHLETS AND PERIODICALS

Bessom, Frank L. *Guide to The Old Burying Hill*. Marblehead: n.d.

Bowden, William Hammond. *Marblehead Town Records 1635–1876*. Salem: Essex Institute Historical Collections, 1933.

Bowen, Nathan. *Almanacks.*

Caulfield, Ernest, M.D. *Pediatric Aspects of the Salem Witchcraft Tragedy.* American Journal of Diseases in Children, 1943.

Chadwick, John W. *Marblehead, Mass.* Harpers Magazine, June, 1874.

Chamberlain, Narcissa G. *The Neighbors of Jeremiah Lee and The Boundaries of His Property.* Essex Institute Historical Collection, Salem: c. 1969.

Cheever, Samuel. *Almanacs.*

Dana, Samuel, A.M. *A Discourse on The History of The First Christian Church and Society in Marblehead, Mass.* Boston: Samuel T. Armstrong, 1816.

Dwight, Timothy. *Travels in New England and New York.* n.d.

Harris, William. *Historical and Critical Account of Hugh Peter.* London: 1751.

Hatch, John B. *Old Witchcraft Jail and Dungeons.* Privately printed, 1955.

Hathaway, Stephen A. *The Second Congregational Church in Marblehead.* Marblehead: June 17, 1885.

Hayward, John. *The New England Gazeteer.* 1839.

Holyoke, Edward. *Almanacs.*

Jenkins, Lawrence W. *A Marbleheader Meets The Last of The Sea Pirates.* Salem: Peabody Museum, 1873.

Kimball, F. H. *Handbook of Marblehead Neck.* Marblehead: 1882.

Laskey, Edith DeBlois. *The Service of Jacob: a story of Marblehead in The Old Fishing Days.* Marblehead: N. Allen Lindsey Co. n.d.

Lee, Thomas Amory. *Colonel William R. Lee of the Revolution.* Salem: Essex Institute, 1917.

Marblehead Academy, 1788–1865. Essex Institute Historical Collection, Vol. C, No. 3. Salem: July, 1964.

Peabody, Robert E. *Peach's Point, Marblehead.* Salem: Essex Institute, 1966.

Perley, Sidney. *Essex Antiquarian, Vol. III,* Salem: March, 1899.

Potter Zulette. *The Communion Service (Old North).* Marblehead, n.d.

Rawlyk, G. A. *Yankees at Louisburg.* Orno: University of Maine. Series No. 85, 1967.

Searle, Richard W. *History of Catta Island off Marblehead.* Essex Institute, 1947.

Searle, Richard W. *Marblehead Great Neck.* Salem: Essex Institute, 1937.

Siebert, W. H. *The Underground Railway in Massachusetts.* American Antiquarian Society. Worcester: April, 1935.

Smith, Philip C. F. and Russell Knight. *In Troubled Waters: The Elusive Schooner Hannah.* Salem: Peabody Museum, 1970.

Stearns, Ray P. *Hugh Peter was a Wit.* Worcester: American Antiquarian, Vol. 77, April, 1967.

Sturbridge Village. *Rum and Reform in Old New England.* Sturbridge, 1966.

PRIVATE PAPERS AND UNPUBLISHED MANUSCRIPTS

Alley, Mary A. *Diary of Mary A. Alley.*

Barnard, Rev. John *Autobiography of the Rev. John Barnard:* written to Rev. Dr. Stiles, Pres. of Yale College, 1770.

Bentley, William, D.D. *The Bentley Correspondence.*

Bradlee, Francis B. C. *Marblehead Foreign Commerce:' 1789–1850.*

Brown, Frank Chouteaux. *Pencil Points for May*, 1938.

Buxton, Bessie. *James J. H. Gregory.*

Chichester Papers, The. No. 45. *Dame Agnes Frankland.* Chichester, England, 1964.

Coburn, Frank Warren. *The Battle of April 19, 1775.*

Damon, Frank C. *Mrs. Sarah E. E. Gregory: 50 Years Abbot Librarian,* 1950.

Essex Institute Original Manuscripts.

Frankland, Sir Charles Henry. *Diary, 1740–1760.*

Lane, Bruce M. *The Flying Cloud.*

Laskey, Edith DeBlois. *The Powder Ship: a drama concerning the life of young James Mugford.*

New York Public Library Manuscripts.

Norton, David W., Rev. *The Early Years of St. Michael's Church.*

Old North Church Original Records and Documents. Marblehead.

Origin and Development of the Almanack.

Registry of Continental Officers.

Richardson, Eben F. *Nicknames of Marblehead.* Marblehead, Jan. 1, 1921.

Roads, Wilson H. *Justice Joseph Story.*

Roads, Wilson H. *Parson Barnard.*

Roberts, David. *Historical Discourse on Life of Sir Mathew Cradock,* 1856.

Robie, Thomas. Letters written during the Revolution. Sent from Halifax to England and to Marblehead.

Sanborn, Nathan P. *The Fountain Inn,* 1905.

Schouler, James. *Massachusetts Convention of 1853.* Massachusetts Historical Society Procedures, 1905.

Second Congregational Church—Unitarian Records and Documents. Marblehead.

Shipton, Clifford K. A. *Colonial Society of Massachusetts.* A Paper, Dec., 1933.

Tutt, Richard. *General Glover. The Indians of Essex County. The Ancient Ways of Marblehead. The Fishing Industry.*

Tutt, Richard, Jr. *Commodore Samuel Tucker.* Marblehead Shoe Industry. Gerry No. 5 Fire Company.

Verbatim Transcripts of Witchcraft Cases.

Widger, Thurlow S. *Marblehead's Fishing, Foreign Commerce and Shoe Industries, 1952.*

Winthrop, Gov. John. *Governor John Winthrop's Journal, 1630–1644.*

Index

Virginia Clegg Gamage

Soon after graduating from Smith College, Mrs. Gamage moved from free-lance writing into business where she became an executive with a national network and then with an international advertising agency. Later, a wife and mother of four, she became involved in community and regional activities and in new administrative responsibilities, serving as national president of the Alumnae Association and a trustee of Smith College, as well as trustee of the Museum of Science in Boston. Mrs. Gamage travels extensively and, in various official capacities, has spoken in thirty states. Apart from recent free-lance writing, her real labor of love has been the writing of *MARBLEHEAD: The Spirit of '76 Lives Here.* Her years of residence and research have only deepened her affection for Marblehead, which she claims has a charisma unmatched by any other town. Mrs. Gamage is currently serving on the Marblehead Bicentennial Committee for the nation's 200th anniversary, though Marblehead itself will soon be preparing for its 350th celebration.

Digging back through the centuries, Virginia C. Gamage and Priscilla Sawyer Lord have unearthed fascinating facts and stories of Marblehead, in some instances never known to the general public before.

PRISCILLA SAWYER LORD

History and tradition, especially in relation to folk culture, have long held a special kind of lure for Priscilla Sawyer Lord. She has cultivated this interest assiduously since her student days at Boston University. Experience in many phases of library science and launching a story hour at the Abbot Public Library have made possible many intimate contacts for collecting facets of history, legend and lore seldom found in print. As a result, *Marblehead: The Spirit of '76 Lives Here*, written with Virginia Clegg Gamage, is her latest book. Her enthusiasm for Easter lore resulted in *Easter Garland* (1963) and *Easter The World Over* (1971), both written in collaboration with Daniel J. Foley, as was *The Folk Arts and Crafts of New England*, which appeared in 1965.

Her affiliations include the Massachusetts Society for University Education for Women (Board of Directors), National Girl Scouts, Essex Institute Ladies Committee, the Herb Society of America, and the Society of Mayflower Descendants. Mrs. Lord enjoys traveling and has appeared on the lecture platform, radio and television. Sailing is a "way of life" she shares with her husband and family.